"So many introductions to exegesis are earnest, thorough, excellent, and, . . . well, boring. In a delightful change of pace, Brown's has all those virtues, but it has the wonderful distinction of being fresh, engaging, and even fun. Brown beautifully integrates the classic concern for the discovery of the otherness of the text with exercises that help readers to discover their own situatedness in history and society. Then he guides the reader to see how reading oneself as well as reading the text can shed new light on how both can respectfully converge to illumine topics of mutual concern. This is the exegetical and hermeneutical handbook I've been waiting for. I look forward to teaching it in my courses."

—**Carol A. Newsom,** Charles Howard Candler Professor of Old Testament,
Candler School of Theology, Emory University

"Bill Brown brings both his vast erudition and his meticulous attentiveness to the art and craft of Bible reading. The outcome of his prodigious work is a book that has no parallel among our current resources. Brown walks us through the conventional modes of critical reading with impressive textual specificity. Beyond that he offers access to his signature scholarship concerning science, evolution, and ecology with immense learning and acute artistic sensitivity. Potential readers should not be misled by the ordinariness of the book's title. In addition to being an introduction for new students, it will be a welcome resource for those trapped in so-called 'objective' criticism and for those who have been at it so long that they think they know ahead of time what texts will say. Brown brings his own wonder and capacity for surprise that will be contagious for his readers. It may be that the book will evoke a new epidemic of excitement and engagement for Bible readers; it is in any case an enormous gift to us all!"

—**Walter Brueggemann,** William Marcellus McPheeters Professor Emeritus
of Old Testament, Columbia Theological Seminary

"We have long been in debt to William Brown's masterful works of exegesis. With his latest book, he puts us in his debt once more with a masterful work *about* exegesis. Brown covers everything from getting started (exegeting the self and initial impressions) to translation to textual criticism, stylistic and structural analysis, compositional and comparative approaches, and of course literary, historical, and canonical investigations. If all that wasn't enough, Brown takes us from analytical approaches to the text itself to the open table of interpretation, explaining and illustrating an impressive range of 'readings in place'—from science to theology and everything in between. Still further, Brown does not leave unmentioned the culminating act of communicating the text to others. Throughout the book he conducts a master class of his own by relating all of the approaches to Genesis 1–3. There are numerous exegetical handbooks on the market, but they can now retire happily. Brown's work sets the standard and will remain the standard for years to come. Vast in scope, hermeneutically savvy, theologically adept, ecclesially centered, artfully crafted, and beautifully written, this is the exegetical handbook we've all been waiting for."

—**Brent A. Strawn,** Professor of Old Testament,
Candler School of Theology, Emory University

"The wait is over! Bill Brown's *Handbook to Old Testament Exegesis* provides students a trustworthy, practical guide to the 'practiced art' of interpreting biblical texts, yet without being ponderous or cumbersome. Fresh, accessible, and graceful, the handbook walks readers through the technical aspects of exegesis as well as the larger questions of contexts and interpretive frameworks, with an eye on the pressing questions of our time. I can't wait to use it in the classroom to help students develop their own abilities to access the wondrous depths of the Bible."

—**Jacqueline E. Lapsley,** Associate Professor of Old Testament and Director of the Center for Theology, Women, and Gender, Princeton Theological Seminary

"In this comprehensive volume, Brown moves biblical exegesis into the twenty-first century. Brown introduces a fresh understanding of exegesis that acknowledges the multivalence of texts and supports the reader in seeking creativity, adventure, and wonder. Well-researched and filled with helpful textual examples, *A Handbook to Old Testament Exegesis* is a welcome addition to the library of any student of biblical interpretation."

—**Nyasha Junior,** Assistant Professor of Hebrew Bible, Temple University, and author of *An Introduction to Womanist Biblical Interpretation*

A Handbook to
Old Testament Exegesis

William P. Brown

WESTMINSTER
JOHN KNOX PRESS
LOUISVILLE · KENTUCKY

© 2017 William P. Brown

First edition
Published by Westminster John Knox Press
Louisville, Kentucky

17 18 19 20 21 22 23 24 25 26—10 9 8 7 6 5 4 3 2 1

Scripture translations not obviously literal or otherwise identified are from the New Revised Standard Version of the Bible, copyright © 1989 by the Division of Christian Education of the National Council of the Churches of Christ in the U.S.A., and used by permission—with "YHWH" in place of "the Lord."

Scripture quotations marked CEB are from the *Common English Bible*, copyright © 2011 Common English Bible, and used by permission.

Scripture quotations marked NIV are from *The Holy Bible, New International Version*, copyright © 1973, 1978, 1984, 2011 by Biblica, Inc.® Used by permission. All rights reserved worldwide.

Scripture quotations marked NJPS are from *The TANAKH: The New JPS Translation according to the Traditional Hebrew Text*, copyright 1985 by the Jewish Publication Society. Used by permission.

Book design by Sharon Adams
Cover design by Lisa Buckley Design

Library of Congress Cataloging-in-Publication Data
Names: Brown, William P., 1958– author.
Title: A handbook to Old Testament exegesis / William P. Brown.
Description: Louisville, KY : Westminster John Knox Press, 2017. | Includes bibliographical references and index.
Identifiers: LCCN 2016052019 (print) | LCCN 2017004071 (ebook) | ISBN 9780664259938 (pbk. : alk. paper) | ISBN 9781611647990 (ebk.)
Subjects: LCSH: Bible. Old Testament—Hermeneutics.
Classification: LCC BS476 .B7155 2017 (print) | LCC BS476 (ebook) | DDC 221.601—dc23
LC record available at https://lccn.loc.gov/2016052019

♾ The paper used in this publication meets the minimum requirements of the American National Standard for Information Sciences—Permanence of Paper for Printed Library Materials, ANSI Z39.48-1992.

Contents

Contents

Acknowledgments

This book could not have been written without the many students I have had the privilege of teaching at Union Presbyterian Seminary in Richmond, Virginia, and Columbia Theological Seminary in Decatur, Georgia. Their questions and insights, interests and commitments, curiosity and convictions, have greatly informed the writing of this handbook. My hope is that what I have gained from my students will carry over to readers of this book.

In addition to students, I gratefully acknowledge the mentors who have shaped my teaching and exegetical work over the years, beginning with S. Dean McBride and W. Sibley Towner, who graciously welcomed a junior colleague and patiently modeled for me what biblical exegesis could and should be. Other teaching colleagues at Union, past and present, include John Carroll, Carson Brisson, Jane Vann, Rodney Sadler, Frances Taylor Gench, Carol Schnabl Schweitzer, Katie Cannon, Dawn DeVries, Stan Skreslet, and Paul Achtemeier. My recent or current OT colleagues at Columbia Seminary, Kathleen O'Connor, Christine Roy Yoder, Walter Brueggemann, Brennan Breed, and Ryan Bonfiglio, have shown me ways of doing exegesis that have profoundly expanded my hermeneutical horizons. As for those outside of my own teaching area, I thank Marcia Riggs, Stan Saunders, Raj Nadella, Beth Johnson, Mark Douglas, Martha Moore-Keish, Haruko Ward, Kim Long, David Bartlett, Kathy Dawson, Ralph Watkins, and Rodger Nishioka for widening and sharpening my interpretive lenses ever more so. Mentors beyond these two institutions include Carol Newsom, John Hayes, Patrick Miller, Gene Tucker, Max Miller, Brent Strawn, Leong Seow, Jacqueline Lapsley, Dennis Olson, Mark Smith, Chip Dobbs-Allsopp, Kathie Sakenfeld, Alan Cooper, Susan Niditch, Randall Bailey, Samuel Balentine, Sam Adams, and Richard Middleton. There are, of course, many others whose writings I have found enormously helpful in crafting this handbook. They are featured in the citations and bibliographies.

I am grateful for my institution, Columbia Theological Seminary, which granted me a leave of absence (2015–16), and for the Center of Theological Inquiry in Princeton and its director, William Storrar, who made it possible for me to complete the project in a timely manner. The collaborative ethos at CTI was an ideal context to expand my theological purview in truly "astronomical" ways.[1]

---

1. I was one among a group of diverse scholars who were invited to explore the "societal implications of astrobiology" at CTI during 2015–2016.

I am also grateful to Westminster John Knox Press for the timely invitation to write this book. Thanks particularly to Bridgett Green, who initiated the invitation and gave me plenty of moral support throughout the project; to Daniel Braden, who shepherded the project to its publication with care and grace; and to S. David Garber, who doggedly corrected the manuscript, wrestling with the devil in the editorial details. Many thanks for their hard work and forbearance in seeing this project to its completion.

Finally, thanks to my lifelong partner, Gail, who gladly shared in this sabbatical adventure. Without her patience and support this project would not have been possible.

This book is dedicated to the memory of James Luther Mays (1921–2015), whose inaugural lecture at Union in 1960, "Exegesis as a Theological Discipline," was the inspiration behind this work. In his teaching and writings, Dr. Mays consistently modeled what truly could be called the "ministry of exegesis."

Preface and Plan

All too often exegesis is taught as a series of discrete analytical techniques designed to help the interpreter "unlock" the text's meaning. But this is not how exegesis, biblical or otherwise, works. Moreover, there is nothing particularly transformative about an exegetical framework that has more to do with merely explaining the biblical text than with exploring its various capacities for meaning. If isolated from the broader activity of theological inquiry and self-critical reflection, biblical exegesis fails to be a sustaining discipline in the practice of ministry. The need remains for an exegetical guide framed by a hermeneutic of wonder, a generative and generous hermeneutic that explores the text's "wondrous depths" (*mira profunditas*) in community.

While the teaching of biblical exegesis remains foundational in theological education today, it is also ripe for reenvisioning, particularly as the need for greater integration is felt in the theological curriculum. In addition to the practical and curricular reasons, the motivation behind this project also has its theoretical underpinnings, among them: (1) the explosion of methods beyond the "analytical" approaches that have held sway in biblical scholarship; (2) the dismantling of the interpreter's "objective" position vis-à-vis the biblical text; (3) the multiple roles that context plays at every level of interpretation; and (4) the rise of biblical reception history as a way of reconceptualizing the interpretive enterprise, from text-criticism and translation to modern commentary and artistic use.

All these reasons for reenvisioning exegesis boil down to how the biblical text itself is viewed, not as a static entity whose meaning is fixed but as a lively partner in dialogue with readers in dialogue with each other. A hermeneutic of wonder (see chap. 1) views the biblical text as inexhaustible in its depth and incalculable in its breadth of contexts. The emphasis falls not so much on what the text *is* but on what it can *do* (see Breed 2014, 117). Read and interpreted, texts are productive. Readings (re)organize texts as much as texts (re)orient readers. The dialogical dynamic of reading texts with others invariably generates a plurality of outcomes. Accounting for interpretive differences should be a fundamental task of biblical exegesis.

The aim of this handbook is to develop a fresh, example-filled introduction to exegesis of the Hebrew Bible that brings together various exegetical perspectives (methods, criticisms, reading strategies, etc.) in a way that cultivates the reader's curiosity, critical engagement, and empathic imagination. As they currently stand, exegetical introductions basically fall into two camps: (1) handbooks focused primarily on analytical modes or "tools" of exegesis and (2) surveys of various methods operative in biblical scholarship. The first camp is too limited in its focus, and the second often remains detached from the student's hands-on engagement. Exegesis is a practiced art, a learned craft, and teaching it involves much more than presenting a survey or providing tools and techniques.

By addressing more explicitly the various capacities of the biblical text for meaning, capacities that become evident when the text is read in various contexts, exegesis is able to host an enlivening, ever-broadening conversation among diverse readers. Generative dialogue with the text should naturally lead to generative dialogue with others regarding the text, including those who view the text quite differently. In other words, dialogue with others about the text is integral to one's own dialogue with the text. The two are not to be isolated. Put another way, the reader's sense of *wonder of the text* naturally leads to *wondering about the text* with others. This is not to say that the text can simply be conformed to the reader's expectations, but it does affirm that the text can mean more than one thing when read in community.

Exegesis, in short, should foster an expectancy of surprise. Broadly speaking, this handbook aims to reframe exegesis in order to facilitate more generative, if not transformative, encounters with the text and with others around the text. Since wonder is a sustaining force in theological inquiry and ministerial practice (Barth 1979, 63–73), fostering imagination and resilience (Sinclair 2014), it should also be a sustaining force in exegetical study, fostering lively curiosity, critical engagement, and imaginative reflection. Wonder, I am convinced, is integral to the careful and creative work of exegesis, for wonder is the "*eros* of inquiry" (Miller 1992, 15, 53), the enlivening, expectant journey toward discovery and transformation, the *eros* that leads to *caritas* (Scarry 1999, 81; Davis 2007, 40). Exegesis is both a tremendous responsibility and an incredible joy, a praxis most fully realized in community. Exegesis should model such open, wonder-driven inquiry as it facilitates the necessary movement from text to table.

FOR THE INSTRUCTOR

This book is designed to be a resource for the teaching and learning of exegesis. Because it is a handbook for beginning students and not a technical introduction to biblical hermeneutics, it is meant to be practical. That means that this book tries to provide enough background without saying too much theoretically. Freedom is left for the instructor to build upon, comment on, bypass, or disagree with what is discussed. No doubt the instructor will deem certain chapters insufficient given one's own expertise. This book is simply an enabling introduction, not a comprehensive one. There are many gaps; other chapters need to be included.

In addition, I suspect that not all chapters will be deemed equally useful or important by the instructor and, for that matter, by the student. They are written so that the instructor can profitably skip some chapters, such as the one on translation (chap. 4), which presupposes a rudimentary knowledge of Hebrew. Nevertheless, even for an English-based exegesis class, this chapter can still be profitably read. (All Hebrew references are transliterated.)

This handbook is both theoretically conversant, but not technically so, and practically oriented, but not exhaustively so. There are several introductions that attempt some level of theoretical comprehensiveness and diversity, with each essay written by a different author. This book is not an edited collection of methodologies. Instead, it is written by one person, but I have written it in consultation with others whose specific expertise far exceeds my own. This, I hope, provides some measure of cohesion across the various approaches discussed. The trade-off, of course, is that the handbook is not as diverse as one might hope, including myself.

PLAN

This handbook is a show-and-tell book, or better, tell-and-show. It is structured such that each chapter introduces and discusses a distinctive approach to biblical exegesis and then shows how it might work with various texts, including two common texts. Together, these chapters form an expanding narrative of discovery and practice. To achieve that, the book is organized around four sequential steps: (1) Getting Started, (2) Analytical Approaches, (3) Readings in Place, and (4) Communication. "Getting Started" enables readers to identify their own hermeneutical context and to articulate first impressions about certain biblical texts prior to analytical study. "Analytical Approaches" employs the various tools and practices of exegesis, including translation for those who know Hebrew and certain critically based—some would say "classical"—methods. "Readings in Place" explores particular self-identified contextual approaches, from feminist to ecological, including theological interpretation as a culminating, integrative step. Last, "Communication" focuses on the necessity of communicating the results of one's exegetical work, such as in the form of a sermon or lesson plan, within a particular context, namely, a community that also needs to be "exegeted."

One innovation of this handbook is its focus on the reader's self-understanding and experience as an exegete. A chapter is dedicated to helping readers see themselves as a bona fide exegetes equipped with various interpretive lenses and self-critical capacities (chap. 2). Readers are invited to respond to a series of questions regarding their own personal, cultural, and theological backgrounds. This step is meant to help readers articulate the hermeneutical perspectives that help determine what each one looks for and finds meaningful in the text and why.

A core conviction is that as exegetes are multifaceted in their individual approaches to biblical interpretation, so the biblical text is multivalent when it is read and interpreted in the company of others. By exploring various ways of interpreting the text that emerge from different social locations ("places"), the beginning exegete will become aware of the wide range of readings that are possible, depending on the questions posed and the perspectives adopted, and be able to engage them dialogically and self-critically.

Every chapter contains a series of questions that highlight the distinctive aims and accents of a particular exegetical perspective or reading strategy, accompanied by discussion and concluding with specific examples of practice. Various biblical texts are featured to illustrate how they "work" from a particular interpretive perspective or analysis. Another innovation is that two common texts are explored in every chapter. While a variety of biblical texts are covered in the handbook, each chapter concludes with a (re)examination of two common texts: Gen. 1:1–2:4a and Gen. 2:4b–3:24. After much deliberation, I chose these two texts because they well accommodate each and every method discussed. In addition, they were selected because of their contrast in content and style, as well as their interrelatedness and contemporary significance. They serve as the connecting thread throughout the handbook. Finally, each chapter concludes with a bibliographical list of works, both cited and consulted, and recommended resources for further study.

BIBLIOGRAPHY FOR PREFACE

Barth, Karl. 1979 [1963]. *Evangelical Theology: An Introduction.* Translated by Grover Foley. Grand Rapids: Eerdmans Publishing.

Breed, Brennan W. 2014. *Nomadic Text: A Theory of Biblical Reception History.* Bloomington / Indianapolis: Indiana University Press.

Davis, Ellen F. 2007. "Soil That Is Scripture." In *Engaging Biblical Authority*, edited by William P. Brown, 36–44. Louisville, KY: Westminster John Knox Press.

Davis, Ellen F., and Richard B. Hayes, eds. 2003. *The Art of Reading Scripture.* Grand Rapids: Eerdmans Publishing.

Miller, Jerome A. 1992. *In the Throe of Wonder: Intimations of the Sacred in a Post-Modern World.* New York: SUNY Press.

Scarry, Elaine. 1999. *On Beauty and Being Just.* Princeton, NJ: Princeton University Press.

Sinclair, George R., Jr. 2014. *Walking in Wonder: Resilience in Ministry.* Eugene, OR: Cascade Books.

Abbreviations

AAAS	American Association for the Advancement of Science
ABD	*Anchor Bible Dictionary*. Edited by D. N. Freedman. 6 vols. New York, 1992
ABRL	Anchor Bible Reference Library
alt.	a quotation slightly altered
ANE	ancient Near East
ANET	*Ancient Near Eastern Texts Relating to the Old Testament*. Edited by James B. Pritchard. 3rd ed., with supplement. Princeton, NJ: Princeton University Press, 1969
AOAT	Alter Orient und Altes Testament
AT	author's translation
AYBRL	The Anchor Yale Bible Reference Library
BA	*Biblical Archaeologist*
BCE	before the Common Era
BDB	Brown, Francis, S. R. Driver, and Charles A. Briggs. *The Brown-Driver-Briggs Hebrew and English Lexicon*. Peabody, MA: Hendrickson, 1996
BHS	*Biblia Hebraica Stuttgartensia*. Edited by K. Elliger and W. Rudolph. Stuttgart: Deutsche Bibelstiftung, 1983
BJS	Brown Judaic Studies
BTC	The Bible in the Twenty-First Century
BZAW	Beihefte zur Zeitschrift für die altestamentliche Wissenschaft
c.	century
ca.	circa, approximately
CE	in the Common Era
CEB	Common English Bible
chap(s).	chapter(s)
DCH	*The Dictionary of Classical Hebrew*. Edited by David J. A. Clines. 8 vols. Sheffield: Sheffield Academic Press, 1993–2011
DJD	Discoveries in the Judean Desert
e.g.	*exempli gratia*, for example
Eng.	English
et al.	*et alii*, and other persons

etc.	et cetera, and the rest/others
FOTL	Forms of the Old Testament Literature
GBS	Guides to Biblical Scholarship
GBSOTG	Guides to Biblical Scholarship: Old Testament Guides
HALOT	Koehler, Ludwig, Walter Baumgartner, and Johann J. Stamm. *The Hebrew and Aramaic Lexicon of the Old Testament*. Edited and translated by M. E. J. Richardson. 5 vols. Leiden: Brill, 2000
HBT	*Horizons in Biblical Theology*
IBHS	B. K. Waltke and M. O'Connor. *An Introduction to Biblical Hebrew Syntax*. Eisenbrauns: Winona Lake, IN, 1990
IBT	Interpreting Biblical Texts
ICC	International Critical Commentary
IDB	*The Interpreter's Dictionary of the Bible*. Edited by G. A. Buttrick. 4 vols. Nashville, 1962
IEJ	*Israel Exploration Journal*
ITC	International Theological Commentary
JANES	*Journal of the Ancient Near Eastern Society*
JBL	*Journal of Biblical Literature*
JCS	*Journal of Cuneiform Studies*
JSNTSup	Journal for the Study of the New Testament Supplement Series
JSOT	*Journal for the Study of the Old Testament*
JSOTSup	Journal for the Study of the Old Testament Supplement Series
KAI	*Kanaanäische und aramäische Inschriften*. Edited by Herbert Donner and Wolfgang Röllig. 2nd ed. Wiesbaden: Harrassowitz, 1966–69
KAT	Kommentar zum Alten Testament
KJV	King James Version
Lat.	Latin
LH	Laws of Hammurabi
LHBOTS	Library of Hebrew Bible Old Testament Studies
LXX	Septuagint
mg.	marginal note/reading
MT	Masoretic Text (in Hebrew)
mya	millions of years ago
NIDB	*New Interpreters Dictionary of the Bible*. Edited by Katharine Doob Sakenfeld. 5 vols. Nashville, TN: Abingdon, 2006–2009
NIV	New International Version
NJPS	*Tanakh: The Holy Scriptures; The New JPS Translation according to the Traditional Hebrew Text*
NRSV	New Revised Standard Version
NT	New Testament
NTL	New Testament Library
OBT	Overtures to Biblical Theology
OG	Old Greek (version)
OT	Old Testament

OTL	Old Testament Library
OTP	*Old Testament Pseudepigrapha*. Edited by J. H. Charlesworth. 2 vols. Garden City, NY: Doubleday, 1983
pl.	plural
r.	reigned
RBS	Resources for Biblical Study
RSV	Revised Standard Version
SAACT	State Archives of Assyria Cuneiform Texts
SAAS	State Archives of Assyria Studies
SBLBSNA	Society of Biblical Literature Biblical Scholarship in North America
SBLCP	Society of Biblical Literature Centennial Publications
SBLSS	Society of Biblical Literature Symposium Series
SBLWAW	Society of Biblical Literature Writings from the Ancient World
sg.	singular
Smr	Samaritan Pentateuch
UBS	United Bible Society
v(v).	verse(s)
vol(s).	volume(s)
VT	*Vetus Testamentum*
VTSup	Supplements to Vetus Testamentum
ya	years ago; *see also* mya
ZAW	*Zeitschrift für die alttestamentliche Wissenschaft*

Part I

Getting Started

1

A Hermeneutical Adventure

What we observe is not nature in itself,
but nature exposed to our method of questioning.
Werner Heisenberg[1]

Reading can be a sublime and complex process.
Renita J. Weems[2]

The early rabbis commended the study of Scripture in no uncertain terms.

> Study it, study it—for everything is in it! Examine it diligently until you are worn
> out with old age by it, and do not be distracted from it; you could have no better
> measure than it. (Mishnah *'Abot* 5:22)

The verb translated here as "study" ($\sqrt{hpk}$) literally means "turn," as if to say that the Bible
is a finely crafted jewel that, when carefully turned, sparkles with the light of incom-
parable wisdom, the sum total of truth. But the metaphor is also apt in another sense.
In the practice of Bible study, "turning" not only involves the text; it also involves the
interpreter. Interpreting the text entails "turning things over in one's mind," from con-
jectures to new perspectives, from fresh questions to surprising conclusions. Interpreting
the Bible requires discipline and focus, on the one hand, and pondering and creativity, on
the other. It invariably involves change, "turning."

Welcome to the exciting world of biblical interpretation, a world that is expanding
at an accelerated rate! Biblical interpretation today covers a dizzying array of methods,
orientations, and strategies—the various "angles" from which the biblical text is viewed
and the various ways it is understood and lived out by readers. When a single biblical text
meets differently situated readers, it is hard to predict what will happen. The reason is
that textual meaning is never fixed. Meaning is not something contained within the text,
as if it were waiting to be unlocked and released from literary confinement. Meaning,

1. Heisenberg 1962, 26.
2. Weems 1991, 59.

rather, emerges from one's encounter with the text. It is evoked within the interactive space between reader and text. Meaning is relational. When a book falls from the shelf and lands with its pages wide open but no one is there to read it, does it convey meaning?

Truth be told, a reader is required for a text to be meaningful. By itself a text contains merely marks on a page or pixels on a screen. It does not exist as meaningful without its readers. The text comes alive, as it were, when it is read (or heard or sung, etc.), whenever it is communicated or interpreted. In the encounter, the text becomes a partner in the construction of meaning. On the one hand, the text's meaning, when discerned for the first time, strikes the reader as something outside of the familiar range of experience. On the other hand, it is the reader who decides how the text is to be read (and communicated), like a musician playing from a score. Not unlike musical notations regarding tempo, phrasing, and volume, which determine certain parameters of a performance, there are textual signs and rhetorical conventions that cue the reader in the act of interpretation. Nevertheless, every reader creatively invests something of oneself in the interpretation of a text, in the "performance" of the text's meaning. While the relationship forged between a biblical text and a particular reader is unique and ever evolving, it is also a relationship worth sharing with others around the table.

TEXT TO TABLE: THE MINISTRY OF EXEGESIS

With respect to biblical study, the practice of interpretation involves something called "exegesis." The Greek term *exēgēsis* is derived from the verb *exēgeisthai*, which means "to lead out." Formally speaking, then, exegesis is about drawing meaning from the text. But in practice (and in principle), this is far more complex than what the term itself suggests. Although exegesis is a discipline, it is not a strictly objective one (and certainly not a disinterested one), for it necessarily involves the interpreter's active, creative, even intuitive work. While exegesis is a science that requires various tools of analysis, it is also something of an art that involves the interpreter's imagination and creativity. Perhaps it is best to say that exegesis is neither entirely a science nor an art. It is a craft, a learned discipline cultivated over time through practice and gained from considering the practice of others. Exegesis is a lifelong venture that carries the reader from the details of translation and analysis to the creative work of communication. Decisions—both judicious and speculative, careful and creative—must be made at every step along the way. Even the tedious work of translation requires imaginative effort as much as the creative work of communication requires focus and precision.

Exegesis involves listening. It treats the biblical text as a voice, albeit distant and foreign yet in full dialogical partnership with the reader. As with any new conversation, exegesis begins with introductions: the introduction of the text and the introduction of the exegete. That is why first impressions are important, although they may not be definitive in the long run when the dialogue often proceeds in unanticipated directions. Every exegesis begins with a guess or first impression and then concludes with validation or, more often, a change of understanding. The exegesis of the text also involves, necessarily so, an exegesis of the self. Like a conversation between two strangers, exegesis is all about becoming a better listener, but not only of the text. Exegesis also involves coming to know yourself as an interpreter every time you engage the text and identifying the influences and interests that shape how you read texts. Finally, exegesis involves listening well to others at the table, a welcoming roundtable in which every seat is open and filled.

From start to finish, exegesis is a communal enterprise. You are not the first interpreter to work with a biblical passage. You follow countless other interpreters from generations past who have grappled with the text, some of whom have written about it. The commentary literature, both ancient and recent, is vast and available. Consider it a gift. Moreover, you have the privileged opportunity to work with others in dialogue, sharing your insights and listening to theirs. Do not take others for granted, especially when you are convinced that you are right about a biblical text. Often the best insights are recognized only after your own interpretive conclusions come to be questioned by others. Finally, for those who interpret texts for the sake of preaching, worship, or teaching, the community remains ever present in the mind (and heart) of the interpreter. Exegesis is inquiry in communion.

As you develop the craft of exegesis, you are entering a particularly exciting time in the history of biblical interpretation, a revolutionary time in fact, as is the case with other disciplines of inquiry. In act 2, scene 1, of the play *Legacy of Light* by Karen Zacarías, Dr. Olivia Hasting Brown addresses a group of Girl Scouts about her profession as an astrophysicist. She concludes with Einstein's discovery of relativity and what it reveals about the universe:

> Suddenly you have a more chaotic, volatile universe; not a Puritan on a bicycle, but a Hells Angel on a Harley. Throw in the fact that the universe is still expanding and you have a complex, interconnected universe gunning on all cylinders and making one hell of a wheelie while barely respecting the dynamics of physical law. (Zacarías 2007, 65)

This riveting description of a dynamic universe applies well to the contemporary world of biblical interpretation. Exegesis too has become more volatile and complex, gunning on all cylinders and roaring forth in all directions.

A number of factors have contributed to such dramatic change: the shift away from apologetics toward a more open-ended and dialogical approach to Scripture, a move away from defending the Bible to bringing the Bible into honest conversation. Also, the world is changing, culturally, economically, and physically. As the world has become more globalized, so it has become more interconnected. More and more readers from diverse contexts are entering the "House of the Interpreter."[3] That is to say, awareness of the multicultural community of readers has dramatically heightened within the last several decades. The assured results of exegesis of past generations are contested and destabilized by new generations of readers from various contexts. Voices long marginalized or silenced are being heard. Readers from across the global South and East are joining those from the North and West to sit at table together. The multiple ways of interpreting the

---

3. The reference is found in John Bunyan's Christian classic *The Pilgrim's Progress* (1678); cf. https://en.wikipedia.org/wiki/The_Pilgrim%27s_Progress.

biblical text reflect this growing diversity of readers, making every exegetical insight at once generative and provisional.

A cursory glance at the myriad approaches available today, from critical to cultural, literary to ideological, may seem overwhelming. But here we are, and jump in we must. Nevertheless, the active fray of exegesis need not be cause for bewilderment, but ultimately cause for wonder. If exegesis is fundamentally "reading seeking understanding" (cf. Acts 8:30), akin to Anselm of Canterbury's definition of theology,[4] then the joy of understanding, the excitement of new insight, and the thrill of new perspectives are more than simply by-products. For all its hard work, exegesis can be and should be an exercise of "inquisitive awe."[5]

THE HERMENEUTICAL ADVENTURE

Exegesis is only the beginning; it marks the start of an adventure that interpreters, from biblical scholars to philosophers, have reflected on over the centuries. How does one arrive at meaning or gain understanding of a text? The structure of the journey is the stuff of "hermeneutics." This rather technical-sounding name comes from the god Hermes, son of Zeus and the Olympian messenger known for his cunning, swiftness, and agility. In Greek mythology, Hermes delivered messages from the gods to mortals. Regarding the Bible, however, or any ancient text for that matter, the hermeneutical work of interpretation is neither swift nor cunning. Slow and stumbling are more like it. The text is never fully accessible; it will always be more than what we think we know about it. A historical and cultural chasm separates the modern interpreter and the ancient author, filled only partially (and sometimes erroneously) by the long and venerable history of interpretation. We cannot fully grasp what an ancient text said to its intended audience any more than we can transport ourselves back in time and conduct interviews.

Still, by attempting to peer across the hermeneutical divide, we can catch a glimpse of what the ancient text *could* have meant through language study (philology), literary analysis, historical research, and comparative work. Such lines of investigation help us to develop a matrix of possible meanings, some more plausible than others. But we can never overcome the hermeneutical divide; the full meaning of the ancient text remains ever elusive. When a telescope probes the night sky, it not only brings into view objects from great distances; it also looks back in time, measured in light-years. Given the great distances traversed by light, telescopes are the only time machines we have. The more distant the galaxy, the older and more obscure it is to the observer and the faster it is moving away. Such is the built-in limitation of sight, thanks to the finite speed of light. Similar is the limitation of hermeneutical understanding, thanks to the span of time and our own cultural distance. Call it the finite speed of life.

There is, moreover, something broader about the hermeneutical enterprise than simply determining what the text *could* have said in its earliest or originating contexts. If that

---

4. "Faith seeking understanding," from *fides quaerens intellectum*, the original title to Anselm's *Proslogion* as referenced in his preface. See Anselm 1998, 83–87.
5. My brief definition of "wonder." See Brown 2015, 1–14.

were all there is to hermeneutics, biblical interpretation would be strictly a historical enterprise, an antiquarian's quest. For many of its readers, however, the Bible is more than an ancient artifact; it bears profound relevance, and in ways not necessarily reducible to author's original intent, however partially that can be "retrieved." What the text *means*, in other words, is as critical as what it once meant.[6] Discerning the text's meaning includes interpreting the text in the light of one's experience and within one's community. One cannot interpret the biblical text without interpreting oneself and one's context.

While exegesis is a matter of best interpretive practices, hermeneutics is more theoretically oriented: it explores how the process of interpretation is to be understood. While this handbook is devoted primarily to the practical level of interpretation, some hermeneutical overview is needed. Interpretation, specifically exegesis, is "a practical skill," whereas hermeneutics operates more on the philosophical level (Conradie 2010, 298). For our purposes, we recognize that the act of interpreting Scripture is a peculiar one. It is different from interpreting other ancient (or modern) texts, for it requires more than simply studying from a distance, as if biblical texts were simply ancient documents housed in a stuffy museum. For communities of faith, biblical texts are considered authoritative and transformative. They teach and move people; lives are changed. They have relevance and currency. Walter Brueggemann talks of texts that "characteristically erupt into new usage" (2000, 1, 18). They "explode" with new meaning, propelled beyond the interpreter's own analytical or critical insight. Interpreting biblical texts requires creative and empathic imagination as well as analytical acumen and lexical proficiency. All together they help make the agile exegete.

Nevertheless, reading is not the only way biblical texts are interpreted. Biblical interpretation can take place in many ways and among various genres, such as liturgy, sermons, confessions, testimonies, sacraments, hymns, prayers, catechisms, testimonies, public speeches, films, media reports (Conradie 2010, 298). Biblical interpretation is going on all the time and all around, rightly or wrongly, for better or for worse. By necessity, the focus of this handbook is on the dynamics that unfold between text and reader, but even this narrow field of vision is filled, or (better) fraught, with background. In the encounter between text and reader, worlds intersect and sometimes collide.

Drawing from the work of Paul Ricoeur, a French philosopher who had much to say about hermeneutics, one can speak of at least three worlds that interact in the encounter between text and reader: (1) the world behind the text, (2) the world in or of the text, and (3) the world in front of the text (see, e.g., Ricoeur 1976, 88, 92–94). The world "behind" the text refers to the historical context of the text's origin, retrieved through the work of historical investigation. The world "of" or "in" the text designates the text itself, disclosed through close readings. The world "in front of" the text includes the contexts in which the text is interpreted and appropriated, its history of interpretation or reception, including the world of the reader. That is to say, by reading the text you are making history!

Others refer to the "hermeneutical circle." Originally cast by Friedrich Schleiermacher and developed by Martin Heidegger and Hans-Georg Gadamer, the hermeneutical circle acknowledges the reader's investment in the construction of the text's meaning by highlighting the interplay between the whole and the parts in the eye of the interpreter.

6. See Stendahl 1962.

While one's understanding of the text as a whole is made possible only in relation to the text's individual parts, one's understanding of each part is gained in relation to the whole. The result is an unbroken circle of interpretation. The metaphor has also been used to include the ongoing interaction between the text, its context(s), and the reader, whereby the text is read and reread with new understanding. Some prefer to talk of a spiral rather than a circle (e.g., Schökel 1998, 74). Gadamer regarded interpretation as a "fusion of horizons" (1989, 306): the horizon of the past melding with that of the present, resulting in a creative synthesis. The thing about a horizon, however, is that as one is drawn to it, it continues to extend beyond one's reach. The hermeneutical journey is never ending.

Simply by scratching the surface, then, the hermeneutical process becomes complicated. Perhaps a diagram will help.

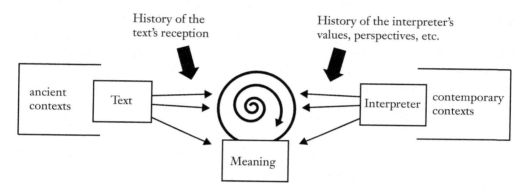

Simplistic as it is, the attempt here is to illustrate how the encounter between text and interpreter is one of mediated and interactive engagement. Call it a "hermeneutical convolution." A tidy circle this isn't. On the far left side, the ancient contexts, including that of the author and/or authorial community, constitute the world "behind" the text. On the far right side is the interpreter's world, the world "in front of" the text, including the interpreter's perspectives, values, cultural background, and so forth. The rotating circle, ever "turning" (!) in the center, illustrates the dialogical dynamic between text and reader, the "hermeneutical circle," if you will, in which the formation of meaning is ongoing, in which preunderstandings, critical examination, and new understandings all come to bear (see Conradie 2008, 107). Equally important is the fact that the circle in the center is supported and mediated by trajectories illustrating the history of the text's reception and the history of the interpreter's own perspectives and values. This is all to say that the text does not come to the interpreter unmediated but filtered and shaped by the text's own history from generation to generation and by the interpreter's own perspectives, values, and prejudgments.

FOR THE LOVE OF EXEGESIS

So much for the hermeneutical lay of the land. As the disciplined beginning point of interpretive inquiry, exegesis should not be encumbered with urgent and anxious expectations, for example, that it will make you a better preacher or teacher. No doubt good exegesis will help. But there is something more fundamental and less functionalistic at work that sustains the best practices of exegesis. New Testament scholar Beverly Gaventa puts it well:

> [The] experiences of delight and wonder solve no doctrinal debate and settle no pressing question of polity. They fall alike on the just and the unjust, the novice and the scholar. They are not limited to believers, to be sure, but for believers they are occasions for enjoying not only language itself but [also] the God whose ways are revealed through that language. Failing to attend to the aesthetics of Scripture places the act of interpretation in jeopardy, since the text is not separable from its language and the multiple wonders of that language. (Gaventa 2007, 111)

Gaventa's plea to invigorate biblical exegesis with a sense of wonder addresses two broad hermeneutical issues: the aesthetics of the text and the self-critical awareness of the exegete. Viewing the text as an aesthetic expression of meaning "performed" in interpretive dialogue and communication, rather than as a repository of meaning to be drawn out once and for all, allows for a more transformative encounter with the text. An arresting piece of visual art, for example, draws the viewer in, engaging both intellect and emotion. In a moving piece of music, the listener loses self in the music's cadences and rhythms and at the same time attains a heightened level of awareness. Indeed, a work of art can inspire one's own creativity and imagination. So also does a text, particularly a biblical text. If the various perspectives, methods, and reading strategies practiced today, from the traditional to the ideological, from the analytical to the intercultural, can be framed as ways of exploring the text's aesthetic lure and versatility for meaning, as well as the interpreter's self-critical engagement, then the practice of exegesis will have a more sustaining, if not transformative, impact. Ultimately, I want to show how the practice of biblical exegesis can be part of the practice of ministry, a practice of empathy, wonder, and hospitality.

Good exegesis requires effort and discipline, yet it also requires delight and patience. If anything, exegesis requires a deliberate slowing down of the reading process, a reveling in the details and subtle nuances of the text, as well as a stepping back to ponder the forest and not just the trees. For the sake of transparency, I confess that my ecclesial tradition (Reformed) lifts up the enjoyment and glorification of God as the "chief end" of humanity (see the first question of the Westminster Catechism). Reading and interpreting Scripture is a part of that enjoyment, a transformative joy to be shared with others. When Scripture is read and communicated with understanding, clarity, and fresh relevance, such joy is beyond measure (see Neh. 8:12).

BIBLIOGRAPHY FOR CHAPTER 1

Anselm. 1998. *Anselm of Canterbury: The Major Works*. Edited by Brian Davies and G. R. Evans. Oxford World's Classics. Oxford: Oxford University Press.

Brown, William P. 2015. *Sacred Sense: Discovering the Wonder of God's Word and World*. Grand Rapids: Eerdmans Publishing.

Brueggemann, Walter. 2000. *Texts That Linger, Words That Explode*. Edited by Patrick D. Miller. Minneapolis: Fortress Press.

Conradie, Ernst M. 2008. *Angling for Interpretation: A First Introduction to Biblical, Theological and Contextual Hermeneutics*. Study Guides in Religion and Theology 13. Stellenbosch, South Africa: Sun Press.

———. 2010. "What on Earth Is an Ecological Hermeneutics? Some Broad Parameters." In *Ecological Hermeneutics: Biblical, Historical and Theological Perspectives*, edited by David G. Horrell, Cherryl Hunt, Christopher Southgate, and Francesca Stavrakopoulou, 295–313. London / New York: T&T Clark International.

Gadamer, Hans-Georg. 1989. *Truth and Method*. 2nd, rev. ed. Translated by Joel Weinsheimer and Donald G. Marshall. New York: Crossroad.

Gaventa, Beverly R. 2007. "To Glorify God and Enjoy God Forever: A Place for Joy in Reformed Readings of Scripture." In *Reformed Theology: Identity and Ecumenicity II: Biblical Interpretation in the Reformed Tradition*, edited by Wallace M. Alston Jr. and Michael Welker, 107–15. Grand Rapids: Eerdmans Publishing.

Goldingay, John. 1995. *Models for Interpretation of Scripture*. Grand Rapids: Eerdmans Publishing / Carlisle: Paternoster.

Heisenberg, Werner. 1962. *Physics and Philosophy: The Revolution of Modern Science*. New York: Harper & Row.

Martin, Dale. 2008. *Pedagogy of the Bible: An Analysis and Proposal*. Louisville, KY: Westminster John Knox Press.

McKenzie, Steven L., and Stephen R. Haynes, eds. 1999. *To Each Its Own Meaning: An Introduction to Biblical Criticisms and Their Applications*. Louisville, KY: Westminster John Knox Press.

McKenzie, Steven L., and John Kaltner, eds. 2013. *New Meanings for Ancient Texts: Recent Approaches to Biblical Criticisms and Their Applications*. Louisville, KY: Westminster John Knox Press.

Ricoeur, Paul. 1976. *Interpretation Theory: Discourse and the Surplus of Meaning*. Fort Worth: Texas Christian University Press.

Schökel, Luis Alonso, with José María Bravo. 1998. *A Manual of Hermeneutics*. Translated by Liliana M. Rosa. The Biblical Seminar 54. Sheffield: Sheffield Academic Press.

Soulen, Richard N., and R. Kendall Soulen. 2011. *Handbook of Biblical Criticism*. 4th ed. Louisville, KY: Westminster John Knox Press.

Stendahl, Krister. 1962. "Biblical Theology, Contemporary." *IDB* 1:418–32. Reprint in *Meanings: The Bible as Document and as Guide*, 11–44. Philadelphia: Fortress Press, 1984.

Weems, Renita J. 1991. "Reading Her Way through the Struggle: African American Women and the Bible." In *Stony the Road We Trod: African American Biblical Interpretation*, edited by Cain H. Felder, 57–77. Minneapolis: Augsburg Fortress Press.

Zacarías, Karen. 2007. *Legacy of Light*. A Play Commissioned by Arena Stage. New York: Graham Agency.

2

Self-Exegesis

> We are drenched in contexts.
> *Kathleen O'Connor*[1]

The Bible can never be read and interpreted impartially. Indeed, how can it be? By any definition, interpretation is a subjective activity. As the object of one's attention, the text as read and understood (or not) invariably reflects something of the reader's own perspective. Consequently, any full exegesis of the text requires, in some form or manner, an exegesis of the self. Exegesis is all about becoming a better reader not only of the text in all its otherness but also of the reader's subjectivity in all its familiarity. Hence, listen to yourself as you listen to the text. Become aware of your interpretive tendencies, and reflect on what might account for them as you engage the text. What do you typically listen *for* when you listen to the text, and why? Exegesis involves coming to know yourself as an interpreter as you engage both the text and the factors (personal, cultural, religious, etc.) that shape how you read.

This chapter marks the first step in the exegetical venture, but it is one that is frequently overlooked in practice. The initial step is to help you identify yourself as a bona fide exegete equipped with certain interpretive lenses. It is not an isolated step that, once taken, can then be discarded throughout the remainder of the interpretive process. No. It is a step meant to accompany every step in the exegetical process. The self-aware exegete is the exegete who can host an honest and open conversation with the text as well as with other interpreters of the text. The self-aware exegete is not a defensive interpreter. The self-aware exegete can identify his or her own tendencies to interpret a text in certain ways while remaining open to dialogue with others who may read the same text quite differently. The self-aware interpreter, finally, can appreciate how one's own understanding of the text has changed throughout the course of study and dialogue. The self-aware exegete is confidently self-critical.

To facilitate this initial step of self-awareness, I invite you, the reader, to respond to a series of questions listed below regarding your personal, cultural, and religious background.

---

1. O'Connor 1998, 324.

They are meant to help you identify how your background and current context(s) shape the way you approach the text. This "exegetical self-profile" draws its inspiration from Norman Gottwald's "Student Self-Inventory on Biblical Hermeneutics," whose aim is to "stimulate . . . students' self-reflection on the ways they frame biblical interpretation" (1995, 251). The questions below are not as exhaustive as Gottwald's, but the aim is comparable: to help you articulate your own interpretive perspective(s) based on your multi-faceted background and commitments. These questions should help you account for what you look for and find meaningful in the biblical text in light of your cultural, ecclesial, familial, and personal histories. Moreover, such a self-profile will help you enter into productive conversations with other interpreters. The text encountered by different interpreters, accompanied by mutual understanding of each other's background and perspectives, invariably leads to genuine, if not transformative, dialogue.

The care you devote to developing your exegetical self-profile will reflect the care that you devote to exegeting the text. It is important to do so candidly and appreciatively, knowing that God is ever "at work in you" (Phil. 2:13; cf. 1:6). You are a work in progress, from your family of origin to your present commitments and convictions. Innumerable factors have come to play in your development, and this self-profile is a mere scratch on the surface of the *mira profunditas* (wondrous depth) that is you. You are "fearfully and wonderfully made" (Ps. 139:14). Developing an exegetical self-profile acknowledges that. Read yourself with deep respect and an ongoing commitment to "know thyself."

EXEGETICAL SELF-PROFILE

Try your hand at developing a self-narrative that addresses the following questions.

1. What is your family background ethnically, socially, and economically?
2. What was your first exposure to the Bible as you remember it, and in what context (e.g., home, worship, classroom)?
3. Is there a defining experience or event that has influenced the way you read Scripture?
4. How does your ethnic background and culture inform the way(s) you interpret Scripture? What has been your most meaningful experience of cultural diversity?
5. Does your gender inform the way you interpret Scripture? If so, how so?
6. How do your political views inform your biblical interpretation (or vice versa)?
7. What do you consider to be the most pressing social or ethical issue today? Is Scripture relevant to it?
8. What is your vocation or sense of call, and how does that shape the way you read Scripture?
9. What personal values direct your attention toward Scripture? Relatedly, what is your working theology as you read and interpret biblical texts?

Below are five exegetical self-profiles that address in narrative fashion and in varying degrees the questions given above. They are profiles developed by former students.[2] And, truth be told, one of the self-profiles is of me. They are offered not as models but simply as examples to encourage you on your way toward becoming a more self-aware exegete.

---

2. I thank C. G. Gim, Brandon Perkins, Kathryn Threadgill, and Claudia Aguilar for their contributions.

Exegetical Self-Profile A

I was born in mid-1970s near Seoul, South Korea, into my Christian family of origin. My older brother and I made our family fourth-generation Christians. This was a big deal because my paternal grandfather, who lived with us, and his brothers persevered in the face of persecution for believing in Christ. My father's side of the family is from parts of Korea that became North Korea after the (Korean) War, and for some time during and after the war, they were refugees in the southern part of the peninsula. Their very survival hung on their hope and trust in Christ, their strength and redeemer.

As such, I grew up learning that weekly corporate worship at church was more important than anything else. Serving God and others in and through our church life, even when physically sick, was considered the highest priority of our lives. Also, nearly all family gatherings—including gatherings for traditional holidays like *Choosuck*, or Harvest Festival, as well as for significant family events such as the memorial day of a relative—were centered on worship. This was our family culture.

At bedtime my mother regularly read Bible stories to us, and for several years we even had a daily family worship time reserved after dinner. So it was second nature for me to start reading the Bible around school age, though I did not understand many of the words. At first my curiosity in reading the Bible was to learn how to be a "good girl" that God would like and approve. I read the Bible literally.

In Korea, my parents were solidly middle class. Dad taught Western philosophy in a university, and my mother taught middle-school home economics. They strongly emphasized education for my brother and me, and this eventually motivated them enough to decide to immigrate to the United States when I was nine years old. As new immigrants in the suburbs of a Midwestern city in North America, my family became lower-middle class since my parents took minimum-wage jobs.

One might think that immigration would have been the major event that exposed me to cultural and ethnic diversity, but in college I became friends with other Asian Americans and became more aware of my own Asian-ness. My brother and I had attended public primary and secondary schools where over 95 percent of the students were Euro-Americans, and I only remember feeling vaguely anxious about how I looked different from most of my peers and wondering whether I would be better liked by boys if I were white.

My seminary places a heavy emphasis on social justice, and this has helped me to feel empowered to be an Asian American female. Clinical Pastoral Education (CPE) has helped me understand further that I have the responsibility for feeling self-empowered, and that "the system" and "culture" are not the only principalities contributing to the way I have been experiencing the world. Moreover, I've come to understand that while I feel oppressed in some ways, I am also in a place of privilege as an educated, middle-class, Asian heterosexual woman.

These experiences have led me to seek a call in chaplaincy, the context in which I received pastoral care and grew in self-awareness. Now I read the Bible and view the world through the lens of pastoral care, including the domestic issues of immigration, as well as racial, gender, and sexual orientation inequalities. I look to God as one who empowers, supports, joins, and frees persons to regard themselves and others as God's creation and cocreators. I look to God as one who "disempowers" fear.

Exegetical Self-Profile B

I was raised in an upper-middle-class family in southern Arizona. My father was a university professor, and my mother stayed at home while my brother and I were growing up. My first real exposure to the Bible was in Sunday school, not at home. Although we regularly attended a Presbyterian congregation throughout my childhood years, we did not pray at mealtime or talk about matters of faith. That was left for church. In my sixth-grade confirmation class, I received a copy of the *Good News for Modern Man* version of the New Testament. Attracted to its accessible language, I eagerly read it and used it for personal devotions throughout my middle-school and high-school years as I became more active in the youth group at church. My love for Scripture and the church began to develop then, and I clearly read the Bible for answers and support during those tumultuous teenage years. At the same time, a deeper yearning to know and understand the ways of God in the world, as well as a thirst for knowledge about the meaning and purpose of life, was nurtured in my early reading of the Bible.

As a white male, I grew up in an insulated and privileged environment unaware of the prevalence of racial discrimination, sexism, and poverty. Being blind to these realities also blinded me from the ways Scripture addresses the interlocking realities of oppression. I read the Bible individualistically and "apolitically" for many years. My first experience with cultural diversity was becoming friends with an African American boy in my first-grade class. He and I regularly walked home together from school. I remember asking him, "Why is your skin black?" His response was immediate: "Because my mom and dad are black." And we left it at that. Although it sounded like an innocent question of curiosity at the time, I have come to realize that such a question was asked from a position of white privilege: being black was an anomaly to me. Before long he and his family moved, which saddened me greatly. There is something of a counterpart to that experience that occurred many years later: I had the privilege of attending worship in a South African township. As I entered the congregation in a group of North Americans and Europeans, the Black pastor noticed us and said from the pulpit with his arms wide open, "Welcome home! Welcome to the birthplace of humanity!" I will always remember that.

Living in the arid Southwest is different from living in the deep South, where I currently reside, and yet social change was afoot everywhere when I was a teenager. I remember my father complaining of student riots at the university. My public schooling was predominantly Anglo by makeup, with some Hispanic representation. Spanish was the primary "foreign" language, which I learned but never achieved fluency. I do remember marveling over my third-grade Latina teacher sharing with us certain Latin-American customs of celebrating Christmas. Through her, cultural diversity became a matter of intrigue and wonder.

Educationally, I came to seminary with a strong background in science, and so learning theology and biblical interpretation was new to me. I had to learn, among other things, how to write essays. Throughout my theological education, I was never quite sure how to incorporate my science background. I've always appreciated how science is driven by a sense of wonder and curiosity about the world. Now I'm discovering ways in which science can deepen my theological reflection.

A crisis in my faith erupted when my brother was killed in a fluke accident when he was eighteen years old. "Why?" I cried out to God. I've yet to receive an answer. I do not believe it was God's will to take my brother. After many years, the tragedy has brought my family closer. Today, as I deal with aging parents, I consider life to be a fragile, precious gift. These experiences have directed my attention particularly to the Psalms and the Wisdom literature of the Hebrew Bible, from which I gain much comfort and insight.

Speaking of Scripture, I see God's preferential option for the poor strongly represented. I'm all for government efforts addressing the growing problem of economic inequality, which the church must also address more concertedly. In addition, environmental degradation of our planet is of great concern to me. I grew up in the glorious Southwest desert, but now the land surrounding my parents' home is fully developed with cookie-cutter homes and condos. Because of urban sprawl, the desert I loved to explore at home no longer exists. I suffer occasional bouts of what some call "solastalgia" (Google it). My love of nature also directs my focus on Scripture.

Exegetical Self-Profile C

As I climbed into the fifteen-passenger van, I can remember thinking, "My family is so far from normal." That is still the case. I was only eight years old and dressed in an elf costume that Mom had sewn. The truly embarrassing part was when Santa Claus got behind the wheel to drive us. For 364 days out of the year, he was simply "Dad," but this one day each Christmas season our family dressed in costumes and delivered Christmas baskets to the underprivileged families of my father's congregation. Seeing a Caucasian man in south Alabama—a commissioned lay pastor for thirty years in an African American congregation, now driving through the lower-income parts of town—baffled most people. Yet when they saw him dressed as Santa Claus with a van full of his mixed-race children dressed as elves and handing out presents, it is a wonder I am here to recount that experience.

I realized early on that there was nothing normal about my family. This is how I learned to interpret the Scriptures. The gospel was a social gospel: it called for liberation of and justice for the oppressed, the widow, the orphan. We were taught how to interpret the living Word for our lives with the practices of servant leadership exemplified in Christ. From the time we were small, I was Ruth, literally, gleaning in the farmers' fields with Mom and delivering the produce to needy families in our community who could not otherwise afford fresh produce.

My parents were missionaries in the Congo (now the Democratic Republic of the Congo). Dad was a history teacher and lay pastor; Mom was a registered nurse. While in the Congo, they adopted my oldest sister from Vietnam. They would go on to adopt ten other children and have two birth children of their own. I am number ten of the thirteen. I was adopted from South Korea when I was thirteen weeks old. My biological mother was Korean, and my biological father was an African American soldier. However, the only culture and heritage I know comes from Caucasian parents and mixed-race children growing up in the racist South. As Democrats, my parents shattered dividing walls of economic classes, social norms, race, and political views. My hermeneutical lens is completely devoid of labels or normative boxes. As I interpret life and Scripture, there is but one essential identity: beloved child of God.

When I went away to a small conservative liberal arts college in the mountains, it was the first time I experienced blatant racism, sexism, and classism. My liberal stance with a social gospel interpretation was put to the test as I was challenged to know my role as a woman in the church. My Christian values of justice for the marginalized were challenged by a historical fundamentalist interpretation of Scripture. However, it brought forth an even greater awareness as I moved into my liberal progressive seminary, where I was deemed far more conservative than my classmates! Race continued to play a role in my first few weeks of seminary education as I was approached and asked to join the African American group on campus and then the Korean American group. I continued to baffle my peers as I talked about my white parents and my not-so-normal upbringing. In an institution striving for intentional diversity and inclusiveness, I learned to embrace my unique background and perspectives. I could not, for example, settle for many liberation theologies, which seemed only to perpetuate divisions. Instead, my hermeneutical lens was framed by a world that God created, where all parts fit together in a "luminous web," as Barbara Brown Taylor puts it, an undivided wholeness.

In my life and education, I have been blessed to encounter many different people from various walks of life, with unique stories and backgrounds to share. However, when my seminary sent me to Kikuyu, Kenya, for my church internship, the gospel truly became the living Word for my life. God's grace became embodied in a woman with a story of faith that would alter my life forever. Walking home from church one night, she was robbed near a cornfield by two men. One of the men took out a machete and slashed her leg, which later become infected. Doctors called her family and told them to say their good-byes. Grace told me that she heard God's voice explain to her that now was not her time to die. The next day her fever broke, and she recovered. Grace spoke of how she lived her life in loving service in response to the grace and mercy God had shown her. She told me this on the anniversary day of that horrific event. We gathered at my house and sang praises, prayed, and celebrated. Later that summer, I had the privilege of witnessing another amazing event in Grace's life, her wedding day. "Surely the Lord has blessed me, beyond what I deserve or imagine," Grace said as we delighted in the most colorfully festive wedding I had witnessed. It was then that Grace became a sister in Christ to me, a person marked by the very grace Christ offers to us all.

As Scripture interprets Scripture, as faith seeks understanding, as the living Word takes on flesh in Jesus Christ and is lived out in the body of Christ, my hermeneutical perspective opens me to infinite interpretations. It is a social gospel that knows no boundaries and seeks to build bridges in the grace and mercy given through Jesus Christ. And it calls me to walk humbly, to seek justice, love mercy, and listen to those whom God calls beloved children.

Exegetical Self-Profile D

I was raised in a lower-middle-class family in the "Buckle of the Bible Belt," Nashville. My Bible-college educated father tried his hand at becoming a senior pastor before ultimately holding numerous jobs ranging from serving as a corrections officer to becoming a long-bed truck driver. My mother, who has an associate's degree in accounting, worked as a bookkeeper and was a devoted Sunday school teacher. My father and mother made sure that my siblings and I knew the Bible before ever stepping into the church. Our breakfast and dinner table was not only filled with prayer but also punctuated with my father telling us stories from the Hebrew Bible to warn us about the sinful transgressions of our ancient Jewish ancestors.

As a child who had been brought up to revere the Bible as inerrant, I took its accounts of history and prophecies for the future as a matter of grave importance. I would pick up the KJV in the pew during Sunday service and begin reading the book of Revelation as a way to stay engaged during our long worship services. I had been told that this book laid out how God once and for all would rid the earth of evil. But Revelation scared the hell out of me, a nine-year-old at the time. From churches being spewed out of God's mouth, to a mark on a person's forehead, to the beasts of the sea, I recognized that the God of the Bible was not to be trifled with.

My fear-induced understandings of Scripture became tempered when I enrolled at Fisk University. In the Introduction to History course, I made the *fortunate* mistake of telling my professor during class introductions that I was a preacher, to which she replied, "You do know that the Bible is a book of social control?" I had no response that day because I felt as if she had insulted a member of my family. Over the next four years of study, however, I came to see how the Bible that we as a people love so much has been, is currently, and may very well continue to be used to sanction the oppression of the very folks who regard it as holy.

As a male I have come to understand that the Bible I was taught to revere so highly is replete with stories and patriarchal laws that, if taken literally, could negatively affect the well-being of my mother, grandmother, sisters, aunties, cousins, and so many other women that I know and love. When I still encounter pastors and leaders who want to hold women to the biblical mandates for modesty in their dress and silence in the pews, I shudder to think how many women throughout history have had to spend their lives swimming upstream to fight against these prescriptions. As a Black male who has been in church all his life, I have yet to see a female pastor question, let alone deconstruct, the relationship between the Bible and patriarchy.

My lower-middle-class background taught me that politically and theologically there was always value in hoping for a better tomorrow. When voting for the first time in 2008, I cast my ballot for then Senator Barack H. Obama because his "change we can believe in" narrative was one that I had first grown to love through Scripture. I knew of a God through Scripture who promised time and again that our current situation in life would be made more beautiful and more abundant if we would only follow this God.

As a millennial I have grown increasingly distressed at the mistreatment that youth and young adults in general and Black youth in particular suffer. Seeing youth discriminated against, such as Ahmed Mohamed because of his religious identity, and lamenting over Michael Brown and Renisha McBride, who were killed in part because of their kissed-by-the-sun embodiment, I turn back to the Bible and ask God, "What do you have to say about this?" In my distress I look for answers and comfort from the book that first introduced me to a loving God. I see a God through Scripture who repeatedly is said to come to the aid of Her children when they are crushed by empires and principalities, and this gives me comfort and hope. But such comfort is always short lived, because the Scriptures that remind me of this God of comfort are the same Scriptures that point only to hope and not to reality.

As a preacher, Christian educator, and emerging religious ethicist, I continue to look to Scripture to find good news for those engaged in the struggle for justice. The good news that I thought was once self-evident in Scripture is now harder to come by. The narratives contained within this sacred book have the potential to do immense damage to persons and communities if we are not careful to consider the complexity of their theological claims within their particular sociological worldviews. I have no choice, therefore, but to wrestle with Scripture. I am committed to this wrestling because I believe that the good news of our God can be found in those ancient words when we are daring enough to engage wholly with Scripture, to critique it when necessary, and to utilize it in connection with the vast lexica of human experience. Then and only then will the oppressed and oppressor be able to sit together and hear Scripture proclaimed and to reply in unison, "Thanks be to God!"

Exegetical Self-Profile E

My encounters with the Bible have always been through the eyes of two cultures: I grew up in a Roman Catholic family, but my mother was forced to convert to Roman Catholicism in order to marry my father, and her Baptist background never left her. I grew up in Mexico City, one of the largest cities in the world, with all the beauty and problems that a big city has, but spent long periods of time in rural Sonora, the state where my extended family still resides. I lived in Mexico City until my midtwenties, but have lived in the American South for almost a decade. My readings are always bicultural and always bilingual, from a place of exile.

My exegetical lenses have been formed over generations. My family's history influences my reading of the Bible just as much as my individual history. For at least three generations my family has been engaged in revolutionary movements seeking social justice. My family knows that the status quo is not what God intends. While I grew up in a loving family in an upper-middle-class environment, attending private schools and having every basic need provided for, my parents grew up surrounded by physical abuse, persecution, and extreme poverty. I cannot read the Bible without thinking about my mother being mocked and beat up for being the illegitimate child of a Protestant single mother, or the calluses that my father developed from walking barefoot for miles every day in order to go to school in the desert, or the many meals both of them missed while growing up. To me, the poor are always at the heart of the gospel.

In my current context, the poor and marginalized are often people of color. Living in Atlanta has opened my eyes to the difficult and complex realities of racism in this country: it permeates economics, politics, transportation, housing, access to food, pedagogy, and every sphere of life. And when you are the majority, you are mostly blinded by it. I know because it happened to me. It took me a long time of living in a foreign land and becoming a minority, "the other," to see the systems from which I was benefiting, the discrimination that happened right in front of my eyes, and the cultures of oppression that my privilege helped perpetuate in Mexico, where I was the majority. Suddenly my eyes were opened to see the indigenous people whose lives depend on one crop, the disabled who struggle to access buildings and buses, the families living on landfills, the corruption that has become part of our ethos, the erosion of mountains, the pollution of lakes, and the cloud of smog that paints my hometown gray. Now my call is to encourage others in my context to open their eyes to the realities that surround them.

INVITATION

We do not come to the Bible as blank slates. We are shaped decisively by our backgrounds and experiences, by our commitments, communities, and convictions—theological, political, and personal. Our various backgrounds may not mean much when we read a stop sign and understand its implications for driving, but they matter greatly when we read something as profoundly deep and powerfully life-transforming as Scripture. What is your exegetical self-profile? To be self-aware as an exegete is to be more aware of Scripture's impact upon you and your impact upon its meaning.

BIBLIOGRAPHY FOR CHAPTER 2

Gottwald, Norman K. 1995. "Framing Biblical Interpretation at New York Theological Seminary: A Student Self-Inventory on Biblical Hermeneutics." In *Reading from This Place: Social Location and Biblical Interpretation in the United States*, edited by Fernando F. Segovia and Mary Ann Tolbert, 251–61. Minneapolis: Fortress Press.

Kitzberger, Ingrid Rosa, ed. 1999. *The Personal Voice in Biblical Interpretation*. London: Routledge.

O'Connor, Kathleen. 1998. "Cross Borders: Biblical Studies in a Trans-Cultural World." In *Teaching the Bible: The Discourse and Politics of Biblical Pedagogy*, edited by Fernando Segovia and Mary Ann Tolbert, 322–37. Maryknoll, NY: Orbis Books.

3

First Impressions

> What we call the beginning is often the end
> And to make an end is to make a beginning.
> The end is where we start from. . . .
> *T. S. Eliot, "Little Gidding"*[1]

Now that you have taken the time to "exegete" yourself, you are ready to begin the journey of biblical exegesis, to begin to "listen" to the text. Exegesis invariably slows down the process of reading so that a substantive dialogue between you and the biblical text can unfold. Such dialogue involves asking questions. Think of exegesis as an interview process, yet one whose outcome can never be fully predicted. Any exegetical perspective should be open to surprise. The steps discussed in this handbook should be viewed not as prescribed rules to be mechanically followed but as guides to posing questions and pursuing possible lines of inquiry. Imagine exegesis as a map of possible pathways in and through the text's rugged, fertile terrain. But exegesis also invites readers to blaze new trails, asking new questions not thought of before and making new discoveries. By any measure, exegesis is an adventure that begins with an initial encounter filled with first impressions and questions and concludes with knowing the text well enough that you can effectively communicate its meaning(s) in a variety of contexts. The best exegetes are the agile exegetes who recognize the text's versatility in the construction of meaning. They know that for every end there lies a new beginning in the exegetical journey.

In view of its intended audience, this handbook aims to help the reader reach a critically informed and theologically generative understanding of the text that is relevant to the ongoing work of preaching and teaching, which feeds back into the ongoing work of exegesis. One specific goal is to discern and communicate a message from the text for a particular occasion and context, a word for "such a time as this," rather than to establish a once-and-for-all-time meaning of the text. The aim of communication is to offer a *timely* word, not necessarily a timeless word. I usually cringe, for example, when I read through

---

1. Http://www.columbia.edu/itc/history/winter/w3206/edit/tseliotlittlegidding.html.

an old sermon of mine on a particular biblical text. For a new context, including my own, I invariably look at the text with new eyes and discover new meaning. We can never exhaust the meaning of the text. To think otherwise would be to "tame" the text, to lock it in a box and keep the key. "Exegesis does not allow us to master the text so much as it enables us to enter it" (Hayes and Holladay 2007, 22).

This brief chapter encourages you to describe your initial "entrance" into the text, to open the door and linger at the threshold instead of charging in armed with your analytical tools and methodologies ready to deploy. Before turning to issues of translation, form, genre, and other critical approaches, take time simply to read Gen. 1:1–2:4a in the version with which you are most familiar. After reading this first creation account, consider the following seven sets of questions (an appropriate number for Genesis), questions that can be applied to any biblical text.

1. What seems most familiar about this text? Can you recall a time and place in which you encountered this text before? If so, how do you remember the text?
2. What struck you as new, unfamiliar, or surprising about the text? Are there problems of intelligibility or questions of understanding that emerge as you read the text? What would you like to know more about the text?
3. Do you notice any gaps in the text? What do you see as gaps between the text's world and yours?
4. What about the text speaks to you most meaningfully? What do you find objectionable? Do you find yourself reading with or against the "grain" of the text? Do you see yourself as an "outsider" or an "insider" vis-à-vis the text? Why?
5. Do you see anything going on "between the lines" of the text? Can you imagine any subtexts within the text?
6. State in two or three sentences what you consider to be the central message of the text. Was that easy or difficult to do?
7. Finally, compare your version of the text with another translation that you are not so familiar with. (If you know another language, try reading the passage in that language.) Note any discrepancies between them (e.g., 1:1, 26–28; 2:1–3). How do they change or question the way you understand the text?

After you have completed this series of questions for Gen. 1:1–2:4a, do the same for Gen. 2:4b–25. There are no right or wrong ways of responding to these questions. They are simply meant to begin a dialogue with two biblical texts. How you answer them indicates your first impressions before you begin the work of translating the Hebrew, and in any relationship such impressions can change over time. You will have opportunity to reassess them as you move toward posing new questions and reaching new conclusions. Change is expected. Shift happens. Welcome to the exegetical adventure!

BIBLIOGRAPHY FOR CHAPTER 3

Hayes, John H., and Carl Holladay. 2007. *Biblical Exegesis: A Beginner's Handbook*. 3rd ed. Louisville, KY: Westminster John Knox Press.

PART II

Analytical Approaches

4

Translation

For whatever may be said of the inadequacy of translation, it remains one of the most essential and most worthy activities in the general traffic of the world.

J. W. Goethe[1]

The verb "translate," related to the Latin verb *transferre* (transfer), literally means "to carry across." To translate, thus, is to "carry" meaning from one language to another. But as any translator knows, the task is always imperfect, for what one "carries" in translation, like water cupped in one's hands, can never be fully contained. Meaning leaks.

It gets worse. A well-known Italian saying expresses well the problematic nature of translation: *Traduttore, traditore* (translator, traitor). This proverb, when translated, illustrates its own truth: the wordplay becomes obscured in English, a vivid illustration that translation is an act of betrayal. Equally pessimistic is the statement attributed to the Jewish poet Hayyim Nahman Bialik: "Reading the Bible in translation is like kissing your bride through a veil" (D. Parker 1995, 4). If true, then perhaps the best that can be hoped for is found in Geddes MacGregor's response, "Still, when a veil there must be, the translator's task is to make it as gossamer-fine a veil as may be" (1968, 190). Even with the thinnest of veils, translation comes with a cost: a loss of both sense and sound. Translators, while enthusiastic in their task, do their work with a healthy degree of reluctance, knowing full well that their work can never measure up to the original document. Every translator is an interpreter, if not a traitor.

Over the centuries the work of translation has proved time and again to be a risky business, even life-threatening. Ask William Tyndale (1494–1536), who was burned at the stake, partly for his English translation. Nearly every translation of the Bible has been condemned by someone. In Islam, any rendering of the Qur'an in a language other than its own, Arabic, is considered an "interpretation of its meanings," not a translation proper. While this may sound restrictive to non-Muslims, it is a truthful admission of what is involved in translation. There is no translation without interpretation.

1. Quoted in Berman 1992, 57.

But this has not prevented the proliferation of Bible "translations." In the English-speaking world the Bible is typically identified with a particular translation rather than with its source language. Mention the "Holy Bible," and many think of the King James Version (1611), despite the fact that Hebrew, Aramaic, and Greek are the Bible's native languages. The Bible remains the most widely translated book in history, and the story of its translations is ongoing. Translations are part of the Bible's legacy to generations, past, present, and future, a living legacy.

ISSUES AND TASKS

To translate the Bible is to join in the work of a long line of translators that stretches all the way back to the mid-third century BCE, if not earlier. Greek translators were responsible for the so-called Septuagint, the Greek Old Testament and source of Scripture for the early church (see chap. 5). As of 2015, the whole (Protestant) Bible has been translated into 554 languages,[2] and at least 900 translations are available in English alone![3] Some translations are produced by committees, others by individuals. Moreover, the whole spectrum of translational approaches, from literal to paraphrase, is well represented.

The challenges of translating the Bible are legion. Translators today are separated from the ancient writers of Scripture by a cultural chasm that prevents complete understanding of what the ancient authors and editors were trying to communicate in their Hebrew and Aramaic dialects. Translators of contemporary works are at a distinct advantage: they have access to the living author to ask questions for clarification. But biblical translators cannot resurrect the dead. If an "authorized" translation is one that meets the approval of the author, then every Bible translation from the Old Greek to colloquial English is by necessity *un*authorized!

In addition to our lack of complete linguistic and cultural knowledge, another challenge is the limited corpus of biblical literature. Yes, the Bible is a big book, but it is also limited in its literary scope. If the canonical corpus had been more extensive, translators would have more material to work with, resulting in greater facility with Biblical Hebrew and Aramaic.[4] The only way to get to know the meaning of a word is to see how it is used, and the more places it is used, the more often a word is attested, the more it becomes semantically familiar. Yet many words in the Hebrew Bible are used only a few times, and some only once, where each is called a *hapax legomenon* (said once; pl., *hapax legomena*) and is devilishly difficult to translate.[5] In addition, the Bible features a wide range of literary genres and styles, from liturgy to love poetry. Words and phrases can take on

---

2. See http://www.wycliffe.net/statistics.

3. See http://news.americanbible.org/article/number-of-english-translations-of-the-bible.

4. There is a limited corpus of ancient extrabiblical Hebrew and Aramaic inscriptions that one can consult as well. See, e.g., Davies et al. 1991–2004; Dobbs-Allsopp et al. 2004; Gibson 1971, 1975, 1982; Donner and Röllig 1966–69 (*KAI*); Lindenberger 2003.

5. Recourse to cognate (i.e., Semitic) languages such as Aramaic, Syriac, Ugaritic, Akkadian, Arabic, and Ethiopic may help the translator determine the meaning of an enigmatic word in Biblical Hebrew. Also of help are the ancient translations of the Hebrew texts, particularly the Greek, Syriac, Aramaic, and Latin versions, which are also indispensable for text-critical purposes (see chap. 5).

different shades of meaning and function in various ways across different kinds of literature. Finally, the language of Biblical Hebrew itself has its own broad development across
the Bible's vast compositional history, including everything from spelling (morphology)
to semantics and syntax (see, e.g., Sperber 1966).

To conclude: translating an ancient text is a daunting task. It is, in fact, impossible
if one thinks of translation as simply a matter of taking words from one (source) language and finding equivalent words in another (target) language. Such "equivalence" is
never precise and therefore never fully achievable. And yet a biblical transition aims to
bridge the yawning chasm of cultural difference between an ancient text and contemporary contexts. By necessity the biblical translator is an intermediary for the most daring
cross-cultural dialogue ever to be conducted. With the ancient Scriptures as the source,
the translator serves as a "secondary source" for those who rely on the new translation
(de Waard and Nida 1986, 3). The translator, in other words, proceeds in two directions
simultaneously. On the one hand, the translator tries to remain "faithful" to the text by
crafting a translation that is as accurate as possible to the original text. On the other hand,
the translator remains faithful to the community of readers, for whom the translation is
intended, with self-commitment to finding effective ways to communicate the text. Cumbersome translations that revel in archaic obscurities or show off the translator's technical
prowess with the ancient language have no place. Certainly a crucial aim of this nearly
impossible enterprise is this: "a translation should communicate" (10–11).

Yet not just communicate. The larger task of translation is to *represent*, however possible, the ancient text, both communicatively and aesthetically. There is no consensus on
how the latter can or should be done. Some have made attempts to replicate Hebrew word
order in English, such as Susan Niditch in her Judges commentary, in which she provides
two separate translations: one that adheres to the standard conventions of English syntax
and another that pushes the boundaries of English convention in order to reflect Hebraic
word order. Compare, for example, her two translations of Judg. 6:1.

> And the descendants of Israel did evil in the eyes of Yhwh,
>   and Yhwh gave them into the hands of Midian for seven years.
>
> And evil did the descendants of Israel in the eyes of Yhwh,
>   and give them did Yhwh into the hands of Midian for seven years.

Regarding the second example, Niditch admits to a certain "bumpiness" regarding her
literal translation (2008, 25). She employs an auxiliary verb ("did") in her more literal
transition to aid in readability while preserving the distinctive syntax of Hebrew prose.
With the latter translation, she intends to convey something of the biblical rhythm and
syntax of the language, as well as the "oral and aural aspects of the text" (25). There is,
in other words, an aesthetic interest behind such a translation, specifically an interest in
cultivating an appreciation for Hebrew word order.

Robert Alter develops this appreciation further. He decries what he calls "the heresy of
explanation" committed by most English translations of Biblical Hebrew (2004, xvi–xlv).
In their striving for complete philological clarity, modern translators have given up conveying the literary power and beauty of Biblical Hebrew. The aesthetic quality of biblical

prose cannot be captured by contemporary colloquial usage; it should not be reduced to "the language of quotidian reality" (xxxi). Biblical Hebrew has a "distinctive music, a lovely precision of lexical choice, a meaningful concreteness, and a suppleness of expressive syntax that by and large have been given short shrift by translators" (xlv). While fully recognizing that no translation can replicate the aesthetics of Biblical Hebrew, Alter does suggest certain ways of capturing something of its supple syntax and concrete language. He encourages the translator to retain the repetitive nature of biblical prose, including translating the *waw* conjunction consistently as "and," regardless of whether it serves to introduce a parallel, adversative, or subordinate clause. Also, according to Alter, it is paramount for translators not to clarify in the translation itself the metaphors and concrete images with which biblical poetry and prose are replete (xxxii). For biblical prose, "cadenced English prose [must] at least in some ways correspond to the powerful cadences of the Hebrew," since biblical literature was composed to be heard, "not merely to be decoded by a reader's eye" (xxxii).

Although Alter overstates the issue, his point is well taken: the *aural* aesthetics of the text cannot be disregarded in the task of translation. On the one hand, the translator strives for communicative clarity in the target language (e.g., Eng.), and on the other hand, aims to retain something of the aesthetic, "mesmerizing" quality of the original language. Achieving a balance is always a judgment call, yet it should not be thought of as walking a tightrope for fear of falling but rather as an adventure in literary expression and experimentation that rests on the interface between clarity and beauty. The Bible should not be translated as if it were a museum relic, filled with obscurities, beautiful as they may be. But neither should it be cast in the language of text messaging.

While the task of translating the Bible is to be approached with great care, it can (and should) also be approached with great joy. And why not? To be able to apply one's growing knowledge of Hebrew and Aramaic in translating the ancient texts of Scripture is a privilege and delight, for there is so much to discover when working with the original language. Many subtleties and linguistic connections are discernible only in the Hebrew and Aramaic, regardless of whether they can be captured in translation. To *hear* the text in its variegated rhythms and cadences is a joy beyond measure. While greater semantic precision and nuance are to be had, knowing the original languages can also help one discern how multivalent the biblical text can be. Although it may seem counterintuitive, it is possible that a Bible passage in Hebrew can accommodate several possible senses, which a given translation often collapses into one. This is particularly the case with Hebrew poetry, which often revels in ambiguity. On the other hand, many cases of ambiguity arise because of our limited knowledge of how the ancient languages work, and we can only make educated guesses. In any case, good translations require the exercise of the translator's agile verbal capacity.

Syntax

As a testament to the creative capacities of translators, the range of translation types available today is exceedingly wide, from the literal to a paraphrase and to culturally defined interpretations. In any case, a literal word-for-word translation, which one finds in interlinear translations, is insufficient. Such "translations" are helpful only to those who know next to nothing about Hebrew but want to gain some sense of Hebraic word order and vocabulary. They tend to ignore matters of semantic nuance and syntax, how words are structured together to function meaningfully in clauses and sentences. As any student of Biblical Hebrew knows, Hebrew syntax is distinctive; it covers everything from word order to the versatile use of clause conjunctions, issues treated in most basic grammar textbooks but more extensively in reference grammars (see bibliography). Take, for example, the very first verse of Genesis. Strict word order given in interlinear fashion would result in the following "translation":

běrēʾšît	bārāʾ	ʾĕlōhîm	ʾēt haššāmayim	wěʾēt	hāʾāreṣ
In beginning	created	God	the heavens	and	the earth.

Such a "literal" translation largely ignores issues of syntax, both Hebrew and English. The first thing to notice is that Hebrew word order typically locates the verb before the subject. It is the reverse in English prose. Hence, the translation "God created the heavens and the earth" is faithful to the target language (Eng.) in communicating the verbal action of the source language, even though the word order is reversed in Hebrew.

What about the syntactical relationship between this verse and what follows? The first verse of the Hebrew Bible has generated a number of translations in English, each featuring different syntax. The following five are representative:

> In the beginning God created the heavens and the earth. (KJV, NIV)
> In the beginning when God created the heavens and the earth . . . (NRSV)
> At the beginning of God's creating of the heavens and the earth . . . (Fox 1995, 11)
> When at first God created the heavens and the earth . . . (Smith 2010, 44–45)
> When God began to create the heavens and the earth . . . (CEB; Alter 2004, 17;
> cf. NJPS)

What are the primary differences among them? The KJV and NIV are unique in positing a complete, self-contained sentence for the first verse. The rest do not. They render, each in its own way, the first verse as a dependent clause that leads directly into the next verse.

It all hinges on the very first word in Hebrew, which consists of a preposition (bě = "in") prefixed to a noun (rēʾšît = "beginning"), translated literally and in isolation as "in (a) beginning." Although vocalized as an indefinite noun in Masoretic Hebrew, this makes little sense in the context of the verse as a whole. And so the KJV and NIV translate "beginning" (rēʾšît) as a definite noun in absolute form: "the beginning." But as any student of Hebrew knows, that would require a different vocalization in Hebrew prose, namely, bārēʾšît instead of běrēʾšît, which certain Greek transliterations and the Samaritan textual tradition admittedly seem to indicate (see the apparatus of the BHS). Of note, however, is that the Septuagint translation (see chap. 5) does not translate the Hebrew with an article (en archē instead of en tē archē).

What makes the most syntactic and semantic sense is that the compound word běrēʾšît is in construct with the following verbal clause.[6] This could literally be rendered, "In (the)

---

6. In contrast to the absolute state. For this noun, the spelling is identical in either construct or absolute state.

beginning *of*" (see, e.g., Prov. 8:22; Jer. 26:1; 27:1). A close parallel is found in Hos. 1:2, in which the word *těḥillat*, also meaning "beginning," is in construct with the verbal clause that follows, meaning "the beginning of YHWH's speaking through Hosea," which can be rendered in more readable English as "when YHWH began to speak through Hosea." Similarly for the first verse of Genesis: of all the translation options listed above, Fox's translation is the most literal while the final example (CEB et al.) would be the smoothest.[7] Either way, the opening compound word in Hebrew is best viewed as grammatically dependent upon the following verbal clause as a whole, thereby rendering the entire verse as a dependent clause.

This is Hebrew syntax at an advanced level, which might seem ironic for the very first verse of the Hebrew Bible. But its complex syntax has, to put it mildly, significant interpretive implications. Rather than a sweeping statement that God created everything at the absolute beginning of time, as implied in the KJV and NIV translations, Genesis begins more modestly with a temporal clause that simply marks the first step of creation proper, a step that takes place in a formless watery state, as indicated in the following verse (v. 2). In other words, the first verse sets the timing for the second, which in turn sets the stage for everything that follows, beginning with the creation of light. Yes, syntax matters.

Word Studies

Translation does not exist by word study alone, but conducting word studies is a necessary part of translation. In any given passage, words that typically warrant further study are those that are central to the text or are ambiguous or multivalent in their context. Such words are critical to understanding the passage as a whole and also interesting in and of themselves. The exegete can refer to theological wordbooks and Bible dictionaries, of which there are many, as well as Hebrew concordances (see bibliography). Nevertheless, the first recourse should always be to consult a Hebrew lexicon, preferably *HALOT* and, less so, BDB, which provide basic definitions replete with numerous citations, some of them exhaustive, depending on the word in question. A word study involves both examining instances of the word in question that occur outside of your particular text, noting its range of distribution and meaning, and identifying the closest contextual parallels in relation to your text. A common temptation is to assume that the entire range of meaning a particular word has applies to the word's meaning in your text. Not so. A word's meaning is contingent on how it is used *specifically* in your text and context (see, e.g., Barr 1961). To illustrate this, here are two examples of word study from Gen. 1:2.

Tōhû wābōhû. One of the most intriguing phrases in the second verse of Genesis is *tōhû wābōhû*, which in Hebrew has a nice alliterative ring that is impossible to replicate in English.[8] The conjunction of these two similar-sounding words in Hebrew constitutes what some grammarians call a *farrago*, "wherein two usually alliterative words combine to give meaning other than their constituent parts" (Sasson 1992, 188). Think of *tōhû*

---

7. A comparable syntactical analysis identifies the verbal clause "(that) God created . . ." as a restrictive clause, resulting in virtually the same translation. See Holmestedt 2008, who cites among several examples 1 Sam. 25:15 and Hos 1:2.

8. French has the archaic expression *Le tohu-bohu*, meaning "hubbub."

and *bōhû* as fraternal twins joined at the hip. Below are examples of how they have been translated together:

> formless void (NRSV)
> formless and empty (NIV)
> without form, and void (KJV)
> void and vacuum (Smith 2010, 52)
> welter and waste (Alter 2004, 17)
> unformed and void (NJPS)
> wüst und wirr (German *Einheitsübersetzung* trans.)

As can be seen, some translations have tried to reproduce something of the alliterative quality of the Hebrew, most notably Smith, Alter, and the German translation, while others aim for stricter semantic clarity. Before making our own contribution to the array of possibilities, we need to gain a better understanding of how these two words function elsewhere.

A word study is needed, actually two. Any word study involves looking at how a particular word functions in its various contexts. But it is best done selectively. *Tōhû*, the first half of the farrago, is attested a number of times in Biblical Hebrew and spans a wide range of meaning. The challenge is to identify those instances in which the term is found in a context similar to Gen. 1:2. For example, Jer. 4:23a refers to the earth reverting to *tōhû wabōhû* (NRSV waste and void), paralleled by the heavens plunged in darkness in the very next line (v. 23b). Clearly the expression refers to the opposite of creation.

Tōhû by itself is also found in another creational context.

> For thus says YHWH,
>> who created the heavens (he is God!),
>>> who formed the earth and made it.
>> He established it;
>>> he did not create it a *tōhû*;
>>>> he formed it to be inhabited! (Isa. 45:18)

Here *tōhû* refers to a state that is uninhabitable. This also seems to be the case in Ps. 107:40 and Job 12:24 (very similar verses), which depict persons of high stature wandering about in *tōhû*, places that have "no way." Similarly, in Job 6:18 *tōhû* designates a place of death. From a more cosmic perspective, Job complains that God "stretches out Zaphon over *tōhû*, and hangs the earth upon nothing" (26:7). Note the parallel between *tōhû* and "nothing" (*bĕlî-mâ*). There are other instances of *tōhû* that take us farther away from the context of creation. Ruined cities and desolate kingdoms are rendered *tōhû* (Isa. 24:10; 34:11). Idols are deemed *tōhû* or "worthless" (1 Sam. 12:21; Isa. 44:9). In Isa. 29:21, *tōhû* has something to do with committing injustice against the righteous (cf. 59:4).

It would be a mistake to claim that all senses of this one word play a role in Gen. 1:2. A word means what it means in its *specific* context. Since Gen. 1:2 paints a picture of non-creation, it seems that *tōhû* has something to do with an uninhabitable condition, devoid of life, akin to "void"—the opposite of creation, as in Jer. 4:23 and Isa. 45:18. Remarkably, however, the overall picture in Gen. 1:2 is not of a desolate wasteland but of dark waters.

Always paired with its partner in Biblical Hebrew, *bōhû* is semantically wedded to *tōhû* (see Jer. 4:23a). It may very well be a nonce term, a word coined specifically to rhyme with the first, thereby reinforcing it (so Alter 2004, 17). The only place where *bōhû* is split from *tōhû* is in Isa. 34:11, but it doesn't wander far. In short, the alliterative mash-up of these twin words, one of them a bona fide stand-alone word, the other not so much, adds another semantic dimension. As a farrago, the semantic result is more than the sum of the parts. The alliterative quality of *tōhû wābōhû* suggests a topsy-turvyness in the depicted scene in Gen 1:2. How to translate? Perhaps, "the earth was an *empty mishmash*." This is simply another option to consider, as one weighs the relative merits of semantic clarity and particular aesthetic concerns, such as alliteration and phonetic assonance.

Rûaḥ. Another critically important term in Gen. 1:2: is *rûaḥ*, whose translations are evenly split:

> a *wind* from God swept over the face of the waters (NRSV; cf. CEB)
> the *Spirit* of God was hovering over the waters (NIV)
> the *Spirit* of God moved upon the face of the waters (KJV)
> a *wind* from God sweeping over the water (NJPS)
> God's *breath* hovering over the waters (Alter 2004, 17)
> rushing spirit of God hovering over the face of the waters (Fox 1995, 13)

As any quick word study would indicate, *rûaḥ* can mean various things: breath, spirit, wind, desire.[9] In connection with God, *rûaḥ* typically means spirit, particularly in the context of prophecy or royal leadership and the imparting of wisdom.[10] But our passage has little to do with prophecy. Within the Priestly narrative, the next time God's *rûaḥ* shows up is in the flood narrative: "and God made a *wind* blow over the earth, and the waters subsided" (Gen. 8:1). This matches something of the context of 1:2, with *rûaḥ* set in relation to the waters. "Wind," then, would seem to be a logical choice for Gen. 1:2. But there is one other aspect to the creation narrative that invites consideration, and it has to do with the way in which God is repeatedly depicted as creating throughout the account, by uttering commands (1:3, 6, 9, 11, 14, 20, 24, 26), which suggests that "breath," specifically breath associated with the utterance of divine speech,[11] could be at play here (see Alter's translation).

But a translation of the second verse is by no means complete without due consideration of the verb that accompanies the subject, namely *rāḥap* in the Piʿel. What is God's "breath" or "wind" actually doing in 1:2? Like *rûaḥ*, the verb in question is also subject to a variety of translations, as can also be seen in the examples cited above (e.g., "swept," "sweeping," "hovering," "moved"). The lexicon identifies two entirely different meanings for the verb such that two distinct roots are identified in BDB: *rḥp* I and *rḥp* II.[12] The first, evident only in Jer. 23:9, means "grow soft" and occurs in the Qal. For the second root, in only Gen. 1:2 and one other verse, BDB suggests "hover." The other verse is Deut. 32:11 (AT).

9. See BDB 924–26; *HALOT* 1197–1201.
10. E.g., Exod. 31:3; Judg. 3:10; Num. 11:17, 25–26, 29; 1 Sam. 10:6, 10; 19:20, 23; Isa. 11:2.
11. See also Tsumura 2005, 74–76.
12. BDB 934; but cf. *HALOT* 1219–20, which does not differentiate the root etymologically, finding "tremble" to be a common meaning.

As an eagle rouses its nest, hovering [yĕraḥēp] over its young;
    as it spreads its wings, taking them up,
      and bears them aloft on its pinions . . .

The parallel with Gen. 1:2 is tight, since the verb in both passages appears in a common stem (Piʿel), which leads one to believe that the verb holds some semblance of semantic similarity in both passages. In the Deuteronomy passage the image is that of a raptor—an eagle or vulture (same word in Hebrew)—"hovering" protectively over its nested brood. With God's "breath" as its subject, the verb generates a mixed metaphor, not uncommon in Hebrew poetry: wind, to be sure, does not literally "hover." Nevertheless, Gen. 1:2 could describe God's "breath" suspended over the waters like a bird of prey suspended gently upon an updraft of air. Far from a violent wind roiling the waters (so NRSV), the picture may be that of God's breath poised to be released in speech (see v. 3). Hence, my translation of vv. 1–2:

When God began to create the heavens and the earth,
    the earth was an empty mishmash,
      with darkness over the surface[13] of Deep[14]
        and God's breath hovering over the surface of the waters.

Here I have tried to achieve communicative clarity with a degree of aesthetic elegance, which, to be sure, lies in the eye (and ear) of the beholder. Some might say I have not done enough to replicate the "mesmerizing" quality of the Hebrew; others might take issue with certain literalities that I've retained. But it was fun, in any case, to negotiate a balance. Now the stage is set for God's first act of creation to take place, tersely told in the next verse. The syntax of the first three verses, convoluted as it may seem, makes a startling claim: light is the first act of creation, an event that has its own suspenseful buildup in the previous two verses.

This little exercise in translation, limited to just the first three verses of Genesis, vividly illustrates that translation is not an exact science (otherwise all translations would ultimately agree). There remains room for creativity and speculation. Translation depends on competing values: clarity, literality, context, communicative quality, and aesthetics, to name a few. Among translations available today, as is clear in their variety, there remains widespread disagreement. But regardless, developing one's own translation through careful word study, syntactical analysis, and contextual considerations is a good place to start, and your translation, thoughtfully done, can rival the best of them.

INCLUSIVE LANGUAGE

One translational issue that presents itself in nearly every biblical text is the use of masculine language for God and humankind. In the Hebrew Bible God is consistently

---

13. Literally, "face."
14. Or "Abyss." Since the word (tĕhôm) lacks a definite article, as it typically does elsewhere, it is likely a proper noun. Whether this implies personification, however, is another question. See chap. 10.

referenced with the masculine pronoun (he/his) or with the masculine verbal inflection, not to mention a preponderance of masculine imagery. For strict literalists, this may be a nonissue. But for others, it is a major concern, particularly those committed to gender equality (see chap. 18).

The issue presents itself on two fronts: (1) source language and context (i.e., Biblical Hebrew/Aramaic and ancient Israelite culture) and (2) target language and context (i.e., Eng. language and contemporary cultures). To complicate matters further, the "source" side of the issue divides itself into two. First, Hebrew, like every Semitic language, is a gender-inflected language. Every noun is either masculine or feminine; every finite verb can take on masculine or feminine form. Second (and not unrelated), the ancient cultural context of the Bible was deeply patriarchal (see chap. 18).

The "target" side of the issue is also manifold. Here is a case in which culture influences the translator's "secondary text," and justifiably so. One could choose to adopt a literal translation that reflects the grammatically masculine language as found in Hebrew and simply leave it at that (and keep it to yourself). But if the work of translation has to do with communication to a wider audience, then consideration of your audience is unavoidable. Put more specifically, if translation, in addition to being faithful to the text, is also about being faithful to a context that values gender equality, then striving to develop a translation that employs inclusive language—language that acknowledges the dignity and equality of women and men in all contexts—is a worthy and faithful goal.

There is, moreover, a deeply theological issue at stake: Is God male? The seeming absurdity of such a question is not irrelevant. Ask Michelangelo. Attributing biologically male characteristics to God will always be a consequence, whether intended or not, whenever masculine language is used in reference to God. The boundary between "masculinity" and "maleness" is ever penetrable, despite objections to the contrary. But how to reflect God's genderless or beyond-gender character is complicated in English, a language that forces either masculine or feminine gender in the use of personal pronouns: "he" or "she," "his" or "her." "It" or "its" is, of course, too impersonal, although the neuter pronoun is occasionally used in English for pets and even young children. God is neither.

Solutions vary. Examples include using "humankind" instead "mankind" when the Hebrew term for "man" (*'ādām, 'ĕnôš*) is used collectively; pluralizing references to a single masculine reference (e.g., "him" to "them," "he" to "they") in contexts that may imply gender inclusion; or adding a feminine reference to a masculine reference. The frequent Hebrew expression "sons of Israel" (e.g., 1 Kgs. 6:13; Isa. 17:3, 9), for example, can be translated as "children of Israel," or better as "Israelites."

As for masculine references to God in the Bible, the first line of defense is simply to replace the masculine reference "he" or "him" with "God," which admittedly can make for cumbersome sentences in which "God" might seem repetitive within a single sentence. The judgment call rests on the translator. Nevertheless, regarding (overly) repeated reference to "God," Gen. 1 actually provides support. Notice the first four verses, translated literally:

When *God* began to create the heavens and the earth, the earth was an empty mishmash, . . . and *God's* breath hovered over the waters' surface, and *God* said,

"Let light be," and there was light. And *God* saw that the light was good; and *God* separated the light from the darkness.

The author could have easily used the masculine pronoun or pronominal suffix after the first reference to God or simply relied on the masculine-inflected verbal forms as sufficient for designating the divine subject. In fact, compared to other narrative compositions in the Hebrew Bible, such would be expected. The author of Gen. 1, however, reveled in repeating "God" (*'ĕlōhîm*) in comparative excess. In fact, nowhere in the Priestly account of creation do we find the third independent personal pronoun. But that is not the case in most English translations. This is due, in part, to the limitations of English grammar, which unlike Hebrew does not have a gender-inflected verbal system. In the NRSV, the first time a pronoun is used to refer to "God" is in v. 5. "God called the light Day, and the darkness *he* called Night." But the Hebrew lacks the pronoun; it has only the verb (with masculine inflection). And so the verse can more literally be translated: "God called the light Day and called the darkness Night."

What is sacrificed, however, is word order. The NRSV, as well as most translations, reflects the Hebrew word order in the second clause of v. 5, which opens with the verbal object "darkness." In that case, a possible translation move would be to eliminate the repeated verb "called" altogether for a smoother English translation that is also gender neutral: "God called the light Day and the darkness Night." Again, it is the translator's judgment call.[15]

Actually, the only place in Gen. 1 where a masculine pronoun appears with reference to God is only in suffixed form in v. 27. In context, we read:

> So God created humankind [*hā'ādām*] in *his* image,
> in the image of God [he] created him;
> male and female [he] created them. (AT)

As in v. 5, English translations typically supply the third-person masculine pronoun (here offset in brackets) where there actually is no pronoun in Hebrew. Nevertheless, the suffix form does appear in v. 27 ("in *his* image" [*bĕṣalmô*]). Clearly, specific maleness is not intended, since the verse specifically states that humankind is created "male and female." Together, *they* are created in God's image. Notice also how "his image" is preceded in parallel fashion with the earlier verse that features God referring to "our image" (v. 26). The only gender-inclusive option is to (re)translate: "So God created humankind in *God's* image." Redundant, yes. But, as noted above, much of Gen. 1 is replete with references to "God," and this translation simply carries it one more step. More cumbersome is handling the bracketed personal pronouns in the last verse. Two options present themselves:

> So God created humankind in God's image,
> in God's image God created him;
> male and female God created them.

---

15. The other challenge is in the final section of the Priestly creation account, in which Eng. translations supply the 3rd-person masculine pronoun (see 1:31; 2:2–3).

Such a translation preserves Hebrew word order. The other option is to eliminate the redundancy by shifting the order:

> So God created humankind in God's image,
>> created him [ʾōtô] in the image of God,
>>> created them [ʾōtām] male and female.

The remaining issue regarding inclusive language is the explicit reference to humankind as "him" in the middle line of v. 27. Observe that it is set in parallel with "them" in the final line, which specifically includes both genders. The clearest option is simply to translate both suffixed pronominal objects as plural.

> So God created humankind in God's image,
>> created *them* in the image of God,
>>> created *them* male and female.

There is, however, a literary cost for such a translation: the result glosses over the difference in object pronominal reference that is so beautifully clear in the Hebrew, a difference inherent in the text's natural transition from the singular "him" to the plural "them," since "humankind" (ʾādām) is singular and grammatically masculine. Verging on the poetic, the Hebrew delicately balances the unity and diversity that characterize human creation, a gendered unity.

In sum, the process of translation is fraught with competing values that the translator must negotiate self-critically and with cultural competence. Yes, there is value in developing a slavishly literal translation as a way of advancing one's facility with the Hebrew. Nevertheless, for a translation to be "put out there," considerations that extend beyond the grammatical and the philological come into play. The translator will need to determine the right balance that preserves something of the text's distinctive rhetorical and aesthetic power, while at the same time clarifying and communicating what the translator discerns as the point or message of the text, fully recognizing the limitations of language, both Hebrew and English.

FROM ADAM TO MAN: A WORDPLAY

Overlooked by most translations, Hebrew references in Gen. 2 to the human being (ʾādām) invite careful reflection. Because the term ʾādām often, but not always, has an article attached to it in Gen. 2–3, it is best not to translate it as a proper name (Adam), which does not occur until 4:25 (cf. 3:17, which is probably a scribal error). Below is a translation of the pertinent passages, which for the moment leaves ʾādām untranslated.

> [2:4b] On the day YHWH Elohim[16] made Earth and Heaven—[5] before any pasturage was on the earth and before any field crops had sprouted, for YHWH Elohim

---

16. Typically translated "the Lᴏʀᴅ God," following the Old Greek translation (*kyrios ho theos*), YHWH Elohim is the literal Hebrew compound name given to God in Gen. 2–3.

had not sent rain upon the earth, and there was yet no ʾādām to serve the ground [ʾădāmâ], ⁶though a spring would emerge from the land and saturate the ground's entire surface—⁷YHWH Elohim formed the ʾādām out of the dust of the ground [ʾădāmâ] and blew into his nostrils the breath of life, and the ʾādām became a living being. . . .

¹⁸YHWH Elohim said, "It is not good that the ʾādām be alone; I shall make for him a cohelper."¹⁷ ¹⁹So YHWH Elohim formed from the ground [ʾădāmâ] every wild animal and every winged creature of the heavens and brought (each one) to the ʾādām to see what he would call it, and whatever the ʾādām called each living creature,¹⁸ that was its name. ²⁰The ʾādām gave names to every domestic animal and winged creature of the heavens and to every wild animal, but for the ʾādām no cohelper was to be found.

²¹So YHWH Elohim caused a deep sleep to fall upon the ʾādām, and he slept. [YHWH Elohim] took one of his sides¹⁹ and closed up flesh in its place. ²²And YHWH Elohim constructed the side that he had taken from the ʾādām into a woman and brought her to the ʾādām. ²³Then the ʾādām proclaimed,

"This now is bone of my bones and flesh of my flesh;
  this one shall be called 'Woman' [ʾiššâ], for from 'Man' [ʾîš] this one was taken."
²⁴This is why a man [ʾîš] leaves his father and his mother and clings to his wife,²⁰ so that they become one flesh. ²⁵And the two of them, the ʾādām and his wife, were naked and were not ashamed.

Most English translations render ʾādām as "man," but this is incorrect in light of the Hebrew. The word for "man" (or "male") in our narrative is ʾîš, which does not appear until 2:23, when the woman (ʾiššâ) is created. So how should one translate ʾādām? Its base meaning is "human being" or collectively "humanity" (see Gen. 1:27), what has traditionally been translated as "man" in the generic sense, though occasionally the word can apply in the gendered sense (cf. Eccl. 7:28).

The real translation challenge is how to acknowledge the ingenious wordplay that the Hebrew narrator has set up. The ʾādām is formed "out of the dust of the ʾădāmâ [ground]." A wordplay is born in 2:5. The ʾādām is created from the ʾădāmâ. Grammatically, the latter term, "ground," resembles what could be taken as a feminized form of the former, "human being," but it is a different word with a different meaning. But not *altogether* different: regardless of whether they share something etymologically in common, that is, a common root (ʾdm), they do share plenty of semantic play in the narrative. Is there a way of capturing the contextual pun in English, a way of choosing a specific translation for

17. NRSV: "a helper as his partner." The noun ʿēzer refers to "help" or "helper." Beyond Gen. 2, the term most often refers to God or divine aid (e.g., Exod. 18:4; Deut. 33:7, 26, 29; Pss. 33:20; 70:5 [6 MT]; 115:9–11; 146:5). The preposition neged in the composite phrase kĕnegdô literally means "in front of" or "opposite to," here in the sense of correspondence.

18. Hebrew nepeš ḥayyâ, the same phrase used of the ʾādām in v. 7.

19. The enigmatic term ṣēlāʿ is used to designate the part of a building or hill: from "side" and "ridge" (Exod. 25:12; 2 Sam 16:13) to the "planks" of a wall (1 Kgs. 6:15) to the "leaves" of a door (1 Kgs. 6:34). Only in Gen. 2 is the term used anatomically, designating either "side" or, less likely, "rib." The OG translation of the Hebrew, pleura, is equally ambiguous. Early and medieval Jewish exegesis, such as found in the commentary work of Philo, Rashi, and Kimchi, interprets ṣēlāʿ as "side." A notable exception is found in *Targum Pseudo-Jonathan*, which identifies the man's "thirteenth rib on the left" (most humans have 12 ribs on each side) for the woman's creation. The midrash on Genesis, *Bereshit Rabbah*, features a discussion of the first human being cut in two to create the woman. In the context of Gen. 2, the translation "rib" seems overly specific.

20. Or "his woman" (ʾištô).

ʾādām that is imminently relatable to the word for "ground" in the narrative? My suggestion is "groundling," much in the same fashion as "earthling" is related to "earth." And so I translate:

> ^{2:4b} On the day YHWH Elohim made Earth and Heaven— ⁵ before any pasturage was on the earth and before any field crops had sprouted, for YHWH Elohim had not sent rain upon the earth, and there was yet no *groundling* to serve the *ground*
> . . .
>   ⁷ YHWH Elohim formed the *groundling* out of the dust of the *ground* and blew into his nostrils the breath of life, and the *groundling* became a living being.

And so forth. A further reason for not translating ʾādām as "man" is to preserve another wordplay that occurs in v. 23.

> This now is bone of my bones and flesh of my flesh;
>   this one shall be called "Woman" [ʾiššâ],
>   for from "Man" [ʾîš] this one was taken.

"Man" and "woman," ʾîš and ʾiššâ: one is, grammatically speaking, the feminized version of the other. To erase in one's translation, as is typical with many translations, the distinction between the human groundling and the masculine "man" with the common designation of "man" is to obscure the two dramatic wordplays that unfold within the narrative. The narrator purposely delays the use of the term "man" (ʾîš) until the woman is created, highlighting the second wordplay and capturing the developmental characterization of the "groundling" turned "man."

HOW A MISSING WORD CAN MAKE ALL THE DIFFERENCE

The task of translation involves, in part, taking account of each word in the source text, but not with the aim of producing a wooden, word-by-word translation, as one finds in interlinear versions. English syntax and grammatical conventions must also be taken into account in order to produce a readable translation. Redundancies, for example, need not be replicated in English, such as one finds with the Hebrew preposition *bên* (between), as in Gen. 1:7. In other cases, however, the omission of a word in translation can have significant consequences. Compare the following two standard translations of Gen. 3:6, followed by Robert Alter's translation of the same verse.

> So when the woman saw that the tree was good for food, and that it was a delight to the eyes, and that the tree was to be desired to make one wise, she took of its fruit and ate; and she also gave some to her husband, who was with her, and he ate. (NRSV)

> So when the woman saw that the tree was good for food, and that it was a delight to the eyes, and that the tree was to be desired to make one wise, she took of its fruit and ate; and she also gave some to her husband, and he ate. (RSV)

And the woman saw that the tree was good for eating and that it was lust to the eyes and the tree was lovely to look at, and she took of its fruit and ate, and she also gave to her man, and he ate. (Alter 2004, 24–25)

Can you spot the difference? The first two translations are identical except for one significant omission in the RSV. The same goes for Alter's translation (and in many other translations, for that matter). Absent are four words in English, as translated in the NRSV, but in Hebrew it is only one word: ʿimmāh, a suffixed preposition translated in the NRSV as "who was with her." Compare Everett Fox's elegant translation: "beside her" (1995, 21). Translations that omit this one Hebrew word allow for the interpretation that the man was separated from the woman and therefore may not have known about the woman's actions in partaking from the tree of knowledge. But with the full translation, a very different picture emerges. Yes, it is the woman who eats first, but she does so with the full awareness and complicity of the man, "who was with her."[21] The narrator makes clear that the woman did not act alone, even though the focus is on her initiative. In the end, *both* the woman and the man are fully culpable. The lesson? A careful translation may undermine your own preunderstanding of the text.

BENEATH AND BEYOND TRANSLATION

As the case of inclusive language pointedly illustrates, translating texts is never a neutral, objective venture. In their groundbreaking work over thirty years ago, authors Eugene Nida and Charles Taber, champions of the "dynamic equivalence" approach to translation, insisted that whenever the question is posed regarding the accuracy of a particular translation, one also needs to ask, "For whom?" For whom is this a "correct" (i.e., an appropriate) translation? While Nida and Taber were mostly concerned with the issue of intelligibility in the target language, the question "For whom?" has taken on greater significance ever since it was posed in 1982.[22] Moreover, the question "For whom?" is inextricably bound up with the question "By whom?" As translators, we invariably translate ourselves into our translations. Translation marks the interface between text and translator, and the translator's context and community are defining factors in the act of translation. This is particularly explicit in so-called cultural interpretations of Scripture, perhaps most well-known being Clarence Jordan's *The Cotton Patch Gospel*, in which Matthew, Luke, and John are "translated" from the ancient Palestinian setting of the first century CE into the rural Georgian landscape of the 1960s. It has been called "a colloquial translation with a Southern accent." Jordan himself, however, preferred to call it a "version," and appropriately so. "Jew and Gentile" is replaced by "white man and Negro." "Crucifixion" is converted to "lynching." Jesus is born in Gainesville and lynched in Atlanta (Jordan 2004, 2011).

21. For a survey of various translations with accompanying analysis, see J. Parker 2013.
22. For a trenchant critique of the "dynamic equivalence" approach and its overemphasis on message vis-à-vis the medium, see Boer 2012.

An example pertinent to our initial foray into Gen. 1 is P. K. McCary's rendering of vv. 1–4 in the *Black Bible Chronicles*.

> Now when the Almighty was first down with his program, He made the heavens and the earth. The earth was a fashion misfit, being so uncool and dark, but the Spirit of the Almighty came down real tough, so that He simply said, "Lighten up!" And that light was right on time. And the Almighty liked what He saw and let the light hang out a while before it was dark again. (McCary 1993, 2)

Not a literal translation, to be sure, but one that is creatively engaging and captures certain aspects of the biblical text that might otherwise be missed in a more familiar translation, such as God's creativity and resolve. "Fashion misfit" is a creative way of interpreting *tōhû wābōhû* in v. 2. "Lighten up!" creatively engages the dramatic surprise of God's first command in v. 3. To be sure, this translation is not attempting to capture the fine nuances of Hebrew syntax, as is clear in the rendering of the first verse.[23] It is concerned, rather, with communicating the relevance of the biblical message for the African American community (McCary 1993, v). This version of the Pentateuch is, according to the book jacket, a "survival manual for the streets." Dynamic equivalence indeed!

"In the act of translation, we create the texts that create us" (Elliot and Boer 2012, 1). In relation to the source text, a translation becomes a secondary text that serves as a window, however distorted, to the primary text while also reflecting something of the translator and the readership. There is no such thing as a translation free from interpretation. Indeed, translation *is* an act of interpretation that sees itself bound to the text as much as it seeks to communicate to a particular audience. A "literal translation" that does not attend to the task of effective communication teeters on the edge of incomprehensibility, whereas a "dynamic" translation that is overly concerned with communication verges on being more a paraphrase or version. Translation is not just about communicating the meaning or message of the text—that is also the business of a commentary and a sermon. Most theories of translation, in fact, are too narrowly focused on matters of meaning. Translation comes from the broader desire to *replicate* the text in another medium (i.e., another language), perhaps akin to painting a landscape (see Scarry 1999, 1–9). In so doing, the act of translation fashions a new text, one that is meant to be both accessible and accurate, however that is to be determined by the translator.

BIBLIOGRAPHY FOR CHAPTER 4

Alter, Robert. 2004. *The Five Books of Moses: A Translation and Commentary*. New York: W. W. Norton.

Berman, Antoine. 1992. *The Experience of the Foreign: Culture and Translation in Romantic Germany*. Translated by S. Heywavert. Albany, NY: SUNY Press.

Boer, Roland. 2012. "The Dynamic Equivalence Caper." In *Ideology, Culture, and Translation*, edited by S. S. Elliot and R. Boer, 13–23. SBL Semeia Studies 69. Atlanta: Society of Biblical Literature.

---

23. A translation that is more sensitive to Hebrew syntax might read, "Now when the Almighty was first down with his program making the heavens and the earth . . ."

Brenner, Athalya, and Jan Willem van Henten, eds. 2002. *Bible Translation on the Threshold of the Twenty-First Century: Authority, Reception, Culture and Religion*. JSOTSup 353. BTC 1. Sheffield Academic Press.

Brunn, Dave. 2013. *One Bible, Many Versions: Are All Translations Created Equal?* Downers Grove, IL: IVP Academic.

Davies, Graham I., Markus N. A. Bockmuehl, D. R. De Lacey, and A. J. Poulter. 1991–2004. *Ancient Hebrew Inscriptions: Corpus and Concordance*. 2 vols. Cambridge: Cambridge University Press.

Dobbs-Allsopp, F. W., J. J. M. Roberts, C. L. Seow, and R. E. Whitaker, eds. 2005. *Hebrew Inscriptions: Texts from the Biblical Period of the Monarchy with Concordance*. New Haven: Yale University Press.

Donner, Herbert, and Wolgang Röllig. 1966–69. *Kanaanäische und aramäische Inschriften*. Vols. 1–3. 2nd ed. Wiesbaden: O. Harrassowitz (*KAI*).

Elliot, Scott S., and Roland Boer. 2012. "Introduction." In *Ideology, Culture, and Translation*, edited by S. S. Elliot and R. Boer, 1–10. SBL Semeia Studies 69. Atlanta: Society of Biblical Literature.

Fox, Everett. 1995. *The Five Books of Moses: Genesis, Exodus, Leviticus, Numbers, Deuteronomy: A New Translation with Introductions, Commentary, and Notes*. The Schocken Bible. Vol. 1. New York: Schocken Books.

Gibson, John C. L. 1971, 1975, 1982. *Textbook of Syrian Semitic Inscriptions*. Vols. 1–3. Oxford: Clarendon Press.

Holmestedt, Robert D. 2008. "The Restrictive Syntax of Genesis i1." *VT* 58, no. 1:56–67.

Jordan, Clarence. 2004 [1970]. *The Cotton Patch Gospel: Matthew and John*. Macon, GA: Smyth & Helwys.

———. 2011 [1968]. *The Cotton Patch Gospel: Luke and Acts*. Macon, GA: Smyth & Helwys.

Knobloch, Frederick W., ed. 2002. *Biblical Translation in Context*. Bethesda, MD: University Press of Maryland.

Kumar, Santhosh S. 2012. *A Guide to Inclusive Language for Theological Students, Christian Ministers and Lay Leaders: Building an Inclusive Community*. Bangalore, India: Santhosh S. Kumar.

Lindenberger, James M. 2003. *Ancient Aramaic and Hebrew Letters*. 2nd ed. SBLWAW 14. Atlanta: Society of Biblical Literature.

MacGregor, Geddes. 1968. *A Literary History of the Bible*. Nashville: Abingdon.

McCary, P. K. 1993. *Black Bible Chronicles*. Book One, *From Genesis to the Promised Land*. New York: African American Family Press.

Metzger, Bruce M. 2001. *The Bible in Translation: Ancient and English Versions*. Grand Rapids: Baker Academic.

Neufeld, Dietmar, ed. 2008. *The Social Sciences and Biblical Translation*. SBLSS 41. Atlanta: Society of Biblical Literature.

Nida, Eugene A., and Charles R. Taber. 1982. *The Theory and Practice of Translation*. Helps for Translators 8. Leiden: Brill.

Niditch, Susan. 2008. *Judges: A Commentary*. OTL. Louisville, KY: Westminster John Knox Press.

Parker, Don. 1995. *Using Biblical Hebrew in Ministry: A Practical Guide for Pastors, Seminarians, and Bible Students*. Lanham, MD: University Press of America.

Parker, Julie Faith. 2013. "Blaming Eve Alone: Translation, Omission, and Implications of ʿmh in Genesis 3:6b." *JBL* 132:729–47.

Porter, Stanley E., and Richard S. Hess, eds. 1999. *Translating the Bible: Problems and Prospects*. JSNTSup 173. Sheffield: Sheffield Academic Press.

Sasson, Jack. 1992. "A Time . . . to Begin." In *"Shaʿarei Talmon": Studies in the Bible, Qumran, and the Ancient Near East Presented to Shemaryahu Talmon*, edited by Michael Fishbane and Emanuel Tov, 183–94. Winona Lake, IN: Eisenbrauns.

Scarry, Elaine. 1999. *On Beauty and Being Just*. Princeton, NJ: Princeton University Press.

Smith, Mark S. 2010. *The Priestly Vision of Genesis 1*. Minneapolis: Fortress Press.

Sperber, Alexander. 1966. *A Historical Grammar of Biblical Hebrew*. Leiden: Brill.

Tsumura, David Toshio. 2005. *Creation and Destruction: A Reappraisal of the Chaoskampf Theory in the Old Testament*. Winona Lake, IN: Eisenbrauns.

Waard, Jan de, and Eugene A. Nida. 1986. *From One Language to Another: Functional Equivalence in Bible Translating*. Nashville: Thomas Nelson.

HEBREW RESOURCES

Hebrew Lexica

Brown, Francis, S. R. Driver, and Charles A. Briggs [BDB]. 1907. *A Hebrew and English Lexicon of the Old Testament*. Oxford: Clarendon Press.

Clines, David J. A., ed. 1993–2011. *The Dictionary of Classical Hebrew*. 8 vols. Sheffield: Sheffield Academic Press (*DCH*).

Clines, David J. A., David M. Stec, and Jacqueline C. R. De Roo. 2009. *The Concise Dictionary of Classical Hebrew*. Sheffield: Sheffield Phoenix Press.

Holladay, William L. 2000. *A Concise Hebrew and Aramaic Lexicon of the Old Testament*. 2nd ed. Leiden: Brill.

Koehler, Ludwig, and Walter Baumgartner. 1994–2000. *Hebrew and Aramaic Lexicon of the Old Testament* [*HALOT*]. Revised by Walter Baumgartner and Johann J. Stamm. Translated by M. E. J. Richardson. 5 vols. Leiden: Brill.

———. 2001. *The Hebrew and Aramaic Lexicon of the Old Testament* [*HALOT*]. Study Edition. Revised by Walter Baumgartner and Johann J. Stamm. Translated by M. E. J. Richardson. 2 vols. Leiden: Brill.

Reference and Intermediate Hebrew Grammars

Arnold, B. T., and J. H. Choi. 2003. *A Guide to Biblical Hebrew Syntax*. Cambridge: Cambridge University Press.

Ben Zvi, Ehud, Maxine Hancock, and Richard Beinert. 1993. *Readings in Biblical Hebrew: An Intermediate Textbook*. Yale Language Series. New Haven: Yale University Press.

Gesenius, H. F. W. 1910. *Hebrew Grammar*. Revised by E. Kautzsch. Edited and translated by A. E. Cowley. Oxford: Clarendon Press.

Gogel, Sandra Landis. 1998. *A Grammar of Epigraphic Hebrew*. RBS 23. Atlanta: Scholars Press.

Joüon, Paul. 2006. *A Grammar of Biblical Hebrew*. 2nd ed. 2 vols. Translated and revised by T. Muraoka. Subsidia biblica 14.1–2. Rome: Pontificio Istituto Biblico.

Merwe, Christo H. J. van der, Jackie A. Naudé, and Jan A. Kroeze. 1999. *A Biblical Hebrew Reference Grammar*. Sheffield: Sheffield Academic Press.

Putnam, Frederic Clarke. 1996. *A Cumulative Index to the Grammar and Syntax of Biblical Hebrew*. Winona Lake, IN: Eisenbrauns.

Sperber, Alexander. 1966. *A Historical Grammar of Biblical Hebrew*. Leiden: Brill.

Waltke, Bruce K., and M. O'Connor. 1990. *An Introduction to Biblical Hebrew Syntax*. Winona Lake, IN: Eisenbrauns (*IBHS*).

Williams, Ronald J. 2007. *Williams' Hebrew Syntax*. 3rd ed. Toronto: University of Toronto Press.

Hebrew in Its Semitic Context

Bennett, Patrick R. 1998. *Comparative Semitic Linguistics: A Manual*. Winona Lake, IN: Eisenbrauns.

Bergsträsser, Gotthelf. 1983. *Introduction to the Semitic Languages: Text Specimens and Grammatical Sketches*. Translated by Peter T. Daniels. Winona Lake, IN: Eisenbrauns.

Kaltner, John, and Steven L. McKenzie, eds. 2002. *Beyond Babel: A Handbook for Biblical Hebrew and Related Languages*. RBS 42. Atlanta: Society of Biblical Literature.

ARAMAIC RESOURCES

Comprehensive Aramaic Lexicon Project [*CAL*]. 1986–. Cincinnati: Hebrew Union College—Jewish Institute of Religion. Online: http://cal1.cn.huc.edu/.

Frank, Yitzchak. 2003. *Grammar for Gemara and Targum Onkelos*. New York: Ariel Institute / Feldheim Publishers.

Greenspahn, Frederick E. 2003. *An Introduction to Aramaic*. 2nd ed. RBS 46. Atlanta: Society of Biblical Literature.

Jastrow, Marcus. 1950. *A Dictionary of the Targumim, the Talmud Babli and Yerushalmi, and the Midrashic Literature*. 2nd ed. 2 vols. New York: Pardes. Also online: http://www.tyndale archive.com/tabs/jastrow/. And http://www.dukhrana.com/lexicon/Jastrow/index.php.

Johns, Alger F. 1982. *A Short Grammar of Biblical Aramaic*. Berrien Springs, MI: Andrews University Press.

Marcus, David. 1981. *A Manual of Babylonian Jewish Aramaic*. Washington, DC: University Press of America.

Rosenthal, Franz, and D. M. Gurtner. 2006. *A Grammar of Biblical Aramaic with an Index of Biblical Citations*. 7th ed. Wiesbaden: Harrassowitz.

Schuele, Andreas. 2012. *An Introduction to Biblical Aramaic*. Louisville, KY: Westminster John Knox Press.

Sokoloff, Michael. 1990. *A Dictionary of Jewish Palestinian Aramaic of the Byzantine Period*. Baltimore: Johns Hopkins University Press.

———. 2002. *A Dictionary of Jewish Palestinian Aramaic of the Talmudic and Geonic Periods*. 2nd ed. Baltimore: Johns Hopkins University Press.

Stevenson, William B. 2000. *Grammar of Palestinian Jewish Aramaic*. Eugene, OR: Wipf & Stock.

Van Pelt, Miles V. 2011. *Basics of Biblical Aramaic: Complete Grammar, Lexicon, and Annotated Text*. Grand Rapids: Zondervan.

CONCORDANCES AND WORD STUDIES

Computer Concordances (including Hebrew/Aramaic)

Accordance Bible Software (for Macintosh and Windows). OakTree Software. For the latest versions, see www.accordancebible.com.

BibleWorks (for Windows and Macintosh). Hermeneutika. For the latest versions, see www.bible works.com.

Bibloi (for Windows). Silver Mountain Software. For the latest versions, see www.silvermountain software.com/bibloi.html.

Logos Bible Software (for Windows and Macintosh). Faithlife. For the latest versions, see www.logos .com.

Book Concordances

Even-Shoshan, Abraham, ed. 1989. *A New Concordance of the Old Testament*. 2nd ed. Jerusalem: Kiryat Sefer Publishing House / Grand Rapids: Baker (in Hebrew).

Kohlenberger, John R., III, and James A. Swanson. 1998. *The Hebrew-English Concordance to the Old Testament*. Grand Rapids: Zondervan.

Lisowsky, Gerhard. 1958. *Konkordanz zum hebräischen Alten Testament*. Stuttgart: Württembergische Bibelanstalt.

Mandelkern, Solomon. 1988. *Veteris Testamenti concordantiae Hebraicae atque Chaldaicae*. 8th ed. Brooklyn: P. Shalom Publications.

Word Studies

Barr, James. 1961. *The Semantics of Biblical Language*. London: Oxford University Press. Reprinted 2004. Eugene, OR: Wipf & Stock.

Botterweck, G. Johannes, Helmer Ringgren, and Heinz-Joseph Fabry, eds. 1974–2006. *Theological Dictionary of the Old Testament [TDOT]*. Translated by J. T. Willis, G. W. Bromiley, and D. E. Green. 15 vols. Grand Rapids: Eerdmans Publishing.

Gibson, Arthur. 2002. *Biblical Semantic Logic: A Preliminary Analysis*. Sheffield: Sheffield Academic Press.

Jenni, Ernst, and Claus Westermann, eds. 1997. *Theological Lexicon of the Old Testament* [*TLOT*]. 3 vols. Peabody, MA: Hendrickson Publishers.

Silva, Moisés. 1994. *Biblical Words and Their Meaning: An Introduction to Lexical Semantics*. 2nd ed. Grand Rapids: Zondervan Publishing House.

VanGemeren, Willem A., ed. 1997. *New International Dictionary of Old Testament Theology and Exegesis* [*NIDOTTE*]. 5 vols. Grand Rapids: Zondervan Publishing House.

Bible Dictionaries

Achtemeier, Paul J., ed. 1996. *HarperCollins Bible Dictionary*. San Francisco: HarperSanFrancisco.

Buttrick, George A., et al., eds. 1962. *The Interpreter's Dictionary of the Bible* [*IDB*]. 4 vols. Nashville: Abingdon.

Crim, Keith, ed. 1976. *The Interpreter's Dictionary of the Bible: Supplementary Volume*. Nashville: Abingdon.

Freedman, David Noel, et al., eds. 1992. *The Anchor Bible Dictionary* [*ABD*]. 6 vols. New York: Doubleday.

Freedman, David Noel, Allen C. Myers, and Astrid B. Beck, eds. 2000. *Eerdmans Dictionary of the Bible*. Grand Rapids: Eerdmans Publishing.

Sakenfeld, Katharine Doob, et al., eds. 2006–9. *The New Interpreter's Dictionary of the Bible* [*NIDB*]. 5 vols. Nashville: Abingdon.

5

Text-Critical Analysis

Textual criticism is the doorway to exegesis,
and there is no back door.
Alexander Achilles Fischer[1]

Every biblical text reflects a rich history of development, from its composition to its transmission. Speaking of the latter, a biblical text typically reflects a plurality of manuscript witnesses, which could range from Qumran fragments dating a couple of centuries before the Common Era to standardized codices from the medieval period. Indeed, the Hebrew text used today by most students (*Biblica Hebraica Stuttgartensia*, or *BHS*) is a formatted representation of a medieval text that preserves over a thousand years of textual transmission, thanks to countless copyists transmitting texts over centuries upon centuries of painstaking work.

Translation involves translating a text. Simple enough, but behind this tautology lies a rather complex question. Which text should be used for our translation and interpretive work? More properly speaking, which *form* of the text? Should it be the Received Text, that is, its "final" form, or should it be its "original" exemplar? Should it be the presenting manuscript (e.g., the Leningrad Codex or the Aleppo Codex), or should it be a text reconstructed from its variant readings? Textual criticism typically favors the latter option. The task of the text critic is to dig deeply into the complex history of the text's transmission. But for what specific purpose remains a matter of discussion.

Some suggest that the text critic is like a detective at a "crime scene," working with only few clues to determine "the exact reading of a text in order to know what God has said and expects from us" (Wegner 2006, 23). More modestly put is the expressed aim to provide "the most reliable reading of the text" (Würthwein 2014, 168) or to enhance "the integrity of the text" (McCarter 1986, 12), which is typically identified with its "original" form, the so-called *Urtext*. But the question remains whether a singular original text is at all recoverable, or ever existed.

---

1. Quoted via Würthwein 2014, 157.

However it is to be defined, the text critic's task is crucial because of two simple facts: (1) no original witnesses of the biblical text have been recovered, and (2) most extant witnesses do not agree with each other. Put generally, I submit that the goal of text criticism is to account for differences among the witnesses of a given biblical text. While determining the "original" form of a text may never be within reach, it is the comparison of the variant readings that helps to identify or reconstruct possibly earlier forms of the text. At its most basic level, text criticism addresses the question of how one form of the text relates to another form of the text. Perhaps the various forms of the same text can be related historically or even "genetically," something like what a paleoanthropologist does using fossil records to trace the convoluted lineage of a certain genus with its various species. And like the evolutionary tree of life, the lineage of a biblical text tends to branch out, resembling more a broad bush than a towering tree.

TEXTUAL ORIENTATION

How does one arrive at a text that on the one hand is free of scribal errors and on the other hand is reflective of its pluriformality, the text's various forms that have evolved in the course of transmission? Is it possible to arrive at an original, singular form of a biblical text? We will return to these all-important questions, but first a brief overview of the textual traditions that constitute the early history of the biblical text is in order.

The Masoretic Tradition

The Hebrew Bible as we have it is called the Masoretic Text (MT), since it is the product of the so-called Masoretes,[2] the name for Jewish scholars who maintained the tradition that governed the production of copies of the biblical text beginning perhaps as early as ca. 500 CE and lasting until 1425 (*ABD* 4:595). The Masoretes strove to preserve the biblical text as accurately as possible and, at the same time, make it readily usable for new generations when Biblical Hebrew became more difficult to read. Their goal of preserving the text also required innovating the text. The Hebrew Bible they inherited, having been in circulation for centuries, was strictly consonantal, devoid of vowel markings or points. By then Hebrew was primarily a literary language, reserved for liturgy and poetry. (Aramaic had superseded Hebrew as the region's lingua franca at least by the third century BCE, and thereafter Greek and Latin came to serve that role.) As part of their innovative work, the Masoretes were responsible for (1) the vocalization of Hebrew words through vowel points, (2) the punctuation or accentual marks that structured the meaning (and reciting and singing) of clauses and sentences, and (3) the division of textual units, both small and large. Because Hebrew syllables, consonantly framed, can be pointed and punctuated in different ways, the Masoretes established a relatively unambiguous and authoritative way of reading (and thus interpreting) the text.

---

2. The etymology of the word is unclear, but the verbal root *msr* came to mean "hand down" or "transmit" tradition (*HALOT* 608).

In addition, the Masoretes supplied marginal notations to preserve the unusual spelling of words and their attestations across the biblical canon and to make consonantal corrections to (but not in) the written text (e.g., *ketiv/qere*). These marginal notes constitute what is called the Masorah. Most obvious are the notes found in the side margins of the *BHS*, known as the Masorah Parva (Mp). These notes contain a storehouse of information regarding the frequency and distribution of various words and their spellings. Deciphering the Masorah, written in abbreviated Aramaic, is the challenge, and the most helpful resources for doing so are Kelley, Mynatt, and Crawford 1998 and Yeivin 1980.

The significance of these innovations, designed to preserve the textual tradition of the MT, should not be underestimated. Take the following example of an English sentence indicated only by its consonants (from Law 2013, 22).

Jn rn t th str t by brd.

How should one vocalize and punctuate this text? Let us count the ways:

Jon ran to the store to buy bread.
Jon, run to the store to buy bread!
Jon ran to the store to buy a board (or a bird).
Jan ran to the stair, at a bay beard.
Jane, I run to thee, a star to obey, a bride!

And so forth, from the straightforward to the nonsensical. Can you think of other ways? By vocalizing the Hebrew text, the Masoretes significantly narrowed the range of reading possibilities, thereby establishing an authoritative interpretation.

The development of the Masoretic Text by no means happened overnight; it developed over at least five generations of working scholars across two families active in Tiberias (on the western coast of the Sea of Galilee): Ben Asher and Ben Naphtali. The former was responsible for the Leningrad Codex, completed in 1008 CE, the manuscript upon which the *BHS* is based. Among the medieval codices, this codex is the only one that is preserved in its entirety. The Aleppo Codex (900–925 CE), a model codex in its own right, lacks, among other texts, Gen. 1:1–Deut. 28:16 and Song 3:11b–Neh. 13:31, due to a fire in 1947.[3]

Because the *BHS* relies entirely on an extant manuscript, it is called a "diplomatic" edition, in contrast to an "eclectic" edition. The latter is a reconstructed text that is considered to be the "best" reading derived from all the available witnesses. The critical editions of the New Testament are "eclectic,"[4] the result of choices made by scholars in their evaluation of variant readings, the significant ones of which are listed in the "apparatus" below the biblical text. Yet even as a "diplomatic" edition, the *BHS* makes reference to variant readings that pertain to a given passage. While the apparatus of an eclectic edition provides evidence for the decisions made to reproduce a "reliable" text, the apparatus of a diplomatic text thrusts the critical decision-making primarily upon you, the exegete.[5]

---

3. The Aleppo Codex serves as the base for a critical edition of the Hebrew Bible being developed by the Hebrew University in Jerusalem.

4. The Nestle-Aland *Novum Testamentum Graece* and the UBS *The Greek New Testament* are examples.

5. The current project *The Hebrew Bible: A Critical Edition*, formerly called the "Oxford Hebrew Bible," is working to produce a thoroughly "eclectic" text (Hendel 2008; 2013).

The apparatus of the *BHS* enables you to situate the Masoretic Text within its sweeping and complex textual history and to make your own critical choices that together would form the text of your translation. The place to begin is by first decoding the apparatus itself. This will not be discussed here, but a helpful resource is Reinhard Wonneberger's manual (2001). Although a bit unwieldy, it contains all the relevant information to begin your own text-critical work with the *BHS*.

Other Textual Witnesses

To make informed text-critical decisions, the translator needs to be aware of the background and distinctive characteristics of other various textual witnesses. Each witness, or better family of witnesses, has a story to tell, some of them quite legendary. And each one takes us into the rich history of textual development, some over a thousand years before the work of the Masoretes. The following discussion identifies the major textual traditions that pertain to the Hebrew Bible. The reader is encouraged to read more in depth (see bibliography).

Qumran

Sometime in the early first century BCE, a group of disaffected Jews founded a community in the inhospitable desert just northwest of the Dead Sea,[6] setting themselves apart from the Jerusalemite priesthood in order to live a life based on uncompromised piety, ritual purity, and the sharing of property. Led by the "Teacher of Righteousness," the members of the community at Qumran (the Arabic name for the adjacent wadi) preserved as well as produced a library of literature, including most of what is now known as the Hebrew Bible.[7]

The discovery of the scrolls, ca. eight hundred so far, began in the winter of 1946–47 when a young bedouin by the name of Muhammad Ahmed al-Hamed came across a nearby cave that contained clay jars, one of which protected the complete scroll of Isaiah (1QIsa[a]), one of the few scrolls to have survived intact. So far eleven caves have been discovered to contain manuscripts (i.e., scrolls and fragments): Caves 4–10 in a terrace of Wadi Qumran close to the settlement, and Caves 1–3 and 11 a few kilometers to the north. They were presumably placed there for safekeeping just before the Roman invasion of the settlement in 68 CE (Würthwein 2014, 58–59).

Before this momentous discovery, the oldest biblical manuscripts available were from the fourth century CE and were Greek. The oldest manuscripts found at Qumran date back to the mid-third century BCE. Apart from the book of Esther, all the books of the canonical Hebrew Bible are represented among the scrolls and fragments, the Psalms being the most common, followed by Deuteronomy. Deuterocanonical books (e.g., Tobit, Baruch, and Sirach) are also represented, along with commentaries and para-

---

6. Although the issue remains hotly debated, Qumran during this period was most likely inhabited by a particular group of Essenes, as described in certain Greek and Latin sources (e.g., Philo, Josephus, Pliny).

7. The connection between the scrolls or manuscripts found in the eleven caves and the actual site of Qumran continues to be a topic of debate, but most likely they belong to the same archaeological setting. On the other hand, many of the scrolls predate the establishment of the community, some as early as 250 BCE.

phrases of biblical texts. Approximately 25 percent of the manuscripts share a common system of spelling that is distinct from the more conservative consonantal text reflected in the masoretic tradition. Nevertheless, the roots of the Masoretic Text can be found among the plethora of Qumran witnesses, roughly 50 percent of the biblical manuscripts. Together they are commonly referenced as proto-Masoretic Texts. The remaining biblical manuscripts from Qumran reflect other textual traditions, specifically pre-Samaritan (5 percent) and the Hebrew sources for the Old Greek (or later Septuagint [LXX]) translation (5 percent). Roughly 40 percent of all the Qumran biblical texts, however, are unclassifiable in the sense that they cannot be attributed to any one of these main textual traditions. They are considered "free" or "independent" texts (Würthwein 2014, 73).

In short, the treasure trove of texts discovered at Qumran indicate that, by the time of the Common Era, the proto-Masoretic textual tradition was not the only one in use. The Qumran discoveries show that before the second century CE, the Jewish Scriptures were very much in flux. Only 48 percent of the Torah manuscripts of Qumran reflect the Masoretic Text (Law 2013, 25). Thus the sheer variety of forms found at Qumran makes it difficult to trace these various textual traditions to a single, original form of the text. In any event, for nearly five centuries, something other than textual uniformity reigned. Indeed, different editions of the same text were peacefully cohabiting in the same cave! "Between the third century BCE and the second CE there was no real preoccupation with a fixed text, and authoritative status was shared by different versions of the same books" (Law 2013, 26). Moreover, the variety of Qumran texts, particularly among the independent texts, suggests a very fine line between the transmission of the text and the text's "final" editing (Würthwein 2014, 72, 161). That is to say, the boundary between composition and copying is blurry.

Samaritan Tradition

The Samaritan Pentateuch and the Qumran pre-Samaritan manuscripts represent a Hebrew corpus that is distinct from the Masoretic textual tradition. The former is associated with the Samaritans, a particular community that, by the second century BCE, if not before, was at odds with the centralized Jerusalem leadership and identified its religious and political center with Mount Gerizim in the north (John 4:1–42). Their beginnings were rooted in a mixed community that began to form in northern Israel as a result of conquest and repopulation by the Assyrian Empire after 722 BCE. The community's independence from Jerusalem continued to develop as a result of the exclusionary policies and practices implemented by the exiles returning from Babylon, who wanted no part with "foreigners." As a result of the destruction of their temple on Gerizim by the Maccabean ruler John Hyrcanus I in 111 BCE, the schism was complete. The Samaritan Bible (Smr) is limited to the Torah in a "corrected" form that favors Gerizim over Jerusalem/Zion. No wonder.

The Samaritan Bible or Pentateuch is written in a special paleo-Hebrew script developed in the third century BCE and contains roughly six thousand differences from the MT, most of them having to do with spelling distinctions. Yet it just so happens that a third of these differences agree with the Septuagint (LXX), the Greek translation of the Hebrew text. This is text-critically significant, for it raises the possibility that the Smr and LXX together preserve a textual tradition that predates the proto-MT, or at least is independent of it.

The Smr is distinctive in at least three ways: (1) it tends to harmonize or reconcile disparities evident in the Hebrew text as reflected in the MT; (2) it simplifies unusual spellings; and (3) it makes certain content-oriented "corrections," particularly by replacing references to Jerusalem or Zion with Gerizim. Apart from such corrections, which came later, certain Qumran texts show striking resemblance with the Smr, thereby demonstrating a degree of textual continuity. These texts are appropriately called "pre-Samaritan" texts.[8] They indicate a non-Masoretic textual base in the third/second century BCE shared by the Smr.

Old Greek / Septuagint (LXX)

According to the legendary *Letter of Aristeas* (2nd-c. [century] BCE), a Greek translation of the Torah was initiated by King Ptolemy II (285–247 BCE), who solicited the assistance of Eleazar the high priest of Jerusalem to appoint six men from each of the twelve tribes (thus 72 translators) and send them to Egypt, where on Pharos Island they allegedly completed their work in seventy-two days, "reaching agreement among themselves on each by comparing versions" (*Aristeas* 302 in *OTP* 2:32-33). Philo adds to the account that the translators (rounded down to seventy) were assigned each one to his cell, thereby working independently yet miraculously developing identical translations (*Life of Moses* 2.7.37). The verdict: a divinely inspired translation! The later expansion of the Greek translation to include the entire Bible came to be the Christian Bible of the early church.

The actual history of the Septuagint Torah is considerably less dramatic and more complex. While the translation of the Torah, beginning with Genesis, into Koine (*koinē*, common) Greek occurred sometime in the third century BCE in Egypt, the translation of the Writings, concluding with Ecclesiastes, did not take place until the second century CE (Tov 2012, 129–30). As a whole, the Septuagint is far from a unified version of the Old Testament, instead being a collection of translations, some independent, some interrelated, developed at different times and places. The earliest extant Greek translations come from Qumran. They mark the beginning of a translational trajectory that scholars call the "Old Greek" translation (OG), the precursor to the Septuagint (LXX), which refers to the fully developed Greek Old Testament, as evidenced in various codices of the fourth and fifth centuries CE (e.g., Vaticanus, Sinaiticus, and Alexandrinus).

Of great interest to the text critic is the distinct possibility that many of the Hebrew texts used as the base texts for the Greek translation might have differed significantly from and are older than the proto-Masoretic Texts. A case in point is the book of Jeremiah in the LXX: it is one-sixth shorter than the MT of Jeremiah, whose chapters, moreover, are arranged differently. Certain Qumran manuscripts (4QJer[b] and 4QJer[d]) suggest that this discrepancy was not the result of the Greek translator's penchant for brevity, but that the translator was actually using a shorter Hebrew base text. In addition, other Qumran manuscripts attest a lengthier proto-MT version of the book of Jeremiah. Hence, not one but two Hebrew versions of the book of Jeremiah coexisted at Qumran:

---

8. But not "proto-Samaritan" because the commonalities are looser compared to the similarities between the "proto-MT" texts and the MT.

one that would determine much of the LXX version of Jeremiah and the other the MT. The discoveries at Qumran, in short, have given the LXX (via the OG) its text-critical due as a bona fide textual tradition in its own right. Equally spectacular discrepancies between the MT and LXX can be found in 1 Samuel (see Law 2013, 30, 50).

Given the significant differences between the LXX and the MT, a number of Greek translations have attempted to fill the gap. Called "recensions," these Greek translations reflect greater fidelity to the proto-MT. They include the *Kaige*-Theodotion recension (late 2nd c. CE), Aquila (early 2nd c. CE), Symmachus (late 2nd c. CE), and Origen's Hexaplaric recension (the hybrid 5th column) in the mid-third century CE.[9] Each has its own peculiarities, but together they share a common tendency to assimilate in varying degrees to the Hebrew text. In addition, the (pre-)Lucianic recension or Antiochene text, though post-Hexaplaric (early 4th c. CE), may reflect an early or "purer" form of the LXX and thus an early Hebrew base that differs from and predates the proto-MT (see Würthwein 2014, 114–17; Tov 2012, 142–46).

Targums

In addition to Greek translations, Aramaic translations of the Bible emerged beginning in the fourth/third centuries BCE. This was no surprise: Aramaic was already the common language of the ancient Near East by the sixth century BCE ("Imperial Aramaic"). According to Neh. 13:24, Hebrew was no longer understood by the population at large. Ezra's public reading of the Law in Jerusalem, for example, involved "interpretation," which presumably required oral Aramaic rendering (8:7–8). Hence, the Targum (explanation/translation) played an essential role in promoting basic biblical understanding and interpretation for Jewish communities for several centuries throughout the Levant, while the Septuagint did the same for Greek-speaking Jews and Christians, beginning in Egypt (see above).

Distinctive among the targums is their nonliteral approach to translation. Taken together, they effectively blur the boundary between translation and commentary. In many passages they appear to be "free" translations. Separately, each targum has its own character. In addition to what has been discovered at Qumran, the various targums can be divided into two categories, defined by their region of use, Palestinian and Babylonian. Among the Palestinian Targums are (1) the *Codex Neofiti*, a complete Palestinian Targum of the Pentateuch; and (2) the *Fragmentary Targum*, or *Targum Yerušalmi II*, a collection of fragments of great variety. The Babylonian Targums include (1) the *Targum Onqelos*, a relatively literal treatment of the Pentateuch; (2) the *Targum Jonathan*, a freer "translation" of the Former and Latter Prophets; and (3) the *Targum Pseudo-Jonathan* (or *Targum Yerušalmi I*), the least literal "translation" of the Pentateuch.

---

9. This column is part of a six-columned Bible, or *Hexapla*, codified by the great biblical exegete Origen (ca. 184–254 CE), who arranged the columns in the order of (1) Hebrew (proto-MT), (2) Greek transliteration of the Hebrew letters, (3) Aquila, (4) Symmachus, (5) Septuagint, and (6) Theodotion. The entire work is said to have comprised 6,000 pages in 15 vols. The 5th column is of particular interest, since Origen identified omissions and expansions within the LXX in comparison to the Hebrew Bible of the synagogue by using special symbols (asterisks and obeloi [Gk. sg. *obelos*; Lat./Eng. obelus/i]). What may have begun as a scholarly tool for exegesis, however, backfired because the fifth column was soon copied and dispersed minus the signs. Consequently, Origen unintentionally "contaminated the stream of biblical transmission" by his Hexaplaric recension, which turned out to be a thoroughly "hybrid text" (Law 2013, 145).

The text-critical value of the targums is, as one would suspect, mixed at best. But occasionally one can detect a Hebrew base text that differs from the MT. Two important targumic manuscripts found among the Qumran scrolls are *Targum Leviticus* and *Targum of Job*.

Peshitta or Syriac Translation

With a particularly graceful script, Syriac is an eastern Aramaic dialect that emerged by the early first century CE. It originated in the region of Edessa (now in SE Turkey) among Jews, many of whom converted to Christianity in the second century CE. The Peshitta (simple/common) is a translation that bears both Jewish and Christian influences. Influenced by targumic tradition, as one might expect, the Peshitta draws from the MT and LXX. Among the many cases where the Peshitta and the LXX agree against the MT, the Peshitta cannot be assumed to be an independent witness.

Vulgate

The Vulgate (Vulgata) is the Latin translation of the Hebrew Bible associated with the great biblical translator and Latin scholar Jerome (ca. 347–420 CE), whose full name is Eusebius Sophronius Hieronymus. He was born in Stridon, an Alpine village on the border between Dalmatia and Pannonia, in what is now Slovenia. Jerome was assigned by Pope Damasus I to revise the existing Latin Bible (see Old Latin below), which was based on the Septuagint but did not measure up to classical Latin. (The Old Latin translations of the Psalms and the Gospels were more "vulgar" than the Vulgate!) Jerome did most of his translation work in Bethlehem (390–405), where he also founded a monastic community. Within the church, Jerome was the only one equipped to do such a translation (and evidently the only one with a confidence full enough, or the ego big enough, to pull it off), even though his facility with Hebrew was intermediate at best. (His Greek was better than his Hebrew.) Completed in 405, the result was an elegant, classical Latin translation that, although based on the Hebrew, frequently matched the sentence structure of the LXX.

Although Jerome did not intend his translation to replace the LXX, his work met stiff resistance, particularly from Augustine, bishop of Hippo, who vigorously argued that any new translation for the church had to be based on the Septuagint, which he considered fully inspired. Jerome, however, considered the *Letter of Aristeas* to be a fabrication and vigorously defended himself by pointing out that the LXX was itself no uniform translation and that a faithful Latin translation could only be achieved by consulting the Hebrew text. For Augustine, the very unity of the church was at stake, a legitimate concern.[10] Augustine cited an incident in the North African city of Oea (Tripoli), where Jerome's translation of Jonah was read. When the reading claimed in 4:6 that Jonah was sitting not under a "gourd" (so LXX) but, according to Jerome, under "ivy" in order to seek shade (Hebrew *qîqāyôn*; LXX *kolokynthē*; Aquila *kittos*), a riot ensued. This was irrelevant to Jerome, who considered this an attack on his linguistic competence. It was not until

---

10. Ultimately the church suffered a schism or break of communion in 1054 between the Eastern Orthodox and the Roman Catholic Churches, the former retaining the LXX as its Bible.

the Council of Trent (1545–63) that the Catholic Church made the Vulgate its official Latin Bible. Text-critically, it is evident that Jerome consulted the LXX (and other Greek translations) almost as much as he drew from the proto-MT. Hence, his translation occasionally supports the LXX and Smr against the MT.

Old Latin

The pre-Vulgate Latin biblical texts of the church are a fragmentary collection known as the Vetus Latina (Old Latin), based on the LXX. Text-critically, the Old Latin is at times useful for reconstructing the pre-Hexaplaric period of the LXX, and therefore it may be a witness to the Old Greek text itself (proto-LXX). Occasionally the Old Latin might serve as a witness to a Hebrew textual tradition where its readings differ from *both* LXX and MT, although this is difficult to demonstrate (Würthwein 2014, 146; cf. Tov 2012, 134).

APPLYING TEXTUAL CRITICISM

So what does one do with all these witnesses, variant as they are and in different languages no less? Textual criticism, again, has to do with adjudicating variant readings with the aim of arriving at the most "reliable," if not the earliest or "original" text. But the "original" invariably points to a hypothetical, reconstructed text. At the very least, textual criticism compares variant readings and attempts to explain their differences. It is a discipline of comparative reading that shares a deep inquiry into the text and revels in the diversity of its witnesses.

Scribal Errors

First and foremost, textual criticism aims to detect unintended errors in the text, what scholars call "textual corruptions" (Würthwein 2014, 172). Mistakes in the transmission or copying of a text inevitably arise for a variety of reasons, ranging from the scribe's lack of understanding of the source language (i.e., Hebrew and Aramaic) to haste, fatigue, or inattention. If the copying is done through dictation, then the errors can only mount. Then there is always chance or accident. Regardless of cause, scribal mistakes typically fall into the following categories.[11]

1. Graphic confusion: similar *looking* letters that are confused, whether in the Paleo-Hebrew script or the square script found in critical editions, such as the *BHS*. Similar-*sounding* letters can also be confused.
2. Transposition or reversal of letters (metathesis).
3. Omitting one of two identical letters next to each other (haplography).
4. Duplicating one letter or word (dittography).
5. Omitting a word or series of words due to the copyist's eye skipping from one word to a similar or identical word. This can happen in one of two ways. When the scribe skips over material bracketed by two words with similar endings, it is called *homoioteleuton*. When it occurs with two words that have similar beginnings, it is called *homoioarchton*.

11. For biblical examples, see Würthwein 2014, 172–76; Tov 2012, 219–39.

6. Misdivision of words, which can happen particularly in a line where several words are pressed together.
7. Mistaking vowel letters or *matres lectionis* (i.e., *waw*, *yod*, *aleph*, and *he*) as consonants.

That's the simple part. There are also deliberate scribal changes, which are obviously due not to scribal fatigue or incompetence, but rather to scribal intention, whether to make the text more accessible or more theologically palatable or legally consistent. These can include inserting explanatory additions or glosses, replacing a difficult word with something simpler, correcting the text grammatically, introducing stylistic changes to smooth out the text, harmonizing the text to mitigate contradictions, and introducing euphemisms to avoid impropriety.[12]

There are, however, instances in which it is well-nigh impossible to determine which variant reading is primary (i.e., earlier or more original). This would be a case of holding two or more different readings at an equal level, allowing each to claim its own validity of meaning. This might indicate the lack of a single originating text or, at the very least, the limitation of text-critical analysis to determine the earlier text.

Method and Guidelines

In their close work with the text, practitioners of textual criticism have devised a few principles that have proved useful in adjudicating variant readings or versions of the same text. They are not rules to be slavishly followed but rather guidelines to consider. The most fundamental rule of textual criticism is that any evaluation of variants must be conducted on a case-by-case basis. That is to say, text criticism cannot simply favor a particular manuscript or textual tradition, however "reliable" it may be overall. Indeed, across biblical books, the MT is of inconsistent quality. Although one typically begins with the MT text critically, the quality of this textual tradition, as has been shown, differs from book to book. For example, the Masoretic Text of Joshua is well preserved, whereas the MT of the books of Samuel is filled with scribal errors and omissions, as demonstrated by other textual versions, including from Qumran. Conversely, any manuscript, however "unreliable" or error-filled, cannot exclude the possibility of preserving an "original" reading (Würthwein 2014, 184).

Textual criticism begins by comparing the witnesses, beginning with the MT but by no means limited to it. Do the LXX and Smr offer readings significantly different from the MT? Does Qumran provide evidence of alternative readings? Which textual traditions agree against others? If the LXX, for example, disagrees with the MT, one question to ask is whether this is due to the work of the Greek translator or to the Hebrew text that the translator was using. If you suspect the latter, then a "back translation" is required, which involves retroverting the Greek into Hebrew, that is, reconstructing the Hebrew from the Greek. Frequently the *BHS* apparatus does this for you.

Once you have compared the (variant) witnesses, then the following guidelines should be considered when making your decision regarding the "best" reading of the text. Despite being "immortalized" in Latin, these principles are not hard-and-fast rules.

12. For examples, see Würthwein 2014, 176–81; Tov 2012, 240–62.

1. *Lectio corrupta sive mutata corrigenda.* "A corrupt or altered reading should be corrected." This simply states that texts exhibiting errors or scribal alterations should be considered secondary in comparison to a text lacking such intrusions.
2. *Lectio difficilior probabilior.* "The more difficult reading is the more probable." The more unusual or difficult variant is likely to be the older one. Scribes tend to clarify rather than complexify the texts they are transmitting. Of course, this rule has its limits when it comes to a text that is rendered difficult, if not incomprehensible, through scribal error.
3. *Lectio brevior portior.* "The shorter reading is preferable." Scribes tend to expand the text rather than abbreviate it. However, the rule does not apply when the shorter text is due to unintentional omission (e.g., haplography, homoioteleuton, or homoioarchton).

Text Critical Issues in Genesis 1

Regardless of textual tradition or translation, Gen. 1:1–2:4a is one of the most structured texts of the entire Bible. And yet there are significant variants between the MT and other versions, particularly the LXX. One notable variant is found in Gen. 2:2. The apparatus of the *BHS* reads "Cp2,2ᵃ" and then lists three textual witnesses, each designated by its specific siglum or symbol: Samaritan Pentateuch, Septuagint/Old Greek, and Peshitta (or Syriac). These three textual traditions together point to the variant reading "And God finished on the *sixth* day. . . ." The MT, however, reads "seventh day," as well as the Targums (Onqelos, Pseudo-Jonathan, and Neofiti) and the Vulgate (lacking in the *BHS* apparatus). The text-critical editor of the book of Genesis in the *BHS*, Otto Eisfeldt, provides the variant Hebrew word complete with vowel pointing: *haššišî* (the sixth). Consequently, we have two variant Hebrew readings of one word: *haššĕbîî* (the seventh) of the MT and *haššišî* (the sixth) of the Smr, LXX (*tē hektē*), and Peshitta. This is not likely a case of scribal error. Is there a way of accounting for the difference? The larger context may provide a clue. Below is a translation of 2:1–3 MT.

> ²:¹ Thus the heavens and the earth were completed, as well as all their host. ² And on the *seventh* day [*sixth* day = Smr, LXX, Peshitta] God completed the work that [God] had done and ceased on the seventh day from all the work that [God] had done. ³ So God blessed the seventh day and hallowed it, because on it God ceased from all the work that [God] had done in creation.

The presenting issue is the timing of creation's completion. The previous section regarding the sixth day records the creation of the land animals and human beings, concluding with 1:31: "God saw all that [God] had made, and, *voilà*, [it was] very good! And there was evening and there was morning, the sixth day." As this verse makes clear, it is on the sixth day in which everything is completed, which stands in tension with the 2:2 MT's reference to God's completion on the "seventh" day, the day on which God ceased ("rested," 2:3 NRSV) from all creative activity.

So this is a case in which one textual tradition makes more sense (LXX et al.) than the other. The MT, on the other hand, presents a text that is in chronological tension with itself. Thus the MT presents the more difficult (*difficilior*) form of this final section of the Priestly account of creation, suggesting that it is also the earlier (if not original) form. It is sometimes claimed that the translator made this "correction" in the process of rendering the Hebrew into Greek. However, the fact that the Smr also attests to this change suggests the possibility that the translator was working with a Hebrew manuscript that read "sixth" instead of "seventh," a distinctly non-Masoretic Text. Unfortunately, we have no witness from Qumran to demonstrate this, so the issue remains open. In any case, the MT likely preserves the older reading.

The conclusion seems straightforward enough.[13] This case, however, is not the only instance of disagreement among the versions of Gen. 1, particularly between the LXX and MT. There are four variants between the MT and LXX that actually have bearing upon the structure of Gen. 1.

Variant 1. In Gen. 1:6–7, the MT literally reads:

> 1:6 And God said, "Let there be a firmament amid the waters, and let it separate the waters from the waters."
>
> 1:7 So God made the firmament and separated the waters that were under the firmament from the waters that were above the firmament. *And it was so [wayhî-kēn].*

In contrast, the LXX reads:

> 1:6 And God said, "Let there be a firmament amid the water, and let it separate water and water." *And it was so [kai egeneto houtōs].*
>
> 1:7 And God made the firmament, and God separated the water that was under the firmament from the water that was above the firmament.

The major difference has to do with the placement of what is sometimes called the transition formula, because it is most often found between God's command and the fulfillment of the command (see 1:9, 11–12, 15–16, 24–25, 30–31; but cf. vv. 20–21). Taking its cue from the LXX, the *BHS* suggests that the phrase in question at the end of v. 7 in the MT be placed at the end of v. 6 ("huc tr 7ᵃ⁻ᵃ"). But because the masoretic placement of the transition formula appears out of place, it is commonly suggested that its location immediately after v. 6 represents a harmonizing move on the part of the LXX. It seems, then, that we have a case of *lectio difficilior* in favor of the MT.

Variant 2. The *BHS* makes another suggestion with regard to the end of v. 7 ("ins . . ."), namely, to insert the Hebrew sentence "And God saw that it was good," the formula of divine approval found also in vv. 4, 10, 12, 18, 21, 25, and 31 consistently *after* the fulfillment of God's command. The reference to v. 8 at the end of this entry for v. 7 in the apparatus acknowledges that the phrase also occurs in v. 8 of the LXX, which is where one would expect it (see v. 10).[14] In either case, the divine approval formula is missing in this section of the MT.

> 1:7–8 MT So God made the firmament and separated the waters that were under the firmament from the waters that were above the dome. And it was so. And

---

13. One could argue, albeit with greater difficulty, that the LXX and other versions preserved the earlier reading and that the MT made the change in order to emphasize all the more the concluding significance of the seventh day.

14. The suggestion by the *BHS* that the divine approval formula be placed at the end of v. 7 rather than within v. 8, as in the LXX, is without merit.

God called the firmament heaven. There was evening and then morning, second day.

> 1:7–8 LXX So God made the firmament, and God separated the water that was under the firmament from the water that was above the firmament. And God called the firmament heaven. ***And God saw that it was good.*** And evening came and morning came, second day.

With the addition of God's approval, the LXX again proves to be more structurally consistent.

Variant 3. In its second entry for v. 9, the *BHS* apparatus notes that the LXX features a fulfillment report, whereas the MT does not. The MT reads:

> 1:9 And God said, "Let the waters that are under the heavens gather themselves together[15] into one place, and let the dry land appear." And it was so.

The LXX is twice as long because it features the fulfillment report of God's command.

> 1:9 And God said, "Let the water that is under the heaven be gathered into one gathering, and let the dry land appear." And it was so. ***And the water under the sky was gathered into their gatherings, and the dry land appeared.***

The editor of the *BHS* has kindly retroverted the line into Hebrew, to be translated as follows:

> ***And the waters under the sky gathered themselves into their gatherings, and the dry land appeared.***

By back-translating the Greek into Hebrew, Eisfeldt is suggesting that the Greek translator relied on a more complete Hebrew text, or *Vorlage*. But such a claim is made without any corroborating external evidence; otherwise it would have been cited.[16] There is also the curious case of the LXX's reference to "*their* gatherings" in v. 9b, since "water" in Greek is singular.[17] Moreover, instead of the MT's "place" (*māqôm*), the Greek translates "gathering" (*synagōgē*), which retroverted into Hebrew would be *miqweh*.[18] These two words in Hebrew are consonantally different only in the final consonant: the final *mem* in the MT and the *he* in the Hebrew base text of the LXX. It is highly possible that a case of "graphic confusion" occurred such that the MT's "place," a much more common word, constituted a misreading of "gathering." Overall, however, with the "addition" of the fulfillment report, the LXX once again features a more structurally consistent form of the text than the MT.

Variant 4. Finally, at the end of Gen. 1:20 the LXX features the transitional formula "And it was so," absent in the MT, which reads:

---

15. The Niphal form of the verbal root √*qwh* takes on reciprocal meaning here (see Jer. 3:17 as a parallel use).
16. But now there is supporting evidence from Qumran. See below.
17. The pl. suffix *autōn* ("their") could only refer to the translator's recognition of the Hebrew pl. "waters" (*mayim*), again suggesting a Hebrew base text that contained the fulfillment report (see below).
18. This seems confirmed by the Qumran fragment 4QGen[h], which features *miqweh*. See Davila 1994a.

1:20 And God said, "Let the waters bring forth swarms of living creatures, and
      birds that fly above the earth across the firmament of the heavens."
1:21 So God created the great sea monsters and every living creature that moves,
      of every kind, with which the waters swarm, and every winged bird of every
      kind. And God saw that it was good.

The LXX reads thus:

1:20 And God said, "Let the waters bring forth living sea creatures, and birds
      flying above the earth across the firmament of the heaven." *And it was so.*
1:21 And God made the great sea monsters, and every living sea creature, which
      the waters brought forth according to their kinds, and every creature that
      flies with wings according to its kind, and God saw that they were good.

With the addition of the transitional formula between the command and fulfillment
regarding the genesis of marine life, it appears that the LXX, once again, has harmonized
the text, making it more structurally consistent.

Analysis. We have noticed four instances in which the Greek translator has produced
a version of Gen. 1 that is more structurally consistent than the MT. Add it all up, and it
seems that in every case the LXX has harmonized the creation account in Gen. 1. That
has led most exegetes to regard the LXX text as secondary, meaning inferior, since the
MT is the shorter (*brevior*) and more difficult (*difficilior*) text. An open-and-shut case, so
it seems.

But questions remain, particularly when one considers other textual witnesses not
listed in the *BHS* (and in many commentaries). One manuscript from Qumran suggests
that the Greek translator was not concerned about harmonizing a structurally inconsistent text (i.e., proto-MT) but instead faithfully rendering a Hebrew text available at the
time (ca. 3rd c. BCE). The recently published fragment of 4QGen[k] (fragment 1) attests
to the "additional" fulfillment report in 1:9 in the Hebrew, which is lacking in the MT
(variant 3).[19] In other words, it is likely that there were two coexisting Hebrew versions of
Gen. 1:1–2:3, one that was structurally consistent (the Hebrew base text or *Vorlage* of the
Septuagint) and one that was not (the proto-MT).

The question of textual relationship can easily be turned to asking why the MT is
so inconsistent. Why, given a text otherwise so rigorously structured and laid out (see
chap. 8), do we occasionally find anomalous placements and omissions of certain formal
elements? Textual criticism cannot give us a definitive answer. Could it be that the one
responsible for the proto-MT version of Gen. 1 as we have it was simply careless in transmitting the text early on? Perhaps the masoretic eye skipped over the fulfillment report at
the end of v. 9 due to the not uncommon scribal mistake of homoioarchton (*wyqww∩wyqr*
[so Davila 1994b, 76]). Perhaps the "transition formula," brief as it is, was misplaced
twice, a case of unintentional error.

Another possibility is that the structural differences in the MT may actually be intentional. *Variant 1*: In Gen. 1:6–7 the MT's placement of the transition formula *after* the

---

19. The fragment, prepared by James R. Davila, features the Hebrew consonants *wtr⁽ hyb[šh]*: "and the dry
land appeared" (Davila 1994b, 76). The final volume (39) of the DJD series provides an invaluable index to all
the biblical texts and where they are published (Tov 2002, 27–114, 165–201).

fulfillment report ("And God made the firmament . . .") gives greater weight to divine activity, more so than in the balanced structure preserved in the LXX.[20] ***Variant 2***: The missing divine approval formula in v. 8 of the MT signals that God's creativity regarding the waters is not complete until the waters have been completely contained in v. 10, where the next approbation formula occurs. ***Variant 3***: The presence of the fulfillment report in v. 9 of the LXX (and of its Hebrew base text) highlights the activity of the waters gathering themselves into discrete bodies, *without* divine activity. Its absence in the MT, conversely, highlights divine activity in place of the waters' activity. ***Variant 4***: In v. 20 the *absence* of the transitional formula in the MT forges a tighter connection between God's command that the waters create marine life and God's activity in creating life, with greater emphasis placed upon the latter. The structure preserved in the LXX and its probable Hebrew base text, by contrast, preserves a measure of parity between natural and divine activity. The proto-MT, however, places more emphasis on divine activity by minimizing the role of creation itself, particularly that of the waters.

So what has just happened? By slavishly following certain text-critical rules and limiting ourselves only to the MT and LXX, we arrive at one conclusion, namely, the allegedly secondary, harmonizing character of the LXX. But by digging more deeply to ponder other possible ways to account for the differences and consulting evidence from Qumran (not yet completely available to the editors of the *BHS*), we come to the opposite conclusion: that the LXX preserves an older, albeit more structurally consistent form of Gen. 1 than we find in the MT. The conclusions that we make to explain textual variants ultimately rest on educated guesses, on informed speculation. But making (and arguing for) those guesses can highlight the intriguing nuances and exciting details of a text's plurality, in this case Gen. 1. Let it be said that textual criticism is more than simply applying procedural rules resulting in assured conclusions. Far from that. Textual criticism invites the skillful work of the "imagination, empathy with the text, and an intuitive understanding of variants" (Würthwein 2014, 204).

TEXTUAL CRITICISM IN TRANSITION: CHALLENGES AND PROMISES

While textual criticism plays an indispensible role in exegesis, questions have been raised about its traditionally set goals. There is growing recognition that any reconstruction that purports to be the "original" form of a biblical text is far from certain. Moreover, the notion of an "original" text presumes a *singular* form of a given text that once existed, from which all other forms and versions, including its variants, can be derived, a questionable assumption. Because all we have are various extant forms of the text, it is entirely possible that the biblical text, even in its earliest stages, was irreducibly pluriform (Breed 2014, 65).

Traditionally defined, the "original" text is the one that lies at the cusp between its composition and its transmission (Tov 2012, 2). But is such a distinction truly categorical?

---

20. Contra Hendel 1998, 21–22, who examines such variants exclusively on the level of scribal error and harmonization.

Does the text's formation cease once it starts being transmitted? The book of Jeremiah proves otherwise, as well as Daniel and Esther, in which the MT and the Greek versions are significantly different (see Tov 2012, 166). The boundary between textual composition (including its editing) and textual transmission is no hard-and-fast division. Truth be told, literary formation and textual transmission are inextricably connected, thus making literary criticism and textual criticism as "interlaced rather than discrete domains of scholarship" (Fox 2013, 341).

Perhaps the most critical question is the question of authority. Why should a reconstructed text reputed to be the text's "original" form be deemed authoritative (or "pure") to the exclusion of all its variants? To do so would limit authority to a reconstruction, allegedly to the author of the text apart from how the text developed further and became transmitted. Perhaps textual criticism should be freed to pursue its most general aim: to account for textual variation, and to do so without reflexively privileging one form over another (see Breed 2014, 55–58). Perhaps textual criticism should move toward a more egalitarian way of handling variants, treating them as voices engaged in textual dialogue. What text criticism does best is uncover the dialogue, from historical to theological, that unfolds among the text's variants. Textual criticism, in short, highlights the various voices *within* the transmitted text. How those voices are hosted (e.g., appreciated and adjudicated) lies in the "imagination" and "intuitive understanding" of the exegete.

BIBLIOGRAPHY FOR CHAPTER 5

Breed, Brennan W. 2014. *Nomadic Text: A Theory of Biblical Reception History*. Indiana Series in Biblical Literature. Bloomington: Indiana University Press.

Brotzman, Ellis R. 1994. *Old Testament Textual Criticism: A Practical Introduction*. Grand Rapids: Baker.

Cross, Frank Moore. 1995. *The Ancient Library of Qumran*. 3rd ed. Minneapolis: Fortress Press.

Davila, James R. 1990. "New Qumran Readings for Genesis One." In *Of Scribes and Scrolls: Studies on the Hebrew Bible, Intertestamental Judaism, and Christian Origins Presented to John Strugnell on the Occasion of His Sixtieth Birthday*, edited by Harold W. Attridge, John J. Collins, and Thomas H. Tobin, S.J., 3–12. College Theology Society Resources in Religion 5. Lanham: University Press of America.

———. 1994a. "4QGen[h]." In *Qumran Cave 4 VII*, edited by Eugene Ulrich and Frank Moore Cross, 61–62. DJD 12. Oxford: Clarendon Press.

———. 1994b. "4QGen[k]." In *Qumran Cave 4 VII*, edited by Eugene Ulrich and Frank Moore Cross, 75–78. DJD 12. Oxford: Clarendon Press.

Flint, Peter W. 2016. *The Dead Sea Scrolls*. Core Biblical Studies. Nashville: Abingdon Press.

Fox, Michael V. 2013. "Textual Criticism and Literary Criticism." In *Built by Wisdom, Established by Understanding: Essays on Biblical and Near Eastern Literature in Honor of Adele Berlin*, edited by Maxine L. Grossman, 341–56. Bethesda: University Press of Maryland.

Ginsburg, Christian D. 1975. *The Massorah*. 4 vols. New York: Ktav.

Hendel, Ronald S. 1998. *The Text of Genesis 1–11: Textual Studies and Critical Edition*. Oxford: Oxford University Press.

———. 2008. "The Oxford Hebrew Bible: Prologue to a New Critical Edition." *VT* 58 (2008): 324–51. See http://ohb.berkeley.edu/ and http://hbceonline.org/.

———. 2013. "The Oxford Hebrew Bible: Its Aims and a Response to Criticisms." *Hebrew Bible and Ancient Israel* 2:63–99.

Kelley, Page H., Daniel S. Mynatt, and Timothy G. Crawford. 1998. *The Masorah of Biblia Hebraica Stuttgartensia*. Grand Rapids: Eerdmans Publishing.

Law, Timothy. 2013. *When God Spoke Greek: The Septuagint and the Making of the Christian Bible*. Oxford: Oxford University Press.

Martin, Gary D. 2010. *Multiple Originals: New Approaches to Hebrew Bible Textual Criticism*. Society of Biblical Literature Text-Critical Studies 7. Atlanta: Society of Biblical Literature.

McCarter, P. Kyle, Jr. 1986. *Textual Criticism: Recovering the Text of the Hebrew Bible*. GBSOTG. Philadelphia: Fortress Press.

Talmon, Shemaryahu. 2000. "Textual Criticism: The Ancient Versions." In *Text in Context: Essays by Members of the Society for Old Testament Study*, edited by A. D. H. Mays, 141–70. Oxford: Oxford University Press.

Tov, Emanuel. 1992. "Textual Criticism (OT)." *ABD* 4:393–412.

———, ed. 2002. *The Texts from the Judean Desert Indices and an Introduction to the Discoveries in the Judaean Desert Series*. DJD 39. Oxford: Clarendon Press.

———. 2003. *Electronic Resources Relevant to the Textual Criticism of Hebrew Scripture*. http://rosetta .reltech.org/TC/v08/Tov2003.html.

———. 2012. *Textual Criticism of the Hebrew Bible*. 3rd ed., rev. and expanded. Minneapolis: Fortress Press.

Wegner, Paul D. 2006. *A Student's Guide to Textual Criticism of the Bible: Its History, Methods, and Results*. Downers Grove, IL: IVP Academic.

Wonneberger, Reinhard. 2001. *Understanding BHS: A Manual for the Users of "Biblia Hebraica Stuttgartensia."* Translated by Dwight R. Daniels. 3rd ed. Subsidia Biblica 8. Rome: Pontifical Biblical Institute.

Würthwein, Ernst. 2014. *The Text of the Old Testament: An Introduction to the "Biblia Hebraica."* Revised by Alexander Achilles Fischer. Translated by Erroll F. Rhodes. 3rd ed. Grand Rapids: Eerdmans Publishing.

Yeivin, Israel. 1980. *Introduction to the Tiberian Masorah*. Translated and edited by E. J. Revell. SBL Masoretic Studies 5. Missoula, MT: Scholars Press.

Septuagint Resources

Brenton, Lancelot Charles Lee. 1971 [1841]. *The Septuagint Version of the Old Testament with an English Translation*. Grand Rapids: Zondervan.

Brooke, Alan E., Norman McLean, and Henry St. J. Thackeray, eds. 1906–40. *The Old Testament in Greek according to the Text of Codex Vaticanus*. 3 vols. in 9. Cambridge: Cambridge University Press.

Dines, Jennifer. 2004. *The Septuagint*. New York: T&T Clark International.

Hatch, Edwin, and Henry A. Redpath. 1989. *A Concordance to the Septuagint and the Other Greek Versions of the Old Testament*. 3 vols. in 2. Grand Rapids: Baker.

Jobes, Karen H., and Moisés Silva. 2000. *Invitation to the Septuagint*. Grand Rapids: Baker Academic.

Kalvesmaki, Joel. 2013. *Septuagint Online*. http://www.kalvesmaki.com/LXX/.

Kraft, Robert, and Emanuel Tov. *Computer Assisted Tools for Septuagint/Scriptural Study*. http://ccat .sas.upenn.edu/rak/catss.html.

Lust, Johan, Erick Eynikel, and Katrin Hauspie, eds. 2015. *Greek-English Lexicon of the Septuagint*. 3rd ed. Stuttgart: Deutsche Bibelgesellschaft.

Marcos, Natalio Fernández. 2000. *The Septuagint in Context: Introduction to the Greek Version of the Bible*. Translated by Wilfred G. E. Watson. Boston: Brill.

Muraoka, Takamitsu. 2002. *A Greek-English Lexicon of the Septuagint*. Leuven: Peeters.

Pietersma, Albert, and Benjamin Wright, eds. 2007. *New English Translation of the Septuagint*. Oxford: Oxford University Press.

Rahlfs, Alfred, ed. 2006. *Septuaginta*. 2 vols. Peabody, MA: Hendrickson Publishers.

Septuaginta: Vetus Textamentum Graecum Auctoritate Societatis Litterarum Gottingensis Editum. 1931–. Göttingen: Vandenhoeck & Ruprecht.

Tov, Emanuel. 1981. *The Text-Critical Use of the Septuagint in Biblical Research*. Winona Lake, IN: Eisenbrauns.

Dead Sea Scrolls

Abegg, Martin G., Jr., James E. Bowley, and Edward M. Cook. 2008. *The Dead Sea Scrolls Concordance*. Vol. 3, *The Biblical Texts from Qumran and Other Sites*. Leiden and Boston: Brill.

Abegg, Martin G., Peter W. Flint, and Eugene C. Ulrich. 1999. *The Dead Sea Scrolls Bible: The Oldest Known Bible Translated for the First Time into English*. San Francisco: HarperSanFrancisco.

Collins, John J., and Timothy H. Lim, eds. 2010. *The Oxford Handbook of the Dead Sea Scrolls*. New York: Oxford University Press.

The Orion Center. 2016. *The Orion Center for the Study of the Dead Sea Scrolls and Associated Literature: Bibliography*. Jerusalem: Hebrew University. http://orion.mscc.huji.ac.il/.

Schiffman, Lawrence H., and James C. VanderKam, eds. 2000. *Encyclopedia of the Dead Sea Scrolls*. 2 vols. New York: Oxford University Press.

Tov, Emanuel, ed. 2002. *The Texts from the Judean Desert Indices and an Introduction to the Discoveries in the Judaean Desert Series*. DJD 39. Oxford: Clarendon Press.

VanderKam, James, and Peter Flint. 2002. *The Meaning of the Dead Sea Scrolls: Their Significance for Understanding the Bible, Judaism, Jesus, and Christianity*. New York: HarperSanFrancisco.

Samaritan Pentateuch

Gall, August von, ed. 1966. *Der hebräische Pentateuch der Samaritaner: Genesis—Deuteronomy*. 5 vols. in 1. Berlin: Walter de Gruyter.

Tal, Abraham, ed. 1994. *The Samaritan Pentateuch: Edited according to MS 6 of the Shekem Synagogue*. Tel Aviv: Chaim Rosenberg School.

Peshitta

International Organization for the Study of the Old Testament by the Peshitta Institute. 1972–. *The Old Testament in Syriac, according to the Peshitta Version*. Leiden: Brill.

Lamsa, George M. 1957. *The Holy Bible from Ancient Eastern Manuscripts*. Philadelphia: A. J. Holman.

Targums

Etheridge, J. W. 1969 [1862–65]. *The Targums Onkelos and Jonathan ben Uzziel on the Pentateuch*. 2 vols. New York: Ktav.

Grossfeld, Bernard, ed. 1973. *The Targum to the Five Megilloth*. New York: Hermon.

McNamara, Martin, et al., eds. 1987–2007. The Aramaic Bible: The Targums (series). 22 vols. Collegeville, MN: Michael Glazier / Liturgical Press.

Sperber, Alexander, ed. 1959–73. *The Bible in Aramaic*. 4 vols. Leiden: Brill.

Vulgate

Knox, Ronald A. 1956. *The Old Testament: A Translation from the Latin Vulgate in the Light of the Hebrew and Greek Originals*. New York: Sheed & Ward.

Weber, Robert, and Bonifatius Fischer, eds. 1994. *Biblia sacra: Iuxta Vulgatam versionem*. 4th ed. Stuttgart: Deutsche Biblegesellschaft.

Biblia Hebraica Stuttgartensia (BHS)

Rüger, Hans Peter. 1990. *An English Key to the Latin Words and Abbreviations and the Symbols of "Biblia Hebraica Stuttgartensia."* New York: American Bible Society.

Scott, William R., Harold Scanlin, and Hans Peter Rüger. 2007. *A Simplified Guide to BHS: Critical Apparatus, Masora, Accents, Unusual Letters and Other Markings*. 4th ed. N. Richland Hills, TX: Bibal Press.

Wonneberger, Reinhard. 2000. *Understanding BHS: A Manual for the Users of "Biblia Hebraica Stuttgartensia."* 3rd ed. Rome: Pontifical Biblical Institute Press.

6

Stylistic Analysis I: Poetry

> They say you can jinx a poem
> if you talk about it before it is done.
> *Billy Collins, "Madmen"*[1]

Whether in English or in Hebrew, every text has its own style. In the art world, style has to do with the distinctive form expressed within a particular medium, whether music, architecture, or literature. In the fashion world, style has to do with the form and arrangement of clothing that best suits the body aesthetically—a subjective judgment, to be sure, as particular styles can go in and out of fashion at the drop of a hat.

In biblical literature, style has to do with rhetoric or the art of discourse, which includes both the aesthetic and persuasive appeals of a given text. The text's rhetoric indicates the way a passage communicates effectively, specifically, how the text both *appeals* and *makes its appeal* to the reader.[2] In other words, the rhetoric of the text refers to the text's gravitational pull, how the text draws the reader into its world. Each text does it differently. Indeed, the various kinds of literature in the Bible reflect marked differences in style or rhetoric. One notable yet relative difference is that between poetry and prose. A narrative text from 1 Kings differs significantly from a psalmic lament. The methodical style of Gen. 1 stands in stark contrast to the lyrical Song of Songs. From liturgy to love poetry, from historiographic narratives to prophetic judgment oracles, the Hebrew Bible is replete with rhetorical diversity.

This chapter and the next explore how the biblical text works aesthetically and persuasively upon the reader, or, to put it another way, how the text engages the reader with a sense of wonder, not unlike how the experience of beauty can stir the imagination. An arresting piece of visual art, for example, draws the viewer in, decentering the mind while also stimulating the intellect and stirring the emotions. In a moving piece of

---

1. Https://www.poetryfoundation.org/poetrymagazine/poems/detail/40284.
2. Frequently the distinction is made between a text's aesthetic qualities on the one hand, and its power of persuasion (i.e., the classical view of rhetoric) on the other. This chapter treats them as parts of a whole. For resources on rhetorical criticism, see Porter and Stamps 2002; Trible 1994; Watson and Hauser 1994; Patrick and Scult 1990.

music, the listener loses oneself in its cadences and rhythms while attaining a heightened sense of attention. The biblical text, too, has its "distinctive music, a lovely precision of lexical choice, a meaningful concreteness, and a suppleness of expressive syntax" (Alter 2004, xlv).

Take, for example, the "numerical proverb" of Prov. 30:18–19:

> Three things are too wonderful for me;
>   four things I do not understand:
> the way of an eagle in the sky,
>   the way of a snake on a rock,
> the way of a ship on the high seas,
>   and the way of a man with a woman.[3]

This artfully crafted saying immediately engages the reader through both its deceptive simplicity and its concrete imagery. First, the use of numbers in the first verse may strike the reader as confusing: is the proverb speaking of three things or four things? The progression from "three" to "four," or more abstractly from "x" to "x + 1," is a standard formula for the "numerical proverbs" found in Prov. 30 and elsewhere (e.g., 30:15, 21, 29; cf. Amos 1:3, 6, 9; etc.). In each case, the latter number (four) gives the true count while at the same time highlighting the final item as climactic. Thus the opening line introduces a degree of suspense about what comes next: four discrete items that evoke four separate scenes, each characterized by a certain movement ("way"), all culminating in the final scene. The progression of these scenes is unmistakable. We begin with sky (heaven), the most humanly inaccessible region of creation, and then come down to earth, concluding with a scene of human intimacy. The overall movement, or "way" (!), of the proverb is from outer realm to human realm and intimacy.

This proverb is both a testimony and a puzzle. Its appeal derives from its power to evoke images that are so wonderful yet so divergent. Moreover, this proverb invites the reader, as it did the rabbis,[4] to ponder what these four "ways" could possibly share in common. But presuming a tidy answer would run counter to the sage's own confession of wonder. These "four things," the sage testifies, retain an element of mystery regardless of how much can be known about them, no matter how well each "way" can be explained. Such is the sage's testimony: there's nothing quite like ships, snakes, and sex to evoke a sense of wonder, not to mention soaring raptors. This proverb awakens the desire to know and at the same time transports the reader into realms of mystery. Such, one could say, is "the way of a proverb in the heart of a reader." Poetry does that: it evokes rather than argues.

POETRY

Basic to any discussion of biblical rhetoric is demarcating the line between poetry and prose, which admittedly can be blurry. We start with poetry. Defining poetry, whether

---

3. Specifically, "young woman" ('almâ). Note the unfortunate translation in the NRSV, here adjusted.
4. The rabbis proposed that each "way" left no trace. Cf. Wis. 5:9–14. See the discussion in Fox 2009, 871.

ancient or modern, is difficult, and arriving at a one-size-fits-all definition is well-nigh impossible. Nevertheless, one can identify certain features that help distinguish a poem from a prose narrative: (1) aesthetic quality, (2) density of expression, and (3) performative power.

Aesthetic Quality

The word "poem" comes from the Greek verb *poieō*, "make" or "do." A poem is an artistic creation, an example of verbal art. A poem is crafted to impress the ear; its diction is frequently conveyed through the use of assonance and alliteration, including rhyme, as well as through its metrical structure or rhythm. Such devices serve to "thicken the verbal texture" of a poem (Kinzie 1999, 140).

In addition, there is the visual side to the poetic aesthetic. Poetry is typically arranged in lines, not paragraphs. The typical format of a modern poem distinguishes itself from prose with shorter lines and uneven right margins. The line, in fact, is the fundamental unit of poetry, and as we shall see in biblical poetry, a verse frequently consists of parallel or corresponding lines.[5] But there is at least one other critical aspect to a poem's graphic texture. More often than not, poems revel in imagery and metaphor, in figurative language. As in the proverb discussed above, a poem features images and evokes feelings. The attuned reader not only *hears* the poem but also *sees* what the poem conjures and is stirred by it. A poem is not only riveting to the ear; it is also arresting to the eye, stimulating the imagination, the product of a peculiar synergy between sense and sound.

Density of Expression

A poem typically has less space to wield its communicative craft than its prose counterpart. With the exception of epic poetry, a poem is generally short and compact. According to J. P. Fokkelman, "Poetry is the most compact and concentrated form of speech possible" (2001, 15), with the exception, I would add, of text messaging. The difference between a poem and an instruction manual is readily evident: a poem's terse style conveys an abundance of meaning. Laurence Perrine defines poetry as "a kind of language that says more and says it *more* intensely than does ordinary language" (1963, 3–4). More condensed than prose, poetry exhibits a "higher voltage" and applies "greater pressure per word" (10–11). A poem thus marks a convergence of verbal density and semantic intensity. Semantically, poetry does a lot of heavy lifting with its verbal economy, and its semantic abundance often results in ambiguity. Poetry invites multiple readings. Poetic language is suggestive.

Performative Power

In poetry, the reader is brought into close relationship with the poem's speaking voice. A poem lends itself first to recitation and only thereafter to interpretation. While the reader "performs" the poem by reading it, the kind of performative reading that a poem requires is first and foremost an attentive recitation. A poem must be sounded; otherwise its

---

5. For a thorough historical discussion of the line in Biblical Hebrew poetry, see Dobbs-Allsopp 2015, 14–94.

palpably oral quality is lost, including its rhythm and rhyme, its assonance and euphony. Such qualities have compelled many to compare poetry with music. Both typically share a sense of rhythm. It is no coincidence that many of the biblical psalms contain instructions for musical accompaniment.[6] But whether musically intended or not, a poem's performative power is its power to actively engage the reader orally and aurally.

Reading a poem is quite different from reading a narrative or an essay. Poetry "is not to be galloped over like the daily news" (Kennedy and Gioia 1999, 651). A poem places a high demand on the reader's active participation. Reading a poem as poetry calls for lingering over its words, reflecting on their sequence and phonetic qualities. There is, moreover, an element of simultaneity when it comes to reading poetry. As we read, the poem unfolds before our eyes and ears, and as the poem unfolds, so does our reading. The art of reading poetry is to find oneself "moving inside the growing poem" (Kinzie 1999, 14). We trace "the path of the poem from among the tangle of possible routes it might have taken but did not" (14). In short, reading poetry is much like writing poetry: it proceeds thoughtfully and creatively word by word, image by image, beat by beat.

These three features are inseparably wedded in poetry. Together they establish a poem's openness to interpretation. Something mysterious transpires when reading a poem, "for when we finish reading a good poem, we cannot explain precisely to ourselves what we have experienced—without repeating, word for word, the language of the poem itself" (Kennedy and Gioia 1999, 1011). The irreducible nature of poetry provides a necessary check on all methods of interpretation. In the end, no method or combination of methods will ever capture the full sense and sound of poetic verse. Every poem retains something of the ineffable, and the most one can hope for is a deepening of that sense of mystery—mystery deepened by understanding.

HEBREW POETRY

Now that we have identified some of the marks of poetry in general, what about Biblical Hebrew poetry in particular? Like poetry in general, biblical poetry reflects a compact style of discourse, employs figurative language, and can be powerfully evocative. Grammatically, the terse language of biblical poetry tends to omit certain linguistic elements frequently found in lengthier Hebrew prose, such as the definite article, relative pronouns, and the direct object marker, to name a few. In addition to what biblical poetry lacks, certain features also distinguish, in relative degree, biblical poetry from prose: line structure, peculiar word order, greater assonance and alliteration (occasionally rhyme), repetition, chiasmus, unusual vocabulary, and word pairs. Notice that "meter" is not included. To be sure, both modern poetry and ancient Hebrew poetry reflect what is called prosody, but in different ways. Broadly put, prosody refers to a poem's movement in verbal time. Derived from the Greek word for "accent," the term is more specifically used to describe a poem's "auditory logic" or set rhythmic style, as determined, for example, by an identifiable system of stresses, such as iambic pentameter.

---

6. See, e.g., the superscriptions in Pss. 22, 45, 56, 60, 69, 80.

Hebrew poetry, however, does not adhere to any metrical system. In some cases, accentual rhythms have been identified, such as the so-called *qînâ*, or "lamentation," in which a divisible line of poetry features an accentual beat of 3:2 (see, e.g., Amos 5:2; Ps. 5:1–2). Some read Ps. 117, the shortest psalm in the Psalter, as reflecting a consistent rhythm of 3:3 (Gillingham 1994, 58–59). But such a count depends on how one assigns the accents, particularly in construct chains. Biblical verse is by and large essentially nonmetrical; its rhythmic patterns (if one can call them that) are far too variable to identify any kind of system. Thus it is best to consider Biblical Hebrew poetry as "free verse" (Dobbs-Allsopp 2015, 9–10).

Reading between the Lines: Parallelism

A more fruitful line of inquiry is to examine the segmentation or division of lines in biblical poetry. This characteristic of Hebrew poetry has captured the attention of modern interpreters for over two centuries. In the words of Robert Lowth (1710–87), a professor of poetry at Oxford University, Hebrew poetry exhibits an "exquisite degree of beauty and grace" (1971, 69). The mark of Hebrew poetry's aesthetic allure, Lowth argued, is found in its structure, specifically in what he called *parallelismus membrorum* (68). Simply stated, poetic parallelism is "the correspondence of one . . . line with another" (Lowth 1834, ix). More broadly, such correspondence is evident in the way the segments or lines within any given verse relate to one another. Lowth placed these poetic "correspondences" into three broad categories: (1) synonymous, (2) antithetic, and (3) synthetic (ix).

A few examples will suffice. A Hebrew verse often consists of two discrete lines or segments, together called "couplets" or "bicola" (sg. of "cola" is "colon"),[7] although "triplets" (tricola) and lengthier units can also be found. In a typical poetic couplet, the second line (colon) repeats, intensifies, modifies, or completes the thought of the first. Furthermore, the relationship between the two lines may not always be obvious or even parallel in any strict sense. Yet such regular pairing of segments conveys a sense of lyrical symmetry. Take, for example, the sentence in Ps. 114:1, translated in strict Hebrew word order (with the subject typically following the verb) for purposes of illustration:

> When went forth / Israel / from Egypt,
> A   a   / b /   c

> the house of Jacob / from a people of unintelligible speech,
> A'   b'   /   c'

This extended circumstantial clause consists of two parallel lines, which could be labeled **A** and **A'**, in which "Israel" and "house of Jacob" serve as corresponding partners (**b** and **b'**), as well as "Egypt" and "a people of unintelligible speech" (**c** and **c'**). A terse way of representing this network of correspondences is as follows: **A (a:b:c) / A' (b':c')**. The first line (**A**) contains three grammatical elements: a circumstantial verbal phrase ("when went

---

7. "Colon" comes from the Greek *kōlon*, meaning "limb" or "member." It is used widely in biblical studies but not much elsewhere, perhaps because, according to Alter, it "inadvertently call[s] up associations of intestinal organs or soft drinks" (1985, 9).

forth" = **a**), the subject ("Israel" = **b**), a prepositional phrase ("from Egypt" = **c**). The second line (**A'**) features a corresponding subject ("house of Jacob" = **b'**) and a corresponding prepositional phrase ("from a people of unintelligible speech" = **c'**). Lacking, however, is a corresponding verb, hence no **a'**. Rather, the verb is simply understood in the second line or colon, making it elliptical: "the house of Jacob [went forth] from a people of unintelligible speech." The second line does not just repeat the first; it develops it. These corresponding lines forge a relationship of identity: Israel *is* the "house of Jacob"; Egypt *is* a "people of unintelligible speech." One also observes a poetic escalation. While the geopolitical entity of Egypt is neutrally referred to in line **A**, it is inscribed in derogatory fashion in the following line (**A'**). The "otherness" of Egypt, consequently, is stressed in the second line.

One also sees synonymous parallelism at work in the main clause that follows (v. 2), which is also cast as two lines with corresponding elements.

> became Judah God's sanctuary,
>   Israel his dominion.

"Judah" and "Israel," as well as "God's sanctuary" and "his dominion," with the second colon cast elliptically, reflect prosodic structure similar to v. 1. One wonders, too, whether the move from "sanctuary" to "dominion" also represents an escalation. In any case, the holy and the royal are suggestively combined in this verse.

A special form of balanced parallelism occurs when one colon or line mirrors the other in the order of arrangement. It is often called a "chiasm," derived from the Greek letter *chi* (χ). One example is Ps. 147:4, translated literally in Hebrew word order:

> [God] who counts the number of the stars;
>   to all of them names he gives.
> **A (a:b:c) / A' (c':b':a')**

Notice that the syntactic ordering of the second line is precisely the reverse of the first. The verb (with its subject) opens the first line and concludes the second (**a** and **a'**). The direct object in the first line ("number") corresponds to the direct object ("names") in the second (**b** and **b'**). And finally, closest to the center of the chiasm, are the prepositional phrases: "of the stars" (**c**) and "to all of them" (**c'**), which in Hebrew is marked also by alliteration: *lakôkābîm* and *lĕkullām*, respectively. Poetic intensification is key to the parallelism. Not only is the total number of stars determined; God names each of them individually.

Both examples illustrate Lowth's classification of "synonymous" parallelism. But as can be readily seen, more is going on than simple repetition. There is a movement or interchange between the segments or lines. Through the positive pairing of lines and their corresponding parts, one line amplifies, expands on, or explicates the other. Consequently, poetic momentum builds from one line to the next.

Examples of Lowth's "antithetical" type of parallelism exhibit correspondence of a negative or contrastive sort. This can readily be seen in the following two examples:

For you a lowly people deliver,[8]
> *but* haughty eyes you bring down. (Ps. 18:27 [28 MT])

Some in chariotry, others in horses;
> *but* we in the name of YHWH find strength.[9] (Ps. 20:7 [8])

In each example, the telltale sign is clearly evident in English translation. However, it is not so immediately clear in the Hebrew. The connecting particle is the same in Hebrew (the simple *waw*), whether serving as a conjunctive, "and," or as an adversative, "but." Context is critical. The correspondence in both examples is clearly contrastive: "humble people" and "haughty eyes" constitute an opposite pair, as well as the verbal elements "deliver" and "bring down." For convenience using the symbol of negation in the field of logic (~), the relationship of correspondence can be illustrated as **A (a:b:c) ~ A' (b':c')**, with **a** designating the independent personal pronoun "you" in the first line, which is absent in the second. (The "you" in the second line indicates a verbal inflection, not a separate pronoun.)

Consisting of two clauses, the second example is syntactically more complex and intriguing: **A (a:b:a':b') ~ A' (a'':b'':c)**. The first line lacks a verb; it is elliptical. The second line supplies the verb (**c**), which can be read back into the first: "Some [find strength] in chariotry; others [find strength] in horses." The second line, thus, fills the gap of the first, a gap that builds suspense. As a whole, the first line sets up the foil for the second, which commends the true source of strength. In both examples, the relationship between the two lines is "antithetical," but as in the case of so-called synonymous parallelism, more is at work than simply flat correspondence between opposites. Indeed, the two examples are contrastive in contrasting ways. Psalm 20:7 charts a movement from false trust to true allegiance, with the latter exposing the former as illusory. The second line deconstructs the first. In 18:27 both lines are held to be equally true; the second is the converse and consequence of the first. Delivering the lowly entails the humiliation of the haughty.

As for "synthetic" parallelism, Lowth recognized examples of Hebrew verse that do not fit into either of the first two categories. Parallelism, whether synonymous or antithetical, does not apply in the following cases:

Blessed be YHWH,
> who has not given us as prey to their teeth.   124:6

From the rising of the sun to its setting,
> the name of YHWH is to be praised.   113:3

In the first example, the two lines are linked by a common subject, but that is as far as the syntactical similarity goes. The first line invokes a blessing, for which the second, as a subordinate clause, provides the warrant. In the second example, the first line prefaces the second, which provides its subject matter. This particular case of nonparallel lines exhibits *enjambment* (literally, "straddling"), whereby a sentence or thought does not end where

---

8. The Hebrew word order begins with the independent personal pronoun "you," followed by the object and then the verb.

9. Read *nagbîr* (strength) for MT *nazkîr* (remember, call upon) to make better sense. See Peshitta.

the first line ends but continues naturally into the next.[10] Enjambment creates, in effect, a certain "'tugging' effect" on the reader (Kinzie 1999, 407).

Lowth's method of classification has its limitations. The categories he defined can foster a taxonomic mentality that misses rather than elucidates the "exquisite degree of beauty and grace" he discerned in Hebrew poetry. Nevertheless, his central observation endures: Hebrew poetry, more often than not, consists of parallel parts. But we have found the correspondences to be more nuanced. The term "synonymous," for example, is misleading if it simply means repetition. The same can also be said of "antithetical," and "synthetic"—classifications too general or rigid to be optimally helpful. As James Kugel readily points out, even the most "synonymous" poetic lines exhibit a semantic climax found in the second line's "seconding" role, which can serve the role of emphasizing or advancing the thought: "A is so, and *what's more*, B is so" (1981, 8). Parallelism—specifically the *"predominance* of parallelism, combined with terseness"—is characteristic of Hebrew poetry (Berlin 2008, 5). If, as Paul Valéry claims, "Poetry is to prose as dancing is to walking" (cited in Kennedy and Gioia 1999, 1011), then Hebrew poetry is largely a two-step, although sometimes a waltz.

Merely identifying various levels of correspondence between poetic lines is one thing; charting the progression from one line to the next is something else. The result is a change of meaning, however subtle. Robert Alter quotes Viktor Shklovsky regarding the purpose of parallelism: "to *transfer* the usual perception of an object into the sphere of a new perception."[11] Parallelism highlights a complexity of corresponding "transfers," from the obvious to the subtle. All in all, parallelism reveals "a dynamic microworld in which many different components function in relation to each other" (Berlin 2008, 2). A single line generates only provisional meaning, at best a "half-meaning," and as such it is only partial, prompting the reader to continue reading, thoughtfully and imaginatively, to the poem's conclusion (Kinzie 1999, 49).

METAPHOR AND IMAGERY

A discussion of the aesthetics of Hebrew poetry would not be complete without some comment on poetic imagery and metaphor. The book of Psalms, for example, is rich with imagery, some of it drawn from the rich iconography of the ancient Near East,[12] and much of it cast as metaphor.

What is a metaphor? In light of its Greek root, "metaphor" originally denoted the "carrying over" or "transference" of property (*meta*, "trans" + *pherō*, "carry"). In the act of reading, metaphors facilitate the transference of meaning from something familiar to something new. Most modern definitions of metaphor include two elements that establish a correspondence or congruity. According to Janet Martin Soskice, "The metaphor is that figure of speech whereby we speak about one thing in terms [that] are seen to be

---

10. For a full discussion with examples, see Watson 1986, 333.
11. Quoted in Alter 1985, 10, emphasis added.
12. See the foundational work of Keel 1997 [1978]. For discussion of the rhetorical dynamics between ancient iconography and biblical poetry, see Brown 2002.

suggestive of another" (1985, 15). Every definition of metaphor acknowledges at least two elements: the "one thing" and "another." What is their relationship? Take, for example, "Time is a thief." In this metaphor time, an abstract concept, is personified as someone who steals. Steals what? Youth, cast as a possession, and ultimately life itself. Cognitive theorists Lakoff and Turner helpfully talk about a metaphor as the act of mapping or superimposing an aspect of a "source domain" onto "a target domain" (1989, 28–29). In this case the source domain of robbery, and more broadly our sense of entitlement and possession, is mapped onto the abstract concept of time, personifying it and turning it into something that infringes upon our sense of justice.

The terms "target domain" and "source domain" illustrate more precisely what happens when something is referenced metaphorically, namely, a superimposing or unilateral "mapping." Such "transference" of meaning results in a new understanding of the target domain, in this case "time." Through the use of metaphor, "time" is perceived differently. Nothing new, however, is said of possessions or thieves. To take a biblical example, the psalmist's statement that "YHWH God is a sun and shield" (Ps. 84:11 [12]) highlights the (royal) efficacy of divine blessing and protection but by itself no more implies solar worship than it suggests the veneration of shields. The source domain illuminates a new, crucial dimension of its target (God).

For the metaphor to work, an understanding of both domains must be gained before new insight is achieved. There must be a recognizable correspondence between the metaphor and its target domain that can be acknowledged by both poet and reader; otherwise the metaphor remains indecipherable. Lakoff and Turner offer the example "Death is a banana," a statement lacking sense, an example of *catachresis*, the improper use of metaphor (1989, 50–51). The true and effective metaphor, by contrast, stands on the ground of shared knowledge and builds on that knowledge in a way that elicits new inferences and connections.

On the one hand, if a metaphor is too enigmatic, it only perplexes the reader. On the other hand, if a metaphor is too obvious or conventional, it packs no punch, leading to no new understanding. Such metaphors are fully lexicalized and literal.[13] They are "dead." In a "living metaphor," "there is dissonance or tension . . . whereby the terms of the utterance used seem not strictly appropriate to the topic at hand" (Soskice 1985, 73). An effective metaphor, thus, effectively weds analogy and anomaly; it creates conceptual and emotional friction by which new meaning is achieved. The creative metaphor is a master of surprise, but it is not meant to be a source of complete puzzlement.

Both characteristic of Hebrew poetry, metaphor and parallelism share common ground. Both involve the "transference" of meaning. In parallelism, meaning is transferred from the first line to the subsequent line(s) invariably with modification. The same thing can be said of metaphor. In the act of reading, metaphors facilitate the transference of meaning from something familiar to something different, and transformation is the result. A metaphor's contribution to the construction of meaning, moreover, is suggestive rather than propositional, more generative than limiting. Indeed, with any literary image, metaphorical or not, there is a "natural polyvalency" that "resists reduction

13. E.g., "the leg of a chair" and the "flow of electricity." See Soskice 1985, 7–83.

to propositional summation" (Newsom 2003, 236). Such is the way of poetry. Through metaphor, poetry generates a surplus of semantic connections.

OF SHEPHERDS AND SHADOWS: PSALM 23

As a prosodic analysis "maps" the dynamic structure of a poetic line, so a metaphorical analysis helps to "map" the images and their significance within, for example, a given psalm. Consider Ps. 23 (AT).

> *A Psalm of David.*
> [1] YHWH is my shepherd;
>   I lack nothing.
> [2] In meadows of grass he lets me lie;
>   to waters of repose he leads me, refreshing my soul.
> [3] On account of his name,
>   he leads me on paths of righteousness.
> [4] Even as I sojourn in the darkest valley,
>   I fear no danger,
> for you are with me;
>   your rod and your staff—they give me comfort.
> [5] You arrange before me a table
>   before my enemies.
> You anoint my head with oil;
>   my cup is well filled.
> [6] Only[14] goodness and kindness shall pursue[15] me
>   all the days of my life,
> so that may I dwell[16] in the house of YHWH
>   as long as I live.

The psalm is well-known for its evocative images: shepherd, grass, meadows, still waters, path, dark valley, rod and staff, table, cup, and oil. Drawn from various source domains, such images give the psalm its distinctive coherence and movement. The psalm is most known, of course, for its stand-alone first verse. Notice its prosodic structure, or lack thereof. It does not conform to either synonymous or antithetical parallelism. It is also not enjambed: the first line can stand on its own as a statement of trust. Furthermore, the verse syntactically lacks a connecting particle to link the two lines together, such as a *waw*. As is typical of much Hebrew poetry, this verse is "asyndetic": it lacks any coordinating words, leaving the reader with the task of discerning the rhetorical relationship between the two lines. What then is the connection between "YHWH is my shepherd" (**A**) and "I lack nothing" (**A'**)? If one were to provide a connecting word to link the two lines explicitly, what would it be? Perhaps "therefore," to suggest that the second line A' is the

---

14. The translation of *'ak* is debatable (cf. NRSV "surely"). For the restrictive sense of "only," which fits the context better (see below), see, e.g., 1 Sam. 18:8; Isa. 45:14; Pss. 37:8; 62:5 (6 MT).

15. Hebrew root √*rdp*, which in this psalm exhibits an ironic intensity that most Eng. translations, including the NRSV, fail to acknowledge (but see CEB).

16. Repoint as *šibtî* (so LXX). MT has "I shall return." Cf. Pss. 27:4b; 61:7 (8 MT).

consequence of line **A**. Are there other possibilities? What about "indeed," giving the second line an emphatic nuance? In any case, while the verse is asyndetically bare poetically, it is suggestively rich semantically.

The Good Shepherd

As for imagery, the psalm richly draws from the pastoral domain. With God as the shepherd, the speaker imagines the security of flourishing in grassy meadows and beside still waters. The bucolic scene serves as the source domain for over half the psalm. Its explicit target is God, but it also includes the speaker, who is cast as a sheep.

An exploration of the shepherd metaphor, particularly in light of its background outside of Ps. 23, also yields a fuller picture of the metaphor's function within the psalm. The pastoral scene, it turns out, is political. This metaphor has deep roots in biblical and ancient Near Eastern literature that fill out not only its source domain but also its target. For example, in his famous law code, Hammurabi, the first ruler of the Babylonian Empire (r. c.a. 1792–1750 BCE), proclaimed himself not only as "the pious prince" (*rubûm naʾdum*) and "king of justice" (*šar mîšarim*) but also as "shepherd of the people" (*rēʾî nišî*).[17] As the good shepherd, Hammurabi boasts of his generous provision for his subjects, granting them rest and peace, prosperity and protection,[18] not unlike what the speaker says of God in Ps. 23. Hammurabi's "staff is straight." It is his scepter. YHWH's "staff" provides comfort and security. The shepherd metaphor turns the privileged office of king into a responsibility of tender care.

In biblical literature, the shepherd metaphor frequently designates a position of leadership, particularly that of king.[19] David is considered the exemplary royal shepherd in Ps. 78:70–72 (cf. 2 Sam. 7:7–8). The passage plays on David's former occupation as qualification and indeed standard for the royal office. To shepherd is to rule with care and guidance. The shepherding role, of course, is not limited to earthly kings. As in Ps. 23, God takes on the role of shepherd in Ezekiel:

> I myself will be the shepherd of my sheep, and I will make them lie down, says YHWH God. I will seek the lost, and I will bring back the strayed, and I will bind up the injured, and I will strengthen the weak. But as for the fat and the strong, I will destroy them; I will feed them with justice. (34:15–16 AT)

Such are the various responsibilities that the divine shepherd resolves to fulfill. Serving as the source domain for the metaphor, the pastoral imagery works well throughout the list until we come to the last two items. Unlike a human shepherd, the divine shepherd in Ezekiel will cull out the choice sheep for the sake of the injured and the weak! The last item on the list, moreover, reveals the target of the shepherd metaphor: the divine king. God's provision is not, literally, rich pasturage, as sheep would want, but "justice," as the weak and the oppressed would want. Drawn from the pastoral domain and applied to the

---

17. LH 4.32; 48.95; 4.45. For translation, see Roth 1995, 80, 135.
18. LH 47.35–58. Translation based, with slight modifications, on Roth 1995, 133.
19. See, e.g., 2 Sam. 5:2; 1 Kgs. 22:17; 1 Chr. 11:2; Ps. 100:3.

domain of divine kingship, the shepherd metaphor highlights God's intention to protect and provide for Israel. Among the psalms, the metaphor of the divine shepherd is by no means confined to Ps. 2 (see, e.g., 28:8–9; 80:1; 100:3). In these passages, the shepherding image is associated with salvation, blessing, governance, and ownership. All these nuances come to bear metaphorically in Ps. 23.

From Pasture to Sanctuary

In consort with the shepherd imagery, the idyllic images that populate the first verses of Ps. 23 map out God's royal protection and guidance. In contrast to the secure path, the valley of darkness evokes danger (v. 4a), setting in sharper relief God's protective role as shepherd. In v. 5, however, the scene shifts abruptly from the pastoral to the domestic domain: the images of table, oil, and cup point to God's abundant provision and hospitality. No longer as shepherd, God is now the gracious host. With enemies held at bay and the speaker seated at the table, protection and provision are served. Finally, the domestic turns sacred as the speaker proclaims his desire to dwell in YHWH's "house" for the remainder of his life. As a whole, the psalm's movement is governed by dramatic shifts in source domains, from pasture to home to sanctuary, all to underscore the speaker's testimony to God's provision and protection.

Most remarkable is the surprising metaphorical turn taken in the final verse, in which the speaker declares that God's "goodness and benevolence [*ṭôb wāḥesed*] will *pursue*" him. The verb itself suggests persecution, specifically of enemies stalking the speaker (cf. vv. 4a, 5b). But as the table scene makes clear, the threat posed by the speaker's unnamed enemies is no more. But now there is another "threat." The source domain of persecution is mapped onto the target domain of divine benevolence! The association seems non-sensical, but this is no act of catachresis. How is it that God's benevolent goodness takes the place of the pursuing enemies? This *is* a surprising turn, and ironic at that! With the choice of this one verb, the psalmist flirts with the idea of God's benevolence taking on an aggressive quality. The metaphor of pursuit, as applied to God, effectively displaces the role that the enemies once had. The speaker joyously declares that he is no longer the target of his enemies but of God's love, from which there is no escape! In dogged pursuit, God's benevolence will track him down and sequester him in the sanctuary. Such a radically ironic twist can only be achieved through poetry.

A POETIC PORTION OF GENESIS

While Gen. 1 is narrative, it is not entirely prosaic. The language of Gen. 1 has sometimes been called "elevated" prose, verging occasionally on the poetic. A case in point is that wonderfully obscure v. 2, translated literally:

> the earth was an empty mishmash,
>   and darkness over the surface of Deep,
>   and God's breath hovering over the surface of the waters.

This triplet, or tricolon, contains no active, finite verb. Indeed, the second line lacks a verb altogether and thus is elliptical. The last line is participial. Altogether, the syntax underlines ongoing yet static action, a state of timeless activity. How do these lines compare to each other poetically? Let's divide the three lines according to syntactical units.

> the earth / was / an empty mishmash,
> **A**   **a**   / **b** /   **c**

> and darkness / over the surface of Deep,
> **A'**   **a'**   /   **d**

> and God's breath / hovering / over the surface of the waters.
> **A''**   **a''**   / **b'** /   **d'**

Or **A (a:b:c) / A' (a':d) / A'' (a'':b':d')**. In each line, element **a** is the subject, and **b** is the verb, which is elliptically missing in the second line. Whereas the first line concludes with a description of the state "of the earth" before creation, the following lines feature prepositional phrases (**d** and **d'**). What does this tell us? An obvious poetic pairing is found with the parallel between **d** and **d'**, since both have to do with the watery depths in relation to its subjects (**a'** and **a''**). A more subtle poetic pairing has to do with the two subjects, "darkness" and "God's breath," suggesting a surprising connection. Whereas elsewhere God is associated with light (cf. Ps. 104:2a), here God's "breath" is poetically aligned with "darkness." How so? Perhaps the key lies in the verb "hovering." Darkness is the state of God's breath suspended or held, merely "hovering." But it is light when God's breath is released, uttered in the first command in v. 3. However the relationship is to be construed, the association between divine breath and primordial darkness powerfully sets the stage for the creation of light in the next verse.

Another poetic piece is the account of God's creation of humankind (1:27). The following is a literal rendering that also replicates Hebrew word order divided up into syntactical units.

> So created God / humankind / in his image,
> **A**   **a**   / **b** /   **c**

> in the image of God / he created / him;
> **A'**   **c'**   / **a'** / **b'**

> male and female / he created / them.
> **A''**   **c''**   / **a'** / **b''**

Or **A (a:b:c) / A' (c':a':b') / A'' (c'':a':b'')**. Notice how each line contains corresponding syntactical elements; only the sequence is changed, due to element **c**, the adverbial phrase, being transferred to the first position in the following two lines.

The poetic surprise comes at the end. The first two lines are synonymous, but the third line carries two surprises. First, the object of God's creation, it turns out, is plural. Humankind is revealed to be a plurality, "them," contrary to what might have been implied in the second line with "him." More intriguing is the poetic association of God's "image" with "male and female" (**c/c'** and **c''**). Because both serve as adverbial descriptors of the kind of human creation that God has created, they are poetically related.[20] What could be the point of relating God's image with gender plurality? Perhaps to say that God's image is more fully embodied in *both* genders. Could the poetic association also serve as a check on the patriarchal tendency to view God as primarily male? One wonders. Poetry is good at prompting more questions than answers. In any case, parallelism is no mere ornamentation: it is the carrier of meaning in Hebrew poetry, meaning formed by association, meaning on the move.

There are also passages in Gen. 2–3 that can be examined poetically. Take a look at Gen. 2:23; 3:15–16, 19. See what surprising associations emerge through prosodic analysis.

BIBLIOGRAPHY FOR CHAPTER 6

Alter, Robert. 1985. *The Art of Biblical Poetry*. New York: Basic Books.
———. 2004. *The Five Books of Moses: A Translation and Commentary*. New York: W. W. Norton.
Berlin, Adele. 2008. *The Dynamics of Biblical Parallelism*. 2nd ed. Grand Rapids: Eerdmans Publishing.
Brown, William P. 2002. *Seeing the Psalms: A Theology of Metaphor*. Louisville, KY: Westminster John Knox Press.
———. 2010. *Psalms*. IBT. Nashville: Abingdon.
Dobbs-Allsopp, F. W. 2015. *On Biblical Poetry*. Oxford: Oxford University Press.
Fokkelman, J. P. 2001. *Reading Biblical Poetry: An Introductory Guide*. Louisville, KY: Westminster John Knox Press.
Fox, Michael V. 2009. *Proverbs 10–31: A New Translation with Introduction and Commentary*. The Anchor Yale Bible 18B. New Haven: Yale University Press.
Gillingham, S. E. 1994. *The Poems and Psalms of the Hebrew Bible*. Oxford Bible Series. Oxford: Oxford University Press.
Keel, Othmar. 1997 [1978]. *The Symbolism of the Biblical World: Ancient Near Eastern Iconography and the Book of Psalms*. Translated by Timothy J. Hallet. Winona Lake, IN: Eisenbrauns.
Kennedy, X. J., and Dana Gioia. 1999. *Literature: An Introduction to Fiction, Poetry, and Drama*. 7th ed. New York: Longman.
Kinzie, Mary. 1999. *A Poet's Guide to Poetry*. Chicago: University of Chicago Press.
Kugel, James L. 1981. *The Idea of Biblical Poetry: Parallelism and Its History*. New Haven: Yale University Press.
Lakoff, George, and Mark Johnson. 2003. *Metaphors We Live By*. 2nd ed. Chicago: University of Chicago Press.
Lakoff, George, and Mark Turner. 1989. *More than Cool Reason: A Field Guide to Poetic Metaphor*. Chicago: University of Chicago Press.
Lowth, Robert. 1971 [1787]. *Lectures on the Sacred Poetry of the Hebrews*. 2 vols. New York: Garland Publishing.
———. 1834. *Isaiah: A New Translation with a Preliminary Dissertation and Notes, Critical, Philological, and Explanatory*. 10th ed. Boston: William Hilliard; Cambridge: James Munroe & Co.
McBride, S. Dean, Jr. 1990. "Prosody." In *The Song of Songs: A Commentary on the Book of Canticles or the Song of Songs*, by Roland E. Murphy, 85–91. Edited by S. Dean McBride Jr. Hermeneia. Minneapolis: Fortress Press.
Newsom, Carol A. 2003. *The Book of Job: A Contest of Moral Imaginations*. Oxford: Oxford University Press.

---

20. The prepositional phrase modifies the verb "create" in the second line; so also "male and female" in the third line: "(as) male and female God created them."

Patrick, Dale, and Allen Scult. 1990. *Rhetoric and Biblical Interpretation*. JSOTSup 82. Sheffield: Almond Press.

Perrine, Laurence. 1963. *Sound and Sense: An Introduction to Poetry*. 2nd ed. New York: Harcourt, Brace & World.

Porter, Stanley E., and Dennis Stamps, eds. 2002. *Rhetorical Criticism and the Bible: Essays from the 1998 Florence Conference*. Library of New Testament Studies. London/New York: Sheffield Academic Press.

Roth, Martha T. 1995. *Law Collections from Mesopotamia and Asia Minor*. SBLWAW 6. Atlanta: Scholars Press.

Soskice, Janet Martin. 1985. *Metaphor and Religious Language*. Oxford: Clarendon Press; New York: Oxford University Press.

Trible, Phyllis. 1994. *Rhetorical Criticism: Context, Method, and the Book of Jonah*. OBT. Minneapolis: Fortress Press.

Watson, Duane F., and Alan J. Hauser. 1994. *Rhetorical Criticism of the Bible: A Comprehensive Bibliography with Notes on History and Method*. Leiden: Brill.

Watson, Wilfred G. E. 1986. *Classical Hebrew Poetry: A Guide to Its Techniques*. JSOTSup 26. Sheffield: JSOT Press.

7

Stylistic Analysis II: Narrative

> A narrative is like a room on whose walls a number of false doors have been painted; . . . but when the author leads us to one particular door, we know it is the right one because it opens.
>
> *John Updike*[1]

Though distinct from poetry, biblical prose narrative wields its own rhetorical power. Like great children's literature, it has a certain noble simplicity, except that the simplicity one finds in biblical prose can be quite deceptive. Biblical narrative draws the reader into what can be a bewildering complexity of narrative dynamics, including plot development, characterization, repetition and variation, ambiguity, irony, tension, and subtle interconnections, to name a few. Biblical narrative is demanding of one's attention. It also invites a sense of wide-eyed wonder.

In his often-referenced study *Mimesis* (1946), the German Jewish scholar Erich Auerbach observed how spare and cryptic biblical narrative is in comparison to Greek literature, specifically Homeric epic poetry. Absent are profuse descriptions of inner motivations and emotions; gone are the introspective musings of the story's characters. Hebrew narrative by comparison is strikingly laconic. Instead, action and outcome, interspersed with dialogue, characterize Biblical Hebrew narrative. And yet, he observed, such simple narrativity is "fraught with background" (Auerbach 1953, 12) and, one could add, filled with "gaps"—gaps to be filled by the reader's active imagination (Sternberg 1985, 186–229).

A number of questions apropos to Biblical Hebrew narrative can be posed. I offer seven (always a good biblical number):

1. Does the narrative flow smoothly, or are there interruptions and/or surprising twists?
2. Does suspense play a role, and is there a climax to the narrative?
3. What is playful about the narrative (e.g., wordplays, irony, satire, surprise)?
4. What is said and what is left unsaid? What is ambiguous or enigmatically expressed?
5. What is repeated, and what is the significance of the variations?

---

1. Updike 2012, 183.

6. How complex are the characters within the narrative, including God?
7. Is the reader omniscient? Is the reader privileged with knowledge beyond what the characters themselves know?

Consider the following examples of Hebrew narrative from Genesis. The first example revels in enigma.

JACOB AT THE JABBOK

While Gen. 32:22–32 is a compact, laconic narrative, it is also a story replete with irony and ambiguity. This enigmatic story, moreover, is rife with interconnections that point beyond itself, signaling a critical turning point within the larger Jacob narrative. While the narrative proper begins at night, with Jacob's encounter at the Jabbok with a mysterious "man" (*ʾîš*) (v. 25), it is nested in the larger narrative of Jacob's homeward-bound journey and his impending encounter with Esau, to whom Jacob sends messengers in v. 3. They return with news that Esau is coming to meet him, along with a considerable army. The suspense mounts.

Prior to our story, human and divine realms are tightly intertwined as Jacob makes repeated reference to Esau as "my lord," eight times no less, and to himself as his brother's "servant" (four times). It is no coincidence that Jacob also refers to himself as YHWH's "servant" in his prayer for deliverance (v. 10). The prayer (vv. 9–12), effusive in its expressions of reverence and humility, anticipates Jacob's encounter with Esau, as if Jacob were practicing before God for his impending encounter with Esau. Jacob, moreover, plans to present Esau with a lavish gift in hopes that his brother will be appeased and that he will "see his face" and "be accepted" by him (v. 20 [21 MT]). The language of appeasement employs a verb that in other contexts designates atonement (*kpr*)[2] and indicates forgiveness.[3] Moreover, Jacob's gift to Esau, his *minḥâ*, elsewhere refers to tribute and political submission to an overlord, human (Judg. 3:15–18) or divine (Gen. 4:3). It can even be used to appease the deity's anger.[4] Jacob's approach to Esau, thus, resembles something of a supplicant's approach to an angry deity. Indeed, Esau is introduced to Jacob in the same manner as the three divine strangers are introduced to Abraham in 18:2. In both scenes, the patriarch "lifted his eyes, and saw, and *voilà!*" (33:1). Esau appears!

The impending crisis that Esau poses constitutes the critical background of Jacob's encounter with the mysterious nocturnal wrestler in our narrative. The stage is set when Jacob is "left alone" at night. The action proceeds tersely: "Jacob was left alone; and a man wrestled with him until daybreak" (32:24). Nothing is said about Jacob's shock or any details about the wrestling match, and certainly nothing about the nocturnal assailant's identity. The reader is left in the dark. So much for the reader's "omniscience"! For all of the drama of an all-night wrestling match, the real drama comes at daybreak in the form of dialogue. The conclusion of the story, not coincidentally, comes to light under

---

2. E.g., Exod. 32:30; Lev. 4:20; 23:28; Deut. 32:43; Ezek. 45:15.
3. E.g., Pss. 65:3 (4 MT); 78:38; 79:9.
4. See 1 Sam. 26:19.

the rising sun. The transition from night to day signals the transition from mystery to revelation.

The mystery "man," it turns out, has strength inferior to Jacob's and also is a wrestler who cheats. Upon seeing that he is "unable to prevail," the "man" dislocates Jacob's thigh with a blow that also packs a certain national import, as the final verse, an etiology, indicates (v. 32). But victory is snatched from the jaws of defeat, for Jacob refuses to release his opponent until he receives a blessing. The predawn blessing marks the turning point in the passage and, for that matter, in the entire Jacob cycle in Genesis (25:19–35:27). Jacob's name change is nothing short of a game changer. He is now deemed the eponymous ancestor of all Israel for having "striven with God and with men and prevailed" (v. 28 AT).[5] And on which side of the divine-human spectrum does the wrestler's identity fall? Evidently both![6] His countenance, to be sure, remains shrouded in darkness. But the wrestler's refusal to surrender his name reveals, paradoxically, his divine status (v. 29; see Judg. 13:18), for immediately thereafter Jacob pronounces the name of the site (v. 30). Is this another narrative gap? The story does not indicate that the assailant is released and where he goes. Instead, we have Jacob now giving a name to the site of his encounter, "Peniel" or "The Face of God" (v. 30a NJPS mg.). In Jacob's own words: "I have seen God face to face, and yet my life has been delivered" (v. 30b AT). Jacob's prayer has been answered: he has been delivered, but not from Esau. His fraternal foe has not yet arrived on the scene. Jacob's prayer was for deliverance from his brother (v. 11), yet in actuality he has been delivered from God! With the sun rising, Jacob leaves with a new name and a limp. Blessed though he is, successful though he is in prevailing over "God and men," Jacob is in no position to either fight or flee as he approaches Esau. The suspense mounts while the irony deepens.

Jacob approaches Esau, bowing to the ground seven times—deference fit for God (33:3). But Esau charges Jacob, as if fit to attack: he "clinches" Jacob (ḥbq), "falling on his neck" (v. 4 AT). Indeed, what turns out to be a fraternal embrace of reconciliation is described by the phonetically similar verb to "wrestle" in the previous scene.[7] A wordplay is born.[8] At this point in the plot, there is little difference between the nocturnal wrestler and Jacob's kin, until the two brothers are said to kiss and weep. Next comes the clincher. Jacob implores Esau, "Take my gift, for truly I have seen your face as one sees the face of God, and you have accepted me" (v. 10 AT). In Jacob's eyes, the face of God and the face of Esau share a striking resemblance. Esau's face reflects the face of God, who, Jacob states, "has dealt graciously with me" (v. 11). Esau, in turn, has "favorably received" Jacob (v. 10b). In Jacob's testimony, Esau and God are cast as parallel agents. Both have spared Jacob's life.

As for the nocturnal wrestler's identity, Hosea's unsympathetic portrayal of the Jabbok/Jacob story overtly associates the divine "messenger" with God in parallel fashion

---

5. This folk etymology (see also Hos. 12:4) is only phonetically related to the name Israel, whose original meaning was probably "El rules."

6. The poetic parallel between "with God" and "with men" in v. 28 suggests a tight coordination regarding the shifting identity of the wrestler in the text.

7. For ḥbq, see, e.g., Gen. 29:13; 48:10; Prov. 4:8; 5:20; Song 2:6; 8:3.

8. The narrator could have easily used the more common verb for wrestling, √ptl (as in Gen. 30:8).

(12:4 CEB). But the Genesis narrative refuses to be so explicit; the links are too thick and numerous to separate the God of heaven from Esau of Seir, divinity from humanity (cf. Deut. 33:2). While approving Jacob's name for the site, Peni-el ("the face of God"), the narrator teases the reader's imagination with the face of Esau. The ambiguity is abundant. In Hebrew prose, the identities of the actors are not clarified except at the ends of verses (Gen. 32:25, 27 [26, 28]). Geller calls them examples of "annoying ambiguity" (1996, 15). But there is nothing annoying about the human-divine interchange that pervades the narrative. No supernatural wonder is performed to signal unequivocal divine status. That itself is a startling surprise. Perhaps the greatest ambiguity is that Jacob's victory seems to mark him as semidivine, in league with Gilgamesh, as Geller suggests (22). But this "pregnant ambiguity" also signals the story's greatest irony. By prevailing over the nocturnal assailant, Jacob is wounded. His prevailing has led to his being injured and thus deprived of strength. Jacob is now damaged goods and is in no position to "prevail" over his brother Esau, even if he wanted to. Instead, he is humbled to the point of giving up his "blessing," the one he had stolen from Esau (33:11; see 27:35).

As it stands, the narrative is set up in such a way as to effect an unexpected reversal. By day, Jacob discerns the face of God in the benevolent face of Esau. But at night, the angry face of Esau is reflected in the hidden face of God. Esau's wrath is played out in a deity's wrestling with a trickster. But wrestling at night, so the larger narrative claims, paves the way for reconciliation by day. Just as Esau's birthright and blessing were stolen, so now his anger has left him; Esau is deprived of his wrath. Nevertheless, something of that anger, as provoked by Jacob, manifests itself in the dead of night, whosever anger it is: Esau's, Laban's, Isaac's, God's. In any case, the results are transformative, even if they constitute a major gap in the narrative. No longer harboring hostility, Esau surprisingly shows himself to be noble and gracious. Unlike Cain, Esau has prevailed over his own anger as much as Jacob has over his opponent (cf. Gen. 4:5–7).

Unexpected grace is written all over this ironic story, God's grace demonstrated in Esau's grace and God's "weakness" resulting in Jacob's uncharacteristic humility. As the night visitor yields a blessing to Jacob, so Jacob gives up his blessing to Esau. Jacob, the underdog, accepts his new status as Israel's eponymous hero but as "the least of all." He is a "trickster in transition" (Niditch 1987, 117). But God, too, engages in trickery: assaulting Jacob at night, engaging him *mano a mano*, or "face to face" in the dark, yet "losing," thereby preserving Jacob's life, but not without a parting injury and a new name, a blessing and a bane. The story of Jacob at the Jabbok is part of a larger narrative in which antagonists are turned protagonists, heroes limp in defeat, and enemies extend grace. The story can be read on so many levels, from the etiological to the psychological to the theological. It is a compact story with a generative capacity for meaning.

A TYPE SCENE IN GENESIS

Narrative repetition is a hallmark of ancient literature, and the Bible is no exception. A telling example in Genesis is the type scene, which designates a distinctive episode that is repeated in parallel fashion elsewhere, sometimes with different players, sometimes in different locations, but always replete with recurring motifs. There is the betrothal type scene in Gen. 24:10–61; 29:1–20; and Exod. 2:15b–21 (Alter 1981, 51–60). Also the incident of Hagar's flight from Sarah, given in both Gen. 16 and 21:9–21, is a type scene that involves the rivalry between a patriarch's vulnerable foreign concubine and his jealous infertile spouse.

Then there's the threefold type scene of the so-called ancestress in danger: the story of a couple sojourning in a foreign land where the patriarch instructs his wife to pretend to be his sister (Gen. 12:10–20; 20:1–18; 26:1–12). Abra(ha)m and Sarai/h figure in the first two episodes, while Isaac and Rebekah are the protagonists in the third. Many points of comparison could be made between these three episodes (see chap. 9), but here I focus on the issue of ambiguity in particular in order to illustrate their stylistic differences.

In Gen. 12, Abram and Sarai are driven into Egypt because of a severe famine (v. 10). On the way, Abram hatches a plan to protect himself: Sarai is to pretend to be his sister in order to cover up the fact that she is his wife (vv. 11–13). The plan works, albeit with unintended consequences. Sarah is noted for her beauty and "taken into Pharaoh's house" (v. 15). Abram is enriched. The situation calls for divine intervention: YHWH afflicts Pharaoh and his household with "great plagues" (v. 17). Nothing is said regarding how Pharaoh himself makes the connection, but he confronts Abram, exposing his ruse and ejecting the couple (vv. 18–19).

As the famine was "severe" (*kābēd*), driving Abram and Sarai into Egypt (12:10), so now Abram is severely rich (*kābēd*) upon leaving Egypt (13:2). This *inclusio*, or repetition of an identical word or phrase, marks the beginning and conclusion of this episode. And within this terse narrative everything that is said counts. So also everything that goes unsaid. What happened to Sarai? All that is said is that "the woman was taken" into Pharaoh's harem (v. 15). The verb "take" (*lqḥ*), here cast as a Qal passive, can have the specific nuance of "wed" in this context (see v. 19). Sarai, in other words, has become wedded to Pharaoh. Has her marital bond with Abram been violated? Has *she* been violated? Such a situation demands intervention, and quickly, hence the direct divine action that immediately follows (v. 17).

Genesis 12 represents the simplest and most ambiguous form of this type scene. By comparison, the two subsequent episodes elaborate the plot and alleviate the ambiguity. This is particularly the case in Gen. 20. Of note is that Abraham and Sarah now sojourn in Gerar. There the Philistine king Abimelech "took Sarah" (v. 2). But before anything illicit can happen, God appears in a dream, warning him of the consequences of adultery (death) while Abimelech protests his innocence (vv. 3–7). The dialogue eliminates all ambiguity: clarification is made that Abimelech "had not approached" Sarah (v. 4). As Abimelech had to explain himself before God, so Abraham must explain himself before Abimelech in the confrontation scene. The narrative is well balanced between these two "alibis." Abraham admits to fearing for his life because "there is no fear of God at all in this place" (v. 11). In addition, however, the patriarch defends his ruse as a half-truth, for Sarah is in fact his half sister (vv. 12–13).[9] The explanation satisfies Abimelech, who declares Abraham exonerated and consequently enriches him along with his restored wife (20:14–15). The

___

9. However, this is nowhere implied in the genealogical account in Gen. 11:29–30.

conclusion of this episode takes a surprising twist: Abraham prays to God to heal Abimelech and his household to bear children (vv. 17–18). God's closing of wombs was not mentioned earlier. In any case, no ambiguity is left unmitigated.

The final episode of this type scene is the strangest of all (Gen. 26:1–11). Not Abraham and Sarah, but now Isaac and Rebekah play their respective roles: the fearful liar and the attractive wife, aka "sister." Moreover, there is no forced "taking" by the king, and hence no need for divine intervention. God's role is played out only at the outset: God tells the couple *not* to head down to Egypt in response to this famine (vv. 2–5). And so back in Gerar, King Abimelech sees for himself the true nature of their relationship through a wonderful wordplay. The king sees "Isaac 'isaac-ing' [*yiṣḥāq mĕṣaḥēq*] his wife, Rebekah" (v. 8). The root *ṣḥq*, which means to "laugh," is shared by both the proper name and the verb (cf. 21:5–6). Is this a euphemism for intercourse or foreplay? Clearly the action of "isaac-ing" involved more than a stand-up comedy routine; otherwise Abimelech would not have been concerned. Rather, it marks the moment of revelation for the peeping king, who with typical type-scene indignation upbraids Isaac for lying about his wife. Here, however, the danger remains only hypothetical, as Abimelech warns Isaac (v. 10) and his people (v. 11). Isaac was afraid to die, his only excuse for the ruse (vv. 7, 9), and the king threatens death to anyone who even "touches this man or his wife" (v. 11). Verging on satire, this version of the "ancestress in danger" type scene has no ancestress in danger.

These three episodes participate, each in its own way, in a common type scene that places the patriarch in the awkward position of lying, whether fully or partially. A stylistic comparison of the three highlights their respective differences. Each episode is paced differently and highlights different moments. Most telling is the mitigation of the ambiguity and alleviation of the tension that characterize the first. Abraham is fully exonerated, and Sarah is fully protected in the second. Isaac clumsily repeats the conduct of his father in the third episode, and Rebekah is not threatened, only exposed, as is Isaac, a humorous twist to a type scene that perhaps by now has outlasted its welcome in Genesis.

One last observation takes us back to the initial episode. While Gen. 12 is the simplest and most ambiguous form of this type scene, it also is the one that points to a larger narrative event, one that extends beyond Genesis: the exodus out of Egypt. The unique twist in this episode is that it corresponds to the narrative structure of the exodus: endangerment in Egypt,[10] deliverance by plagues, ejection by Pharaoh, and even enrichment (see Exod. 11:2; 12:35–36). Far beyond its own boundaries, this episode foreshadows the collective experience of Israel in Egypt. Such is the art of biblical narrative: seemingly simple stories "fraught with background" and filled with connections.

THE CREATION ACCOUNTS OF GENESIS

Comparing the narrative poetics of Gen. 1:1–2:4a and 2:4b–3:24 is a rich study in itself. Both are written in prose, but their aesthetic contours could not be more different. The first account reads like a dispassionate treatise; it resembles a report more than a story.

---

10. Indeed, Sarai's induction into Pharaoh's household can be considered a form of enslavement.

Compared to the lofty cadences of its canonical predecessor, the second account reads more like a Greek tragedy. Methodical progression gives way to narrative bumps and twists. While Gen. 1 teeters on the edge of abstraction, Gen. 2–3 revels in messy drama.

Genesis 1:1–2:4a: A Fugue

How does one describe the narrative style of Gen. 1? Depending on your preference, plodding or methodical comes to mind. Its pace is slow and deliberate, systematically progressing from day to day, with each creative act building on the previous one. Lacking suspense, narrative progress in Gen. 1 is measured incrementally. Repetition is key, particularly in the case of formulaic language. For example, every act of creation is prefaced by divine command. The formula for divine discourse ("God said") is repeated ten times, no less (vv. 3, 6, 9, 11, 14, 20, 24, 26, 28, 29), with the first eight issuing commands of creation ("Let . . ."). Usually the command is followed by a corresponding act of creation, the description of the command's fulfillment. Such systematic presentation is further enhanced with the repeated formula ("and it was so"), sometimes called the "transitional formula" when it occurs in between the command and its fulfillment (vv. 11, 15, 24). In three instances, however, the formula could also be the "execution formula" in vv. 7, 9, 30, where the fulfillment report is entirely absent. Other motifs include the "day conclusion" formula: "and there was evening and there was morning, the X day," which occurs, notably, six times for six days (vv. 5, 8, 13, 19, 23, 31). Also, there is the "divine approval" formula: "and God saw that it was good" or a variant thereof (repeated *seven* times, including its climactic pronouncement, in vv. 4, 10, 12, 18, 21, 25, 31).

All these repetitions serve as building blocks in the construction of a systematically presented account of creation. But there are variations within the repetition, ranging from subtle to obvious. On the subtle side is the occasional variation between the command and its fulfillment. For example take the case of vegetation in 1:11–12:

> [11] Then God said, "Let the earth sprout forth vegetation: plants yielding seed and fruit trees of every kind on earth that bear fruit with the seed in it."
> And it was so.
> [12] So the earth sprouted vegetation: plants yielding seed of every kind, and trees of every kind bearing fruit with the seed in it.
> And God saw that it was good. (alt.)

The "deed report" by and large mirrors the "word report." Only the details vary. More pronounced, however, is the creation of sea life in 1:20–21:

> [20] And God said, "Let the waters produce swarms of living creatures, and let birds fly above the earth across the dome of the sky."
> [21] So God created the great sea monsters and every living creature that moves, of every kind, with which the waters swarm, and every winged bird of every kind.
> And God saw that it was good.

One would expect v. 21 to begin, "So the waters brought forth . . ." Divine action is emphasized in the fulfillment report, which is not anticipated in the command. See also

vv. 24–25. A larger variation is found in the introduction of blessing in the latter parts of the creation account. Three times God blesses: sea and aviary life (v. 22) and humankind (v. 28), both commanded to "be fruitful and multiply." The final blessing is entirely different: the seventh day is blessed and made holy (2:3).

The greatest anomaly comes in the final three verses, the account of the seventh day (2:1–3). Lacking is the "day formula," even though the day is identified no less than twice (vv. 2a, 3a). Also missing is the discourse of divine command and fulfillment, although God remains the subject of active verbs, particularly "bless" and "hallow" (v. 3a). This final section does exhibit its own manner of repetition, however. Verses 2b and 3b are quite similar (but not identical) in emphasizing the cessation and completion of divine activity.

In short, Gen. 1 reads more like a report structured around various motifs and formulas, with variations here and there. Is it fair to ask, then, whether this special kind of narrative has its own climax? Because there is no conflict or tension woven into the "plot," there is no dramatic resolution at the end. And yet the progression of days, with each building upon the previous, does lead to a culmination of sorts. One could point to the creation of humanity in Gen. 1:26–28, the final act of creation, as that climactic moment, along with the God's final approval of creation, declaring it all "very good" (v. 31). Moreover, Gen. 2:1 rounds out the account by using the same language as 1:1 ("the heavens and the earth"), resulting in a tightly wrought and methodically progressive account of creation.

But the account does not end there. It is the seventh day that marks the narrative's completion and the culmination of creation: cessation from work and the consecration of the final day, a day set part from the previous six days. Both the style and the content set this section apart from Gen. 1. The one major element that ties this final section to all that has gone before is the reference to the next day, the "seventh day." Is it the final day? Curiously, the concluding day formula ("there was evening and . . .") is absent. Because of its stylistic anomalies, the seventh day lacks narrative closure.

Nevertheless, closure does pertain to the account as a whole: "These are the generations of the heavens and the earth when they were created," states 2:4a. We have a double *inclusio*: "heavens and earth" (1:1; 2:1, 4a). As many have recognized, Gen. 2:4a would have served as the perfect title for the account as a whole. So why is it placed at the end rather than at the beginning? Is it a retrospective title, rare as that is in Hebrew narrative? Or does it introduce what follows? Or both? One wonders.[11]

Divine Eloquence

A final observation. The divine commands in Gen. 1 exhibit their own style of discourse. Divine discourse in Gen. 1 features a stylistic elegance that sets itself apart from the surrounding narrative material. The following examples stand out:

> Then God said, "Let the earth sprout forth [*tādšēʾ*] vegetation [*dešeʾ*]." (1:11 alt.)
> "And let them be lights [*limʾôrōt*] in the heavenly firmament to illumine [*lĕhāʾîr*] the earth." (1:15 AT)

11. On composition and redaction, see chap. 9.

Then God said, "Let the waters produce [yišrĕṣû] swarms [šereṣ] . . ." (1:20 alt.)

Although not evident in English translation, God's commands utilize a stylized linguistic construction that grammarians call *figura etymologica*, whereby the verb and its object or subject share a common root. Literally these lines can be rendered: "Let the earth sprout sproutlings." "And let them be lights . . . to light the earth." "Let the waters swarm with swarmers." The great biblical scholar Claus Westermann claims that this "etymological formation" serves the "monotonous style that characterizes this chapter" (1984, 124). To each one's own. Overlooked is the lack of such verbal correspondence in the parallel fulfillment reports (cf. vv. 12, 16–17, 21). The result is a heightening of the rhetorical artistry of divine speech, giving it a certain elegance, as I see it, rather than "monotony."[12]

Genesis 2–3: Jazz Improvisation

There is nothing particularly systematic or methodical about the Yahwist's narrative style, at least by Priestly standards (for further discussion see p. 156). What Gen. 2–3 lacks in methodical progression, it more than makes up with narrative convolution and unpredictability. From ingenious wordplays to surprising twists, the narrative keeps the reader off guard. Indeed, the reader's knowledge is as nearly limited as that of the characters.[13] What will God do next? How will the human characters react? It is hard to predict for the first-time reader. As for the narrative's convoluted—or better, improvisational—style, the first sentence is a case in point (2:4b–7 AT).

> [4b] On the day YHWH Elohim made Earth and Heavens— [5] before any pastur-age[14] was on the earth and before any crops[15] had sprouted, for YHWH Elohim had not sent rain upon the earth, and there was yet no 'ādām to work the ground ['ădāmâ], [6] though a spring would emerge from the land and saturate the ground's entire surface— [7] YHWH Elohim formed the 'ādām out of the dust of the ground and blew into his nostrils the breath of life, and the groundling became a living being.

This initial sentence just goes on and on, making Gen. 1:1–3 look simple by comparison. Verse 6 in particular adds an extra convolution—a parenthetical statement within a par-enthetical statement, all describing the state of things before God creates the first human being.

   This account is an eclectic mix (or mess): it contains etiology, dialogue, wordplays, car-tographic details, and divine judgments, all brought together in a narrative that conjures suspense and surprise. Genesis 2–3 is a messy narrative that matches its subject matter: humanity. Perhaps it is no coincidence that the Yahwist reverses the creational order in the opening verse: instead of the Priestly rendering of "the heavens and the earth" (1:1; 2:1, 4a), as fully articulated titles (with the definite article), the Yahwist has the bare

---

12. For further detail, see Brown 1993.

13. Except for one critical difference: the reader knows what it means to be human. The human characters in the narrative have that to discover for themselves in the end.

14. Literally, "plant of the field."

15. I.e., plants for human food, in distinction from cattle feed.

parallel phrase "Earth and Heavens" (2:4b). From the Yahwist's perspective, creation is all about Earth, and it begins with the dirt.

Wordplays

The Yahwist apparently likes to play in the dirt, specifically the fertile layer of narrative discourse. The narrative is littered with wordplays, beginning with the most central: the groundling ('ādām) is fashioned from the topsoil of the ground ('ădāmâ). As made clear in my translation (see chap. 4), the wordplay illustrates how inextricably connected the human creature is to the earth. "He" is bound to the ground by his literary, "genetic"identity. The 'ādām is a child of "dust," a creature of the earth.

Other wordplays follow. The 'ādām undergoes an identity change in the creation of the woman. In his cry of jubilation over her creation, the groundling declares in Gen. 2:23:

> This at last is bone of my bones
>   and flesh of my flesh;
> this one [zō't] shall be called "Woman" ['iššâ],
>   for out of "Man" ['îš] this one was taken.

As much as the 'ādām is related to the 'ădāmâ, so the 'iššâ (woman) is to the 'îš (man). The genetic relationship is chiastically balanced: the (grammatically) masculine is taken from the (grammatically) feminine in the case of the 'ādām, and the feminine is taken from the masculine in the case of the 'iššâ. Moreover, the wordplay in both cases serves to highlight commonality rather than difference. In the case of the 'îš and the 'iššâ, the man's poetic jubilation praises the woman ("this one," [zō't]) for the common substance ("bone" and "flesh") they share together.

Another and rather curious wordplay comes at a critical juncture in the plot, with two words that on the surface seem to have nothing to do with each other: "naked" ('ărûmmîm) in 2:25 and "craft/clever" ('ārûm) in 3:1. The former applies to the human couple and the latter to the serpent. The similarity of sound between these two words—they are near homonyms—is anything but coincidental, since their occurrence is tightly juxtaposed:

> And the man and his wife were both naked ['ărûmmîm], and were not ashamed. (2:25)

> Now the serpent was craftier ['ārûm] than any other wild animal that the YHWH Elohim had made. (3:1a)

> Then the eyes of both were opened, and they knew that they were naked ['êrûmmîm]. (3:7a)

What is the purpose of the wordplay? Perhaps to associate the serpent's cleverness with the couple's realization of their own nakedness. The narrator acknowledges that recognizing one's own nakedness is itself a mark of self-awareness or consciousness (3:7). Indeed, the near homonym would have been the expected result of such awareness: "Then the eyes of both were opened, and they knew that they were *clever*." How wonderful! But no. In the Yahwist's hands, the primal man and woman do not prove to be tricksters like the serpent. The wisdom gained from eating the fruit was a self-awareness not of their clever-ness but of their nakedness, their vulnerability. How ironic.

Narrative Bumps

A major interruption in the flow of the narrative occurs in 2:10–14, which details some-thing of the watershed topography of the area (and beyond): out of a common water source in Eden, four branches flow forth in different directions. The order of the rivers is deliberate: Pishon, Gihon, Tigris, and Euphrates, progressing from the unknown to the well-known. The first river has the most detailed description, with the second follow-ing suit. The Pishon is nowhere elsewhere mentioned in the Hebrew Bible, and its land, "Havilah," remains geographically unfamiliar, perhaps something of a mystery, this place of fine gold (Gen. 25:18; 1 Sam. 15:7). The Gihon is better known, by name at least, but only as a spring on the east side of Jerusalem, connected to the palace (1 Kgs. 1:33, 45). The river that flows through Cush (the area of Sudan) is clearly something different and also bears an aura of mystery. The Tigris and the Euphrates need no introduction. The order is deliberate: the garden is situated somewhere between mythic and geographic reality, between the familiar and the unfamiliar.

Stylistically, this section serves as an interlude that interrupts the flow of the narrative, as can be seen in the immediately surrounding verses (2:8–9, 15 AT).

> [8] YHWH Elohim planted a garden in Eden, in the east, and placed there the groundling whom he had formed. [9] YHWH Elohim caused to sprout from the ground every tree, pleasant to the sight and good for food, including the tree of life in the middle of the garden and the tree of the knowledge of good and bad.[16]
>
> . . . .
> [15] YHWH Elohim took the groundling and placed him in the garden of Eden to serve[17] it and preserve it.[18]

Because of this interlude, v. 15 repeats the substance of v. 8, in addition to defining the groundling's commission, to resume the narrative's flow.

Narrative Pacing and Suspense

Speaking of narrative flow, there are moments when the narrative pauses, causing the reader to linger, such as the moment the woman ponders the tree of knowledge: "The woman saw that the tree was good for food and that it was a delight to the eyes and that the tree was desirable for acquiring wisdom" (3:6a AT). The woman's lingering over the tree is the narrator's cue to describe this particular tree more fully (cf. 2:9, 17): useful, beautiful, and *desirable*. The temptation, if one can call it that, comes not only from the serpent but also from the tree itself.

---

16. To be preferred over "good and evil," which suggests Greek dualistic thinking. See Lapsley 2005, 15, 112n41.
17. The verb in Hebrew (ʿbd) can mean "work" or "serve"; cf. 2:5.
18. The verb (šmr) can also mean "protect" or "guard."

Amid the evocative detail of the tree's appeal, suspense begins to mount. Will the woman partake from the tree or not? Other moments of suspense occur throughout the narrative, such as when God is strolling in the garden while the couple is hiding, and the fateful question is posed: "Where are you?" (3:8–9). The suspense in this encounter is heightened all the more from the fact that the prohibition is punishable by death. Indeed, its articulation already begins to build suspense in 2:16–17. Is death imminent, now that the divine command has been violated (see also 3:2–3)? The narrative keeps the reader hanging.

Perhaps the greatest moment of suspense occurs when the couple partakes of the forbidden fruit. The serpent claimed: "Surely, you will not die, for God knows that on the day both of you eat from it, your eyes will open, and you shall be like gods, knowing good and bad" (3:4b–5 AT). The outcome, however, does not meet expectations. Recognition of nakedness was conveniently unaddressed by the serpent. So did the serpent lie? The answer comes from God's own mouth (3:22 AT):

> YHWH Elohim said, "See, the groundling has become like one of us, knowing good and bad. And now, lest he stretch out his hand and take also from the tree of life and eat and live forever . . ."

Yes, the couple did become "like gods," so God admits, introducing a new pressing concern. It is as if God has once again ascertained the situation as "not good" (cf. 2:18). Now it is not good that the ʾādām remain in the garden. And the punishment of death? It has not come to pass. The narrative keeps the reader pondering, wondering, with only partial resolutions offered.

Repetition

Repetition is key at least for one critical juncture in the narrative. The woman, prompted by the serpent, repeats God's prohibition from eating the fruit of the tree of knowledge. Observe how the woman recasts the prohibition given in 2:16–17 here in 3:2–3 (AT):

> [2] But the woman said to the serpent, "From the fruit of [every] tree of the garden we may eat. [3] But as for the fruit of the tree that is in the middle of the garden, God said, 'You shall not eat from it, nor shall you touch it, lest you die.'"

The woman gives the prohibition a more stringent cast: neither eat *nor touch*. This added detail constitutes a gap between God's original decree and the woman's replication of the decree. What is the significance? At the very least, it casts an entirely positive light on the woman's awareness, while at the same time highlighting the egregiousness of the impending disobedience.

Paradox

Perhaps the most significant paradox in the story is the development of the ʾādām into an ʾîš, a "man." Only in this way can an equal partner be created, a partner fashioned from the ʾādām's own "flesh" and "bone," comparable to the groundling fashioned from the ground. Although deemed a "helper" (ʿēzer, 2:18, 20), the woman is no subordinate creature; she is the man's suitable counterpart. This new creation requires the extraction of a part of the ʾādām, namely, his "side" (Hebrew ṣēlāʿ). This surgical procedure is no one-way derivation, however, for it is from the creation of the woman (ʾiššâ) that the ʾādām finally becomes a "man" (ʾîš). The first time that the ʾādām is actually referred to as a "man" in the Hebrew is in 2:23. Only then is the ʾādām truly a "he," the result of the woman's creation. God's surgical procedure, in other words, marks the mutual engendering of humanity. With the creation of the woman, humanity is now "genderly" separated. Call it the splitting of the ʾādām.

What a paradoxical wonder! Through the act of surgical removal, one would expect the ʾādām to be neutered. Quite the contrary. Precisely in and through his physical loss, the ʾādām gains his masculine identity, and he does so vis-à-vis the woman. The newly fashioned woman bears a direct physical correspondence to this newly fashioned man, and his response is one of utter (and uttered) jubilation. His cry of joy acknowledges their fully shared identity (Gen. 2:23). The man's jubilation focuses on what they share in common: bone and flesh. The woman and the man find themselves to be made in the image of each other, physically and socially. They are family.[19] Having been fashioned as a groundling, the ʾādām now discovers *him*self to be formed in relation to the woman nearly as much as the woman was fashioned from the man. Together, they form a familial partnership.

Characterization

The characterization of the groundling and the woman is also key. Simply put, the two human characters are a work in progress from beginning to end. The garden story traces the tender, painful drama of growing up human. The turning point that led to disobedience and self-consciousness had been building all along within the narrative. As the groundling was placed in the garden to serve, the first human was given a job for which no moral assembly was required. At this point, human identity remained undeveloped. At the moment the prohibition was uttered, however, a new stage was reached: choice became meaningful for ʾādām. Disobedience was now possible. The next stage of the couple's development came with the dilemma posed by both the serpent's countertestimony, eliciting a measure of cognitive dissonance, and the tree's desirability for acquiring discriminating knowledge. By partaking from the tree, the primal couple gained a level of self-consciousness, an awareness of their vulnerable condition and of their newly acquired ability to make decisions on their own. Unwittingly, in their choice to become fully divine, they became fully human.[20]

Narrative Gap

The confrontation scene between God, the couple, and the serpent features a suggestive narrative gap. It opens with God's entrance, remarkable for its informality. God casually

19. See the reference to "bone" and "flesh" in Laban's acknowledgment of Jacob in Gen. 29:14, as well as similar examples of this expression in Judg. 9:2 and 2 Sam. 5:1.

20. As for God's character in the Yahwist narrative (and in the Priestly account), that will be reserved for chap. 23.

strolls through the garden during a comfortable time of day. But this time instead of greeting God, the man and the woman hide in fear. God discerns that they are not immediately present and so inquires as to their whereabouts. The man's response is steeped in irony (3:10). The Hebrew idiom "to hear the voice (or sound) of God,"[21] resembles the expression "to obey God," precisely what the couple did not do.

God demands an explanation. Under interrogation, the man blames the woman ("whom you gave to be with me," 3:12), who blames the serpent (it "misled me," 3:13 AT). This blame game, however, does not come full circle; something is missing. In the punishments that follow, the serpent is addressed first, followed by the woman, and then the man. Missing is God's interrogation of the serpent. God never asks the serpent, "What is this that you have done?" This is a significant gap. If God had questioned the serpent, it could have easily responded with the sure defense "I only told the truth." But the serpent has no opportunity to say it, perhaps because it would have put God on the defensive.[22] The serpent's response would have cast the whole story, from the garden to the expulsion, as a divine setup. And perhaps it is—a setup for becoming tragically human.

Hebrew narrative can be like that. The way it unfolds, the style it adopts, can raise questions more than yield answers, leaving loose ends and open endings for the reader to ponder. In other cases, Hebrew narrative provides closure and stability. In contrast to the fugue-like style of the Priestly account (1:1–2:4a), in which repeating parts build together a well-structured coherence, is the Yahwist's improvisational style. In the former, every word and act of creation counts, making methodical progress toward diversity, stability, and a sense of completion. In the latter, the narrative unfolds in fits and starts, and even "false" steps. In the Yahwist narrative, the characters are given freedom to determine the course of the narrative. God, the main character, does some "experimenting" as well. The Yahwist does not conclude on a note of completion; its "ending" is just the beginning. These two creation accounts, by their narrative style and strategies, are a rich study in contrast and subtlety.

BIBLIOGRAPHY FOR CHAPTER 7

Alter, Robert. 1981. *The Art of Biblical Narrative*. New York: Basic Books.
Auerbach, Erich. 1953. *Mimesis: The Representation of Reality in Western Literature*. Translated by W. Trask. Princeton, NJ: Princeton University Press.
Brown, William P. 1993. "Divine Act and the Art of Persuasion in Genesis 1." In *History and Interpretation: Essays in Honour of John H. Hayes*, edited by M. Patrick Graham, William P. Brown, and Jeffrey K. Kuan, 19–32. JSOTSup 173. Sheffield: Sheffield Academic Press.
Fewell, Danna N., and David M. Gunn. 1997. "Shifting the Blame: God in the Garden." In *Reading Bibles, Writing Bodies: Identity and the Book*, edited by Timothy K. Beal and David M. Gunn, 16–33. London: Routledge.
Geller, Stephen A. 1996. *Sacred Enigmas: Literary Religion in the Hebrew Bible*. London and New York: Routledge.
Janzen, J. Gerald. 1993. *Genesis 12–50: Abraham and All the Families of the Earth*. ITC. Grand Rapids: Eerdmans Publishing.

21. The syntax is slightly different ("obey" includes the use of the preposition ʾel in place of the direct object marker), but the resemblance is unmistakable.
22. See Fewell and Gunn 1997.

Lapsley, Jacqueline E. 2005. *Whispering the Word: Hearing Women's Stories in the Old Testament.* Louisville, KY: Westminster John Knox Press.

Niditch, Susan. 1987. *Underdogs and Tricksters: A Prelude to Biblical Folklore.* San Francisco: Harper & Row.

Sternberg, Meir. 1985. *The Poetics of Biblical Narrative: Ideological Literature and the Drama of Reading.* Bloomington: Indiana University Press.

Trible, Phyllis. 1994. *Rhetorical Criticism: Context, Method, and the Book of Jonah.* GBSOTG. Minneapolis: Fortress Press.

Updike, John. 2012. *More Matter: Essays and Criticism.* New York: Random House Trade Paperbacks.

Westermann, Claus. 1984. *Genesis 1–11: A Commentary.* Minneapolis: Augsburg Publishing House.

8

Structural Analysis

Some say that the origin of life brings order out of chaos
—but I say, "order out of order out of order!"
Günter Wächtershäuser[1]

In addition to style, the aesthetic appeal of a text has to do with its structure and form. "Pattern recognition," neuroscientists tell us, is a highly cognitive process that animals exercise to interpret their environments. It can be a matter of survival, or of fantasy. There is, in fact, a name associated with seeing patterns that do not exist (apophenia), from seeing faces in the clouds to believing conspiracy theories to, in some cases, finding chiasms in biblical narrative.

A text's structure can shed light on how the text is constructed, that is, how it is put together, whether to develop a plot, build an argument, or render prayer to God. Every text, for example, has its boundaries: where the text begins and ends. Internally, every text exhibits some degree of coherence or organization. Important questions to ask include these: *Is the text divisible into its constitutive parts? Is there progression or discernible movement from one part to another? Do the parts fit together in a way that exhibits a pattern of communication, that conforms to a conventional literary or oral genre?*

OUTLINING STRUCTURE

The main task of this chapter is to discern form from content. This can be done by developing an outline of the text, with focus on its structure. Developing an outline does *not* involve replicating the content of the text but rather entails illustrating in an accessible way the text's internal design, its form. This includes at least two things: (1) dividing the text into its parts, and (2) showing how these parts interrelate. Here is a simple example from Jer. 1:4–10:

---

1. Quoted in Tyson and Goldsmith 2004, 247.

The Prophetic Call of Jeremiah
    I. Introduction of YHWH's word to Jeremiah   v. 4
    II. Content of YHWH's word: Jeremiah's Call   v. 5
    III. Jeremiah's objection   v. 6
    IV. YHWH's counterobjection and reassurance   vv. 7–8
    V. YHWH's commissioning of Jeremiah   vv. 9–10

The outline illustrates the back-and-forth nature of Jeremiah's prophetic call report: God initiates, but Jeremiah pushes back, to which God responds with a counterobjection and reassurance. The passage concludes symbolically with Jeremiah's prophetic commission. The structural movement of prophetic call, resistance, and divine response(s) is by no means unique to Jeremiah. We see a similar movement also with the calls of Moses and Isaiah. At the burning bush, Moses objects to God no less than five times; each time he is addressed by God (Exod. 3–4). As for Isaiah, a similar outline unfolds in Isa. 6:

The Prophetic Call of Isaiah
    I. Setting the scene: Temple theophany   vv. 1–4
    II. Isaiah's objection: Unworthiness   v. 5
    III. YHWH's response: Ritual cleansing   vv. 6–7
    IV. YHWH's query   v. 8a
    V. Isaiah's acceptance   v. 8b
    VI. YHWH's commissioning of Isaiah   vv. 9–13

Similar structures call for a generalized pattern or archetype for the "prophetic call narrative." By structurally comparing the call narratives of Isaiah and Jeremiah, one can also begin to discern their differences: different scenes, different kinds of commissioning, differences in order of presentation, and so forth. Three notable differences are readily evident: (1) Isaiah's call includes an acceptance, while Jeremiah's does not; (2) there is no verbal counterresponse on God's part in Isaiah's calling; and (3) God's ritual cleansing of Isaiah sets the stage for his commissioning, which follows, whereas in Jeremiah the ritual and commissioning are more tightly intertwined.

    Let's take an example of another call narrative, the call of Abram in Gen. 12:1–4. My translation, which differs a bit from standard English versions, is featured below.

    ¹YHWH said to Abram:
        "***Go forth***, you,
        from your country, from your kindred, and from your father's house
        to the land that I will show you,
        ²so that I will make you into a great nation and bless you
        and make your name great.
        So be² a blessing,
        ³so that I will bless those who bless you—
        but the one who belittles you I will curse—
        and that by you all the families of the earth can gain a blessing."
    ⁴So Abram went just as YHWH told him . . .

---

2. Imperative use of the verb "to be": *hĕyēh* (see also Gen. 17:1b).

I have formatted my translation in a way that I believe best reflects the text's overall structure, as outlined below.

<pre>
I. Narrative Introduction: Divine Speech   v. 1aα
II. YHWH's Call to Abram   vv. 1aβ–3
   A. First Command: "Go forth"   v. 1aβ–b
   B. Consequences for Abram   vv. 2a
      1. Posterity: "great nation"
      2. Prosperity: "blessing"
      3. Reputation: "name"
   C. Second Command: "Be a blessing"   v. 2b
   D. Consequences for Abram's contacts   v. 3
      1. Blessing others: major
      2. Cursing the other: minor
      3. Universal blessing: "all"
</pre>

The structural outline reveals a remarkable balance. God's call to Abram is evenly divided between two commands: go forth and be a blessing. Each command is followed by three consequential actions on God's part ("so that I . . ."), the first on behalf of Abram and the second for those who come into contact with him. The outline, along with its translation, highlights a tightly wrought interchange between divine and human action. God's blessings, it turns out, are conditional upon Abram's response to these two commands.

Narrative Structure

A structural analysis can also be applied to a much larger swath of material, demonstrating evidence of deliberate design. This is evident, for example, in the Abrahamic cycle in Gen. 12:1–22:19, a narrative tapestry of various traditions woven together in a, yes, chiastic or concentric configuration. A chiasm, as explained in chap. 6, is a particular literary design (prose or poetic) in which the two halves of a passage mirror each other sequentially.

Introduction (11:10–32): genealogical background, setting the stage for the family saga.
A Divine command to Abram and Abram's Response (12:1–9)
   B Sojourn of Abram and Sarai in Egypt (12:10–20)
      C Abram and Lot (13:1–14:24)
         D Promise of an Heir and Birth of Ishmael (15:1–16:16)
            E Divine Covenantal Commitment: (17:1–27)
         D' Promise of an Heir (Isaac) (18:1–15)
      C' Abraham and Lot (18:16–19:38)
   B' Sojourn of Abraham and Sarah in Gerar (20:1–21:34)
A' Divine Command to Abraham and Abraham's Response (22:1–19)
Concluding Episodes (22:20–25:11): broader genealogical context of the family saga.[3]

3. Credit goes to S. Dean McBride Jr. for this concentric breakdown of the Abrahamic narrative.

A chiastic structure highlights a series of thematic correspondences that in its arranged order begins to reverse itself in the middle, yielding a symmetrical structure of sorts. Cast lineally, the Abraham cycle is structured as **A B C D E D' C' B' A'**. This narrative chiasm highlights at least two dimensions of our passage: the "bookends" of the passage and its center. Note that the cycle begins and concludes with a divine command to the patriarch, a bracketing that consists of divine instruction and Abra(ha)m's obedience, an *inclusio*.[4] The turning point of the narrative, the center of the chiasm, is found in Gen. 17 (**E**), the covenant of circumcision (vv. 10–14), which not coincidentally also features a name change for the patriarch and for the matriarch (17:5, 15). The chiasm also explains, at least partially, why we have parallel stories, as in this case the ancestral couple's sojourn in Egypt (12:10–20) and Gerar (20:1–21:34), which contains a common type scene (see chap. 7).

An even lengthier, and more complex, chiasm is found in the Jacob cycle, which covers Gen. 25:12–36:43, as illustrated below:

> **The Unchosen Son (Ishmael): 25:12–18**
> **A** Birth, prediction, and early conflict between Jacob and Esau (25:19–34)
>   **B** Relations with indigenous population: Isaac and the Philistines (26:1–33)
>   **C** Blessing (*bĕrākâ*) obtained through *deception* (27:35–36)
>   **D** Jacob's flight from Esau (27:41–28:5)
>   **E** Encounter with God's "angels" (28:10–22): Bethel
>   **F** Arrival in Haran: Rachel and Laban (29:1–30)
>   **G** Children: Jacob acquires a family (30:1–24)
>   **H Joseph's Birth (30:22–24)**
>   **G'** Flocks: Jacob acquires wealth (30:25–43)
>   **F'** Departure from Haran: Rachel and Laban (31:1–55)
>   **E'** Encounter with God's angelic host: Mahanaim (32:1–2)
>   **D'** Jacob's approach to Esau and the "wrestling match" (32:3–32)
>   **C'** Blessing (*bĕrākâ*) returned (33:11): *reconciliation* (33:1–15)
>   **B'** Relations with indigenous population: Jacob and the Canaanites (chap. 34)
> **A'** Birth, death, fulfillment, Jacob and Esau together bury Isaac (chap. 35)
> **The Unchosen Son (Esau): Chapter 36**[5]

First a caveat: this chiastic outline does not account for all the parts of the narrative. Instead, it highlights those portions of the narrative, particularly motifs, themes, and scenes, that help shape the narrative's overall chiastic pattern. This chiasm, like the previous one, helps to determine the movement of the plot, specifically the symmetry of Jacob's sojourn and the movement from conflict to resolution: **A B C D E F G H G' F' E' D' C' B' A'**. The literary structure itself is shaped by Jacob's movement. His flight from home and his eventual return, his arrival in Haran and his eventual departure, help structure the overall narrative of Jacob's sojourns.

The narrative begins in conflict and concludes with reconciliation. The chiastic center is found in Gen. 30:22–24 (**H**). It is no coincidence that immediately after Joseph's birth, Jacob expresses his intent to return home (30:25). Joseph's birth, thus, marks a turning

---

4. Note that both commands contain the directive *lek-lĕkā* ("go forth, you"; 12:1a; 22:2b).
5. Credit goes to S. Dean McBride Jr. for this concentric structuring of the Jacob cycle.

point, literally, in the narrative. From this outline, one can easily see repetitions that are strategically placed. Notice the two encounters with "angels" in 28:10–22 and 32:1–2. The section concerning Isaac's relationship with the Philistines (26:1–33) is a story of conflict resolved by covenant. Jacob's time with the Canaanites (chap. 34), however, is marked by conflict resolved by violent deception.

A prominent motif in the narrative is the theme of "blessing" (*běrākâ*). A "blessing" is taken from Esau by Jacob in 27:35–36, and a "blessing" (translated as "gift" or "present" in most English translations) is offered by Jacob to Esau in 33:11. The Jacob narrative, in short, contains a chiasm of conflict and reconciliation, of grasping and extending blessing.

STRUCTURE AND FORM

Some texts exhibit a particular form or pattern that is shared in common in varying degrees, and such a pattern may point to a specific genre, that is, a conventional form or pattern of communication that has its "home" in a particular setting.

Lament Psalm

Take, for example, the individual lament psalm. A prototypical example is Ps. 13:

> *To the director. A Psalm of David.*
> [1] How long, YHWH? Will you forget me forever?
>   How long will you hide your face from me? (v. 2 MT)
> [2] How long must I bear counsels[6] within me,
>   sorrow in my heart daily?
>   How often must my enemy rise up against me? (v. 3 MT)
> [3] Take note (and) answer me, YHWH, my God!
>   Restore light to my eyes,
>   lest I fall into the sleep of death, (v. 4 MT)
> [4] lest my enemy say, "I have overcome him,"
>   and my foes rejoice over my downfall.[7] (v. 5 MT)
> [5] But as for me, I trust in your benevolence [*ḥesed*].
>   My heart shall indeed rejoice in your salvation. (v. 6a MT)
> [6] I will sing to YHWH,
>   when[8] he has dealt fully[9] with me. (v. 6b MT)

This short six-verse lament contains various elements or sections arranged in a particular order, outlined as follows:

---

6. So MT. Frequently suggested is the emendation (without textual support) of *ʿēṣôt* for *ʿaṣṣabôt* (so *BHS*) for better sense and parallelism. In psalmic poetry, inner deliberation can indicate crisis, such as in Pss. 42 and 62. Of course, a wordplay is possible.

7. Literally, "and my foes rejoice that I am shaken."

8. Or "for" (*kî*). The conjunction is ambiguous.

9. The perfect aspect of the verb *gml* can imply "good-as-done" activity on the part of God, but the overall syntax suggests that the speaker's praise is contingent upon God's deliverance.

Superscription
- I. Invocation and Complaint   vv. 1–2
- II. Petition   vv. 3–4
  - A. Request
  - B. Motivation
- III. Affirmation of Trust and Praise   vv. 5–6

What makes this psalm an individual lament or complaint psalm is its anatomy and overall structure. One can discern the main parts of the psalm: invocation (v. 1), complaint (vv. 1–2), petition (vv. 3–4), and affirmation of trust and praise (vv. 5–6), all presented in an order that moves from complaint to praise. The complaint is cast as a series of questions and opens with an invocation. It describes the speaker's desperate state: abandonment by God, inner "sorrow," and social hostility (v. 2). The complaint, however, does not stand on its own but serves to introduce the petition that follows: God is called upon to restore the speaker's life. An added feature in the petition is the motivation the speaker deploys to compel God to act (vv. 3b–4a). If God fails, then the speaker will die and his enemies will exult. The speaker makes the case, none too subtly, that God's very reputation is at stake. The psalm concludes with an affirmation of trust and a vow to praise (vv. 5–6).

The distinctive structure of this psalm points to a general form or genre, usually called an individual lament or complaint. Generally speaking, it is a form of prayer designed to motivate God to act on behalf of a speaker amid a dire situation. Yet like all genres, the genre of lament points to a typical form that is not uniformly applicable to every so-called lament. Psalm 88, for example, does not conclude in praise or affirmation of trust, but remains "stuck" in complaint, with only minimal petition, to the bitter end. Seemingly established forms, thus, are meant to be modified, even broken.

There are, of course, many other forms or genres to be found among the psalms, such as communal laments, songs of praise, and thanksgiving psalms. Their forms and possible settings in life are explored in any standard introduction to the psalms, not to mention commentaries. Less well defined are the so-called wisdom psalms, Torah psalms, and royal psalms, which do not exhibit clearly definable forms but are grouped together by common themes and language. While every biblical text exhibits its own structure, it may not exhibit a definable form or genre.

Prophetic Judgment Oracle

Another readily identifiable form is the so-called judgment oracle (or disaster oracle), the most prominent form in prophetic literature. A terse example is found in Hos. 4:1–3 (alt.).

[1] Hear YHWH's word,
　　people of Israel;
for YHWH has an indictment
　　against the land's inhabitants.
There is no faithfulness or loyalty,
　　and no knowledge of God in the land.
[2] Swearing, lying, murder, stealing, and adultery break out;
　　bloodshed follows bloodshed.

³ Consequently¹⁰ the land mourns,
    and all who live in it languish;
  along with the wild animals and the birds of the air,
    even the fish of the sea are dying.

Hosea 4:1–3 follows a movement that opens with a call to attention and concludes with a declaration of judgment or consequence ("consequently" or "therefore"). In between lies a set of reasons that make up the bulk of the prophetic oracle. It can be outlined as follows.

I. Call to attention	v. 1a
A. Proclamation: "Hear . . ."	v. 1aα
B. Identification of addressee: "Israel"	v. 1aβ
C. Reason: YHWH's "indictment"	v. 1aγ
II. Message	v. 1b–3
A. Reasons/indictments: covenantal violations¹¹	vv. 1b–2
B. Judgment/consequence	v. 3

Prophetic oracles typically begin with a call to attention that leads directly to the content of the message or "word." Very often the call is cast in the form of the so-called messenger formula: "Thus says YHWH [kōh ʾāmar yhwh]," whereby the prophet acts as God's spokesperson, whether in judgment or salvation.¹² The content of the judgment oracle typically consists of reasons and a judgment, usually in that order, but not always. They are tightly interrelated. Take out, for example, the reasons given in our passage above (vv. 1b–2), and the concluding judgment becomes something of a non sequitur. The reasons provide the basis for the concluding judgment. They serve as the indictments or accusations behind the judgment; they ensure that judgment is not something carried out willy-nilly. Prophetic judgment is not a prediction of the future but a judgment supported by reasons, punishment that fits the crimes.

In Hosea's case, however, there remains the question of whether the conclusion is, properly speaking, a judgment. If one defines "judgment" as a verdict coupled with divine punishment (see, e.g., Hos. 2:6, 9; Amos 1:4; 4:2), then judgment does not apply in this case. Hosea 4:3 lacks reference to divine intervention in its concluding verse. Instead, the land and the waters are simply said to be degrading. The word translated "therefore" in the NRSV, and in most other translations, may be better translated as "consequently" (ʿal-kēn) in this case: "Consequently¹³ the land mourns, and all who live in it languish." In other words, the oracle's conclusion and its reasons are more tightly interwoven than what is conveyed in the NRSV. That the breakdown of the covenantal communal order leads directly or naturally to the breakdown of the created order is perhaps the point.¹⁴ The reasons, in other words, spell out the consequence, not the result of direct divine

---

10. NRSV "therefore." See discussion below.
11. Hosea apparently references certain violations of the Decalogue or some early version of it.
12. The examples are numerous. See, e.g., Isa. 50:1; Jer. 7:20; Amos 1:3.
13. Wilhelm Rudolph offers a more innovative translation: "No wonder the land . . ." (Rudolph 1966, 94).
14. This does not necessarily rule out divine action at work behind the scenes, but inbreaking divine intervention is not indicated here.

intervention. As a former student of mine titled his sermon on this passage, "Stop and Smell the Dead Fish!"

Judgment in Disguise

As noted above, genres can be tweaked or modified. Amos 3:1–2, for example, is a judgment oracle masquerading as a pronouncement of blessing or salvation up until its surprising conclusion.

> [1] Hear this word that YHWH has spoken concerning you, O Israelites,
>   concerning the entire clan that I brought up from the land of Egypt:
> [2] "Only you have I known[15] from all the clans of the earth.
>   Therefore, I will transfer[16] upon you all your sins." (AT)

Structure

I. Call to attention	v. 1
A. Proclamation: "Hear . . ."	v. 1aα
B. Identification of addressor and addressee	v. 1aαβ
C. Relationship between addressor and addressee	v. 1b
II. Announcement of judgment	v. 2
A. Reason	v. 2a
B. Judgment	v. 2b

This judgment or disaster oracle (see also Amos 4:1–3; 5:10–13) rests on a masterful twist on the audience's expectations. The prophet sets up his audience to expect a word of salvation from the God who saved Israel from Egyptian bondage. But the last line proves otherwise. God's unsurpassed "knowledge" of Israel turns out to be the reason not for salvation but for judgment! The "exodus election" forms the basis of Israel's judgment, and such judgment is cast as the consequence of Israel's sins. This message from Amos *reverses* Israel's expectations by denying Israel the exodus as a basis for claiming God's grace. What looks like an announcement of salvation turns out to be one of judgment. Attention to the structure of this passage highlights the surprising irony all the more: the people's special, indeed liberating relationship to God becomes the very reason for their accountability.

Prophetic discourse consists of more than judgment oracles. Other forms are readily identifiable: salvation oracles, disputations, vision reports, eschatological promises, trial speeches, symbolic-act reports, just to name a few. They are conveniently treated by Nogalski (2015, 57–78). Each prophetic form or genre is never fixed, as if it were a mold into which words are simply poured, thereby yielding another instance of, say, a vision report. No, genres are inherently malleable and flexible. Variation is invariable.

---

15. Force of the verb *yādaʿ* (know) in this context denotes selection/election. See parallels in Gen. 18:19; Exod. 33:12, 17; Deut. 9:24; 10:15 (with synonym *bḥr*).

16. The verb *pqd* here necessitates a word study, given its wide range of connotations, with special attention to context. Possibilities include "transfer, place, 'visit,' hold against." The NRSV and KJV break the syntax of the Hebrew with their respective translations. See Amos 3:14.

THE QUESTION OF GENRE

A text's particular structure *may* point to a form shared by other texts, which in turn *may* reflect a common setting. Classifying texts according to various forms has been, for example, a staple of Psalms research, beginning with the foundational work of Hermann Gunkel (1862–1932). It was Gunkel's conviction that common forms or genres reflect common "settings in life" (*Sitze im Leben*) or institutional contexts of usage, such as worship (cultic), education, family, legal or judicial, royal court, commercial, and so forth.

While genres have traditionally been viewed as a means of classifying texts by placing them into well-defined categories, recent work tends to view genres more flexibly as "tools for communication and meaning making" (Zahn 2012, 276). The relationship between text and genre, in other words, is to be viewed dynamically and organically, not essentially or rigidly. Because of their particularities, texts do not so much *belong* to particular genres as *participate* in them (Newsom 2005, 439). Or put more actively, texts *perform* genres in different ways. Think of genres as "contracts," forged between authors and readers, that lay out certain expectations of what the text is to do (Newsom 2010, 199). Sometimes texts "refuse" to meet particular expectations: they can surprise. Moreover, a text's participation in one genre by no means precludes participation in another. Genres are "probabilistic complexes, not hypothetically pure structures that lie behind the text" (Buss 1999, 255). Genres, furthermore, are dialogically dynamic. Every instance of a genre is a "reply" to other instances within the same genre, as well as to other genres (Newsom 2005, 447).

While classifying texts remains an important form-critical task, it must be recognized that genres themselves are more flexible and dynamic than categories. Genres are not pigeonholes; they change over time as they account for the considerable variety of texts (i.e., so-called mixed forms). They are akin to "fuzzy sets" in mathematics, in which the delineation of types are far from crisp (Fox 1991, 142n2). They can only be drawn approximately, allowing for overlapping features. Put simply, the quest for a genre, somewhat like identifying a genus in biology, attempts to establish family resemblances among texts, whether they are distant cousins or twin siblings. Genres are genetic prototypes, as it were, in a sea of mutations.[17]

Identifying the genre of a text with its setting in life, thus, must be done with caution and with the realization that no genre, let alone an individual text, is exclusively tied to its originating setting. Recent scholarship has shown no tight correspondence between, for example, a psalm's form and its alleged setting (Nasuti 1999). Psalms of similar structure and common language, for example, can reflect different contexts of use, from public worship to individual devotion. A psalm's functional setting, in other words, can be a moving target. Take Ps. 30, for example, which presents itself as an individual thanksgiving psalm. The superscription, however, reads, "A song for the dedication of the temple," suggesting that it was used for an eminently communal event. The identification of a *Sitz im Leben* for a given text is not locked and final: biblical texts lack copyright restrictions.

---

17. Carol Newsom, for example, proposes a "prototype" theory of genre by which "there is a distinction between central or privileged properties and those that are more peripheral" (2005, 443).

Another liability in classifying texts according to genre is the temptation to overlook what makes a particular text distinctive or unique. Genre analysis by itself can make texts appear, well, generic. Still, such study is useful. A genre, as stated above, conveys a set of expectations that help the reader identify and even anticipate how a particular text moves rhetorically from beginning to end, or how it *could* have moved (without claiming how it *should* have moved). In other words, genre classification should always remain descriptive, not prescriptive. Serving as a malleable template, a genre can reveal how a particular psalm, for example, subverts, revises, or tweaks a prototypical pattern, thereby highlighting its distinctiveness within the family of psalms with which it shares certain formal features. In the task of genre analysis, similarity and difference are inseparably connected.

GENESIS ACCOUNTS OF CREATION

As much as there are certain structures or patterns that are (proto)typical among various texts, some other patterns are not so typical, and hence cannot be classified within a specific genre. It is perhaps no coincidence that the genres discussed above correspond to distinctly poetic texts, such as psalms. Narrative texts are not so easily classified in terms of discrete genres or are classified in more general ways. Still, narrative texts give evidence of structure and plot, organization and movement, all of which can be outlined. The Genesis creation texts are no exception.

Genesis 1, as mentioned previously, consists of discrete parts, or "building blocks," that give an intricate coherence to the account as a whole. These units make for a dense and lengthy structural outline, and for good reason: Gen. 1:1–2:3 is the most structurally dense passage in all of the Hebrew Bible. If there is any doubt, see the outline below.

The First Account of Creation
I. Introduction: Precreation	1:1–2
A. Temporal Introduction	1:1
B. Precreative State	1:2
II. Seven Days	1:3–2:3
A. Six Days of Creation	1:3–31
1. First Day (Light)	1:3–5
a. Command	1:3a
b. Fulfillment	1:3b
c. Approval	1:4a
d. Separation	1:4b
e. Naming	1:5a
f. Day Enumeration	1:5b
2. Second Day (firmament/heaven)	1:6–8
a. Command	1:6
b. Fulfillment	1:7a
c. Confirmation formula ("and it was so")	1:7b
d. Naming	1:8a
e. Day Enumeration	1:8b
3. Third Day (seas, land, vegetation)	1:9–13
a. Collection of water	1:9–10

(1) Command	1:9a
(2) Execution formula: "and it was so"	1:9b
(3) Naming	1:10a
(4) Approval	1:10b
b. Vegetation	1:11–13
(1) Command	1:11a
(2) Transition formula: "and it was so"	1:11b
(3) Fulfillment	1:12a
(4) Approval	1:12b
(5) Day Enumeration	1:13
4. Fourth Day (celestial luminaries)	1:14–19
a. Command	1:14–15a
b. Transition formula: "and it was so"	1:15b
c. Fulfillment	1:16–18a
d. Approbation	1:18b
e. Day Enumeration	1:19
5. Fifth Day (sea and winged creatures)	1:20–23
a. Command	1:20
b. Fulfillment	1:21a–bβ
c. Approval	1:21bγ
d. Blessings	1:22
e. Day Enumeration	1:23
6. Sixth Day (land animals and humanity)	1:24–31
a. Land Animals	1:24–25
(1) Command	1:24a
(2) Transition formula: "and it was so"	1:24b
(3) Fulfillment	1:25a
(4) Approbation	1:25b
b. Human Beings	1:26–30
(1) Command	1:26
(2) Fulfillment	1:27
(3) Blessing/Mandate	1:28
c. Provision of Food	1:29–30
(1) Divine declaration	1:29–30a
(2) Execution formula: "and it was so"	1:30b
d. Universal Approval	1:31a
e. Day Enumeration	1:31b
7. Statement of Completion	2:1
B. Seventh Day (cessation)	2:2–3
1. Statement of Completion	2:2a
2. Divine "acts"	2:2b–3
a. Cessation	2:2b
b. Blessing and Consecration	2:3a
3. Reason	2:3b
<<< Priestly Transition to the Yahwist Account	2:4a>>>[18]

Through this outlined structure, one can readily see how the building blocks fit together to form a systematic, methodically arranged narrative. This account of creation is governed by the persistent rhythm of command, fulfillment, approval, and the day enumeration,

18. For details on this verse, see chap. 11 below.

with other variable elements mixed in on occasion (e.g., naming, blessing). Speaking of variability, the formula "and it was so" functions in different ways throughout the account, depending on its placement. It serves to confirm the fulfillment or act of creation in 1:7b, fulfills the act of creation in 1:9b and 1:30b, and most often serves as a transition from God's command to the fulfillment of the command in 1:11b, 15b, and 24b. The formula, thus, is something of a floater. The greatest variable, however, is the seventh day (2:2–3). Its structure sets itself apart from the other six days: no command, no act of creation, no approval, no naming formula. While a blessing occurs on the seventh day, God's act of consecration is unprecedented in the account. Genesis 1 is a highly structured text, replete with measured degrees of variation.

But there may be more to the structure of Gen. 1 than meets the eye that is focused only on the building blocks or formulaic details. Is there a more general pattern at work that is discernible when one steps back to see the whole, a deeper pattern that functions meaningfully within the sphere of ancient Israelite practice?

The Architecture of Sacred Space

A pattern not reflected in the detailed structure outlined above is the text's overall symmetry, particularly for the first six days.

Day 1 (1:3–5)	**Day 4** (1:14–19)
Light	Lights
Day 2 (1:6–8)	**Day 5** (1:20–23)
Waters above (sky)	Aviary Life
Waters below	Marine Life
Day 3 (1:9–13)	**Day 6** (1:24–31)
Land	Land Animals
	Humans
Vegetation	Food

According to their thematic correspondences, the first six days of creation line up to form two parallel columns, establishing a well-coordinated symmetry. Days 1–3 delineate the cosmic domains, which are then populated by various entities or agencies that inhabit these domains (Days 4–6). Vertically, the two columns address the two abject conditions of lack referenced in 1:2, formlessness and emptiness. The left column (Days 1–3) recounts the cosmos being *formed*, while the right column (Days 4–6) describes the cosmos being *filled*. Days 4–6 report the filling of the domains with their respective inhabitants, from the celestial spheres, which "rule" both day and night (1:14–18), to human beings, who exercise "dominion" (1:26–28). With the stars set in the heavens and the various forms of life, each according to its kind, filling sky, land, and sea, creation proceeds from emptiness to fullness in the right column, just as it had proceeded from formlessness to form-fullness in the left.

Missing from this symmetrical structure, however, is the seventh day (2:2–3). Having no corresponding partner, the seventh day stands alone. It is unique both in content and form: God "says" nothing to formally introduce this new day, and nothing gets created on it. Apart from introducing the theme of holiness, the addition of the seventh day serves to restructure the entire schema of creation itself. The result can be illustrated as follows.

"Day" 0
Creation Incomplete (1:2)

Day 1 (1:3–5) Light	**Day 4** (1:14–19) Lights
Day 2 (1:6–8) Sky Waters below	**Day 5** (1:20–23) Aviary life Marine life
Day 3 (1:9–13) Land Vegetation	**Day 6** (1:24–31) Land animals Humans Food

Creation Complete (2:1–3)
Day 7

This final odd day establishes a *vertical* correspondence with creation's initial, precreative condition described in 1:2, which could paradoxically be called "Day 0" for the sake of illustration, the "day" before time, or "Day minus 1," as it were, a "day" that does not count as a day of creation yet sets the stage for those that do. Together, these two "days" form a subtle correspondence: nothing is created on either day. The time*less* character of "Day 0," moreover, shares a particular kinship with Day 7. Both lack the temporal formula "evening came and then morning." As Day 0 is "before" created time, so Day 7 is suspended above time. The Priestly account of creation is thus bracketed by precreation (Day 0) and postcreation (Day 7). Symmetry abounds!

But there is more. The final day serves as the capstone for an entirely new structure. Without this seventh day, the resulting pattern would lose a distinction that remains largely hidden to most modern readers. Ancient readers of Genesis would have recognized the pattern as the common threefold structure of the temple (1 Kgs. 6–8) and tabernacle described in the latter chapters of Exodus.[19] In the instructions for building the tabernacle given in Exodus, three discrete areas are identified: the outer court (*ḥāṣēr*), the "holy place" (*haqqōdeš*), and the inner sanctuary or "most holy place" (*qōdeš haqqodāšîm*) (Exod. 26:33–34; 27:9, 12–19). Similarly, Solomon's temple is described in 1 Kgs. 6–8 as consisting of three parts: the vestibule or portico (*ʾûlām*), the nave (*hêkāl*), and the innermost sanctum located at the far back of the temple, the "inner sanctuary" (*děbîr*; e.g., 6:5, 16, 20–23; 7:50; 8:6–8).

19. For architectural structure of Syro-Palestinian temples, see Hundley 2013, 105–14.

```
┌─────────────────────┐
│      Vestibule      │
│   (Outer Court)     │
├─────────────────────┤
│        Nave         │
│    (Holy Place)     │
├─────────────────────┤
│   Inner Sanctum     │
│  (Holy of Holies)   │
└─────────────────────┘
```

This threefold arrangement of sacred space corresponds precisely to the way in which the various days of creation are distributed chronologically and thematically. The first six days, by virtue of their correspondence, demarcate the architectural boundaries of sacred space. The last day, given its uniqueness, is lodged in the most holy space, a space uniquely unbounded since it lacks final boundaries by virtue of its transcendent status (see below).

Day 1 ——————— Day 4
Vestibule
(Outer Court)
Day 2 ——————— Day 5
Nave
(Holy Place)
Day 3 ——————— Day 6
Inner Sanctum
(Holy of Holies)
Day 7

Here in Gen. 1:1–2:4a, creation is cast in the image of the temple or tabernacle, the tripartite structure of sacred space. The cosmos, according to the Priestly account, is God's cosmic sanctuary! Creation's "entrance," as it were, is demarcated by Days 1 and 4, featuring the creation of light and lights. Not coincidentally, Solomon's Temple in Jerusalem, like many temples of its time and vicinity, faced eastward, toward the rising sun. On the other end chronologically (and spatially), the holy seventh day marks God's completion of creation, God's "rest," which corresponds to the inner sanctum, where God is said to reside in "thick darkness" (see 1 Kgs. 8:12).[20] Divine rest and residence, in other words, find their correspondence in creation and temple. The temple is a microcosmos, and the universe, in turn, is a macrotemple. Biblically speaking, then, creation is God's *first* temple.[21] Yes, structure is key to interpreting Gen. 1 in more ways than one!

---

20. Reference to "thick darkness" in the temple, similar to the description of precreation in Gen. 1:2, preserves God's transcendence over time and space.

21. This observation is nothing new. What is relatively new is the temple nature of creation as demonstrated from the text's own literary structure. See McBride 2000, 12–15.

Genesis 2:4b–3:24

As the Priestly account follows a discernible pattern, so the Yahwist account bears its own overall narrative structure. This can be illustrated by dividing the narrative into various scenes or acts, as in a drama. I count four scenes, each containing parallel elements. Every scene, except for the last, identifies a deficiency followed by God's response. The plot is driven by the fits and starts of creative activity addressing various deficiencies, suggesting more an improvisation on God's part than a meticulously executed program. The four scenes can be indicated as follows:

1. Creation of the ʾādām and the garden (2:4b–17)
2. Creation of the animals and a companion (2:18–25)
3. Temptation and disobedience (3:1–7)
4. Expulsion and punishment (3:8–24)

Each scene features a particular lack or loss, to which a particular response is given to remedy the situation. Take the first scene.

Temporal Introduction ("In the day . . ."):	2:4b
I. Scene 1	2:5–17
A. Lack: no plants, no water, no tiller	2:5
B. Provision	2:6–14
1. Subterranean stream	2:6
2. Creation of the ʾādām	2:7
3. Garden	2:8–9
4. Rivers	2:10–14
C. The ʾādām's commissioning	2:15–17
1. Purpose	2:15
2. Freedom of consumption	2:16
3. Restriction	2:17
a. Prohibition	2:17a
b. Punishment of death	2:17b

Like Gen. 1, the Yahwist account begins with a temporal introduction that leads directly into a description of deficiency. The lack is remedied systematically, beginning with the watering of the land's surface and the creation of the ʾādām, whose purpose is to maintain the garden.

II. Scene 2	2:18–25
A. Lack ("not good"): no companion	2:18
B. Provision of companion	2:19–23
1. Plan A: Creation of animals	2:19–20
2. Plan B: Creation of woman	2:21–22
3. The ʾādām's approval	2:23
4. Etiology of marriage	2:24
C. Result: naked and unashamed	2:25

The next lack also has to do with the ʾādām's welfare, namely, the lack of a companion. God first resorts to creating more animals from the ʾădāmâ. They too are groundlings.

But the ʾādām does not recognize any of them as his companion and counterpart. God thus resorts to another plan, the creation of the woman from the ʾādām's own "flesh and bone." Confirmation of success is given in the ʾādām's approval in v. 23. The narrative pauses to articulate the institutional legacy of the naked man and woman together in the garden: what appears to be an etiology of marriage to explain current practice rooted in primordial origins (v. 24). The final verse describes the condition of the primal couple, which sets up the next scene.

III. Scene 3	3:1–7
A. Lack of divine status	3:1–5
1. Introduction of the serpent	3:1
2. Countertestimony to 2:17	3:2–5
B. Self-remedy	3:6–7
1. Partaking of the tree	3:6
2. Result: consciousness	3:7a
C. Lack: nakedness	3:7bα
D. Self-provision: sewing fig leaves	3:7bβ

A new character enters the stage, the serpent, whose function is to question the divine prohibition by introducing a new lack: the lack of divine wisdom and status. The "provision" this time is not granted by God but rather initiated by the couple, who take matters into their own hands. The result is the couple's self-recognition of nakedness, with accompanying shame. This is followed by another act of provision, this time *self*-provision: sewing fig leaves to provide clothing.

IV. Scene 4	3:8–24
A. Encounter with God	3:8–13
1. God in the garden	3:8
2. The ʾādām's response: fear	3:9–10
3. Interrogation	3:11–13
a. ʾādām's response: blame	3:12
b. Woman's response: deception	3:13
B. God's punishments	3:14–19
1. To the serpent	3:14–15
2. To the woman	3:16
3. To the ʾādām	3:17–19
C. Naming of Eve	3:20
D. God's provision of clothing	3:21
E. Loss of the garden	3:22–24
1. Reason: to prevent full divinity	3:22
2. Expulsion	3:23
3. Guarding the tree of life	3:24

The final scene is less reflective of the structure that is set by the first three scenes, and for good reason. The theme of lack is replaced by its counterpart, loss. This is expressed in two ways: the loss of the garden at the conclusion of the narrative, and the implied loss of intimacy and mutual harmony. (Note that the ʾādām's punishment is the longest.) Yet even amid punishment and loss, God has not given up the role of provider (3:21). From careful attention to structure, one can identify divine provision as a connecting thread in the narrative.

CONCLUSION

While there is more than one way to highlight a text's structure, central is identifying the text's constitutive units and discerning how they interrelate. Studying the text's structure is important for discerning the text's defining contours and shifts, its trajectories and disjunctions, its central and peripheral points. Rendering a structural analysis of a text also prevents the reader from getting lost in the details of text. It involves taking a step back and seeing the forest from the trees. It may also afford one a glimpse of the text's "setting(s) in life," its location and function in ancient Israel's life. Ultimately a structural analysis serves to aid one's reading of the text with greater aesthetic and meaningful depth. One could argue from structure, for example, that the primary reason for the "seven days" of creation is to demonstrate that creation is God's cosmic temple. From the structure of Gen. 2–3, one can discern all the more clearly that God continues to provide even in the face of loss. Form matters.

BIBLIOGRAPHY FOR CHAPTER 8

Brown, William P. 2010. *Psalms*. IBT. Nashville: Abingdon.

Buss, Martin J. 1999. *Biblical Form Criticism in Its Context*. JSOTSup 274. Sheffield: Sheffield Academic Press.

———. 2010. *The Changing Shape of Form Criticism: A Relational Approach*. Edited by Nickie M. Stipe. Sheffield: Sheffield Phoenix Press.

Fowler, Alastair. 1982. *Kinds of Literature: An Introduction to the Theory of Genres and Modes*. Cambridge, MA: Harvard University Press.

Fox, Michael V. 1991. *Character and Ideology in the Book of Esther*. Studies on Personalities of the Old Testament. Columbia: University of South Carolina Press.

Hayes, John H., ed. 1974. *Old Testament Form Criticism*. San Antonio, TX: Trinity University Press.

Hundley, Michael B. 2013. *Gods in Dwellings: Temples and Divine Presence in the Ancient Near East*. SBLWAW 3. Atlanta: Society of Biblical Literature.

Knierim, Rolf, and Gene Tucker, eds. 1981–. Forms of the Old Testament Literature series (FOTL). Grand Rapids: Eerdmans Publishing.

Koch, Klaus. 1969. *The Growth of the Biblical Tradition: The Form-Critical Method*. New York: Charles Scribner's Sons.

McBride, S. Dean, Jr. 2000. "Divine Protocol: Genesis 1:1–2:3 as Prologue to the Pentateuch." In *God Who Creates: Essays in Honor of W. Sibley Towner*, edited by William P. Brown and S. Dean McBride Jr., 3–41. Grand Rapids: Eerdmans Publishing.

Nasuti, Harry P. 1999. *Defining the Sacred Songs: Genre, Tradition and the Post-Critical Interpretation of the Psalms*. JSOTSup 218. Sheffield: Sheffield Academic Press.

Newsom, Carol A. 2005. "Spying Out the Land: A Report from Genology." In *Seeking Out the Wisdom of the Ancients: Essays Offered to Honor Michael V. Fox on the Occasion of His Sixty-Fifth Birthday*, edited by Ronald L. Troxel, Kelvin G. Friebel, and Dennis Robert Magary, 437–50. Winona Lake, IN: Eisenbrauns.

———. 2010. "Rhetorical Criticism and the Dead Sea Scrolls." In *Rediscovering the Dead Sea Scrolls: An Assessment of Old and New Approaches and Methods*, edited by Maxine L. Grossman, 198–214. Grand Rapids: Eerdmans Publishing.

Nogalski, James D. 2015. *Interpreting Prophetic Literature: Historical and Exegetical Tools for Reading Prophets*. Louisville, KY: Westminster John Knox Press.

Rudolph, Wilhelm. 1966. *Hosea*. KAT 13.1. Gütersloh: Gerd Mohn.

Sweeney, Marvin A., and Ehud Ben Zvi, eds. 2003. *The Changing Face of Form Criticism for the Twenty-First Century*. Grand Rapids: Eerdmans Publishing.

Tucker, Gene M. 1971. *Form Criticism of the Old Testament*. GBS. Philadelphia: Fortress Press.

Tyson, Neil deGrasse, and Donald Goldsmith. 2004. *Origins: Fourteen Billion Years of Cosmic Evolution*. New York: W. W. Norton.

Weinfeld, Moshe. 1981. "Sabbath, Temple and the Enthronement of the Lord: The Problem of the *Sitz im Leben* of Genesis 1:1–2:3." In *Mélanges bibliques et orientaux en l'honneur de M. Henri Cazelles*, edited by André Caquot and M. Delcor, 501–12. AOAT 212. Kevelaer: Butzon & Bercker; Neukirchen-Vluyn: Neukirchener Verlag.

Zahn, Molly M. 2012. "Genre and Rewritten Scripture: A Reassessment." *JBL* 131, no. 3:271–88.

9

Compositional Analysis

Nothing goes by luck in composition.
Henry David Thoreau[1]

The Bible reflects a long history of composition and transmission, and every text within it has its history too—a history of formation and development across time, even centuries. We normally think of a text's history beginning with its author, who took the effort to write and revise until feeling sufficiently satisfied to release a text for a wider audience, beyond an audience of one. Comparing the author's notes and rough drafts with the finished product would reveal something of the text's prehistory before it was disseminated publicly.

With a biblical text, however, the situation is more complicated. Though there may be a single author in some cases, biblical texts are typically adopted and adapted by communities, if not created by them. At the very least, the canonical character of these texts defines them as communally validated. Moreover, communities clearly have a hand in shaping the biblical text, guiding it to its received and final form. In fact, the origination of many biblical texts seems rooted in the community from the very outset. How can one, for instance, talk of an individual author for a proverb, folktale, or a law code? Rather than as free creations of creative individuals, such texts are the products and properties of communities. They could be called traditions, which in many cases, if not most cases, originated orally. Oral-based traditions are ever open to emendation and embellishment when they are transmitted to various audiences and to succeeding generations. One might assume that oral "texts" that are eventually written down become frozen, forever preserved in pristine literary form. Think otherwise. Written texts, too, are amenable to revision: expansion, clarification, or whatever constitutes improvement in the eye (and hand) of the scribal community. Whenever biblical texts were copied, opportunities arose to make emendations, whether intentional or not (see chap. 5). Call it "transmission with

---

1. Van Doren 1916, 80.

modification."[2] From its composition to its editing and ongoing transmission, each text has a life, an *evolved* life.

Exploring the dynamics of compositional growth bridges two technical disciplines in biblical studies: traditio-historical criticism and redaction criticism. The former typically designates the preliterary or oral stages of textual development, whereas the latter is focused on the discernible written stages of a text's literary history up to its final form. Hence the compositional history of a biblical text includes both its prewritten and its written development, the entire sweep of a text's growth. However, the daunting challenge of determining the full "compositional context" of a text comes from the fact that we have only literary texts to work with. Yes, the Bible speaks, but not orally. This makes reconstructing the oral form of a written text an exercise in speculation, but not an exercise in irrelevance, as we shall see. On the one hand, ancient Israel, like other comparable societies of antiquity, was primarily an oral-based culture. Hence most biblical traditions, whether songs, laws, or prophetic pronouncements, were oral based. On the other hand, it is thanks to ancient Israel's scribes (e.g., authors, secretaries, editors, copyists—the literati) that we have the literature at all, as they composed, preserved, modified, and redacted these ancient traditions. Hence this chapter treats both disciplines of textual inquiry together.[3]

The following questions are key: *How does the text in its final form make use of and reshape received traditions? Is there evidence of editorial "fingerprints" that indicate the text's literary growth over time? How does an understanding of the compositional stages behind the text contribute to your understanding of the text's meaning in its larger literary context?*

ANCESTRESS-IN-DANGER TRADITION IN GENESIS 12, 20, 26

In chap. 7 we compared the three accounts of the ancestress-in-danger episode or type scene with a focus on literary style, specifically regarding the theme of ambiguity. Now we widen our focus to consider their possible oral roots and literary development.

Oral Tradition

One can easily imagine such a story of deception and intrigue lending itself to retelling, complete with embellishments and variations, as we see in these three accounts preserved in Genesis. Their shared motifs may suggest that they all drew from a common stock of oral tradition, a folktale that depicts an ancestral couple sojourning in a foreign land and concocting a lie to conceal their marital relationship out of fear for their lives. The results of their ruse prove near disastrous not only for the couple but also for the community, including the foreign king. The result is their expulsion, but not without the ironic result that they leave better off, even enriched.

---

2. A play on Darwin's definition of evolution as "descent with modification."
3. For a history of traditio-historical criticism, see Knight 2009, 98–104.

Getting at the oral version of the tale means sifting out the most common or foundational denominators among the three stories: (1) a patriarch and a beautiful matriarch; (2) the lie ("She is my sister") given out of fear; (3) the king's covetousness; (4) exposure of the marital relationship; and (5) confrontation between king and patriarch. There is nothing to suggest, however, which couple (Abra[ha]m and Sarai/h, or Isaac and Rebekah) constitutes the earliest, oral form of the tradition. The same goes for the identity of the royal antagonist. Perhaps the major characters were originally anonymous. "There once was a man who lived with his beautiful wife in a foreign land. . . ." Who knows? If we, for example, discovered a text *outside* the biblical corpus that reflects this narrative tradition, say, of an Aramean couple settling in Babylon, then we could marvel at how widespread such a tradition was throughout the ancient Near East.[4]

Determining an underlying, allegedly oral form as the basis for all three accounts resides, admittedly, on speculation, for the obvious reason that there is no ancient oral version for us to hear. Examining the text in terms of its "tradition history" can involve trying to find (or construct) the simplest version of the account, which may never have existed. There are too many unknowns. On the other hand, the attempt at least has its heuristic value. Let's say that the simplest and earliest version of the story involved a couple who devised a ruse resulting in unintended consequences, necessitating divine intervention, but not without involving a heated confrontation with the king, resulting ultimately in the couple's expulsion. With that in mind, we can see stark differences among the three versions. Compare the three accounts (Gen. 12:10–20; 20:1–18; 26:1–11) and identify what you see as the major differences.

Here are some differences I see. The third account in Gen. 26 features a comparatively lengthy introduction that, in fact, presupposes the first account in Gen. 12. Isaac is told by God *not* to repeat what Abram and Sarai had done by sojourning in Egypt (26:2–3). So Gerar it is. The ruse itself is planned at different times among the accounts: before entering the land (Gen. 12) and in the land (Gen. 20 and 26). More striking is the aftermath of the matriarch being taken into the royal household in the first two accounts: Sarai's abduction triggers divine plagues (12:17), whereas it prompts a divine dialogue in 20:3–8, which includes the threat of death but absolves the king of any violation of the couple's marital bond. More striking still, there is no abduction in the third account! Rebekah is never in danger, and God figures nowhere in the scene that involves the disclosure of the marital relationship. Instead, the king (rather humorously) discovers it himself. Whereas the first two stories reveal the relationship through divine intervention, the third account reveals it through exposure, casting either the king as a voyeur or Isaac as reckless, or a bit of both. In either case, this significant change in the ancestress-in-danger tradition turns entirely on a humorous wordplay based on Isaac's name (26:8).[5] Of the three, the Isaac-Rebekah episode is the most distinctive.

Other less striking differences include (1) the concerted defense of Abraham in 20:11–13, which absolves the patriarch, halfway at least, from lying; (2) the expulsion of Isaac

---

4. Archives of contracts discovered at Nuzi, a Hurrian administrative center in northern Iraq, have been used to explain the "wife-sister motif" found in Genesis, but with mixed success. See Speiser 1963, 19–28.

5. Regarding this issue, see chap. 7.

and Rebekah postponed until much later; (3) the entire lack of divine intervention in the third story; and (4) the way the enrichment is described in the first two stories but lacking in the third (12:16; 20:14–16; cf. 26:12–15). The differences, both major and minor, become all the more striking in light of the common features that allegedly draw from a common base tradition: a foreign man whose beautiful wife attracts unwanted attention devises a "sister" ruse that results in possibly disastrous consequences. But God comes to the rescue, yet not without an angry confrontation with the king, who expels the couple with wealth.

This works only for the first two accounts. The third story uniquely twists the tradition, one could argue, to suit the patriarch's character. Although the first two accounts highlight the patriarch as a trickster of sorts, the third highlights him humorously as, well, a bumbler. Of the two Abra(ha)mic accounts, the first is the simplest and most ambiguous, whereas the second fills in significant gaps, including the protection of the matriarch, the means by which the foreign king finds out, the "half sister" excuse, and the matriarch's exoneration. On the other hand, the first account is uniquely Egyptian in its setting, which, as we have seen, creates a narrative arc extending from Genesis to Exodus. Of the three accounts, the first one makes the most extensive literary impact: the story of the ancestral couple in (and out of) Egypt foreshadows the exodus story. The Egyptian drama of Gen. 12, therefore, is likely a distinctly literary feature, not an originally oral one. Thus Gen. 12 is, one could argue, an Egyptianizing of an earlier (oral?) tale that had the ancestral couple (originally?) in Gerar. Perhaps. In any event, this is another case of looking for allegedly oral commonalities that lead, invariably, to finding literary differences.

Redactional Features

Behind every good book stands a good editor. Focusing on literary features in terms of textual development leads us to another related discipline: redaction criticism. This approach focuses on determining the earlier (or "original") literary integrity of a text by identifying what is added or inserted into the text, hence making a redacted (edited) text. Redaction criticism is to literary features what traditio-historical criticism is to oral features. And because the literary and the oral happily coexisted in ancient Israel, the boundary line between these two disciplines is blurry at best. But whether distinct or overlapping, both modes of analysis have to do with highlighting textual development.

Some texts are so homogeneous that redaction criticism would not apply. However, most texts—the more extensive, the more likely—give evidence of considerable development. To put it another way, redactional analysis looks for the handiwork of an editor. Specifically, a redactional analysis searches for literary tensions, both breaks and bridges, that suggest added material. Take the opening verses of Gen. 26:

> [1] Now there was a famine in the land, ***besides the former famine that had occurred in the days of Abraham***. So Isaac went to Gerar, to King Abimelech of the Philistines. [2] YHWH appeared to Isaac and said, "Do not go down to Egypt; settle in the land that I shall show you. [3] Reside in this land as an alien, and I will be with you, and will bless you; for to you and to your descendants I will give all these lands, and I will fulfill the oath that I swore to your father Abraham. [4] I will make

your offspring as numerous as the stars of heaven, and will give to your offspring all these lands; and all the nations of the earth shall gain blessing for themselves through your offspring, [5] because Abraham obeyed my voice and kept my charge, my commandments, my statutes, and my laws."

[6] So Isaac settled in Gerar. [7a] When the men of the place asked him about his wife, he said, "She is my sister."

The first verse begins in the same way as Gen. 12:10 (AT): "And there was a famine in the land." But whereas 12:10 immediately proceeds to the patriarch's sojourn to Egypt ("So Abram went down to Egypt to reside there as an alien . . ."), the first verse of Gen. 26 takes a literary digression to link the Isaac-Rebekah episode with Abram and Sarai's sojourn to Egypt. Only after this digression does the narrative proceed to Isaac and Rebekah's sojourn in Philistia. Is the digression possibly secondary? If we bracket out (temporarily) the middle portion of this account ("besides . . . Abraham"), we continue to have a smooth narrative line: "Now there was a famine in the land, so Isaac went to Gerar," a famine just as in Gen. 12:10. One could argue that the middle portion was added in order to link the Isaac-Rebekah episode with the account in Gen. 12. However, there is no literary tension evident with its (alleged) addition, so the verdict is out on whether this material was actually added. In any case, the middle portion functions to link the Isaac-Rebekah narrative to the larger narrative of sojourning.

More obvious is the material that follows (Gen. 26:2–5). A narrative tension is evident in the transition from v. 1 to v. 2. So Isaac arrives in Gerar, according to the end of v. 1, but v. 2 presupposes that he hasn't moved yet! God warns Isaac not to travel to Egypt but to "settle in the land that I shall show you." Indeed, all of vv. 2–5 can be considered a block of text added to the larger narrative. Take it out, and the narrative proceeds smoothly—except for the redundancy in v. 6, which serves to resume the narrative flow, beginning where v. 1 ended. Verse 6, one could say, is a resumptive addition.[6] Take 26:2–6 out, and there is no interruption to the narrative flow:

> [1] Now there was a famine in the land, besides the former famine that had occurred in the days of Abraham. So Isaac went to Gerar, to King Abimelech of the Philistines. . . . [7] When the men of the place asked him about his wife, he said, "She is my sister." (alt.)

But what is deemed "secondary" redactionally need not be considered secondary in importance. "Secondary" does not mean dispensable. To the contrary, such added material is just as important as the surrounding earlier material, for it shows evidence of editorial work with the text, and the exegete has opportunity to explore why this material was added, to determine its purpose or function within the passage as a whole. Like the middle portion of v. 1, vv. 2–6 tie the Isaac-Rebekah episode to the Abram-Sarai episode. But now much more is at stake than simply the cross-referencing of separate sojourns. This additional material lays claim that Isaac is also the bearer of God's blessing, as was Abram. Indeed, because of Abraham (v. 5) Isaac is a recipient of God's beneficence, first explicated in Gen. 12:1–3: the promise of land, progeny, and international blessing. And

---

6. It is technically called a *Wideraufnahme*, from the German meaning "resumption."

"so Isaac settled in Gerar" to succeed not only by his wits (or lack thereof) but also with God's blessing in hand (see 26:12–13).

A Wrestling Match Revisited

Let's now turn to the more enigmatic story in Genesis: Jacob at the Jabbok wrestling with an unknown assailant in the night but discovering God at daybreak (Gen. 32:22–32 [23–33 MT]). What kind of tradition lies behind this mysterious story of a nocturnal wrestling match and the patriarch's victory? Are there identifiable digressions that would lead one to discern certain stages of development? Most obvious is the etiological explication found at the conclusion of the text (32:32), which focuses on Jacob's hip dislocation and the dietary restriction that results from it (Di Vito 1999, 99). This is found in the italicized portions below.

> [22] The same night he got up and took his two wives, his two maids, and his eleven children, and crossed the ford of the Jabbok. [23] He took them and sent them across the stream, and likewise everything that he had. [24] Jacob was left alone; and a man wrestled with him until daybreak. [25] When the man saw that he did not prevail against Jacob, *he struck him on the hip socket; and Jacob's hip was put out of joint as he wrestled with him.* [26] Then he said, "Let me go, for the day is breaking." But Jacob said, "I will not let you go, unless you bless me." [27] So he said to him, "What is your name?" And he said, "Jacob." [28] Then the man said, "You shall no longer be called Jacob, but Israel, for you have striven with God and with humans, and have prevailed." [29] Then Jacob asked him, "Please tell me your name." But he said, "Why is it that you ask my name?" And there he blessed him. [30] So Jacob called the place Peniel, saying, "For I have seen God face to face, and yet my life is preserved." [31] *The sun rose upon him as he passed Penuel, limping because of his hip.* [32] *Therefore to this day the Israelites do not eat the thigh muscle that is on the hip socket, because he struck Jacob on the hip socket at the thigh muscle.*

Admittedly v. 25b seems a bit out of place. The assailant's sucker punch and the subsequent dislocation of Jacob's hip would indicate winning, rather than losing, on the part of the nocturnal assailant. Why would the assailant cry out to be let go in v. 26 after he has so severely impaired his opponent? Note also the variant spelling of "Peniel" in v. 31 as "Penuel," another likely indication of editorial work. If for the moment we bracket out these references, the result is a more streamlined if not more coherent text:

> [22] The same night he got up and took his two wives, his two maids, and his eleven children, and crossed the ford of the Jabbok. [23] He took them and sent them across the stream, and likewise everything that he had. [24] Jacob was left alone; and a man wrestled with him until daybreak. [25] When the man saw that he did not prevail against Jacob, [. . .] [26] he said, "Let me go, for the day is breaking." But Jacob said, "I will not let you go, unless you bless me." [27] So he said to him, "What is your name?" And he said, "Jacob." [28] Then the man said, "You shall no longer be called Jacob, but Israel, for you have striven with God and with humans, and have prevailed." [29] Then Jacob asked him, "Please tell me your name." But he said, "Why is it that you ask my name?" And there he blessed him. [30] So Jacob called the place Peniel, saying, "For I have seen God face to face, and yet my life is preserved."

Another etiology concerns Jacob's change of name in vv. 27–29, a feature essential to the larger narrative cycle in which Jacob is the designated father of a nation with his twelve sons, hence the name "Israel." But here in our story, as an isolated account, the (re)naming episode is perhaps not so essential:

> [22] The same night he got up and took his two wives, his two maids, and his eleven children, and crossed the ford of the Jabbok. [23] He took them and sent them across the stream, and likewise everything that he had. [24] Jacob was left alone; and a man wrestled with him until daybreak. [25] When the man saw that he did not prevail against Jacob, [26] he said, "Let me go, for the day is breaking." But Jacob said, "I will not let you go, unless you bless me." [27] *So he said to him, "What is your name?" And he said, "Jacob."* [28] *Then the man said, "You shall no longer be called Jacob, but Israel, for you have striven with God and with humans, and have prevailed."* [29] *Then Jacob asked him, "Please tell me your name." But he said, "Why is it that you ask my name?"* And there he blessed him. [30] So Jacob called the place Peniel, saying, "For I have seen God face to face, and yet my life is preserved."

The result is an even more compact account of Jacob's wrestling match at the Jabbok:

> [22] The same night he got up and took his two wives, his two maids, and his eleven children, and crossed the ford of the Jabbok. [23] He took them and sent them across the stream, and likewise everything that he had. [24] Jacob was left alone; and a man wrestled with him until daybreak. [25] When the man saw that he did not prevail against Jacob, [26] he said, "Let me go, for the day is breaking." But Jacob said, "I will not let you go, unless you bless me." [29b] And there he blessed him. [30] So Jacob called the place Peniel, saying, "For I have seen God face to face, and yet my life is preserved."

Not coincidentally, this abbreviated version corresponds closely with the poetic parallel of the wrestling match found in Hosea:

> In his vigor he strove with God [or "a god"];[7]
>   he strove with a messenger and prevailed;
>   he wept and sought his favor. (12:3b–4a AT [4b–5a MT])

The bare elements of the episode are there: Jacob wrestling with a divine "messenger" and prevailing. The last line is grammatically ambiguous: is the one who "wept" the divine "messenger" or Jacob? Either is possible. Yes, Jacob in Genesis does seek blessing, but in Hosea it is unclear whether Jacob is the subject in the final line in Hosea. In any case, no mention is made of a change in Jacob's name. Nevertheless, the Hosea passage does preserve the pun in the verb "to strive," which hints at Jacob's identification with Israel (the root *śrh* in *yiśrā'ēl*).

Can one reach farther back into the story's oral origins? Here the mist of textual history becomes too thick to see. Some scholars have posited an original folktale about a hero attacked in the dead of night by a river demon and prevailing over his opponent

---

7. Hebrew *'ĕlōhîm*.

(Westermann 1985, 514–21).[8] If that's the case, the composers and editors responsible for Gen. 32 have made a "monotheizing" move to incorporate this heroic tale into Israel's ancestral history. The assailant can be none other than a divine being, indeed God (or God's "messenger"), and Jacob's heroic victory is worked into a tale that involves the transformation of his very identity, limp included—by all measures a costly "victory."

GROWTH IN THE GARDEN

What, then, about our creation texts? Is there evidence of textual change for either of them? Genesis 1:1–2:3 is a difficult text to analyze redactionally, since the structure and language of the text are rather consistent.[9] But that has not stopped scholars from trying to sift out different traditions. For example, the number of divine acts reported (eight) does not correspond to the number of divine commands (ten), a discrepancy that may be the result of a merging of two discrete traditions: a creation account dominated by divine commands and another account characterized by God's acts. Others have suggested that the seven-day schema is a final overlay that chronologically shaped an earlier account of God's words and corresponding deeds. Perhaps. In any case, to reconstruct earlier texts and precursors of tradition that might lie behind Gen. 1 is speculative.

Genesis 2–3, however, is another matter. Replete with literary digressions and repetitions (or "doublets"), the second creation account is not a smooth text by any measure. Thus it is possible to discern particular redactional layers by working backward from the text as we have it to the text in its allegedly earlier forms. We start with two major digressions in the narrative flow as highlighted below:

> [2:4b] On the day YHWH Elohim made Earth and Heaven— [5] before any pasturage was on the earth and before any field crops had sprouted, for YHWH Elohim had not sent rain upon the earth, and there was yet no groundling to serve the ground, [6] *but a spring would emerge from the land and water the ground's entire surface*— [7] YHWH Elohim formed the groundling out of the dust of the ground and blew into his nostrils the breath of life, and the groundling became a living being. [8] YHWH Elohim planted a garden in Eden, in the east, and placed there the groundling whom he had formed. [9] YHWH Elohim caused to sprout from the ground every tree, pleasant to the sight and good for food, including the tree of life in the middle of the garden and the tree of the knowledge of good and bad.
>
> [10] *Now a river flows from Eden to water the garden, and from there it splits and becomes four branches.* [11] *The name of the first is Pishon, which encircles all the land of Havilah, where there is gold.* [12] *The gold of that land is fine; bdellium and onyx stone are [also] there.* [13] *The name of the second river is Gihon, which encircles the whole land of Cush.* [14] *The name of the third river is Tigris, which flows toward Assyria, and the fourth river is the Euphrates.*
>
> [15] YHWH Elohim took the groundling and placed him in the garden of Eden to serve it and preserve it. [16] And YHWH Elohim commanded the groundling,

---

8. Westermann even suggests that the naming of the site in Gen. 32:31a has suppressed an older naming account of the Jabbok (1985, 519).

9. The text-critical situation, however, is far different; see chap. 5 above.

saying, "From every tree of the garden you may most certainly eat, [17] but from the tree of the knowledge of good and bad you shall not eat, for on the day you eat from it you will surely die." (AT)

Genesis 2:10–14 constitutes a narrative break that provides specific geographical information about Eden's watershed, the source of four major rivers. The following verse (v. 15) resumes the narrative's flow, picking up v. 8 by partially repeating it, although with variant language (the verbs *śym* and *nwḥ* both mean "place" or "put"). Moreover, the river geography of this section may be anticipated by v. 6, itself a disruptive verse within the complicated syntax of vv. 4b–7. Indeed, the content of v. 6 is a bit jarring in that the deficiency of water referenced in the previous verse is due to the lack of *rain* (v. 5b), but what follows is not rain as a remedy but a subterranean spring (*'ēd*). Both v. 6 and v. 10, moreover, share in common the verb "to water" (*šqh* in Hiphil). It could be, then, that vv. 6, 10–14 belong to a redactional cluster of verses that show evidence of the text's growth toward its final, full form. Their addition places Eden in a global context, locating it as the center of a water source that provides for various lands, both known and unknown.

Bracketing out, for the time being, these "secondary" portions yields the following reduced and perhaps earlier text. Note the doublet in vv. 8b and 15a, suggesting that the latter is secondary—another case of *Wideraufnahme*, or resumption (so also Carr 1993, 578).

> [2:4b] On the day YHWH Elohim made Earth and Heaven— [5] before any pasturage was on the earth and before any field crops had sprouted, for YHWH Elohim had not sent rain upon the earth, and there was yet no groundling to serve the ground— [. . .] [7] YHWH Elohim formed the groundling of dust from the ground and blew into his nostrils the breath of life, and the groundling became a living being. [8] YHWH Elohim planted a garden in Eden, in the east, and placed there the groundling whom he had formed. [9] *And YHWH Elohim caused to sprout from the ground every tree pleasant to the sight and good for food, and the tree of life in the middle of the garden and the tree of the knowledge of good and bad.* [. . .]
> [15] *YHWH Elohim took the groundling and placed him in the garden of Eden* to serve it and preserve it. [16] *And YHWH Elohim commanded the groundling, saying, "From every tree of the garden you may most certainly eat,* [17] *but from the tree of the knowledge of good and bad you shall not eat, for on the day you eat from it you will surely die."* (AT)

Again, this literary bridging made possible by v. 15a is prompted by the inclusion of vv. 10–14; it serves to resume the narrative that follows, repeating v. 8b with different words: both describe God's placement of the *'ādām* in the garden. Moreover, the garden planting is referenced twice: God "planted a garden in Eden" and God "caused to sprout from the ground every tree. . . ." But this sets up a literary tension: it would be peculiar for the groundling to be placed in the garden (v. 8b) *before* the garden actually grows (v. 9), causing the groundling to wait until the trees are grown enough to provide sustenance. Notice also that v. 8 refers to "a garden in Eden," whereas v. 15 references "the garden of Eden." Hence vv. 9 and 15a appear secondary as well, and if they are, so also vv. 16–17, which together depend on v. 9. Bracketing out these verses results in the following abbreviated text:

.[2:4b] On the day YHWH Elohim made Earth and Heaven—[5] before any pasturage was on the earth and before any field crops had sprouted, for YHWH Elohim had not yet sent rain upon the earth, and there was yet no groundling to serve the ground—[7] YHWH Elohim formed the groundling out of the dust of the ground and blew into his nostrils the breath of life, and the groundling became a living being. [8] YHWH Elohim planted a garden in Eden, in the east, and placed there the groundling whom he had formed [15b] to serve it and preserve it.[10] (AT)

To summarize so far, by noticing subtle disruptions and doublets, as well as linguistic and thematic connections, we can trace something of the literary evolution of the text. The resulting picture suggests that an earlier form of the account made no mention of rivers watering the earth and of the garden's arboreal composition, with its the two special trees, along with God's mandated permission and restriction. Instead, we read of a garden planted by God, who fashions and places a human creature (the groundling) to preserve the ground of the garden.

The following section (2:18–24) coheres nicely with the earlier shape of the creation narrative so far. God searches for a corresponding helper for the groundling to assist in maintaining the garden, and eventually the woman is created. The resulting wordplay of the "man" and the "woman" (ʾîš and ʾiššâ) in v. 23 corresponds nicely with the earlier wordplay of the "groundling" and the "ground" (ʾādām and ʾădāmâ). Verse 24, likely an addition, provides an etiological note that grounds the custom of marriage in the garden. Things change, however, in v. 25. The observation that "the groundling and his wife were both naked, and were not ashamed" serves as a bridge to the following account in the next chapter, the account of the so-called fall. The comment on the couple's lack of shame and clothing in 2:25 anticipates 3:7, 21. This final verse in chap. 2, moreover, joins the previously noted editorial additions (2:6, 9–15abα, 16–17), which together serve to set the stage for what happens next.

So far we have noticed verses added here and there to an existing creation account. If we step back and take stock of the changes, we see a remarkable transformation by which an editor/composer adapted an early creation account of the groundling and the woman in the garden and turned it into a story of crime and punishment, of human disobedience and its painful consequences. This later composer/editor transformed a garden that depended on rain (rather than on a subterranean stream) and required human work (2:5b, 15bβ) into a well-watered fruit orchard (vv. 6, 9, 10–14). Human work required to preserve the garden is transformed into human observance of a divinely mandated prohibition regarding a specific tree in the garden (vv. 16–17). The tragic story in chap. 3 was composed as an extension of the idyllic creation account in chap. 2. The story of human work in the garden ends with human expulsion, a tale of "paradise" lost. The final editor/composer reshaped the received tradition of a garden story in chap. 2 to deliver a painful warning: obedience to divine command is to be valued over the acquisition of wisdom.[11]

---

10. The object suffix is feminine; thus, its grammatical antecedent could originally have been the "ground" (ʾădāmâ) rather than the "garden" (gan), which is typically masculine but in this case came to be the antecedent in the narrative's final form.

11. For more on this, see Carr 1993; Mendenhall 1974.

The edited expansion of Gen. 2 also bears marks of textual unevenness, most notably regarding the prohibition and expulsion. For example, the prohibition given by God is directed toward the ʾādām in 2:17. Yet the woman repeats the command to the snake, employing verbs cast consistently in the plural: "But as for the fruit of the tree that is in the middle of the garden, God said, 'You shall not eat from it, nor shall you touch it, lest you die'" (3:3 AT). When it comes to the description of the couple's expulsion from the garden, however, reference is made only to the man in 3:22–24. Any reference to the woman is absent. This has led some interpreters to suggest that an earlier form of Gen. 3 had only the ʾādām as the protagonist. There is indeed precedent for such a conclusion, for we have a striking parallel elsewhere in the Bible, specifically in Ezek. 28:11–19. This passage is the closest biblical parallel to the garden story in Gen. 2–3. Ezekiel 28:11–19 is a divine judgment oracle directed against the king of Tyre, an island port city of Phoenicia, who is described as a virtual Adam, the first and only human created in the "garden of God." What might we infer about the shape of the Eden tradition that underlies the Ezekiel version? At the very least, it appears to be a form that focuses exclusively on one individual, a primal man: his genesis, his crime, and his punishment.

This suggests that the focus on the woman and her partaking of the fruit in Gen. 3 marks a later development in the early Eden tradition. Perhaps an earlier form featured only the man committing the crime, and perhaps only one tree was involved. (Notice that there is no tree in Ezekiel's version.) Also notable is the figure of the "guardian cherub" in Ezekiel. (28:14, 16), who is responsible not only for driving the king from the garden but also for guarding the "tree of life" in Gen. 3:24. The cherubim (pl. of "cherub") in Genesis guard (šmr) the path to the "tree of life," thereby thwarting any attempt at human encroachment (Gen. 3:24). But the ʾādām in Genesis, it may be recalled, also had a comparable purpose not only to "serve" but also to "preserve" or guard (šmr, 2:15). The "tree of knowledge" and the "tree of life" are both off-limits to the ʾādām (2:17; 3:22), for eating both of them puts one in the company of the gods.

The story of Adam and Even in the garden is a complicated, messy affair, not only from the standpoint of its narrative logic but also in terms of its textual growth (and they are not unrelated). Its literary "seams" point to editorial reworking and expansion of previous textual traditions. While an early creation tradition celebrates the mutual harmony between the ground and the groundling, as well as between the man and the woman, a later reworking of the tradition points to the painful estrangement that occurs in the aftermath of disobedience, a story of crime and punishment. Moreover, further editorial work on the so-called fall introduces the woman as a central character in the plot, a plot that once may have involved only the man.

Much more could be explored, such as the background of the two trees in the garden. While the "tree of knowledge" shares most of the spotlight in the Genesis narrative, the "tree of life" is mentioned at the beginning (2:9) and reappears only at the end (3:22, 24).

> [3:22] Then YHWH Elohim said, "See, the ʾādām has become like one of us, knowing good and evil; and now, he might reach out his hand and take also from the ***tree of life***, and eat, and live forever"— [23] and YHWH Elohim sent him forth from the garden of Eden, to till the ground from which he was taken. [24] And he drove out

the groundling, and at the east of the garden of Eden he placed the cherubim, and a sword flaming and turning to guard the way to the ***tree of life***. (alt.)

Note the redundancy of expulsion: God "sent him forth from the garden" in v. 23 and God "drove out the man" in v. 24. Verses 22 and 24 clearly hang together, since they both reference the "tree of life" as the singular reason for expulsion. On the other hand, v. 23 by itself could very well preserve an earlier account in which it is the disobedience, the partaking from the "tree of knowledge," that is the reason for the expulsion. The implication is that the "tree of life" references may be later additions to the text. Indeed, if we go back to 2:9, we find a syntactical complexity that could indicate redactional work.

> Out of the ground YHWH Elohim made to grow every tree
>   that is pleasant to the sight and good for food, (2:9a)
>   ***including the tree of life in the midst of the garden,*** (2:9bα)
>   and the tree of the knowledge of good and bad. (2:9bβ)

Verse 2:9abβ (without v. 9bα) seems straightforward enough:

> Out of the ground YHWH Elohim made to grow every tree
>   that is pleasant to the sight and good for food, (2:9a)
>   ***including the tree of the knowledge of good and bad***. (2:9bβ)

God cultivates a grove of edible trees, all delightful, including in particular the "tree of knowledge." The addition of 2:9bβ takes the earlier story (see above) in one direction: toward disobedience against God by consuming the fruit of the "tree of knowledge." But with the addition of 2:9bα inserted in between—the addition of the "tree of life"—the narrative turns toward God's "fear" that humanity might become immortal and therefore divine. In other words, we have not one but two narrative directions, each providing a reason for the expulsion. As for the first direction (the "tree of knowledge"), the story could be read to conclude at 3:23 (minus v. 22b), whereas the second direction (the "tree of life") could conclude at 3:22, 24. In other words, the crime-and-punishment story that revolves around the "tree of knowledge" is layered or supplemented by a fear-and-prevention story involving the "tree of life"!

So what lies behind these two trees? It is remarkable that the "tree of knowledge of good and bad" is nowhere referenced in the Hebrew Bible outside of Gen. 2–3, whereas the "tree of life" is firmly planted in the Wisdom literature, specifically in Proverbs:

> She is a tree of life to those who lay hold of her;
>   those who hold her fast are called happy. (3:18)

> The fruit of the righteous is a tree of life,
>   but violence takes lives away. (11:30)

> Hope deferred makes the heart sick,
>   but a desire fulfilled is a tree of life. (13:12)

According to the first saying, the tree of life *is* wisdom—wisdom that includes the capacity to judge between what is good and bad. This is a tree that is fully attainable;

nothing is forbidden about it. Wisdom imparts life—prosperous, abundant, fulfilling life. Genesis 2–3, however, has a different vision. The "tree of life" is the tree of immortality, whereas the "tree of knowledge" marks the acquisition of wisdom, of discerning right from wrong and good from bad (3:6; cf. Deut. 1:39; 2 Sam. 14:17; 19:35; 1 Kgs. 3:9). In the hands of our biblical editor, the "tree of life" as a symbol of wisdom has become *two* trees, one that imparts wisdom but no life, and the other that imparts immortality but no wisdom. The final editor of Genesis has, in effect, taken an ax and split the "tree of life" (= wisdom) in two in order to demote wisdom and, at the same time, elevate the importance of obedience.[12]

But this is only a scratch on the literary surface. There are other ways to account for the text's unevenness through alternative reconstructions of redactional layers.[13] However one reconstructs layer upon literary layer, I find it helpful to think of the redactional growth of the text as cracks or fissures on a seemingly polished surface that enable the reader to peer down into the text's internal formation, its formative stages of development. Yet the cracks are narrow, too narrow to ever allow the exegete to "excavate" every layer with certainty. The redactional complexity of a text reflects its richness of meaning, of meaning in process. Among such layers one can occasionally uncover a hidden debate that may not be fully settled; otherwise only one voice or perspective would be championed. The fact that multiple layers are preserved in a text reveals something of the text's remarkable power to hold a variety of views, to host an ancient yet ongoing dialogue. Moreover, as tedious as it may seem, it is fascinating to speculate about the dialogue, building on what one can discern among the fissures. As analytical as it may seem, even redaction criticism engages the imagination, occasionally resulting in "Aha!" moments of discernment.

BIBLIOGRAPHY FOR CHAPTER 9

Carr, David. 1993. "The Politics of Textual Subversion: A Diachronic Perspective on the Garden of Eden Story." *JBL* 112, no. 4:577–95.

Di Vito, Robert A. 1999. "Tradition-Historical Criticism." In *Each Its Own Meaning: An Introduction to Biblical Criticisms and Their Application*, edited by Steven L. McKenzie and Stephen R. Haynes, 90–104. 2nd ed. Louisville, KY: Westminster John Knox Press.

Hayes, John H., and Carl R. Holladay. 2007. "Redaction Criticism." In *Biblical Exegesis: A Beginner's Handbook*, 115–26. 3rd ed. Louisville, KY: Westminster John Knox Press.

Knight, Douglas A. 2009. "Traditio-Historical Criticism: The Development of the Covenant Code." In *Method Matters: Essays on the Interpretation of the Hebrew Bible in Honor of David L. Petersen*, edited by Joel M. LeMon and Kent Harold Richards, 97–116. RBS 56. Atlanta: Society of Biblical Literature.

Mendenhall, George E. 1974. "The Shady Side of Wisdom: The Date and Purpose of Genesis 3." In *A Light unto My Path: Old Testament Studies in Honor of Jacob M. Myers*, edited by Howard N. Bream et al., 319–34. Gettysburg Theological Studies. Philadelphia: Temple University Press.

Speiser, E. A. 1963. "The Wife-Sister Motif in the Patriarchal Narratives." In *Biblical and Other Studies*, edited by Alexander Altmann, 15–28. Studies and Texts 1. Cambridge, MA: Harvard University Press.

12. For a discussion of the historical significance of these redactional layers, see chap. 12.
13. Cf., e.g., the comprehensive account attempted by Titus 2011 as another option.

Titus, Joseph P. 2011. *The Second Story of Creation (Gen 2:4–3:24): A Prologue to the Concept of Ennea-teuch?* European University Studies 23 (Theology), vol. 912. Frankfurt am Main: Peter Lang.

Van Doren, Mark. 1916. *Henry David Thoreau: A Critical Study.* Boston and New York: Houghton Mifflin.

Westermann, Claus. 1985. *Genesis 12–36: A Commentary.* Minneapolis: Augsburg Publishing House.

10

Comparative Analysis

> If you want to find out what a cat is, put it in front of a mouse.
> *James M. Robinson*[1]

In the previous chapter, we compared biblical texts for the purpose of discerning their literary, and possibly oral, development. They were texts that, for example, shared a type scene or narrative theme. In this chapter we overtly treat the issue of comparison, specifically comparison between biblical and *non*biblical texts, an endeavor that has been a staple of biblical research ever since archaeologists began discovering and deciphering texts of neighboring ancient civilizations, such as Sumerian, Egyptian, Babylonian, Assyrian, Ugaritic, Hittite, Moabite, Phoenician, and Persian. With the decipherment of Egyptian hieroglyphs and Akkadian and Ugaritic cuneiform in the nineteenth century, scholars have been identifying parallels, in both content and form, between biblical and nonbiblical texts.

Moreover, the fact that ancient Israel was historically a latecomer on the cultural scene has led some to infer that biblical scribes may have been familiar with some of the literary and religious traditions of their neighbors, from Egypt to Mesopotamia. This is strikingly clear in at least one case: a significant portion from the book of Proverbs is directly based on an Egyptian set of instructions.[2] Clearly, there were no copyright restrictions in antiquity.

To state it simply, a comparison sets side by side two or more subjects (texts in our case) in order to determine their similarities and their differences. This sounds easy enough: "compare and contrast" has always been a standard exercise in literary studies. But much of biblical scholarship has swung between extremes: an overemphasis on similarity and, conversely, an overemphasis on dissimilarity (Strawn 2009, 118–24; Hayes 2014, 15–37). Finding a middle way between "parallelomania"[3] and "parallelophobia"[4] is

---

1. Robinson 1964, 91–92. Robinson attributes the illustration to Ernst Fuchs 1954, 109.
2. Prov. 22:17–24:22 draws from the Instruction of Amenemope. See Hayes 2014, 297–319.
3. Term from Sandmel 1962.
4. Or "parallel-onoia." See Howard Eilberg-Schwartz 1990.

ever the challenge in comparative research. A fair and balanced approach is needed that on the one hand recognizes the distinctions among various cultures and their traditions and on the other hand discerns the ties that bind these cultures together, from the commercial and the cultural to the literary and the religious.

As far as biblical interpretation is concerned, the task of comparison is never an end in itself. Identifying similarities and differences among texts, biblical and otherwise, is only half the endeavor. A careful comparison needs to be generative, resulting in new exegetical insights for texts that otherwise would go unnoticed in isolation. The comparison of a biblical text and a nonbiblical text, it is hoped, can shed new light on both texts. In biblical interpretation, a comparative approach is a form of contextual study, one that takes seriously the ancient Near Eastern (ANE) context of biblical literature. William W. Hallo offers an apt metaphor:

> The goal of the contextual approach is fairly modest. It is not to find the key to every biblical phenomenon in some ancient Near Eastern precedent, but rather to silhouette the biblical text against its wider literary and cultural environment and thus to arrive at a proper assessment of the extent to which the biblical evidence reflects that environment or, on the contrary, is distinctive and innovative over against it. (1990, 3)

To "silhouette the biblical text" means seeing it against the illuminated backdrop of its ancient context, which geographically spans the entire Fertile Crescent, from Egypt to Mesopotamia. Hallo speaks of the biblical text as on the one hand "reflecting" its larger environment and on the other hand standing distinctively against it. But rarely is it either-or. While similarity and difference, identity and distinction, lie at the core of the comparative approach, they are ineluctably bound together. A case in point is Hosea's strident polemic against the worship of Baal (Ba'al) in 2:16–17 (see also vv. 8, 13). Even as the prophet polemically champions YHWH worship over and against worship of Baal, Hosea also forges a convergent relationship between the two deities. The way in which YHWH is depicted in Hosea resembles, in fact, the character of the Canaanite deity Baal, a god of rain and fertility, as in 2:21–23. This most elegant and uplifting passage details how the rain will commence, not from Baal but from YHWH, whose power of fertility was Baal's hallmark. Far from painting YHWH as Baal's opposite, the prophet describes YHWH as having absorbed Baal's essential qualities. Transformation is dramatically conveyed in the injunction in 10:12 (alt.):

> Sow for yourselves righteousness;
>   reap faithful love [hesed];
>   break up your fallow ground!
> For it is time to seek YHWH,
>   so that he may come and rain righteousness upon you.

The prophet takes up the language of fertility and gives it a profoundly moral twist.

While the craft of comparison in biblical studies is typically limited to texts of roughly proximate time and geographical location, it need not be. Indeed, the possibilities of comparing biblical literature with other literary works are endless, ranging from the Old

Testament Pseudepigrapha of later centuries in antiquity (see Charlesworth 1983–85) to modern works.[5] Each work, in principle, provides the means for reinterpreting the other, resulting in a richer, more complex understanding of both. The craft of comparison undergirds much of what biblical interpretation does on so many levels. The determination of a genre, for example, depends on the comparison of similar patterns across various texts. Translation depends on the informed comparison of two distinct languages, the source and the target. Unpacking the meaning of a metaphor relies on comparing the source and target domains, noticing both similarities and differences. A prosodic analysis involves finding similarities and differences between poetic lines. Relevant interpretation of biblical texts begins by acknowledging the differences between ancient and contemporary contexts. Comparison is done all the time in biblical interpretation.

And so it is with interpreting biblical texts in light of their ANE context, which can cover the historical range from the Early Bronze Age (ca. 3000 BCE)[6] through the Iron Age up until the beginning of the Hellenistic period (ca. 300 BCE) and the geographical range from Egypt and Greece to Anatolia and Mesopotamia. Cultural contact was the norm. A Late Bronze Age fragment of the Epic of Gilgamesh, for example, was discovered at the biblical site of Megiddo.

The framers of the biblical creation accounts inherited many venerable traditions of their cultural neighbors. Instead of creating their accounts ex nihilo, the composers of Scripture developed their traditions in dialogue with the religious traditions of the surrounding cultures, particularly those from Mesopotamia and Egypt, as well as those from their more immediate Canaanite neighbors. This should come as no surprise: geographically ancient Palestine was sandwiched between the superpowers of the ancient Near East, serving as both their land bridge and buffer zone. Before Israel ever entered the historical scene, various kingdoms in the area, both large and small, had developed their own accounts of creation, of which certain biblical writers may have been at least nominally aware. Indeed, some of these traditions could be considered part of a widespread cultural "canon" of Near Eastern antiquity.[7]

I have chosen one ancient nonbiblical account of creation for comparison with Gen. 1: the *Enuma Elish*, otherwise known as the Babylonian Epic of Creation. Other texts, of course, could be enlisted, such as the Ugaritic Baal Epic and various Egyptian creation texts, but limitations of space, alas, preclude this.

ENUMA ELISH

One of Israel's imperial oppressors was Babylon, situated beside the river Euphrates. Babylon's kings include the great Hammurabi (r. c.a. 1792–1750 BCE) of law-code fame, and Nebuchadnezzar II (r. 605–562 BCE) of imperial fame, who conquered Judah and deported much of its populace. From Babylon, beginning in the late second millennium

5. See, e.g., an insightful comparison of Job with the *Wizard of Oz* in Linafelt 2006.
6. Specifically, the Protodynastic period in Egypt, beginning in 3150 BCE, and the Early Dynastic period of Sumer in Mesopotamia, beginning in 2900 BCE.
7. See, e.g., the collection of extrabiblical texts in Hallo and Younger 2003a.

under the reign of Nebuchadnezzar I (r. ca. 1125–1104 BCE), comes an epic narrative of cosmic intrigue that includes a story of creation. Titled *Enuma Elish* for its first two words (when on high), this Akkadian epic was recited publicly, and perhaps dramatically, during the New Year's Festival in April as part of a grand ritual designed to maintain its hegemony throughout the land. The origin of this practice can plausibly be traced to the recovery of the statue of Marduk, Babylon's patron deity, from Elam in the south, an appropriate occasion for Nebuchadnezzar to proclaim Marduk's supremacy over the gods. The epic was likely written in honor of the occasion and served as a foundation story for the exaltation not only of Marduk but also of the Babylonian king, renewing his mandate to rule the country and thus to assert Babylon's dominion over Mesopotamia and beyond. As performed and witnessed annually by a host of governmental officials, the story did much more than entertain. Its purpose was to maintain loyalty throughout the vast extent of the burgeoning empire. The *Enuma Elish*, in short, presents an eminently imperial cosmogony.[8]

To compare the *Enuma Elish* with Gen. 1, one must of course read both. Rather than recounting the entire plot, I urge the reader to enjoy one of the accessible translations of the Babylonian Epic of Creation in modern English. Nothing can compare (!) to reading an ancient account firsthand, albeit in translation. I recommend Dalley 1989b or Lambert 2013, 45–133.[9] The following are some brief remarks about the epic before making comparative observations with Gen. 1.

The *Enuma Elish* opens with the murky emergence of primordial powers, setting the stage for a cosmic *War and Peace*, whose characters proliferate from one episode to the next. The epic begins not as a cosmogony (i.e., creation of the cosmos) but as a theogony, an account of divine origins.

> When on high neither the heavens had been named,
> nor the earth below pronounced by name,
> There was primordial Apsu, their progenitor,
> and creator Tiamat, who bore them all.
> Because their waters were intermingling,
> no pasture-land was yet formed, no marshes yet found.
> When not one of the gods had yet appeared,
> no names yet received, no destinies decreed,
> the gods were created therein.[10]

Pervading this state of deficiency are two primordial powers. They bear names but remain inchoate at this point; they are more domains of potency than divine personae: Apsu, the primordial power of freshwater, and Tiamat, the elemental power of saltwater. Together they form a primordial soup from which all creation is ultimately derived. But first the gods are born.

---

8. The "canonical" status of the *Enuma Elish* is demonstrated in an Assyrian version of the Babylonian epic in which the patron deity Aššur replaces Marduk as the narrative's protagonist.

9. See also Foster 2003, which offers only a section. For the latest critical edition and translation (in French), see Talon 2005, 79–108.

10. AT. The remaining translations are from Dalley 1989a unless otherwise noted.

The first half of the epic is structured as a series of six generations. Emerging successively are two pairs of deities, representing the deposits of silt from the rivers (Laḫmu and Laḫamu) and the circular horizons of the heavens and the earth (Anshar and Kishar). Next is the sky-god Anu, who in turn sires one of the central characters of the plot, the god of wisdom, Ea (or Nudimmud), who "was superior to his forefathers" (I.17). Later in the narrative, Ea fathers Marduk, who becomes the hero of the epic. As generation follows generation, divine power develops in ever greater concentration: Ea is said to have "no rivals" (I.20), and on Marduk, his son, is conferred unsurpassable strength, "mighty from the beginning" (I.88).

To make a long story short, conflict arises between the old generation and the new generation, led by Marduk. Eventually it comes down to a cosmic battle between Tiamat and Marduk. Marduk's victory solidifies his ascendancy as the victorious king over all the gods. Conflict, war, and victory all prepare for the next dramatic scene: creation. After victory, a brilliant idea comes to Marduk.

> The Lord rested, and inspected her corpse.
> He divided the monstrous shape and created marvels (from it);
> he sliced her in half like a fish for drying:
> Half of her he put up to roof the sky;
> Drew a bolt across and made a guard hold it.
> Her waters he arranged so that they could not escape. (IV.135–40)

In addition to fashioning the universe from Tiamat's body, Marduk establishes his own estate, Esharra, a great shrine constructed in the "image of Apsu," and sanctuaries for other gods. Marduk fixes the constellations, including the planets and the moon, and with them the divisions of the calendar year (V.1–4). The moon comes next, named Nannar, who is entrusted with the night (V.13–21). More down to earth, Marduk pierces Tiamat's eyes to form the sources of the Euphrates and the Tigris Rivers. Her tail is bent up into the sky to fashion the Milky Way, and her thigh is used to support the sky. As for the rebel leader Qingu, Tiamat's lover, Marduk divests him of the "Tablet of Destinies." With conquering and creation complete, Marduk is publicly acclaimed king. He is given the name Lugaldimmerankia: "King of the gods of heaven and earth" (V.112). Marduk then declares his intention to establish his own house in front of Esharra. This is "Babylon," the "home of the great gods," "the center of religion" (V.129).

But there is one more matter. Marduk consults Ea, his father, to create humankind. Such a plan is not without cause: imposed upon this earthly creature will be the "work of the gods," thus making rest for the gods possible. Ea suggests that Qingu's blood provide the raw material for humankind's creation. And so it is. Grateful, the gods offer to make Marduk the sanctuary of his dreams, their resting place, Babylon. In two years' time they build a magnificent ziggurat for the Apsu, complete with individual shrines for themselves. The order of the universe has found its completion. In the final act of obeisance, the gods swear an oath of absolute fealty to Marduk. The epic concludes with the conferral of fifty throne names, drawn from the fifty gods in attendance, highlighting different aspects of Marduk's rule over heaven and earth.

In this epic, creation properly begins when conflict ends. Creation is the corollary of conquest. A carcass is required for cosmic creation, and bloodshed is deemed necessary for human creation. Apsu and Tiamat, the elemental powers of creation, are divested of their personae, including their divinity. Construction follows destruction. Creation, moreover, is the exercise of imperial power. Marduk's exaltation and the world's creation are bound together. The victor's prowess on the battlefield is matched by his ingenuity on the construction site. Ingenuity and generosity: the creation of humankind in particular is testimony to Marduk's munificence, which grants freedom to the gods. Their freedom from servitude, however, is humanity's burden. Humankind, made in the image of gore, from the blood of a rebel god, is the quintessential servant of the gods.

GENESIS 1 IN COMPARISON

With the *Enuma Elish* in mind, biblical scholar S. R. Driver observed that "we have in the first chapter of Genesis the Hebrew version of an originally Babylonian legend" (Driver 1907, 31). I suspect, however, that the first-time reader of the Babylonian account might have a different impression. Genesis 1 seems to distinguish itself quite well in both style and content from the *Enuma Elish*. Commonalities seem few and far between. Compared to the Babylonian account, Gen. 1 reads like a dispassionate treatise that studiously avoids the fray of epic conflict.

Style, thus, is a major category for comparison. The biblical text's repetitive structure suggests ancient liturgical usage (Weinfeld 1981). Paradoxically, it might seem, the *Enuma Elish* also has its performative cultic roots: its reading was a prominent feature of the Babylonian *Akitu* Festival, a celebration of the new "equinox year" marking the restoration of the cosmos (see Sommer 2000). Along with its purifying rituals, this festival also dramatized Marduk's rise to prominence in the Babylonian pantheon (Hayes 2014, 155; Bidmead 2002). Hence, both the biblical and Babylonian accounts share a common cultic setting.

One fruitful way of comparing these two magisterial accounts is to have them "talk" to each other about certain issues or themes—"talking points," if you will. I suggest the following: (1) depiction of the beginning, (2) divine character, (3) conflict and chaos, (4) manner of creation, (5) humanity's creation and role, and (6) the theme of rest. There are, of course, other points of comparison to be explored. This is simply a start that, I hope, is suggestive enough to invite the reader to continue exploring.

In the Beginning

The *Enuma Elish* starts off as a theogony: the creation of the gods, up to six generations worth. Nothing of the sort is found in Gen. 1, which begins as a cosmogony. The Babylonian account begins with a list of negatives or lacks: no heavens ("not named") and no earth, as well as no "gods" and "destinies" (I.7–8). Genesis 1:1 begins positively: "When God began to create the heavens and the earth . . ."

Nevertheless, both accounts share a common setting for the beginning of creation: the setting of water. Representing ocean and freshwater, Tiamat and Apsu commingle. In Gen. 1, water is part of the precreative condition before light is created. Curiously, nothing is said about the creation of light in the *Enuma Elish* until the stars, the moon (Nannar), and the sun (Shamash) are referenced in V.1–20 (cf. Gen. 1:14–18). Marking the beginning of creation with water in the Babylonian Creation Epic might reflect the pervasive presence of water in Babylon, a city built on both sides of the Euphrates. Why Genesis begins with water is less clear, at least geopolitically (cf. Gen. 2:4b), except that water may be the image of choice to designate formlessness. Water is the quintessential amorphous substance, which becomes divided and contained in Days 2 and 3. In the *Enuma Elish* the primordial waters are slain, with Tiamat dismembered for the sake of creation.

Divine Character

In the *Enuma Elish*, the birth of the gods comes first, before creation. With each generation, six in total, there is an increase in divine strength to the point that violent conflict becomes inevitable. Ultimately Marduk is proclaimed king of the universe (e.g., IV.14), but it is by no means automatic. He earns it by vanquishing chaos. His acclamation as king brackets both his conquest and his creation (see IV.28 and V.79). Creation is a part of Marduk's ascendancy.

In Gen. 1, God's sovereignty is assumed from the outset. "In the beginning" there was God without rival, who creates by royal decree and deed. Indeed, the *Enuma Elish* and Gen. 1 share in common a royal figuration of the divine protagonist. To be sure, God does enter into battle and slay rebellious opponents elsewhere in biblical narrative, but the creative rhythm of word and deed in Gen. 1 is what gives God a royal character. "Let there be light," "Let the waters produce," "Let the earth sprout forth": all of the divine commands reflect God's sovereignty in and over the creative process, from beginning to end. In comparison to the *Enuma Elish*, divine sovereignty in Genesis is set in sharp relief, a sovereignty, however, that does not emerge from the fray of conflict but simply exists from the beginning.

The relationship between command and fulfillment also features significantly in the *Enuma Elish*, as one would expect. The lesser gods acknowledge Marduk's sovereign rise to power by their submission: "Whatever you command, we will do!" (V.146). Indeed, Marduk's test of his royal authority revolves around the annihilation and re-creation of a constellation, all by divine command (IV.19–26). With the test completed, unanimous royal acclamation ensues: "Marduk is the king!" (V.28). Although God's royal bearing in Genesis might seem comparatively understated, the prominence of divine command and its unimpeded fulfillment throughout the account underlines it.

Conflict and Chaos

Conflict is written all over the *Enuma Elish* but seems strikingly absent in Gen. 1. This may well be the greatest contrast between the two accounts. With Ea murdering Apsu in his sleep, Marduk killing Tiamat on the battlefield, and Qingu slain for his rebellion, the Babylonian account drips with blood, all to pave the way for Marduk's rise to absolute sovereignty. Indeed, the final line sums it up: ". . . [Marduk], who defeated Tiamat and took the kingship" (VII.162).

In Gen. 1, there is no kingship for God to seize and, hence, no necessity to engage in mortal combat. The Priestly creation account lacks any hint of conflict that would necessitate violent engagement on the part of God. No subjugation is required to make progress from "chaos" to cosmos, to achieve a well-ordered universe. I put "chaos" in quotation marks because what is described in Gen. 1:2 (*tĕhôm* and *tōhû wābōhû*) presents no threat to God. "Deep" (*tĕhôm*) and the "waters" (*mayim*) lack the combative chaos found in the *Enuma Elish*, and for that matter in Ps. 74:12–17. The same goes for the "great sea monsters" (*tannînim*) in 1:21. Neither Tiamat nor Leviathan is lurking to rise up and wage battle. Rather, the curtain in Gen. 1 rises to reveal a benign primordial soup, benign, that is, to God. Although there may be nothing salutary about impenetrable darkness (*ḥōšek*), nothing about it is deemed inimical to God.

One "parallel" often noted between the *Enuma Elish* and Gen. 1 is the dismemberment of Tiamat's body and the act of separating the "waters above" from the "waters below" in Genesis. Compare the following:

> [Marduk] divided the monstrous shape and created marvels (from it).
> He sliced her in half like a fish for drying:
> Half of her he put up to roof the sky,
> Drew a bolt across and made a guard hold it.
> Her waters he arranged so that they could not escape. (*Enuma Elish* IV.136–140)

> Then God said, "Let there be a firmament amid the waters to be a divider between the waters." So God made the firmament and divided the waters below the firmament from the waters above the firmament. And it was so. (Gen. 1:6–7 AT)

While the language of separation is striking, the contrast in imagery is stark: on the one hand a corpse, albeit a watery one, and on the other hand a vast expanse of water. In Genesis notice also that God is not directly involved in the act of separation but rather commands into being a "firmament" or divider to do the work of separation. God does not wield a sword. Division or separation is, to be sure, essential in the process of creation for both accounts, yet God's division of the waters does not constitute a dismemberment of conquered chaos but a separation that introduces structure or form amid formlessness.

It has been suggested that the term *tĕhôm* (Deep) is etymologically related to *Tiamat* (Akkadian *ti-amat*) but if it is, it is only indirect (see Tsumura 2005, 36–41). Of note is that the word *tĕhôm* in Gen. 1:2 lacks an article, which suggests that it is a proper name: "the face of Deep/Tehom." Although mythically profiled, any sense of personification is lacking in Gen. 1; indeed, *tĕhôm* is poetically paralleled with "the face of the waters" at the end of the verse. Is *tĕhôm/Tehom* a vestige of Tiamat and her personified role as watery chaos? Perhaps. Nevertheless, no hint of conflict between God and *Tehom* is referenced in Gen. 1. Quite the contrary: God's breath "hovering" over the dark waters, like a mother eagle over her nestlings (Deut. 32:11), could suggest a relationship of intimacy as opposed to enmity. At the very least, the imagery establishes a positive relationship with the deep, as borne out by the waters' constructive role demonstrated later in creation.

A major point of distinction between the two accounts is the role of conflict in the context of creation. In the *Enuma Elish*, conquest is a prerequisite for creation: Marduk must conquer to create; creation requires a corpse. Less graphically, cosmos comes from chaos. But put that way, Gen. 1 finds at least an abstract affinity with the violent epic account: cosmos comes from "mishmash" (*tōhû wābōhû*). Familiarity with the *Enuma Elish* heightens the reader's appreciation of the fact that the Genesis account begins not with nothing (*nihil*) but with a formless, hence watery "chaos" (1:2).

To say, however, that conflict plays no role in Gen. 1 is not quite accurate. Humankind is given the arduous task of "subduing" the earth (1:28). It appears that humankind, rather than God, faces resistance within creation that necessitates force. God creates a creation that requires coercion, but not on God's part, in order to make it viable for human flourishing. Laid out schematically, Genesis reverses the ordering of creation: whereas the *Enuma Elish* places conflict prior to creation, necessitating its defeat for the sake of cosmos-making, Gen. 1 places "conflict" *after* creation, on the sixth day, giving humanity the task of figuring it out.

Manner of Creation

If we take the element of conflict out of the picture, we find a number of contact points between the *Enuma Elish* and Gen. 1. Take the starry heavens, for example, a part of the cosmos that is significantly featured in both narratives. Each of these accounts invests the celestial spheres with the role of organizing the calendar. Marduk sets up "three stars each for the twelve months" (V.4). The planet Jupiter (Neberu) is given the task to "mark out their courses" (V.6). Nannar, the moon, is "entrusted" with the night (V.12). Having created it, Marduk addresses the moon to determine the beginning of every month (V.15–20). Thus the year is "organized" astronomically.

Similarly, Gen. 1 finds a regulatory function for the stars regarding calendrical matters in 1:14–15. The sun and the moon, in particular, have their respective functions.

> So God made the two great lights, the greater light to rule the day and the lesser light to rule the night, as well as the stars. And God set them in the heavenly firmament to illumine the earth, to rule the day and the night, and to divide between the light and the darkness. And God saw that it was good. (1:16–18 AT)

Marduk, too, designates moon and sun (Nannar and Shamash) according to their intertwined roles. There is, however, one major difference. The reader may find it strange that the "two great lights" in Gen. 1 are not named. Instead, they are described with the circumlocutions "greater light" and "lesser light." Would it not have been appropriate for God to have "called the greater light Sun [*šemeš*] and the lesser light Moon [*yārēaḥ*]" (cf. Gen. 1:5, 8, 10)? Perhaps naming these cosmic entities outright would have cast them as (semi-)deities. Shamash in Mesopotamian lore, for example, is the god of justice as well as of omens. Is the vague language part of a deliberate program of demythologization in Genesis? Some interpreters claim that Gen. 1 constitutes a polemic against polytheism.

Others, myself included, discern here a more irenic perspective in the Genesis account, which may have its roots more in Babylonian astronomy than in mythology. In any case, interpreting Gen. 1 within its ancient Near Eastern context poses such questions to ponder.

Place and Role of Humanity

Marduk implements a plan to create humanity in order to provide rest for the gods. The manner by which humanity is fashioned requires the slaying of Qingu, Tiamat's substitute spouse and military ringleader. His punishment as an instigator in the war is death. Ea creates humankind from Qingu's severed blood vessels. Divine liberation is brought about by human bondage.

The language of human service to God is nowhere developed in Gen. 1. Instead, its opposite is declared: "Then God said, 'Let us make humankind in our image, according to our likeness; and let them have dominion . . .'" (1:26). "Dominion" instead of servitude gives humanity a royal stature that is absent in the *Enuma Elish*. Relatedly, the Genesis account describes humanity (*ʾādām*) created "in the image of God" (vv. 26–27), while in the *Enuma Elish* humanity is created from the blood of a god. Both accounts acknowledge humanity's partially divine origin, but the latter is more problematic. It is Qingu's punishment, his punishment for rebellion, that provides the occasion for humanity's creation, creation from a criminal. Being created in God's image, on the other hand, carries no punitive force but rather indicates an iconic relation to the divine. The Hebrew term for "image" (*ṣelem*) is elsewhere used for idols, such as the cult statues of other deities.[11] By virtue of their creation by God in God's "image," human beings take on the status of near divinity; they bear a distinctly theophanic presence in creation.

Although this is not evident in the *Enuma Elish*, scholars have long noticed that the language of divine "image" is frequently applied to the king in Mesopotamia as well as in Egypt. The pharaoh, for example, is spoken of as the image of God or the gods, so also the king in Mesopotamia (Strawn 2009, 130–32).[12] Neo-Assyrian kings frequently erected images (Akkadian *ṣalmu/ṣalmāni*) of themselves in conquered territories to celebrate their victories. Here the Priestly author does something innovative: the image of God typically associated with the conquering king is applied to all humankind. Some have called this a "democratizing" move on the part of the Priestly narrator. Better perhaps is "universalizing": the whole of humankind bears the image, the image of God. All human beings rightfully exercise "dominion" over the world for their welfare (1:28). Humankind is thus "human*king*." The account of humanity's creation in Gen. 1 involves, thus, the *humanization* of royal status and, in turn, the *universalization* of humanity's "dominion."

---

11. E.g., Num. 33:52; 2 Kgs. 11:18; 2 Chr. 23:17; Ezek. 7:20; Amos 5:26. This is not the only nuance of "image." Genesis 5:3 uses the word to highlight the genetic relationship between Adam and his son: "When Adam had lived one hundred thirty years, he became the father of a son in his likeness [*bidmûtô*], according to his image [*kĕṣalmô*], and named him Seth."

12. For more detailed discussion, see Machinist 2006; Middleton 2005, 99–111, 235–69.

Rest

Much of the plot in the *Enuma Elish* turns on the issue of rest, or the lack of it. Resolution of the epic narrative, in fact, involves the restoration of rest. Apsu cannot rest because of the turmoil of the young deities "dancing" too much, roiling Tiamat. The issue is raised once again with Marduk's play with the four fearful winds, with the gods finding "no rest" (I.110). Lack of rest is deemed a burden, an "immovable yoke," a bondage no less even within the divine realm (cf. I.122). Loss of sleep ignites the conflict. Related to the lack of rest, moreover, is the burden of unrelenting toil, which inspires Marduk to create humankind so that the gods may find freedom and rest (VI.25, 33).[13] Finally, Marduk's greatest creation is the establishment of a permanent "resting place" for the gods: Babylon (VI.52, 57). In the giving of Marduk's second name (Marukka), Marduk is known for putting "the Anunnaki at ease" and "the Igigi at rest" (VI.134). Rest is realized in the creation of a city, the "Home of the Great Gods" (V.129).

Rest likewise plays a defining role in the Genesis narrative, but it is not unveiled until the end, in the last two verses of the account (2:2–3). The literal sense of "rest" in this passage is "cease" (*šbt*), formally marking the completion of creation. Nevertheless, cessation is connected to rest elsewhere in the Priestly tradition, as in the Decalogue commandment concerning the Sabbath:

> For in six days YHWH made heaven and earth, the sea, and all therein, but rested [*wayyānaḥ*] on the seventh day; therefore, YHWH blessed the sabbath day and consecrated it. (Exod. 20:11 AT)

In the Sabbath commandment, God does indeed "rest" (verb *nwḥ*) on the seventh day to provide a paradigm for human living. Compare Exod. 31:17 (AT):

> [The sabbath] is a sign forever between me and the people of Israel that in six days YHWH made heaven and earth, and on the seventh day he ceased [*šābat*] and was refreshed [*wayyināpaš*].

Here God's completion of work in creation is coupled with God being "refreshed" or renewed (*npš*, related to the noun *nepeš*, which frequently designates the vitality of self-hood) on the seventh day. Given that connection, "rest" marks the conclusion of the work of creation. It is this "act" that sets this day apart from all other days: a day of cessation, of rest and refreshment, a distinctly holy day. Nothing is said about human toiling so that God can rest. No, God simply "rests" because creation is now complete. So also human beings after their six days of work. Nothing is said in the *Enuma Elish* of humanity receiving such a gift.

Both the *Enuma Elish* and Gen. 1:1–2:3 highlight the critical importance of rest, the lack of which is considered a form of bondage. But the issue is resolved in very different ways. The Babylonian epic is concerned exclusively with rest for the gods. While Gen. 1 alludes to God's "rest" (through the cessation of work), its implications are spelled out

---

13. Similarly, in the Atrahasis Epic, a Babylonian account of the flood (see 1.5.11–12).

later with regard to human rest. How is rest achieved? In part by conquest in the *Enuma Elish*, through the elimination of rivals. But there is a positive, constructive side as well. The building of Babylon marks the culminating achievement of rest for the gods—the construction of a special holy place, a temple no less, that provides a restful "home" for the gods.

In contrast, Gen. 1 does not identify any special *place* for God's rest. Rather, it is a special *time*, one that is deemed holy. The seventh day is the day that God "indwells," as it were, in rest. Whereas the focus in the *Enuma Elish* is on a city, that of Gen. 1 is on a particular day. When it comes to the theme of rest, temple and time—more specifically, city and Sabbath—are the respective foci of these two creation traditions, dialogically linked yet so very different.

Comparative work of biblical texts is ongoing as new conversation partners are brought into dialogue. Comparison with the Babylonian *Enuma Elish* is only one example. The reader is invited to compare Gen. 1 with the Egyptian accounts of creation and the Ugaritic Baal Epic.[14] What are the significant differences and similarities among these ancient texts, particularly with respect to Gen. 1? How might Gen. 1 serve as a response to these nonbiblical accounts?

ADAM AND ADAPA

Much can be done comparatively with Gen. 2–3 as well. However, in this section, I offer a more narrow focus. Comparative work is often conducted in order to answer a particular question or to resolve a particular issue in the biblical text. One vexing issue in the garden story that has plagued interpreters, both ancient and modern, is whether the man and woman in the narrative were created immortal. Therein lies an ambiguity in the garden: the ʾādām is created from the "dust of the ground" (2:7). Furthermore, bone and flesh, which both the man and woman share (2:23), are not the stuff of immortality. On the other hand, whereas the tree of knowledge is prohibited, nothing is said explicitly about prohibiting the fruit of the tree of life (2:9, 16–17) until the very end (3:22, 24). So was the latter tree permitted while the couple remained in the garden?

The prohibition given by God regarding the tree of knowledge includes a threat of punishment that seems to imply immediate execution: "in the day that you eat of it you will surely die" [*môt tāmût*; 2:17 AT]). But they do not. Instead, they are punished, and the final punishment, reserved for the ʾādām (3:17–19), describes the inevitability of death: "You are dust, and to dust you shall return" (v. 19). Finally, God admits that the ʾādām has become semidivine ("like one of us," v. 22a) and therefore resolves to banish him from the garden in order to prevent him from partaking from the "tree of life" and consequently "live forever" (3:22b). So were the man and the woman created immortal, which they lost in their act of disobedience? Or were they created mortal and through their disobedience lost the *opportunity* to become immortal, as 3:22 implies? Such a quandary has generated a host of arguments for both sides of the issue.

14. For the Egyptian accounts, I recommend Allen 2003. For the Baal Epic, see Smith 1997 or Coogan and Smith 2012, 110–53.

One ancient Babylonian tale may be of help: the story of Adapa and the South Wind, a late second-millennium Mesopotamian myth found in four extant fragments from Tell-el Amarna in Egypt and in Nineveh, specifically from the library of the Assyrian king Ashurbanipal (668–627 BCE). Adapa, a priest of Eridu, was a man made "perfect in wisdom." An opening line of the story summarizes both the beginning and ultimate fate of Adapa: "To him [Ea] granted wisdom, eternal life he did not grant him" (A.4).[15] This sage served Ea's temple in Eridu by providing food and drink, which included catching the daily allotment of fish. On one outing, the south wind capsized his boat, to which Adapa responds with a curse, thereby "fracturing the wing" of the south wind (B.1–5). The result is a drought for seven days. Anu, the sky god, queries his messenger as to why the south wind has not blown, who points the finger at "Adapa, son of Ea" (B.12). Anu summons Adapa. Meanwhile, the wise god Ea informs Adapa that he will be summoned to heaven to give account of himself. He advises him, among other things, to adorn mourning attire and not to accept any offer of food and drink from Anu, lest he die. But if he is offered oil and a garment, he can gladly accept them. Adapa ascends to heaven and is eventually received by Anu, who asks, "Come now, Adapa, why did you fracture the wing of the south wind?" (B.59–60). Adapa fully confesses just as it happened: "In my fury, I cursed the wind" (B.67). Upon the recommendation of two vegetation gods (Tammuz and Gizzida), Anu is satisfied and offers Adapa the "food of life," which Adapa declines, and the same for the "waters of life." However, Adapa gladly accepts a garment and oil.

> Anu stared and burst out laughing at him,
> "Come now, Adapa, why did you not eat or drink?
> Won't you live? Are not people to be immortal?" (B.81–83)

Adapa responds: "Ea my lord told me, 'you must not eat, you must not drink.'" Anu responds, "Let them take him and return him to his earth" (B.85; D.5–7).

The Adapa myth is a tale of lost opportunity. This human, and thus mortal, sage is endowed with wisdom, but due to Ea's ruse, he loses the chance to gain immortality. Ea's intentions are left unstated in the narrative, but they can easily be inferred.[16] Adapa, to be sure, is no Adam: Adapa is not the primal human being, and his function is to take care of a sanctuary, not a primeval garden. Their respective stories do not share much in common, except for, possibly, the issue of immortality. And it is on this issue that the similarity is striking, particularly in light of Gen. 3:22, which provides the rationale for the expulsion: to prevent the *ʾādām* from gaining immortality.

Both the *ʾādām* and Adapa stories, one scholar concludes, refer to the "early human forfeiture of the *possibility* of immortality" (Mettinger 2007, 107, emphasis added). In both stories immortality remained merely a potential, a possible outcome, but never to be realized. While such a claim begs the question, it does rather forcefully pose the probability that the primal couple never had immortality to begin with, contrary to traditional Christian interpretation. The *ʾādām* was created from the ground, so also the animals, all created mortal.

15. Translation is from Foster 1996, 430–34.

16. It is likely that Ea deceived Adapa to prevent him from being inducted into the divine assembly and taken into Anu's service, thereby losing his own priest (Mettinger 2007, 105–6).

As for the "tree of life," mentioned only once at the beginning (2:9), it remains in the background until the narrative's very end (3:22, 24), displaced by the tree of knowledge throughout the story. Within the logic of the narrative, one could imagine that the couple ate from the tree of life along with all the other trees as a matter of course, but one would expect the narrator to have made mention of this, and more importantly, such a possibility would have obviated God's resolution to bar the ʾādām from the garden at the end (3:22).

As Adapa refused the food (and water) of life, so Adam forfeited the possibility of eating the fruit of the tree of life because of his disobedience. The parallel with Adapa strengthens such an interpretation. Indeed, since Adapa was unaware of the gift of life contained in the food and water that Anu offered him, perhaps the primal couple was unaware of the significance of the fruit of the "tree of life" and never partook. But is the parallel decisive? Here again, the differences between the two stories come to the fore, while certain narrative points in the garden narrative require some explaining.[17] Let the reader decide.

CONCLUSION

Parallels should be taken with a grain of salt and a dose of sugar, that is, with a degree of openness and wariness (but never weariness). If the similarities outweigh the differences, then perhaps you've discovered a true parallel. But regardless, increasing your familiarity with the rich literature of the ancient Near East, as vast as it is, is hardly a bad thing in exegetical study. At least it provides the opportunity for broadening and deepening the ancient dialogue with a variety of partners, regardless of whether the actual authors and tradents of the Hebrew Scriptures did so directly. I doubt, for example, that the Priestly author of Genesis had a copy of the *Enuma Elish* before him or that the Yahwist knew the Myth of Adapa by heart.

Nevertheless, such extrabiblical works are important conversation partners to engage with as one continues to interpret the biblical texts with greater depth and awareness of ancient issues, genres, and conventions. Indeed, the ancient conversation partners are numerous. For all its distinctiveness, theologically and otherwise, the Hebrew Bible is no isolated piece of literature; it remains a deeply connected corpus, linked indelibly to its larger ancient context. Indeed, the Bible *is* ancient Near Eastern literature, which includes literature that dramatizes Marduk's rise to power, witnesses to Baal's vanquishing of chaos, and recounts the creative acts of Ptah. Biblical traditions did not develop in a vacuum. They are both a product of their rich environment and a response to it.

---

17. As for the punishment given in Gen. 3:19, one could argue that death is simply assumed rather than instituted. The "return" to the ground is the result of being fashioned *from* the ground. The punishment itself is weighted toward the painful reality of agricultural labor (3:17–18), much like the woman's increase of labor pains (v. 16), not toward the reality of death. Indeed, the primary sense behind the reference to death as a "return" is that the ʾādām will die outside the garden, rather than within it, for the ʾādām was in fact created outside the garden (2:7a, 8). Adam's punishment, thus, is not a death penalty but an expulsion penalty. See Wright 1996.

BIBLIOGRAPHY FOR CHAPTER 10

Allen, James P. 2003. "Canonical Compositions (Egyptian)" (1.1–17). In Hallo and Younger 2003a, 5–27.

Bidmead, Julye. 2002. *The Akitu Festival: Religious Continuity and Royal Legitimation in Mesopotamia.* Piscataway, NJ: Gorgias Press.

Charlesworth, James H., ed. 1983–85. *The Old Testament Pseudepigrapha.* 2 vols. Garden City, NY: Doubleday. (See also Delamarter 2003.)

Coogan, Michael D., and Mark S. Smith. 2012. *Stories from Ancient Canaan.* 2nd ed. Louisville, KY: Westminster John Knox Press.

Dalley, Stephanie, ed. and trans. 1989a. "Atrahasis." In *Myths from Mesopotamia: Creation, the Flood, Gilgamesh and Others,* 9–38. Oxford World's Classics. Oxford: Oxford University Press.

———. 1989b. "The Epic of Creation." In *Myths from Mesopotamia: Creation, the Flood, Gilgamesh and Others,* 228–77. Oxford World's Classics. Oxford: Oxford University Press.

Delamarter, Steve. 2003. *A Scriptural Index to Charlesworth's "The Old Testament Pseudepigrapha."* Sheffield: Sheffield Academic Press.

Driver, S. R. 1907. *The Book of Genesis with Introduction and Notes.* 6th ed. London: Methuen & Co.

Eilberg-Schwartz, Howard. 1990. "Beyond Parallel-anoia: Comparative Inquiry and Cultural Interpretation." In *The Savage in Judaism: An Anthropology of Israelite Religion and Ancient Judaism,* 87–102. Bloomington: Indiana University Press.

Foster, Benjamin R. 1996. *Before the Muses: An Anthology of Akkadian Literature.* Vol. 1. *Archaic, Classical, Mature.* 2nd ed. Bethesda: CDL Press.

———. 2003. "Epic of Creation (1.111)." In Hallo and Younger 2003a, 391–402.

Fuchs, Ernst. 1954. *Hermeneutik.* Bad Cannstatt: R. Mullerschön Verlag.

Garr, W. Randall. 2000. "'Image' and 'Likeness' in the Inscription from Tell Fakhariyeh." *IEJ* 50:231–34.

Hallo, William W. 1990. "Compare and Contrast: The Contextual Approach to Biblical Literature." In *The Bible in the Light of Cuneiform Literature,* edited by William W. Hallo et al., 1–30. Scripture in Context 3. Ancient Near Eastern Texts and Studies 9. Lewiston, NY: Edwin Mellen.

Hallo, William W., and K. Lawson Younger, Jr., eds. 2003a. *The Context of Scripture.* Vol. 1, *Canonical Compositions from the Biblical World.* Leiden: Brill.

Hayes, Christopher B. 2014. *Hidden Riches: A Sourcebook for the Comparative Study of the Hebrew Bible and Ancient Near East.* Louisville, KY: Westminster John Knox Press.

Lambert, W. G. 2013. *Babylonian Creation Myths.* Mesopotamian Civilizations 16. Winona Lake, IN: Eisenbrauns.

Linafelt, Tod. 2006. "The Wizard of Uz: Job, Dorothy, and the Limits of the Sublime." *Biblical Interpretation* 14, nos. 1–2:94–109.

Machinist, Peter. 2006. "Kingship and Divinity in Imperial Assyria." In *Text, Artifact, and Image: Revealing Ancient Israelite Religion,* edited by Gary Beckman and Theodore J. Lewis, 152–88. BJS 346. Providence, RI: Brown University Press.

Mettinger, Tryggve N. D. 2007. *The Eden Narrative: A Literary and Religio-Historical Study of Genesis 2–3.* Winona Lake, IN: Eisenbrauns.

Middleton, J. Richard. 2005. *The Liberating Image: The* imago Dei *in Genesis 1.* Grand Rapids: Brazos Press.

Robinson, James M. 1964. "Interpretation of Scripture in Biblical Studies Today." In *Ecumenical Dialogue at Harvard: The Roman Catholic–Protestant Colloquium,* edited by Samuel H. Miller and G. Ernest Wright, 91–109. Cambridge, MA: The Belknap Press of Harvard University Press.

Sandmel, Samuel. 1962. "Parallelomania." *JBL* 81, no. 1:1–13.

Smith, Mark S. 1997. "Baʿal Epic." In *Ugaritic Narrative Poetry,* edited by Simon B. Parker, 81–180. SBLWAW 9. Atlanta: Scholars Press.

Sommer, Benjamin D. 2000. "The Babylonian Akitu Festival: Rectifying the King or Renewing the Cosmos?" *JANES* 27:81–95.

Strawn, Brent A. 2009. "Comparative Approaches: History, Theory, and the Image of God." In *Method Matters: Essays on the Interpretation of the Hebrew Bible in Honor of David L. Petersen*, edited by Joel M. LeMon and Kent Harold Richards, 117–42. RBS 56. Atlanta: Society of Biblical Literature.

Talmon, Shemaryahu. 1978. "The 'Comparative' Method in Biblical Interpretation: Principles and Problems." In *Congress Volume: Göttingen, 1977*, 320–56. VTSup 29. Leiden: Brill.

Talon, Philippe. 2005. *Enūma Eliš: The Standard Babylonian Creation Myth*. SAACT 4. Helsinki: University of Helsinki: The Neo-Assyrian Text Corpus Project.

Tsumura, David. 2005. *Creation and Destruction: A Reappraisal of the* Chaoskampf *Theory in the Old Testament*. Winona Lake, IN: Eisenbrauns.

Walton, John H. 2011. *Genesis 1 as Ancient Cosmology*. Winona Lake, IN: Eisenbrauns.

Weinfeld, Moshe. 1981. "Sabbath, Temple and the Enthronement of the Lord—The Problem of *Sitz im Leben* of Genesis 1:1–2:3." In *Mélanges bibliques et orientaux en l'honneur de M. Henri Cazelles*, edited by A. Caquot and M. Delcor, 501–12. AOAT 212. Kevelaer: Butzon & Bercker; Neukirchen-Vluyn: Neukirchener Verlag, 1981.

Wright, David P. 1996. "Holiness, Sex, and Death in the Garden of Eden." *Biblica* 77:305–29.

Comparative References and Guides

Arnold, Bill T., and Brent A. Strawn, eds. 2016. *The World around the Old Testament: The People and Places of the Ancient Near East*. Grand Rapids: Baker Academic.

Arnold, Bill T., and Bryan E. Beyer. 2002. *Readings from the Ancient Near East: Primary Sources for Old Testament Study*. Grand Rapids: Baker Academic.

Coogan, Michael D. 2012. *A Reader of Ancient Near Eastern Texts*. Sources for the Study of the Old Testament. Oxford: Oxford University Press.

Coogan, Michael D., and Mark S. Smith. 2012. *Stories from Ancient Canaan*. 2nd ed. Louisville, KY: Westminster John Knox Press.

Dalley, Stephanie. 1989. *Myths from Mesopotamia: Creation, the Flood, Gilgamesh and Others*. Oxford World's Classics. Oxford: Oxford University Press.

Foster, Benjamin R. 2005. *Before the Muses: An Anthology of Akkadian Literature*. 3rd ed. Bethesda: CDL Press.

Gordon, Cyrus H., and Gary A. Rendsburg. 1997. *The Bible and the Ancient Near East*. 4th ed. New York: W. W. Norton.

Hallo, William W., and K. Lawson Younger Jr., eds. 2003a. *The Context of Scripture*. Vol. 1, *Canonical Compositions from the Biblical World*. Leiden: Brill.

———. 2003b. *The Context of Scripture*. Vol. 2, *Monumental Inscriptions from the Biblical World*. Leiden: Brill.

———. 2003c. *The Context of Scripture*. Vol. 3, *Archival Documents from the Biblical World*. Leiden: Brill.

Hayes, Christopher B. 2014. *Hidden Riches: A Sourcebook for the Comparative Study of the Hebrew Bible and Ancient Near East*. Louisville, KY: Westminster John Knox Press.

Lambert, W. G. 2013. *Babylonian Creation Myths*. Mesopotamian Civilizations 16. Winona Lake, IN: Eisenbrauns.

Matthew, Victor H., and Don C. Benjamin. 1997. *Old Testament Parallels: Laws and Stories from the Ancient Near East*. 2nd ed. New York: Paulist Press.

Parker, Simon B., ed. 1997. *Ugaritic Narrative Poetry*. SBLWAW 9. Atlanta: Scholars Press.

Pritchard, James B., ed. 1969. *Ancient Near Eastern Texts Relating to the Old Testament*. 3rd ed., with supplement. Princeton, NJ: Princeton University Press. [*ANET*.]

———, ed. 1994. *The Ancient Near East in Pictures Relating to the Old Testament*. 2nd ed., with supplement. Princeton, NJ: Princeton University Press. [*ANEP*.]

Sparks, Kenton L. 2005. *Ancient Texts for the Study of the Hebrew Bible: A Guide to the Background Literature*. Peabody, MA: Hendrickson Publishers.

Talon, Philippe. 2005. *Enūma Eliš: The Standard Babylonian Creation Myth*. SAACT 4. Helsinki: University of Helsinki: The Neo-Assyrian Text Corpus Project. (Translation in French.)

Walton, John H. 1994. *Ancient Israelite Literature in Its Cultural Context: A Survey of Parallels between Biblical and Ancient Near Eastern Texts*. Grand Rapids: Zondervan.

Online Resources

Achaemenid Royal Inscriptions Project. https://oi.uchicago.edu/research/projects/achaemenid-royal
-inscriptions-project.
Cuneiform Digital Library Initiative. http://cdli.ucla.edu/.
The Electronic Text Corpus of Sumerian Literature. http://etcsl.orinst.ox.ac.uk/.
Electronic Tools and Ancient Near Eastern Archives (ETANA). http://www.etana.org/.

11

Literary Analysis

Location, location, location
Anonymous[1]

No text stands on its own, isolated and hermetically self-contained. Rather, a text stands in line with other texts, before and after it, all interconnected, explicitly or implicitly. A text might be an episode within a larger narrative, a discrete point in a larger argument, a section of a lengthy liturgy, a polemical response to a nonextant text, a letter in an ongoing correspondence. In biblical studies, literary context has first and foremost to deal with what lies beyond the boundaries of a given text, to determine how the text fits within its larger literary environment. It asks two basic interrelated questions: (1) *What does the text contribute to its larger context?* (2) *What does the larger context contribute meaningfully to the text?*

For both questions, we begin by looking for connecting threads, from catchwords to common themes, as well as for disjunctions and tensions between the text and its literary surroundings. In some cases, a text may constitute an interruption, a disruption or digression within the larger flow. In other cases, a text may "melt" into its surroundings to the point that its boundaries are barely distinguishable, in which case you would look for other, wider boundaries. In any case, it is only natural to ask why this text is here and not somewhere else. In other words, *location, location, location*! Finding connections prompts the question of whether a text depends upon or presupposes what has gone before. Conversely, does the material that follows depend on the text for it to make sense? How does the text set up what follows? What would happen, as an experiment, if you took out the text from its location? Would there be a gaping hole, or would the larger narrative flow smoothly? These are some of the questions to consider when examining the text within its literary context.

Literary context is fundamentally about looking beyond a text to surrounding texts. While there is no limit to how far one can and should look, it is best to begin by looking

1. It was thought that British real estate tycoon Lord Harold Samuel originated this phrase, but it has been traced to a 1926 real estate classified ad in the *Chicago Tribune*, according to William Safire. Http://www.nytimes .com/2009/06/28/magazine/28FOB-onlanguage-t.html?_r=0.

at what immediately surrounds the text, including the preceding verse and the following verse. Take, for example, the call of Abram in Gen. 12:1–3 (AT).

> YHWH said to Abram: "Go forth, you, from your country, from your kindred, and from your father's house to the land that I will show you, so that I will make you into a great nation and bless you and make your name great. So be a blessing, so that I will bless those who bless you—but the one who belittles you I will curse—and that by you all the families of the earth can gain a blessing."[2]

The text seems discrete enough. Within the larger narrative, this episode marks a break, a new chapter, literally, in the family history of Abram and Sarai.[3] How does the immediate material relate to Abram's call? The previous verse records the death of Terah, Abram's father (11:32); hence, a natural transition occurs from father to son as the attention shifts to Abram in 12:1. Indeed, our passage has an important backstory that begins in 11:27 and provides important genealogical background, including the crucial observation that Sarai was barren (11:30). Thus the preceding material prepares the reader for one of the narrative's primary issues: Sarai's barrenness and God's blessing, introduced in 12:1–3.

Are there other connecting threads that tie our passage with the preceding material? Indeed, there is at least one, an important catchword in fact: "name." An integral part of God's promise to the patriarch is to "make [Abram's] name great" (12:2). The issue is also addressed in the previous episode of the Tower of Babel:

> Then they said, "Come, let us build ourselves a towering city with its top in the heavens, and *let us make a name for ourselves*; otherwise, we shall be scattered abroad upon the face of the whole earth." (11:4 AT)

While the Babel building program failed in its intended purpose (the participants did get "scattered"), the theme of the great name is picked up in God's promise to Abram in 12:2.

One can look even farther back to find the theme of blessing running throughout the prior Genesis narratives, particularly in 1:22, 28; 5:2; 9:1. In all these instances, God's blessing is tied to procreation, frequently supported by the command, "Be fruitful and multiply." Something of that same blessing is operative in God's blessing to Abram (and Sarai): indeed, to be a great nation entails being a populous nation. Hence the theme of blessing in the previous material highlights a particular component of blessing in Gen. 12: the blessing of progeny, an issue that will become increasingly central in later chapters.

Can we find other connecting threads that tie our passage to what precedes it? How are the "families of the earth" in 12:3, for example, developed prior to our passage? What about the theme of land, which figures prominently at the beginning of our passage (12:1)? Looking forward, how does our passage set the stage for what follows? What role does the next verse play in relation to our text? "So Abram went, as YHWH had told him; and Lot went with him" (v. 4a). The first half of this half-verse provides the fulfillment of what God commanded in v. 1: "Go forth, you, from your country . . ." with the matching verb (*hlk*): God says, "Go," and Abram "went." One must therefore ask whether v. 4a

---

2. For translation issues, see chap. 4.

3. Genesis 1–11 is frequently referred to as the "primeval history," and Gen. 12–50 as the family history of Israel's ancestors. The precise boundary, however, blurs under close examination. Does Gen. 11:27–32 go with the former or the latter? It is at the very least transitional.

should be considered the genuine ending of our passage. The argument can go both ways. On the one hand, 12:1 and 4a together form an *inclusio*, a literary envelope that connects God's command and its fulfillment; hence v. 4a could be included as the appropriate end-boundary to our passage. On the other hand, v. 4a begins a new episode in the narrative, one that launches the couple's adventure-filled travels, which cover a considerable amount of material in Genesis. Another clue is to look at the following verse:

> Abram took his wife Sarai and his brother's son Lot, and all the possessions that they had gathered, and the persons whom they had acquired in Haran; and they set forth to go to the land of Canaan. (12:5a)

Contentwise, v. 5a repeats and expands on v. 4a. Lot's accompaniment is referenced twice; in fact, Lot is introduced in v. 5 as if he were not mentioned at all in v. 4a! This might suggest that v. 4 serves as a bridge between vv. 1–3 and what follows, beginning with v. 5. It is transitional.

Finally, we can vastly extend our discussion of literary context by tracing themes or, better, trajectories throughout the book of Genesis, such as blessing, land, and progeny. The charge for Abram to "go" to a "land," for example, finds its concluding parallel in 22:2, the beginning of the *Akedah*, the story of Isaac's binding.

> [God] said, "Take your son, your only son Isaac, whom you love, and **go forth**, **you**, to the **land** of Moriah, and offer him there as a burnt offering on one of the mountains that I shall show you." (AT)

The command to "go" is identical to the command given in 12:1, including the use of the so-called ethical dative construction (lek-lĕkâ). As in 12:4, Abraham obeys without hesitation: he takes his son and goes to Moriah to sacrifice him. Having passed the "test," Abraham receives a reinstatement of God's blessing with specific reference to abundant progeny, national power, and a blessing to the nations (22:17–18), all echoing 12:2–3.

More literary connections can be explored. The theme of blessing can be traced throughout Genesis, forward and backward, concluding with Jacob's blessing of his twelve sons (49:1–28) and beginning with God's command to be "fruitful and multiply" (1:22, 28). What does Gen. 12:1–3 contribute to its larger context? It inaugurates a family history that extends throughout the rest of Genesis. Abram and Sarai, accompanied by God's promise of blessing, go forth on a sojourn that extends far beyond their lives, for four generations in fact.

AMOS 9:11–15

Some texts stand out sharply from their context. One example is the final section of Amos, two units that seem totally out of character with the rest of the book.

> In that day I will raise up the fallen booth of David, and I will repair their breaches, raise his ruins, and rebuild it as in the days of old, so that they will repossess the remnant of Edom and all the nations over which my name has been called. [This is] an utterance of YHWH, who will do this.

Voilà, the days are coming (an utterance of YHWH)
   when the plower will overtake the reaper,
    and the one who treads grapes [will overtake] the one who carries the seed.
The mountains will drip with sweet wine, and all the hills will melt.
I shall restore the fortunes of my people Israel:
   they will restore devastated cities and dwell [there],
    and plant vineyards and drink their wine,
    and cultivate gardens and eat their fruit.
Thus I shall plant them on their ground
   and they shall never again be plucked up from their ground,
   which I have given to them, so says the YHWH your God. (9:11–15 AT)

Instead of an oracle of judgment, so typical of Amos, the book concludes with two oracles of salvation, announcing national and agricultural restoration. The unique nature of this concluding section cannot be fully appreciated unless one has read Amos from beginning to end. The book is a collection of judgment oracles, vision reports, and admonitions that give little hope to the northern kingdom. Two examples will suffice.

Amos 3:1–2 could be called the fulcrum point to the book as a whole. It provides the conclusion to the series of harsh judgment speeches against various neighboring countries, concluding with Israel (2:6–11). At the same time, these two verses serve as preface to the series of speeches against Israel that follows.

Hear this word that YHWH has spoken concerning you, O Israelites,
   concerning the entire clan that I brought up from the land of Egypt:
"Only you have I known from all the clans of the earth.
   Therefore, I will transfer upon you all your sins." (3:1–2 AT)

As explained in chap. 8 (above), this judgment or disaster oracle (see also 4:1–3; 5:10–13) effectively reverses Israel's expectations by denying Israel the exodus as a basis for claiming God's blessing or salvation. Judgment, instead, is called for.

But that's just one example. Another "word" comes two chapters later. Here the prophet casts his judgment in the form of a "lamentation."

[1] Hear this word that I take up over you in lamentation,
   O house of Israel:
[2] "Fallen, no more to rise,
   is maiden Israel;
forsaken on her land,
   with no one to raise her up." (5:1–2)

Such words of lament are cast in the form of a funeral dirge, or qînâ, which carries a 3:2 rhythmic beat in both poetic lines in v. 2. Here the medium is the message. These two passages were selected as representative of Amos's overall message of judgment against the northern kingdom. Throughout the book a host of social sins deserving of judgment are identified, from economic oppression and the amassing of wealth to the suppression of prophecy and the violation of justice (e.g., 2:6–7, 12; 4:1; 5:11–12; 6:4–5, 12; 8:4–6).

Our passage, moreover, is immediately preceded by a horrendous judgment (Amos 9:9–10) that implies no survivors ("no pebble shall fall"). Nothing seems to be shared in common between this final judgment oracle and what follows. Nevertheless, there is a connecting catchword. Compare the following two verses:

> All the sinners of my people shall die by the sword,
>   who say, "Evil shall not *overtake* or meet us." (9:10)

> Voilà, the days are coming (an utterance of YHWH)
>   when the plower will *overtake* the reaper,
>   and the one who treads grapes [will overtake] the one who carries the seed.
> The mountains will drip with sweet wine, and all the hills will melt. (9:13 AT)

The common verb "overtake" (*ngš*) is used in starkly different ways in vv. 10 and 13. The plower "overtaking" the reaper signifies no violent takeover but rather agricultural abundance! The planting season will spill over into the harvest season because the latter will be so abundant (see Lev. 26:5). See also the verb "melt" (*mwg*) in 9:5a and 9:13.

Perhaps most dramatic is the link between 5:2 and 9:11.

> *Fallen*, no more to rise, is maiden Israel. (5:2a)
> In that day I will raise up the *fallen* booth of David. (9:11a AT)

By taking up the common word "fall" (root *npl*), our passage reverses the dirge given in 5:1. However, one should also observe that 9:11–12, at least, has its focus on the southern kingdom, not necessarily the northern kingdom. In any case, the conclusion to Amos picks up earlier words of judgment and turns them into words of restoration.

The ultimate question is how these final passages in Amos (9:11–12 and 13–15) contribute meaningfully to the book as a whole. Specifically, how do these two oracles of salvation inform our reading of the judgment oracles preceding them? Do they reverse them or mitigate them? Do they overturn them or simply "overtake" them? At the very least, these final passages give assurance that God's salvific orientation toward Israel ultimately outweighs all the pronouncements of disaster given earlier in Amos. Judgment is rendered, at most, penultimate. God's final word is restoration. And how do the preceding judgment oracles inform our reading of the final salvation oracles? At the very least, they lay claim that God's salvific turn can never be taken for granted. Salvation follows judgment.

Psalm 23

Literary context even applies to texts that seem quite isolated from each other, such as the psalms, each one a self-contained unit.[4] A literary contextual analysis addresses how psalms in proximity meaningfully relate to each other. Take, for example, Ps. 23. This well-known psalm of trust is bracketed by an agonizing lament (Ps. 22) and a soaring entrance liturgy (Ps. 24). On the surface, they seem to be entirely independent from each other. But their juxtaposition opens up new possibilities of interpretation, whether originally intended or not, thanks to those responsible for arranging them in their present order—the editors of the masoretic Psalter. Another way to put the literary question is this: why is Ps. 23 placed where it is, specifically between Pss. 22 and 24?

---

4. Except for Pss. 9–10, 42–43: each of these pairs originally constituted a single psalm.

Psalm 22 opens with the most anguished cry of the Psalter and concludes with the most uplifting pronouncements of praise (vv. 22–31 [23–32 MT]), which include a universal call to praise regarding YHWH's dominion over the nations (v. 28 [29]) and deliverance to all, including "a people yet unborn" (v. 31 [32]). Central is the testimony given in v. 26 (27).

> The afflicted [mg.] shall eat and be satisfied;
>   those who seek him shall praise YHWH.
>   May your hearts live forever! (alt.)

Provision and protection, not coincidentally, constitute the pervading theme of Ps. 23, cast in the pastoral metaphor of the sheep cared for by the shepherd (vv. 1–3) but also set at the table in the temple (vv. 5–6). Moreover, trust pervades not only Ps. 23 but also Ps. 22 (vv. 4–5 [5–6]); it is trust that enables the speaker to cry out in bitter lament as much as it undergirds peals of praise. As in Ps. 22, the Shepherd Psalm acknowledges the reality of danger, the dark valley, yet while claiming God's accompaniment and protection (23:4). The shepherd does not abandon or forsake the sheep, even in the darkest of valleys. Much to the contrary: the shepherd's presence is felt all the more in moments of greatest danger: "Your rod and your staff—they comfort me" (v. 4). Perhaps it is no coincidence that Ps. 22 is filled with dangerous animals: bulls, lions, feral dogs, and wild oxen (vv. 12–13 [13–14], 16 [17], 20 [21], 21 [22]); sheep need protection from predatory animals (see 1 Sam. 17:34). In addition, as Ps. 22 sets the speaker's praise within the context of the "great congregation" (22:25), so Ps. 23 testifies to God's "goodness and benevolence" within the "house of YHWH" (23:6).

In its literary context, Ps. 23 provides an answer to Ps. 22; it is the testimony of unyielding trust that Ps. 22 elicits. The anguish of Ps. 22 is met with the confidence of Ps. 23. The proclamation of praise at the end of Ps. 22 leads to a testimony of trust in Ps. 23. Psalms 22 and 23 are not unrelated texts. The same goes also for Pss. 23 and 24: the Shepherd Psalm concludes with the speaker's prospect or wish to "dwell in YHWH's house" forever. Not coincidentally, Ps. 24 identifies the qualities of those who are qualified to enter the temple, "the hill of YHWH" (24:3), ranging from pure hearts to true lives (v. 4). Some have argued that Ps. 23 is a pilgrimage psalm to Zion, specifically to the temple. Such a view becomes all the more compelling when Pss. 23 and 24 are read together.

There are, curiously, connecting threads between Pss. 22 and 24 that are *not* evident in Ps. 23, including references to God's dominion (22:28 [29]; 24:1) and to "those who seek" God (22:26 [27]; 24:6). The latter is particularly suggestive, since Ps. 23 stresses the converse, namely, the God who seeks (i.e., accompanies, comforts, and guides) the sheep. Even more explicit, the speaker testifies to God's "goodness and benevolence" in "pursuit" (23:6). Thus Ps. 23 seems to provide a counterpart to the way in which the surrounding psalms depict the divine–human relationship: there are those who devote their lives to "seeking" God; they are the ones who constitute the genuine worshiping community (22:26 [27]; 24:6). Yet as Ps. 23 claims, the God who is sought in the temple is also the God who seeks the needy, providing for them, protecting them, and guiding them to the Shepherd's "house."

There is more. Psalm 24 concludes with a resounding blast of liturgy that invites the "King of glory" to enter into the temple (vv. 7–10). It is a surprising turn since the psalm is earlier devoted to identifying those who are worthy enough to enter (vv. 3–6). Now God is entering! God in Ps. 24 is profiled as the divine warrior and king, "mighty in battle," coming home in victory. Such militant imagery is not unrelated to the shepherd imagery in Ps. 23, since both profiles are royally oriented, each set within a certain context and function. While the shepherd imagery highlights God's caring relationship to God's people, the royal imagery of Ps. 24 stresses the militant side of God vis-à-vis the nations. Finally, while Ps. 23 highlights the temple as the speaker's most desired dwelling place (v. 6b), Ps. 24 claims the temple as God's dwelling place.

A literary contextual analysis reveals the connections, some explicit, some subtle, between discrete texts and asks about the place of a particular text within its larger context. In light of our observations above (and many more that could be said), one could argue that Ps. 23 helps to facilitate the movement from lament to praise and trust. It serves as the bridge of trust between a sense of abandonment to a sense of communion, of coming home to God's "house." The Shepherd Psalm leads the reader to the "house of YHWH," where Ps. 24 marks a formal entrance.

Finally, there is a larger network of connections to be explored in which Ps. 23 plays a significant part. It is part of a chiastic clustering of psalms, specifically Pss. 15–24, that reflect a deliberate aesthetic and theological arrangement. In this cluster Ps. 23 shares certain affinities with Ps. 16, its corresponding partner.

> A Psalm 15 (Entrance Liturgy)
>   **B Psalm 16 (Song of Trust)**
>   C Psalm 17 (Prayer for Help)
>   D Psalm 18 (Royal Psalm)
>   E Psalm 19 (Creation and Torah)
>   D'Psalms 20–21 (Royal Psalms)
>   C' Psalm 22 (Prayer for Help)
>   **B' Psalm 23 (Song of Trust)**
> A' Psalm 24 (Entrance Liturgy)

Psalm 16, by no coincidence, is also a song of trust, replete with comparable language. Compare, for example, the affirmations of trust in 16:2 and 23:1.

> I say to YHWH, "You are my Lord;
>   I have no good apart from you." (16:2)

> YHWH is my shepherd;
>   I lack nothing. (23:1 NIV)

See also the shared references to "cup" in 16:5 and 23:5, and "path" in 16:11 and 23:3. Reference to the "darkest valley" in Ps. 23 is matched by reference to Sheol and the Pit in 16:10. The final reference in Ps. 16 to God's "presence" points to the setting of God's presence given in Ps. 23: the temple. With the psalms, separated as they are individually, connections abound, connections generated by their specific placements and arrangements. Context has all to do with location.

GENESIS 1:1–2:4A AND 2:4B–3:21

Finally, our two creation texts, tightly juxtaposed as they are, cry out for a literary contextual analysis. Both creation stories, to be sure, can stand quite well on their own. They are strikingly different in so many ways in content and style. But amid their vast differences, connections are also evident, some obvious and some not so obvious.

Both accounts have contrasting points of departure. When the curtain rises in Gen. 1, we see a watery mishmash (1:2), whereas in Gen. 2:5 we find a dry patch of land, a situation of deficiency (no plants, no rain, no tiller). When they are combined, however, they resemble in content the opening lines of the *Enuma Elish* (see chap. 10). Notice the pervasive presence of water (in the form of two commingled deities) in the opening scene of the Babylonian creation account as well as the negative list of lacks: no pasture, no marshes, no gods. Observe also that all three accounts begin with a lengthy temporal clause. It is as if our two biblical accounts split up what was united in the *Enuma Elish*, each emphasizing one aspect at the expense of the other: on the one hand the presence of water, and on the other hand a situation of dire lack. The difference in Gen. 2 is that among the lacks listed is the lack of water. Instead, we begin with dry land, which has no place either in Gen. 1 or in the *Enuma Elish*.

Regarding focus and scope, Gen. 1 is expansively cosmic, while Gen. 2–3 is more narrowly focused on human origins in the setting of a garden. Their respective foci may have something to do with the remarkably different sequences of events given in both accounts. In Gen. 1 human beings (*ʾādām*) are created last, on the sixth day (1:26–28); in Gen. 2 the *ʾādām* is created first, before plants and animals (2:7–9, 19). Also, the very act of creating humanity is notably different: In Gen. 1 male and female are created together. In Gen. 2 the woman is created after the *ʾādām* (2:21–23), and consequently the *ʾādām* becomes a "man" (*ʾîš*). Most significantly, Gen. 1 says nothing about human disobedience, and Gen. 2 says nothing about being made in God's "image." No punishment is meted out in Gen. 1. One could go on, but the conclusion is unmistakable: not one but two very distinctive creation traditions constitute the opening chapters of Genesis.

A literary analysis suggests that, given their differences in style and content, these two accounts developed independently. They are self-contained wholes, signaled in no small measure by their respective opening lines: "When Elohim began to create the heavens and the earth . . ." (1:1 AT) and "In the day that YHWH Elohim made Earth and Heavens . . ." (2:4b AT). Notice the change of name for God: Gen. 1:1–2:3 employs *ʾĕlōhîm*, whereas Gen. 2:4b–3:24 employs *yhwh ʾĕlōhîm*. The name YHWH is introduced for the first time in Gen. 2:4b (cf. Exod. 6:2–3).

For all that can be said about their differences and independent status, these two stories are placed together. The literary critic asks "Why?" Why are they placed in this way and not, say, in reverse order? Why both and not just one? What do they have to do with each other? What do they say to each other? Let's begin with connections. Both accounts are bona fide creation accounts. Both detail the creation of the world and humanity: the elements of earth/land/ground, water, vegetation, animals, and human beings are all held in common. Both say something about air/wind/breath, although with different terminology: the primordial "breath of God" (*rûaḥ ʾĕlōhîm*), which "hovers" over the waters in 1:2, and

God's breath, the "breath of life" (*něšāmâ ḥayyîm*), which animates the *ʾādām* in 2:7. The former can also be translated "spirit of God."[5] Both accounts feature God as the central character, even though the *ʾādām* and the woman in the second account also share the narrative spotlight.

The successive placement of these two stories forges a movement from the most expansive, cosmic purview to a narrowly human one. While creation in Gen. 1 concludes with the creation of humanity as the final creative act of God, creation in Gen. 2–3 is primarily about humanity, from beginning to end. One could take the second account as a recapitulation of the first, a sort of narrative rewind that picks up and elaborates on what happens specifically on the sixth day (Gen. 1:26–28). Whereas the narrative tensions remain regarding when the animals and plants are created vis-à-vis humanity, the overall movement is such that the second account more or less picks up where the first account ends.

How do the two stories of *human* creation relate to each other? The contrasting pictures suggest a degree of complementarity. One depicts a very elevated view of humanity, created "in the image of God" no less (1:27). The other, by contrast, describes the first human being created "from the dust of the ground" (2:7). One depicts humanity as nearly divine, theomorphic by design, the other as a groundling, an earthling. To put it more abstractly, humanity according to both accounts is intimately connected both to God and to the earth. The literary juxtaposition is both stark and generative. Could it be that these two creation accounts were brought together to illustrate humanity's genesis somewhere "in the middle" between God and the rest of creation? That humanity is both a creature apart from the rest of creation yet also a part of creation seems to be the message generated by the coupling of these two accounts.

Broadly speaking, at some point in the literary development of Genesis, it was felt that one creation tradition alone was not sufficient, that two accounts were needed, two with quite different foci and orientations. So one question to ask is, How does one creation text complete the other? Genesis 2–3, for example, opens a narrative strand that is left unaddressed in Gen. 1, namely, the problematic nature of human nature: disobedience, shame, fear, alienation, hardship. All figure in the Yahwist account of creation; all are factors in shaping the human condition. A suggestive connection, however, can be seen by comparing the final curse, the curse of the ground, and the Priestly mandate for humanity in relation to the earth. Compare 1:28 and 3:17b–19. The curse of the ground that results in backbreaking toil may lead one to reread Gen. 1:28 with special attention directed toward the key word "subdue." The verb itself suggests resistance that must be overcome in order for humanity to flourish. Is it coincidental that Gen. 3 specifies the challenges involved in cultivating the land, a land resistant to human labor: "thorns and thistles," not to mention rocks and forests to be cleared? Could it be that, in this case, humankind's asymmetrical relationship to the land, alluded to in Gen. 1, is actually spelled out in Gen. 3? Such would be another inference generated by coupling these two stories.

One contextual issue that has invited much debate is the status of Gen. 2:4, translated literally below:

---

5. See chap. 4 for the translational issues.

> These are the "generations" of the heavens and the earth
>   when they were created, (2:4a)
> when YHWH Elohim made Earth and Heavens. . . . (2:4b)

Some interpreters take the first half (v. 4a) as the conclusion of the first account of creation. Others, however, take it to be the prefatory line for the second. The language of v. 4a is more closely aligned with the first account: the order and form of the words "the heavens" and "the earth" match Gen. 1:1, suggesting an *inclusio*. However, the key word in v. 4a is "generations" (*tōlĕdôt*), a genealogical term that can be found throughout the book of Genesis and once in the book of Numbers, as shown in these examples (AT):

> This is the list of Adam's descendants (*tōlĕdôt*).
> When God created humankind,
>   he made them in the likeness of God. (5:1)
> These are Noah's *descendants*.
> Noah was a righteous man, blameless in his generation;
>   Noah walked with God. (6:9)
> These are the *descendants* of Noah's sons, Shem, Ham, and Japheth;
>   children were born to them after the flood. (10:1)
> These are Shem's *descendants*.
> When Shem was one hundred years old,
>   he became the father of Arpachshad two years after the flood. (11:10)
> Now these are Terah's *descendants*.
> Terah was the father of Abram, Nahor, and Haran;
>   and Haran was the father of Lot. (11:27)
> These are the *descendants* of Isaac, Abraham's son:
>   Abraham was the father of Isaac. (25:19)
> These are the *descendants* of Aaron and Moses
>   when YHWH spoke with Moses on Mount Sinai. (Num. 3:1)

The change in translation, from "generations" to "descendants," simply acknowledges that the term *tôlĕdôt* typically refers to human lineage, but when applied to a cosmic context, it is best translated as "generations." But imagine replacing "generations" with "descendants," and you can see the shared sense of these passages: "These are the 'descendants' of the heavens and the earth. . . ." In all cases, use of the term *tôlĕdôt* (or *tôlĕdōt*) points forward, introducing the following section. Moreover, the term is tied to the progenitor rather than to the progeny. These are the "generations" *of* Adam, the descendants *of* Aaron and Moses, . . . the generations *of* the heavens and the earth. Note also the similar syntactical construction shared by Gen. 2:4; 5:1; and Num. 3:1: the reference to "generations/descendants" is followed by the temporal construction *bĕyôm* ("when" or, literally, "on the day of . . .").

Thus Gen. 2:4a seems to refer to what follows, that is, to what happens *after* the earth and the heavens are established, rather than to their own genesis, already recounted in Gen. 1.[6] It signals, for example, that the earth is already in existence when the second account begins. Moreover, nothing further is said about the heavens in the second account, except perhaps in 3:22 by implication.

---

6. For detailed argumentation, see Stordalen 1992, 163–77.

So what? These observations suggest that 2:4a serves in its position to introduce the second creation account rather than to conclude the first, despite the fact that the language of 2:4a closely resembles that of the first. Some have argued that vv. 4a and 4b themselves constitute an original unity by pointing out, for example, that the merism[7] "the heavens and the earth" in v. 4a is chiastically related to "Earth and Heavens" in v. 4b.[8] To be sure, the second pair represents a reversed sequence of the first, but the mirroring is not precise, for the second pair lacks the definite article ("the") in v. 4b. In any case, Gen. 2:4a appears to be transitional. It was added to make possible the joining of the two accounts, and in so doing set the two accounts in sequential order: Gen. 1:1–2:3 recounts the *genesis* of the heavens and the earth, while 2:4b–3:21 tells of the *generations* of the earth and the heavens—yet mostly the earth, it turns out. By its addition, Gen. 2:4a preserves the cosmic perspective of the first account for the more anthropocentrically focused second account.

BEYOND THE CREATION ACCOUNTS: THE "SOURCES" OF THE PENTATEUCH

These first two creation accounts—and there are other creation accounts in the Bible—represent two literary streams that flow mightily through much of the Pentateuch, at times commingling, other times running distinctly parallel in separate sections. Scholars refer to them variously as "sources," "documents," "compositional layers," or "literary strata" and "strands," to name a few. Identifying these distinct literary layers began with analyzing the literary contexts of various passages and noting repetitions ("doublets"), such as two creation accounts, as discussed in this chapter; double genealogies in Gen. 4–5 and 10–11; two interwoven yet distinct versions of the flood story in Gen. 6–9; three accounts of the ancestress-in-danger story in Gen. 12, 20, and 26; and the two accounts of God's covenant with Abra(ha)m in Gen. 15 and 17. One could go on. As was noted centuries ago, different names for God, such as YHWH (the Lord) and Elohim (God), can reflect different sources or traditions.

The Documentary Hypothesis, as it is classically called, is the sweeping result of literary contextual analysis of the entire Pentateuch. The development of this theory in biblical research has a fascinating history, and there are many resources that recount it.[9] I simply lift up a frequently overlooked figure in the history of research: Henning Bernard Witter (1683–1715). His groundbreaking study *Israelite Laws in Palestine: Comments on the Eternal Genesis* (*Jura Israelitarum* . . . [Hildesiae: Schröderus, 1711]) preceded the French physician Jean Astruc's similar discoveries by over forty years and helped launch the identification of separate sources in the Pentateuch by developing formal criteria. Pastor Witter was no ivory-tower academic; he was a Lutheran pastor of a church in Hildesheim, Germany.

---

7. A merism contains two opposite subjects that together are meant to designate a totality. Here "heaven" and "earth" together designate the totality of creation.

8. So Titus 2011, 87.

9. See, e.g., Viviano 1999, 37–42; Campbell and O'Brien 1993, 1–19.

The Documentary Hypothesis is not itself a method. It is what it is called, a hypothesis, or better, a theory that has emerged from careful literary analysis over a broad sweep of biblical material, both narrative and legal. It is, it turns out, an economical way of explaining the contradictions, consistencies, and repetitions throughout the Pentateuch as the compilation of sources, not excluding supplements (Baden 2012, 30–33). Whether all these sources were originally independent or not remains the focus of much discussion. For our purposes, a few illustrative cases in Genesis will suffice, using the two creation accounts as our starting point.

Genesis 1:1–2:3 marks the beginning of the so-called Priestly document, or P source, which includes such programmatic pieces as Gen. 9:1–17 (the covenant with Noah); 17:1–27 (the covenant with Abraham), and Exod. 25–31, 35–40 (the instructions and construction of the tabernacle). It is called Priestly because it reflects particular theological interests, such as the proper performance of cultic ritual and the establishment of sacred space. Its style is characteristically repetitive and enumerative.

Genesis 2:4b–3:21 is frequently called the Yahwist document, or J Source (from the German "Jahwist," pronounced as a "Y"), since it consistently refers to God as YHWH, in this case "YHWH Elohim" in Gen. 2–3. The following table sorts out the two "sources" through the flood story.[10]

Priestly	Yahwist
1:1–2:3	2:4b–3:24
	4:1–24
5:1–28	5:29
5:30–32	6:1–4 (?)
	6:5–8
6:9–22	7:1–5
7:6–7	7:8abα
7:8bβ	
7:9	7:10
7:11	7:12
7:13–16a	7:16b
	7:17a
7:17b	
7:18–21	7:22–23
7:24	
8:1–2a	8:2b–3a
8:3b–5	8:6
8:7	8:8–12
8:13a	8:13b
8:14–19	8:20–22
9:1–17	

Let's compare a few passages to note their distinctive emphases as each "source" tells the story of the flood.

---

10. For detailed discussion, see Wright 2015.

Reason(s) for the Flood

Priestly	Yahwist
	[6:5] YHWH saw that the wickedness of humankind was great in the earth, and that every inclination of the thoughts of their hearts was only evil continually. [6] And YHWH was sorry that he had made humankind on the earth, and it grieved him to his heart. [7] So YHWH said, "I will blot out from the earth the human beings I have created—people together with animals and creeping things and birds of the air, for I am sorry that I have made them." [8] But Noah found favor in the sight of YHWH.
[6:11] Now the earth was corrupt in God's sight, and the earth was filled with violence. [12] And God saw that the earth was corrupt; for all flesh had corrupted its ways upon the earth. [13] And God said to Noah, "I have determined to make an end of all flesh, for the earth is filled with violence because of them; now I am going to destroy them along with the earth."	

The Priestly rationale for the flood is that God "*saw* that the earth was corrupt" and "*filled* with violence," language reminiscent of Gen. 1. "All flesh" is to blame, and so "all flesh" is to be destroyed. Of note is the wordplay: the terms for "corrupt" (6:11, 12) and "destroy" (v. 13) come from the same root (*šḥt*). The Yahwist account, by contrast, finds the problem resting primarily on human beings, due to the evil "inclination" of their hearts, concerning which YHWH expresses deep regret.

Noah's Instructions

Priestly	Yahwist
[6:17] "For my part, I am going to bring a flood of waters on the earth, to destroy from under heaven all flesh in which is the breath of life; everything that is on the earth shall die. [18] But I will establish my covenant with you; and you shall come into the ark, you, your sons, your wife, and your sons' wives with you. [19] *And of every living thing, of all flesh, you shall bring two of every kind into the ark, to keep them alive with you; they shall be male and female.* [20] *Of the birds according to their kinds, and of the animals according to their kinds, of every creeping thing of the ground according to its kind, two of every kind shall come in to you, to keep them alive.* [21] Also take with you every kind of food that is eaten, and store it up; and it shall serve as food for you and for them." [22] Noah did this; he did all that God commanded him.	[7:1] Then YHWH said to Noah, "Go into the ark, you and all your household, for I have seen that you alone are righteous before me in this generation. [2] *Take with you seven pairs of all clean animals, the male and its mate; and a pair of the animals that are not clean, the male and its mate;* [3] *and seven pairs of the birds of the air also, male and female, to keep their kind alive on the face of all the earth.* [4] For in seven days I will send rain on the earth for forty days and forty nights; and every living thing that I have made I will blot out from the face of the ground." [5] And Noah did all that YHWH had commanded him.

Both passages conclude with Noah fulfilling God's command, but the command is different in each one. In case readers miss the glaring inconsistency, I have italicized the contrasting parts. Noah is given two very different sets of instructions. In the Priestly account, Noah is instructed to take "two of every kind into the ark, . . . male and female, . . . according to their kinds." The language, again, is reminiscent of Gen. 1. In the Yahwist account, it is "seven pairs of all clean animals" plus a pair of "unclean animals." Why the discrepancy? Later in the Yahwist narrative, Noah offers sacrifice to God (8:20). There is no episode of sacrifice in the Priestly account, since the institution of sacrifice and hence the distinction between clean and unclean animals are not established until Lev. 11. Thus no distinction is made in Genesis, according to P. Simply "two of every kind," without distinction, are admitted into the ark.

The Beginning of the Flood

Priestly	Yahwist
	7:10 And after seven days the waters of the flood came on the earth.
7:11 In the six hundredth year of Noah's life, in the second month, on the seventeenth day of the month, on that day all the fountains of the great Deep burst forth, and the windows of the heavens were opened.	
	12 The rain fell on the earth forty days and forty nights.

According to P, the flood comes in both directions: from above ("windows of the heavens") and from below ("great Deep [tĕhôm]"). This recalls the watery condition prior to creation in Gen 1:2, before a distinction is made of the "waters below" and the "waters above." In the Yahwist account, the flood is due to a lengthy period of rain.

The End of the Flood

Priestly	Yahwist
8:1 But God remembered Noah and all the wild animals and all the domestic animals that were with him in the ark. And God made a wind blow over the earth, and the waters subsided; 2a the fountains of the Deep and the windows of the heavens were closed.	7:23b Only Noah was left, and those that were with him in the ark.
	8:2b The rain from the heavens was restrained, 3a and the waters gradually receded from the earth.
3b At the end of one hundred fifty days the waters had abated;	

The flood's cessation in P mirrors how the flood began: the waters below and above become contained. Moreover, the "wind" that effects this is rûaḥ, recalling the language of God's "breath" in 1:2. In the Yahwist's account, the rain simply ceases.

Aftermath of the Flood: Covenant versus Sacrifice

Priestly

[9:8] Then God said to Noah and to his sons with him, [9] "As for me, I am establishing my covenant with you and your descendants after you, [10] and with every living creature that is with you, the birds, the domestic animals, and every animal of the earth with you, as many as came out of the ark. [11] I establish my covenant with you, that never again shall all flesh be cut off by the waters of a flood, and never again shall there be a flood to destroy the earth." [12] God said, "This is the sign of the covenant that I make between me and you and every living creature that is with you, for all future generations: [13] I have set my bow in the clouds, and it shall be a sign of the covenant between me and the earth. [14] When I bring clouds over the earth and the bow is seen in the clouds, [15] I will remember my covenant that is between me and you and every living creature of all flesh; and the waters shall never again become a flood to destroy all flesh."

Yahwist

[8:20] Then Noah built an altar to YHWH, and took of every clean animal and of every clean bird, and offered burnt offerings on the altar. [21] And when YHWH smelled the pleasing odor, YHWH said in his heart, "I will never again curse the ground because of humankind, for the inclination of the human heart is evil from youth; nor will I ever again destroy every living creature as I have done. [22] As long as the earth endures, seedtime and harvest, cold and heat, summer and winter, day and night, shall not cease."

The most extensive difference between the two accounts has to do with how the flood story concludes. In P, the narrative ends with God's formal covenant, whereas J concludes the narrative with Noah's sacrifice and YHWH's promise. In both cases, God promises to never again destroy creation. In P, God's promise is guaranteed by covenant, which extends not just to Noah and his family but to all living creatures, and it is signaled by the "bow in the clouds." In J, the divine promise is illustrated by the consistent turning of the seasons.

LITERARY CONTEXT REVISITED

Examining passages within their larger literary contexts can lead to discerning discrete compositional layers. Yet a full literary analysis is not satisfied with simply separating out "sources" without also accounting for their conjoining, their layering or interweaving, their redacted unity. In the flood story of Gen. 6–9, the two strands are interwoven, whereas earlier the Priestly and Yahwist narratives are juxtaposed in blocks, as is also the case after the flood story. As for their relationship, it has been argued that the Priestly account of the flood was developed as a response to the Yahwist account, perhaps even to serve as its replacement. If so, it did not quite work. Both ended up preserved, tightly interwoven and playing off each other. The final editors or redactors of the primeval history (Gen. 1–11), who no doubt shared priestly concerns, saw fit to combine them, differences and all. That the Priestly account is lengthier and has the last word in the narrative of the flood (Gen. 9:1–17) suggests priority given to the P source. Nevertheless, the final editor(s) saw fit that the Yahwist account not be lost. That it too was preserved also says something, but what that something is remains elusive. At the very least, weaving the two accounts together, in spite of their discrepancies, reflects both a compromise and an interpretive openness in the retelling of the flood, as is also the case in the recounting of creation.

BIBLIOGRAPHY FOR CHAPTER 11

Baden, Joel. 2012. *The Composition of the Pentateuch*. AYBRL. New Haven: Yale University Press.

Campbell, Antony F., and Mark A. O'Brien. 1993. *Sources of the Pentateuch: Texts, Introductions, Annotations*. Minneapolis: Fortress Press.

Levin, Christoph. 2009. "Source Criticism: The Miracle at the Sea." In *Method Matters: Essays on the Interpretation of the Hebrew Bible in Honor of David L. Petersen*, edited by Joel M. LeMon and Kent Harold Richards, 39–61. RBS 56. Atlanta: Society of Biblical Literature.

Stordalen, Terje. 1992. "Genesis 2, 4: Restudying a locus classicus." *ZAW* 104, no. 2:163–77.

Titus, P. Joseph. 2011. *The Second Story of Creation (Gen 2:4–3:24): A Prologue to the Concept of Enneatuch?* European University Studies 23 (Theology), vol. 912. Frankfurt am Main: Peter Lang.

Viviano, Pauline A. 1999. "Source Criticism." In *To Each Its Own Meaning: An Introduction to Biblical Criticisms and Their Application*, edited by Steven L. McKenzie and Stephen R. Haynes, 35–57. 2nd ed. Louisville, KY: Westminster John Knox Press.

Wright, David P. 2015. "Profane versus Sacrificial Slaughter: The Priestly Recasting of the Yahwist Flood Story." In *Current Issues in Priestly and Related Literature: The Legacy of Jacob Milgrom and Beyond*, edited by Roy Gane and Ada Taggar-Cohen, 125–54. RBS 82. Atlanta: Scholars Press.

12

Historical Analysis

History is the intellectual form in which a civilization renders account to itself of its past.

J. Huizinga[1]

So far we have talked about biblical texts as literary products without much consideration of the times in which they were produced and the histories they reflect or construct. Biblical texts are texts of antiquity that reflect an ancient and diverse culture, a culture that is foreign to contemporary readers. Thus certain questions arise of a historical bent. *What were the historical conditions in which a particular text was written? What cultural, social, and economic forces were at play that helped to shape the text as we have it? What social values, customs, or beliefs are assumed in the text? Can we learn something historically by peering "through" the text into the historical period in which the text was written or developed?*

One fundamental and unavoidable question is *What is history?* We typically think of "the history of" something as an account of the major events or episodes in the life of an individual, community, or nation. But history has many faces: it can refer to everything from major battles to family rituals. History comes in "big" and "small" packages, but it all has to do with life in the past. Actually, not even necessarily "life." The choice of timescale is critical. There's political history, and then there's geological history (4.5 billion years for Earth) and even cosmic history (ca. 13.8 billion years ago for the visible universe). For historians, ancient Israelite history constitutes part of the larger ancient Near Eastern history, which begins with Sumerian and Egyptian history, beginning in the fourth millennium with the so-called Uruk period (ca. 4000–3100 BCE) and the Protodynastic period in Egypt (3150 BCE), the beginning of the Bronze Age. But anthropologists would want to go farther back, at least to the Neolithic period (10,200–8800 BCE), and paleontologists even farther back.

"Old Testament [Hebrew Bible] History" is to be distinguished from the "History of Ancient Israel." It all depends on where the historian thinks Israel's history begins

---

1. Huizinga 1963, 9.

and how far it extends. Typically the latter ranges from the Egyptian Merneptah stele (ca. 1208 BCE), currently considered our earliest reference to "Israel" in an extrabiblical source, to the end of the Hellenistic period. Old Testament history, on the other hand, extends the "history" farther back to the time of the ancestors, beginning with Abraham and Sarah. Below is a typical timeline of biblical history with *approximate* dates informed by both reconstructed history and the Bible's history:

1800 BCE	Period of the Ancestors
1250	Moses and the Exodus
1200–1000	Period of the Judges
1000	King David and the United Monarchy
922	Beginning of the Divided Monarchy
722	Fall of the Northern Kingdom (Israel) to Assyria
586	Fall of the Southern Kingdom (Judah) to Babylon
539	Beginning of the Persian Period
538	Edict of Cyrus II and the Return from Babylonian Exile
520–515	Rebuilding of the Jerusalem Temple
450 (?)	Ezra/Nehemiah
332	Beginning of the Hellenistic Period
167–160	Maccabean Revolt
63	Beginning of the Roman Period

There are many issues at stake, too numerous and complex to be treated here. Suffice it to say, much about the history that underlies the Hebrew Bible's historical witness remains widely debated. As such, it is helpful to make a categorical distinction, at least in principle. Two senses of history have often been used to articulate the relation of the biblical text to "history": (1) the history *of* the text, and (2) the history *in* the text.[2] That is, external and internal history. In the latter case, history is inscribed by the text itself, such as the "history" of the patriarchs and matriarchs in the book of Genesis. It is history depicted *within* the narrative. "Historiography" would be another term for it. It is what the text itself claims historically, that is, the situations the text describes with its references to events, places, persons, customs, activities, and so forth.

The "history *of* the text" refers to the *external* historical conditions or circumstances in which the text originated, was preserved, and was transmitted. It examines the historical, cultural, sociological "world(s) behind the text." It asks *why* the text was produced (i.e., written, edited, preserved, redacted, and transmitted). Was the text produced in response to certain events or situations? Was it produced to influence history in a certain way, such as to bring about political change? In addition, it is only natural to ask regarding any text, *for whom and by whom was the text written?* For biblical texts, the answer to the question "By whom?" need not refer to an individual author, since biblical texts do not come with a colophon detailing scribal authorship and date of publication. To be sure, certain biblical books and passages are attributed to well-known individuals, such as David's psalms and Solomon's proverbs,[3] but they cannot be historically demonstrated,

---

2. Hayes and Holladay 2007, 53, 56–58.

3. Note that the book of Proverbs, although attributed to Solomon (1:1), also contains collections of proverbial poetry attributed to other figures (25:1; 30:1; 31:1).

and moreover, attributing works to notable historical figures was a common practice in antiquity.

Despite the uncertainties surrounding their origin and formation, each biblical text has its history. No text was written in a vacuum. Every text emerged out of settings located concretely in time and place. As we have already noticed, many texts themselves exhibit signs of their own formation and growth; each text, in other words, has its own historical "career." And this is not reserved exclusively for the text's origin and formation. Texts continue to have a life of their own after their production: they are appropriated by various communities of faith; they are used in both empowering and oppressive ways. They are interpreted. In other words, a historical analysis can take many forms: it can use the text (along with other texts, in addition to archaeological artifacts) to reconstruct the text's historical context, such as the historical context of its production. A historical analysis can also assess the accuracy of the "history" that the text itself recounts, identifying, in other words, its revisionist work. To boil it down, the text can be used historically either as a "window" or as a "world": (1) as a window into the complex sociocultural, historical milieu from which the text arose and was received, or (2) as a world unto itself, the history that the text itself depicts, the story that unfolds within the text. Think of the biblical text as a stained-glass window: there's what lies beyond the window, filtered as it is, and there are the intricate patterns and colors of the window itself. Of course, this is an imperfect example, because typically the window's own aesthetic qualities have little to do with what can be seen *through* the window. In any case, basic to the historical task is to determine how the text's own story, its internally depicted history, relates to the history behind and beyond the text.

The Case of Daniel

One challenge of any historical analysis is to determine whether the historical situation described in the text and the situation out of which the text arose may and/or may not be the same. If the historical "distance" is wide, the text may have more to say about the time in which it was produced rather than the time it allegedly reports. One extreme example is the book of Daniel, which purports to depict the life and events of an individual, a sage, whom King Nebuchadnezzar took captive during the invasion of Jerusalem. The book begins with its superscription: "in the third year of the reign of King Jehoiakim of Judah," which would place the story around 605 BCE.[4] However, much of the book refers to events that actually took place from 167 to 164 BCE, during the period of the *Maccabean revolt* rather than the period of the Babylonian exile. For historical purposes, Daniel is best viewed in light of the political and cultural turmoil of the second century rather than of the sixth century BCE. But as for the "history in the text," Daniel is fertile ground for exploring the ways in which the history of the sixth century BCE is retold four hundred years later.

---

4. This itself is problematic historically, since 2 Kings describes Nebuchadnezzar's siege of Jerusalem taking place *after* Jehoiakim's death in 598 BCE and during his son's brief reign, Jehoiachin (2 Kgs. 24:1–12).

The Case of Amos: Beginning and End

Most prophetic books bear a superscription that provides critical historical information regarding the placement of the prophet, particularly in relation to the reigns of individual kings.

> The words of Amos, who was among the shepherds of Tekoa, which he saw concerning Israel in the days of King Uzziah of Judah and in the days of King Jeroboam son of Joash of Israel, two years before the earthquake. (Amos 1:1)

The superscription identifies a southern and northern king: Uzziah and Jeroboam II, respectively. Their reigns are roughly estimated thus:

Uzziah	783–742 BCE
Jeroboam II	786–746 BCE

As for the earthquake, we do not have enough evidence for its precise dating. The most and least that we can say about the prophet's career is that it was lodged squarely in the eighth century, a period of escalating political and economic power in both Israel and Judah. Fortunately, more specific historical information is given in the body of the book, in 7:10–15. This narrative interlude stands out amid the plethora of prophetic oracles in the book of Amos. It recounts a confrontation between Amos and Amaziah, a priest of Bethel, a royal and religious center of northern Israel (vv. 10, 13). Amaziah observes the effect of Amos's words upon the kingdom: they are words of "conspiracy," unbearable to the land, and no wonder, given Amos's message, which declares oncoming death for the king and exile for Israel (v. 11). The scene reveals that Amos is a southerner, from "the land of Judah," for which the superscription in 1:1 gives more specific information: Amos is from Tekoa, about six miles south of Bethlehem. So Amos is an eighth-century "prophet," a shepherd and agriculturalist, a southerner who felt called to travel north to proclaim judgment against the northern kingdom.

To fill out the historical picture, one would need to gain some familiarity with the reality of the conflict that characterized the relationship between northern Israel and Judah, beginning with the schism in 922 BCE (see 1 Kgs. 11–13). The separation or division of the two kingdoms had been in place for over a century and a half before Amos arrived upon the scene. Both kingdoms fell separately: the northern kingdom to the Assyrians in 722 BCE (see 2 Kgs. 17) and the southern kingdom to the Babylonians in 586 BCE (2 Kgs. 24–25).

Most of the book of Amos reflects not only the time frame of the eighth century but also the provenance of the north. The judgments throughout Amos largely target the northern kingdom, except in the notably rare instance of Amos 2:4–5, which some scholars consider a later insertion, given its brevity and vague language, particularly compared to what follows (vv. 6–16), whose focus is on Israel. And this brings us back to a text we have already discussed (chap. 11 above): Amos 9:11–15. As recognized earlier, these final two passages are out of character alongside the numerous judgment oracles that characterize Amos as whole. Quite distinctive, moreover, is the reference to the "fallen booth of David," which opens the first oracle of restoration. The expression "booth of David" is unique in the Hebrew Bible; one would expect the common phrase the "house of David," which refers to the Davidic dynasty (see, e.g., 2 Sam. 7). A booth, or lean-to, is a much more fragile image, suggesting its imminent collapse. But the metaphor quickly turns urban with reference to breached walls and ruins, referring to a city, most likely Jerusalem, the "city of David" (2 Sam. 5:9; 6:10, 12, 16). In any case, the focus is on the Davidic dynasty and its restoration in Amos 9:11–12. Another historical reference is the "remnant of Edom," a neighboring kingdom south of Judah historically linked to Judah, along with Moab, Syria, and Ammon. The term "remnant" often presupposes a situation of population loss (e.g., 2 Kgs 19:4, 30, 31). These two references suggest the aftermath of exile, over a century after Amos's own time. This oracle of restoration offers hope in a time of collapse and displacement coupled with an imperial vision of Davidic sovereignty over "the nations."

The final passage in Amos, however, refers not to Judah but to "my people Israel" (9:14). Its focus is not so much on monarchic restoration as on agricultural restoration, with a passing reference to urban rebuilding. Does "Israel" here refer to the northern kingdom, as it does throughout most of Amos (e.g., 2:6, 11; 3:12), or could it include *all* Israel, that is, the territorial extent of both kingdoms? That is a question that remains historically and literarily open for further discussion.

Psalms 117 and 23

Some texts simply cannot be anchored historically. That does not mean that they are ahistorical, but rather that they lack historical markers that would indicate the time and place of their origination. Take, for example, Ps. 117, the shortest psalm in the Psalter:

> Praise YHWH, all you nations!
>   Acclaim him, all you peoples!
> For mighty is his benevolence toward us;
>   YHWH's faithfulness endures forever.
> Praise YHWH! (AT)

There is nothing to indicate when this praise psalm was produced. The "nations" have existed throughout all of ancient Israel's existence. This psalm could have originated any-time from the monarchic period to the postexilic period.

Take Ps. 23. Can you place this psalm historically? There is clearly not enough evidence to restrict this psalm to a specific historical setting. On the other hand, a related question to ask is, Can you imagine a time presupposed by this psalm? Does it reflect, for example, the situation of exile? The last line seems to suggest otherwise: the psalmist expresses a desire to "dwell" in the temple. One could argue that Ps. 23 presupposes the existence of the temple; hence, one could date the psalm as preexilic or postexilic (before 586 BCE or after 515 BCE, when the temple was restored), particularly if it functioned as a pilgrimage psalm.

However, one can't be too sure. The psalm could very well have expressed the hope that the temple would be restored, so that a return to the temple could be possible. It is possible that Ps. 23 could have been exilic in origin. In any case, such lack of evidence prompts the interpreter to consider different scenarios for the psalm's provenance and function. But locating historical provenance is not the only thing at stake in a historical analysis. Even if Ps. 23 were preexilic, an important question to ask is how this psalm would have played out in an exilic context, in a situation without the temple, a situation in which pilgrimage was not possible. The fact that this psalm was preserved at all suggests that it was used, or at least could be used, in a variety of historical situations. The longing to "dwell in the house of YHWH" in a time when the "house" lay in ruins makes the psalm a profound and poignant testimony of hope for future restoration, the restoration of the temple, and with it the restoration of pilgrimage and national worship. At least, an exilic origination cannot be ruled out. Such is the openness of historical study.

THE GENESIS CREATION ACCOUNTS

Like Ps. 23 (and many other psalms), creation texts are notoriously difficult to date, since their subject matter is not the history of the present or recent past but that of the primordial past. Nevertheless, such accounts have much to do with the self-perceptions of the communities that composed and preserved them, perspectives of communal order that carry social interests, locate ethical values, and express political perceptions. That is to say, a cosmology reveals something of a community's sociology, including its vision of order and life as it was and is and should be.

Genesis 1

Although there remains some debate, the Priestly account of creation is most often dated to the exile or early postexilic period. This is in part due to the likelihood that the P source is later than the D, or Deuteronomic, source (7th c. BCE). As Julius Wellhausen pointed out over a century ago, whereas D legislates and advocates for the centralization of worship, the Priestly composition presupposes centralization.[5]

In chap. 10 (above), we compared Gen. 1 with the *Enuma Elish*, a Babylonian creation account, noting both connections and contrasts. The connections suggest that the Priestly cosmogony was composed by writers having some familiarity with the Babylonian theogony. The distinct absence of polemics, however, indicates that Gen. 1 was written not as a direct response to it, as if it were addressed to the Babylonian priesthood, but for an Israelite audience perhaps feeling the pressure of assimilation and/or searching for hope and identity in the wake of exile.

Distinct from the Babylonian account, creation according to Gen. 1 is founded not on the conquest of watery "chaos" but on its enlistment (e.g., vv. 9, 20–21). Such an irenic view of creation perhaps reflects a profound effort on the part of the (former) exiles to put the painful past behind and to point the way to a new future. Genesis 1, in other words,

---

5. For details, see Campbell and O'Brien 1993, 4–5.

offers a powerfully edifying and inclusive vision of a community poised to reestablish itself in the land. The Babylonian exile of 586 BCE had left the land of Judah more than decimated. In the eyes of those most affected, imperial conquest and deportation rendered the land for all practical purposes *tōhû wābōhû* (1:2). The survivors experienced this national trauma as nothing less than a resurgence of cosmic chaos, leaving the land "empty," stripping the community of its national identity, and leaving the temple in ruins.[6] The good news of Gen. 1 is that God can work with such chaos to bring forth (new) creation. Heard in the time of exile or thereafter, the message of *imago Dei* in Genesis no doubt was a "clarion call to the people of God to stand tall again with dignity and to take seriously their royal-priestly vocation as God's authorized agents and representatives in the world" (Middleton 2005, 231).

For an exiled people, this "clarion call" also had a more specific function. The edict of release issued by Cyrus II in 538 BCE offered an unprecedented opportunity for the exiles: they could return and rebuild their homeland. In its historical context, Gen. 1 offered a hopeful vision of how to proceed, namely, by appealing to all sectors of the dispersed community and enlisting them in the great collaborative task of reconstruction, a monumental, if not cosmic, task. For former exiles, Gen. 1 would have provided a cosmic, programmatic vision for communal restoration, one that did not require a monarchy (forbidden under Persian hegemony) but instead affirmed the royal dignity of all under God's sovereign rule. At the same time, the account reminded the returning exiles that God's temple was far more than anything they could ever rebuild on site. It was creation itself. For them, God's cosmic temple in Genesis was an edifice of hope. The God of creation "in the beginning," Genesis seems to claim, is also the God of new beginnings, bringing order out of "chaos," whenever it erupts.

Such is one way of reading Gen. 1 in the light of a particular historical situation, the exile and its aftermath. To be sure, it requires speculation, but speculation that is informed by what we currently know of ancient Israel's history. It is a helpful exercise in reminding us that biblical texts were composed and preserved to address issues on the ground, in the struggle for both survival and meaning in challenging and even brutal times. By reading Gen. 1 amid the backdrop of the exile, we can recognize it as a form of nonviolent resistance against Babylonian hegemony and its legacy. Such a reading opens up new considerations of appreciation and understanding for a text that itself might seem to the uninformed reader to be too abstract for its own good.

Genesis 2–3

Because Gen. 2–3 has a more complicated history of literary growth than Gen. 1 (see chap. 9 above), it is harder to pin down historically. Specifically, there is no *one* historical period in which the garden story "originated," since it evolved over two, if not three, stages of development. But for simplicity's sake, I will aim at the two major stages of composition (an early creation story that over time came to be extended into a crime-and-

---

6. For a full discussion of the historical and theological trauma of exile, see Smith-Christopher 2002; Albertz 2003.

punishment story), but also offer a few observations regarding the possible background of a third stage.

As discussed in chap. 8, the bare-bones creation story of Gen. 2 highlights the creation of the *'ādām* from the ground (*'ădāmâ*, 2:7), the planting of a garden (v. 8), the fashioning of animals also from the ground (v. 19), and the creation of the woman from the man (vv. 22–23). In these verses, God does not begrudge the messy work of creating life. Moreover, the God of Gen. 2, in contrast to Marduk in the *Enuma Elish*, creates humankind not to relieve God of God's own labors, but for humanity to flourish in community.

This earliest form of the Yahwist creation account acknowledges the solidarity that humankind and animals have with the land or "ground" as well as celebrates the common substance between the man and the woman ("bones" and "flesh"). There is nothing specifically historical about the narrative in the sense that one can point to a particular situation or date in which the story would have been composed. However, it is clear that this portrayal of creation reflects an agrarian setting that celebrates the fecundity of the soil, specifically the ground as the source of life. Could it have reflected an ethos or vision of ancient Israel's agricultural life that was untrammeled by the rise of urbanization and monarchical power?

It might be too romantic a view of the historical situation to suggest that this early creation story was fashioned, say, before the monarchy and extensive urbanization. Nevertheless, the "history *in* the text" does recall or envision a time of agrarian work that was unimpeded by political disruption, such as the conscription of farmers by kings for military and monumental building projects (e.g., 1 Kgs. 5:13; 9:15). If this earlier version had been composed sometime during the monarchy, that is, with a preexilic provenance, such an account could have served as a potent reminder to the powers that be of the primacy of agrarian work over and against urban development or monarchic consolidation, perhaps as an appeal to safeguard the land's integrity in the face of imperial threat. Or perhaps, on the other hand, such an account would have served to further a royal program designed to increase the productivity of the land, as under Uzziah's reign, according to 2 Chr. 26:10. One can only wonder. One need only ask the historical questions to see where they might lead: What historically could be reflected in this text? Whose interests are served by this text? The answers are uncertain, but they do highlight the historical possibilities within, behind, and beyond each text.

With the added compositional or redactional layer, the plot most certainly thickens. This literary revision and extension transforms this idyllic portrayal of agrarian life into a crime-and-punishment story, whose major movement is the *'ādām's* placement in the garden (2:15a) and his expulsion (3:23). It is in this narrative turn that God sets down the law, specifically a prohibition accompanied by the punishment of death (2:17b). A specific tree is forbidden, and the violation of divine law becomes cause for the couple's eviction. That tree, of course, is the tree of knowledge (2:17a).

The narrative dynamic of the *'ādām's* placement in the garden, of disobedience of God's prohibition in the garden, and of expulsion from the garden may point toward the historical reality of Israel's exile from the land, as recounted in the Deuteronomistic History (2 Kgs. 24:14–16; 25:11–21). The *'ādām's* placement described in 2:15a employs the verb *nûaḥ* (Hiphil), literally, "cause to rest." Its nominal form, *mĕnûḥâ*, is sometimes used to designate the secure possession of the land by Israel (e.g., Deut. 12:9; 1 Kgs. 8:56; cf. Deut. 25:19). Moreover, this version introduces the theme of law and obedience, particularly prohibition and penalty. The following parallel is at least worth considering: as the ʾādām's life *in the garden* is conditioned upon his observance of God's commandment, so Israel's life *in the land* is dependent upon successful observance of the law or Torah (see, e.g., Lev. 18:25–30; Deut. 4:25–27; 6:24; 30:15–20).[7] But neither case turned out well: expulsion in one case (Gen. 3:23) exile in the other (2 Kgs 25:21b).

If this redaction was actually composed in the wake of Israel's exile, then new shades of meaning within this most primordial story begin to emerge. The Genesis story of expulsion from God's garden anticipates the larger Deuteronomistic story of Israel's exile from God's gift of the land. It describes an exile that involves humanity as a whole. In so doing, the account in its penultimate form universalizes the tragedy of Israel's exile while also explaining it. Disobedience is to blame. God's prohibition against appropriating wisdom autonomously highlights the supreme value of obedience, which ultimately points to the value of God's Torah as the source of Israel's livelihood. Both Gen. 3 and Deuteronomy value law over wisdom (see Deut. 4:5–6). For Deuteronomy, observance of Torah, God's authoritative instruction, is the primary or even exclusive source of Israel's wisdom, which the Genesis story expands into a universal claim.

Finally, a possibly additional redaction can be discerned, one that introduces the "tree of life" as the reason for the couple's expulsion, which involves an expansion of 2:9 and the addition of 3:22, 24—the only references to this other tree in Genesis. With this new focus on the "tree of life" as the reason for the ʾādām's expulsion, this second redaction steers the reader's attention away from Israel's national tragedy of exile and points it toward the issue of human immortality, specifically God's concern that humans *not* become immortal. This second redaction has, in effect, remythologized the story by moving away from the theme of "promised land lost" toward that of "immortality lost," specifically the loss of opportunity to gain immortality.[8] Such a redaction might have spoken most powerfully to the Diaspora, the community of Jews in Babylonia, Egypt, and elsewhere under Persian hegemony, who did not feel the need to or could not for whatever reason settle in the land of promise. The interesting historical question to ask is this: At what time or in what setting would the concern for immortality be of particular interest? Perhaps it was in response to tenets of Persian religion (the roots of Zoroastrianism), which included the soul's immortality in the spiritual world after death. But the same can also be said of Egyptian perspectives on life after death. One can only wonder.

All historical reflections on a biblical text involve speculation and reconstruction. Whether accurate or not, given the lack of hard evidence, this exercise in historical exploration and explanation proves helpful by imagining possible scenarios in which biblical texts were composed and functioned meaningfully. Historical study, in other words, reveals that the biblical text invariably has more depth and complexity than appears on the literary surface. There are always backstories to the biblical stories, the worlds "behind" the text.

---

7. For further detail, see Titus 2011, 464–67.
8. Titus 2011, 481. According to Titus, this serves to "soften" the "nationalistic nostalgia" of the former.

BIBLIOGRAPHY FOR CHAPTER 12

Albertz, Rainer. 2003. *Israel in Exile: The History and Literature of the Sixth Century B.C.E.* Translated by David Green. Studies in Biblical Literature 3. Atlanta: Society of Biblical Literature.

Campbell, Antony F., and Mark A. O'Brien. 1993. *Sources of the Pentateuch: Texts, Introductions, Annotations.* Minneapolis: Fortress Press.

Chavalas, Mark W., ed. 2006. *The Ancient Near East: Historical Sources in Translation.* Malden, MA: Blackwell.

Hayes, John H., and Carl R. Holladay. 2007. *Biblical Exegesis: A Beginner's Handbook.* 3rd ed. Louisville, KY: Westminster John Knox Press.

Huizinga, J. 1963. "A Definition of the Concept of History." In *Philosophy and History: Essays Presented to Ernst Cassirer,* edited by Raymond Klibansky and H. J. Paton, 1–10. New York: Harper & Row.

Middleton, J. Richard. 2005. *The Liberating Image: The* Imago Dei *in Genesis 1.* Grand Rapids: Brazos Press.

Miller, Maxwell J. 1999. "Reading the Bible Historically: The Historian's Approach." In *To Each Its Own Meaning: An Introduction to Biblical Criticisms and Their Application,* edited by Steven L. McKenzie and Stephen R. Haynes, 17–34. 2nd ed. Louisville, KY: Westminster John Knox Press.

Smith-Christopher, Daniel L. 2002. *A Biblical Theology of Exile.* OBT. Minneapolis: Fortress Press.

Titus, P. Joseph. 2011. *The Second Story of Creation (Gen 2:4–3:24): A Prologue to the Concept of Enneateuch?* European University Studies 23 (Theology), vol. 912. Frankfurt am Main: Peter Lang.

History Textbooks and References

Ancient Israel

Albertz, Rainer. 1994. *A History of Israelite Religion in the Old Testament.* 2 vols. Louisville, KY: Westminster John Knox Press.

Bright, John, with William P. Brown. 2000. *A History of Israel.* 4th ed. Louisville, KY: Westminster John Knox Press.

Coogan, Michael D., ed. 1998. *The Oxford History of the Biblical World.* New York and Oxford: Oxford University Press.

Gottwald, Norman K. 2001. *The Politics of Ancient Israel.* Library of Ancient Israel. Louisville, KY: Westminster John Knox Press.

Kessler, Rainer, and Linda M. Maloney. 2008. *The Social History of Ancient Israel: An Introduction.* Minneapolis: Fortress Press.

Long, V. Philips, ed. 1999. *Israel's Past in Present Research: Essays on Ancient Israelite Historiography.* Sources for Biblical and Theological Study. Winona Lake, IN: Eisenbrauns.

Miller, J. Maxwell, and John H. Hayes. 2006. *A History of Ancient Israel and Judah.* 2nd ed. Louisville, KY: Westminster John Knox Press.

Miller, Patrick D. 2000. *The Religion of Ancient Israel.* Louisville, KY: Westminster John Knox Press.

Provan, Iain, V. Philips Long, and Tremper Longman. 2015. *A Biblical History of Israel.* 2nd ed. Louisville, KY: Westminster John Knox Press.

Ancient Near East

Boardman, John, et al., eds. 1988. *Persia, Greece, and the Western Mediterranean c. 525–479 B.C.* 2nd ed. Vol. 4 of *Cambridge Ancient History.* Cambridge: Cambridge University Press.

———. 1991. *The Assyrian and Babylonian Empires and Other States of the Near East from the Eighth to the Sixth Centuries.* 2nd ed. Vol. 3, part 2, of *Cambridge Ancient History.* Cambridge: Cambridge University Press.

Briant, Pierre. 2002. *From Cyrus to Alexander: A History of the Persian Empire.* Translated by Peter T. Daniels. Winona Lake, IN: Eisenbrauns.

Hallo, William W., and William K. Simpson. 1998. *The Ancient Near East: A History.* 2nd ed. Fort Worth, TX: Harcourt Brace.

Kuhrt, Amélie. 1995. *The Ancient Near East: 3000–330 BC*. 2 vols. London: Routledge.

Redford, Donald B. 1992. *Egypt, Canaan, and Israel in Ancient Times*. Princeton, NJ: Princeton University Press.

Sasson, Jack M., ed. 2000. *Civilizations of the Ancient Near East*. 4 vols. in 2. Peabody, MA: Hendrickson Publishers. Reprinted from New York: Scribner, 1995.

Snell, Daniel C. 1998. *Life in the Ancient Near East, 3100–332 B.C.E.* New Haven: Yale University Press.

Soden, Wolfram von. 1993. *The Ancient Orient: An Introduction to the Ancient Near East*. Grand Rapids: Eerdmans Publishing.

Archaeology

Albright, William F. 2006 [1942]. *Archaeology and the Religion of Israel*. With a new introduction by Theodore J. Lewis. OTL. Louisville, KY: Westminster John Knox Press.

Ben-Tor, Amnon. 1992. *The Archaeology of Ancient Israel*. Translated by R. Greenberg. New Haven: Yale University Press.

Master, Daniel M., ed. 2013. *The Oxford Encyclopedia of the Bible and Archaeology*. 2 vols. New York: Oxford University Press.

Mazar, Amihai. 1992. *Archaeology of the Land of the Bible*. Vol. 1. ABRL. New York: Doubleday.

Meyers, Eric M., ed. 1997. *The Oxford Encyclopedia of Archaeology in the Near East*. 5 vols. Oxford: Oxford University Press.

Stern, Ephraim, ed. 1993. *The New Encyclopedia of Archaeological Excavations in the Holy Land*. 4 vols. Jerusalem: Israel Exploration Society & Carta; New York: Simon & Schuster.

———. 2001. *Archaeology of the Land of the Bible*. Vol. 2, *The Assyrian, Babylonian, and Persian Periods (732–332 B.C.E.)*. ABRL. New York: Doubleday.

13

Canonical Analysis

> The canon establishes a platform from which exegesis is launched
> rather than a barrier by which creative activity is restrained.
>
> *Brevard Childs*[1]

A text interpreted within its canonical context requires a widening of its literary boundaries to include, in principle, the entire Bible. But a canonical approach is more than simply a literary analysis writ large. Because "canon" is a normative term,[2] canonical analysis is also evaluative. It involves adjudicating the text's most central contributions to the larger canon, exploring how a particular text contributes *meaningfully* to Scripture as a whole. Emphasis is placed not so much on the text's oral or literary formation, or on its historical background, although such matters cannot be ignored. Rather, a canonical approach focuses on the text's "final form," the text as it is situated within the context of Scripture.[3]

The canonically oriented exegete looks for connections that the text has with other parts of the Bible through direct quotations, echoes, imagery, literary allusions, and themes, as well as theological disagreements. The range is wide. Pertinent questions include: *How does the text complement, enhance, or modify the claims of other texts? Are there countertestimonies to the text, and how does one adjudicate them in relation to each other?* Such questions involve evaluating a text in light of other texts throughout the canon.

Put simply, canonical interpretation has to do with interpreting the part (i.e., a particular text or texts) in light of the whole. The whole constitutes a rich network of texts, all in dialogue with each other as hosted by the canonical critic. Canonical interpretation is synchronic: various texts are read together without direct concern for their redactional development, historical backgrounds, and preliterary origins, for example. Nevertheless, there remains a deeper dimension to canonical interpretation. A canonical perspective acknowledges the inseparability of text and community as much as a historical

---

1. Childs 1979, 83.
2. Literally meaning "reed" or "measuring stick," the word "canon" establishes the outer boundaries of what is deemed authoritative as Scripture.
3. Whether the literary formation of the text (see chap. 9) plays a role in contributing to the canonical significance of the text remains a debated point. See Sanders 1972.

perspective does, except that it is the contemporary synagogue and the church (in all their various forms), rather than the ancient Israelites, that constitute the primary communities. Canonical texts are by definition sacred texts—texts deemed authoritative by communities of faith. Jews and Christians, the peoples of the Book, are the self-identified interpretive agents, with each religious tradition having its own canonical boundaries and arrangements. The Jewish Bible does not include NT writings. The expansive Roman Catholic and Orthodox Christian Bibles include the deuterocanonical (or apocryphal) writings, such as 1–2 Maccabees, Sirach, and Wisdom of Solomon. Certain individual books, such as Esther and Daniel, differ in content from one canon to another. The Septuagint, or Greek, translation of the Bible (see chap. 5) served as the canon of the early church, and later the Latin Vulgate for the Roman Catholic Church. For Protestants, the Reformation lifted up the Hebrew canon. The nature of biblical canon itself has proved to be quite fluid historically.

Finally, canonical readings of texts invariably involve theological considerations (see also chap. 22). Biblical texts are deemed foundational for communities of faith because they facilitate an encounter with God and serve as a means for understanding God's will. Canonical readings, thus, are meant to be instructive, because the texts are regarded by communities of faith that read them as authoritative.

BIBLICAL AUTHORITY

What "authoritative" means when applied to biblical interpretation, however, remains a matter of interpretation.[4] Below are two dictionary definitions of authority:

> The power and a right to command, act, enforce obedience, or make final decisions; jurisdiction . . . authorization . . . the power derived from opinion, respect, or esteem; influence of character or office.[5]

> Power to influence or command thought, opinion, or behavior . . . freedom granted . . . convincing force . . . grounds, warrant.[6]

One notices the wide semantic range spanned by the word "authority," but essential is the notion of power. Etymologically, the term is even more richly nuanced. The Latin connotes a creative sense. The word comes from *auctoritas*, meaning "origination," from which the word "author" derives. It is also related to the verb *auctorare*, "to bind." But such richness is easily depleted in the most common uses of the word in contemporary discourse. "Authority" frequently has its home in legal discourse, particularly when a specific decision is sought. People, for example, seek an authoritative precedent or reason that results in a binding decision. Journalists seek an authoritative or credible source for their research and reporting. Certain individuals assume authoritative status because they have become experts in their respective disciplines. Authority is domain specific.

4. For in-depth study on biblical authority and its various nuances, see Brown 2007.
5. *Webster's New Universal Unabridged Dictionary*, 2nd ed. (New York: Simon & Schuster, 1983).
6. *Webster's Seventh New College Dictionary* (Springfield, MA: G. & C. Merriam Co., 1969).

When "authority" is applied to the Bible, certain questions naturally emerge: To what domain(s) does the Bible's authority pertain? Does it apply to scientific and legal matters as it does to matters of faith and moral conduct? That may be easy to answer, but what about murkier matters such as sexuality, climate change, and stem-cell research, where ethical and theological reflection needs to engage the natural and social sciences? To complicate matters further, whereas the recourse to authority frequently involves seeking specific decisions or answers for a specific issue, how does one seek such things from biblical storytelling or the lament psalms? How does one "squeeze" authority out of the love poetry of the Song of Songs? Or is only the legal or instructive material of the Bible to be deemed authoritative? But then, what does one do when such material is not consistent? As a whole, the Bible is a unique source of wisdom, quite different from things we usually regard as authoritative, such as legal texts and scientific reports.

Perhaps a way forward is to acknowledge at the outset that Scripture is authoritative primarily with respect to its theological subject, God, who lies beyond the purview of scientific and historical inquiry. Nevertheless, because God is the creator of all things, respect for the authority of Scripture does not exclude but in fact requires respect for the authorities of the sciences. Indeed, the Bible does not reveal everything about the world in which we live and move, and what it does reveal can be misleading. Is infertility a sign of divine affliction? Must we adopt a geocentric worldview because the sun "stood still" at Gibeon when Joshua defeated the Amorites (Josh. 10:12)? The so-called skydome model of the waters above and below separated by a celestial firmament (Gen. 1:6–8) finds little correspondence with the structure of the cosmos as understood by science. The Bible fully acknowledges that there are many aspects about our world that can be discerned only through empirical observation and that there are realities that remain unexplained. This is indeed the premise of the Old Testament's wisdom tradition, as represented by Proverbs, Job, and Ecclesiastes.

"Authority" in the biblical sense, thus, takes on a different nuance from its normal usage in contemporary legal discourse. Solomon's decree to cut the infant in half was not in itself the right *legal* decision—indeed, it would have been horrifically wrong had it been *literally* carried out (1 Kgs. 3:25)! Rather, it served to provoke a response from the contesting parties to resolve a particular conflict. The Bible's "authority" thus is more at home with the original sense of the term, one connoting a creative, formative power that elicits a response and, in so doing, shapes the conduct and character of the reader or reading community. Simply put, biblical authority is reader-responsive: through our genuine engagement with Scripture, God "authors" us. Scripture's authority is dynamic and life shaping; it provokes a response that carries with it the acknowledgment, if not the conferral, of the Bible's authority. After all, authority must be acknowledged in order for something to be authoritative.

One of the few places in which the Bible directly speaks about itself is found in 2 Tim. 3:16–17.

> All Scripture is inspired by God and is useful for teaching, for reproof, for correction, and for training in righteousness, so that everyone who belongs to God may be proficient, equipped for every good work.

On the face of it, this passage makes a modest claim. Scripture is a gift from God that functions to teach and equip the community of faith. Its inspiration is defined in terms of what it can do for the body of Christ. The Bible's authority is demonstrated by its usefulness, by Scripture's capacity to edify and sustain, to teach and equip people for the life of faith.

According to this brief epistle, the Bible's authority is fundamentally a *functional* authority or, more accurately, a *formative* authority. What makes the Bible the Word of God does not depend upon any particular theory of inspiration so much as testify to what the Bible does in the lives of people. Talking about the Bible as a normative document stresses what is formative about the Bible, what it can *do* for "training in righteousness" and equipping the community "for every good work." Scripture's authority denotes the Bible's capacity to shape and transform people into mature communities of faith. Biblical authority is evidenced in practice as it is lived out by readers of Scripture. It is not something that adheres to the printed words of the text, like font size or the color of its letters, even if it is red. Biblical authority thus does not entail blind submission. The difference between authoritative and authoritarian is deep. The Bible gives reasons or warrants for its claims, for proper authority is *freely* acknowledged; it is not forced. This does not imply, however, that the Bible must be renegotiated on a day-to-day basis. The Bible is more than a friendly persuader; it mediates no less than God's living presence.

Speaking of biblical authority in a certain way amounts to viewing the nature of Scripture in a certain way. The biblical canon is complex and, as such, so is its authority. The Bible is not a systematic book of definitions and diagnoses, answers and prescriptions, complete with a handy index. It is a book filled with narrative and polity, reflective musings and situated letters, songs of praise, protest, and love. As an anthology, the Bible is a thoroughly mixed corpus by any measure: historically, literarily, and theologically. The literature spans nearly a millennium and a half of historical struggle and theological inquiry. It reflects centuries upon centuries of communal struggle and theological discernment. It speaks in many voices, some harmonious, others dissonant.

Discerning the many voices with which Scripture "speaks" is part of the challenging task of interpretation. Challenging even more so is discerning how these voices can "sing" together. That is the task of canonical interpretation, a project that takes seriously scriptural authority. The Bible's authority is realized in its canonical interpretation, and interpretation gives concrete expression to the Bible's authority. The canonical interpreter builds on the fact that Scripture interprets itself as earlier traditions are reformulated for new generations and contexts. Scripture is dialogical. Jewish interpreters have a pointed way of describing this: the Bible *debates* itself (Brettler 2007). Case in point: "Do not answer fools according to their folly, or you will be a fool yourself" is an admonition in Proverbs that is followed immediately by opposite counsel: "Answer fools according to their folly, or they will be wise in their own eyes" (Prov. 26:4–5). To respond or not to respond, that is the question with regard to "fools," and there is no one mind on the issue. Or take the example of John the Baptist's declaration: "The voice of one crying out in the wilderness: 'Prepare the way of the Lord, make his paths straight'" (Matt. 3:3; cf. Isa. 40:3). Ecclesiastes, however, observes: "Consider the work of God; who can make straight what [God] has made crooked?" (Eccl. 7:13).

The dialogical quality of Scripture complicates the issue of biblical authority, for the task of canonical interpretation requires the exegete to find ways to mediate the Bible's contesting voices, its testimonies and countertestimonies. The canonical critic wrestles with whether there are theological perspectives and claims that should be privileged over other perspectives and claims, all represented in Scripture. And what about the voices muted in Scripture that cry out for a hearing, such as the voice of the resident alien or the Canaanite consigned to destruction, as well the countless voices of nameless, marginalized women?

Every interpreter of Scripture must adjudicate the plethora of voices that make up the great canonical family called Scripture. A canonical approach to the text is, in the end, constructive. It hosts a dialogue between a particular text and other texts, irrespective of their literary or historical distance, and aims to fashion coherence from discrepancy, resolution from tension, and relevance from antiquity. Ultimately such coherence lies in the mind and heart of the canonical interpreter and in the community of which one is a part.

CANONICAL CASE STUDIES

A canonical approach, in short, treats the various, and in some cases quite disparate, texts of Scripture as interpretive partners by allowing them to engage each other dialogically. The image that comes to mind is that of a roundtable whose seats are filled by various biblical texts or traditions engaged in active conversation. The canonically minded interpreter serves as host, finding ways to encourage open dialogue with the expectation of discovering new connections and gaining new theological insights, indeed new wisdom and instruction. The following examples illustrate how a canonical "hosting" might be undertaken.

"I Am Doing a New Thing"

This well-known text from Isaiah, a prophetic announcement addressed to the exiles in Babylon, bears relevance that extends beyond its historical context.

> Thus says YHWH,
> the one who makes a way in the sea,
>   a path through the mighty waters,
> who draws out chariot and horse,
>   army and warrior together.
> [But] they lie down, unable to rise;
>   they are extinguished, snuffed out like a wick.
> "Do not remember the former things,
>   or ponder the things of old.
> Voilà, I am doing a new thing!
>   Now it's springing forth! Do you not know it?
> I will make a way in the wilderness,
>   rivers in the desert.
> The wild animals will honor me,
>   [including] the jackals and the ostriches;

> for I provide water in the wilderness, rivers in the desert,
> > to give drink to my chosen people." (43:16–20 alt.)

This passage looks both backward and forward. The prophet looks back at the event of the exodus, that paradigmatic event of Israel's deliverance from Egypt, which concludes with the parting of the sea. Tersely and poetically the prophet describes the climactic event, encapsulating in just a few brief lines what is described in far greater detail in Exod. 14–15. In the prophet's version, everything that happened is attributable solely to divine action. It is entirely God's doing that Egypt's military might is mustered, and it is also God's doing that Egypt's might is wiped out, "snuffed out like a wick."

But God is not done. Through the mouth of the prophet, God announces "a new thing" (ḥădāšâ), something so unprecedented that it is meant to replace the past, rendering it forgettable. Of all the things that God commands to be forgotten, it is this: the very event of Israel's birth—birth by divine deliverance! Yet this tremendous event of triumph is to be forgotten. Why? We may never know, but whatever the reason, the old must give way for the new. Through Isaiah, God announces an entirely new exodus, one that calls for a replacement of the past. Isaiah 43:16–20 is a canonical countertestimony to the book of Exodus. For Isaiah, the new renders the old obsolete: it is without precursor.

As much as Isaiah is a countertestimony to Exodus, another canonical voice serves a countertestimony to Isaiah, offering a far different notion of "newness."

> [9] What has been is what will be,
> > and what has been done is what will be done.
> > > There is nothing new under the sun.
> [10] If there is a thing of which it is said,
> > "See this; it is new!"
> it has already been,
> > in the ages before us.
> [11] There is no remembrance of those before [us],
> > nor of those who will come after.
> There will be no remembrance of them
> > by those who will come afterward. (Eccl. 1:9–11 AT)

Qoheleth, the melancholic sage, exposes the new as illusory, even a delusion. His denouncement appears as a concluding statement regarding how the world works (vv. 4–7). Amid all the cosmic flow and flux, Qoheleth sees nothing new; it is all a recycling of the old, the same thing over and over again. Human life, as the sage later demonstrates, is caught in this never ending, relentless recycling of activity, a world without pause and effect. And then there's death. Qoheleth depicts life as repetitive absurdity. Everything is "vanity" (hevel).

How, then, does one read the Isaianic text canonically in the light of Ecclesiastes and Exodus? Could Qoheleth honestly say to Isaiah, "This can't be new. It has already been, long ago"? Perhaps, but at the very least Qoheleth would challenge the reader to find something *old* in Isaiah's description of the *new* exodus. In fact, if one looks hard enough, one finds that this utterly "new" exodus is actually the mirror image of the old. The elements of sea and land remain, but now they are reversed: whereas the mighty waters were split by a dry path to provide safe passage in the old exodus, now rivers cut through the parched land, providing sustenance and a way home. A "path through the mighty waters" is matched by "rivers in the desert." The new exodus is a reversal of the old, while the old exodus is, in fact, a hidden precursor to the new. The pattern of a safe and sustaining passage pertains, whether old or new. Only the roles have been reversed, those of water and land. As radical as it is presented in the eyes of the prophet, the "new" is *not* created from nothing (ex nihilo), neither does it simply appear out of the blue. Rather, the new is fashioned *from* the old. The "new," it turns out, is a reconfiguration of the old. Qoheleth shows Isaiah that God's "new thing," however radical, always has its precedent.

Such would be one way of reading the Isaiah text canonically, specifically in relation to Ecclesiastes and Exodus. But the conversation can (and should) cut both ways. Canonically, Isaiah has every right to "challenge" Qoheleth to find something new within the world as the sage sees it. The repeated cycles of creation, including that of life, do include *new* phenomena, the new created from the old (*creatio ex vetere*), from evolution to technology, paradigm shifts in human understanding of reality, anthropogenic changes in climate, to name a few. And so the canonical conversation continues, as long as the exegetical ear can bear it.

The Cry and the Cross: Psalm 22 and Mark 15

For Christians, reading the Hebrew Bible or Old Testament in light of the New Testament (and vice versa!) is a necessary and challenging part of biblical interpretation. It is necessary because both Testaments constitute the Christian canon; it is challenging because the temptation is to override the Old Testament in favor the New. Such is the lamentable legacy of Christian supersessionism (see Soulen 1996). The two Testaments are bound together, making possible mutual interpretive interaction.

The New Testament takes up the Old Testament in various ways, from direct quotation to subtle allusion, from citations to echoes. Regarding one end of the intertextual spectrum, the New Testament is replete with quotations drawn from the Old Testament, usually via the Septuagint. Isaiah is quoted most often, and the Psalms come in second. Take one of the most well-known psalms in the Psalter, Ps. 22, which famously begins:

> My God, my God, why have you forsaken me?
>   So far [are you] from my cry,[7] the words of my screaming?[8]
> My God, I cry [to you] by day, but you do not answer,
>   and at night I have no relief. (22:1–2 [2–3] AT)

These words open an anguished and lengthy lament that extends through v. 21a (22a), but abruptly turns toward praise for the remainder of the psalm. The opening words reappear in Mark in Jesus' cry from the cross in 15:34 (also Matt. 27:46).[9]

---

7. MT reads: "from my deliverance." However, the form *mšwʿty*, slightly emended from *myšwʿty*, establishes a better parallel with the following phrase.

8. Literally, "roaring" like a lion (e.g., Isa. 5:29; Ezek. 19:7; Zech. 11:3; Job 4:10). See also Ps. 22:13b (14b MT). The term can be applied to a person's discourse (Ps. 32:3; Job 3:24). The OG or LXX reads "wrong-doings," apparently reading a transposition of two letters as *šĕgiʾōtay* (see Ps. 19:13). The context, however, argues against such a reading.

9. The crowd ironically misunderstands Jesus' cry of dereliction, which is cast in Aramaic, thinking that he is calling upon Elijah rather than "my God" (*Eloi*) (Mark 15:35).

When it was noon, darkness came over the whole land until three in the afternoon. At three o'clock Jesus cried out with a loud voice, ***"Eloi, Eloi, lema sabachthani?"*** which means, ***"My God, my God, why have you forsaken me?"*** When some of the bystanders heard it, they said, "Listen, he is calling for Elijah." (Mark 15:33–35)[10]

But that's not the only place where Mark borrows from the psalm. The reference to the soldiers dividing up Jesus' clothes in Mark 15:24 echoes another verse from the psalm.

They divide up my garments among themselves,
  and for my clothing they cast lots. (Ps. 22:18 [19])

And they crucified him, and ***divided his clothes among them,*** ***casting lots*** to decide what each should take. (Mark 15:24)

In this case we do not have a direct quotation, but something close to it, the major difference being the shift in person: the psalmist speaks in the first person, whereas Mark recounts this moment of abject humiliation in the third person, along with a more prosaic rendering of the second line of the psalmic verse.

More subtle in the Markan crucifixion account is the depiction of derision that Jesus suffers on the cross.

All who see me mock me;
  they open (their) lips and shake their heads.
"He has committed himself to YHWH,
  so let him deliver him.
Let him save him, for he delights in him." (Ps. 22:7–8 [8–9] AT)

Those who passed by derided him, ***shaking their heads*** and saying, "Aha! You who would destroy the temple and build it in three days, save yourself, and come down from the cross!" In the same way the chief priests, along with the scribes, were also ***mocking him*** among themselves and saying, "He saved others; he cannot ***save himself.*** Let the Messiah, the King of Israel, come down from the cross now, so that we may see and believe." Those who were crucified with him also ***taunted him.*** (Mark 15:29–32)

The allusions are subtle but unmistakable, so also the transformation that takes place in Mark's narrative! Whereas the mockers in the psalm taunt the speaker by appealing to God as his deliverer ("Let [YHWH] save him"), Mark has Jesus' deriders make the appeal to Jesus himself ("Let the Messiah, the King of Israel, come down"). In Mark's telling, the irony becomes more fully recognizable.

In his account of Jesus' crucifixion, Mark draws three times from Ps. 22 and in so doing unites Christ on the cross with the psalmist in anguish.[11] By reciting the cry of the psalmist, Mark identifies Jesus with the afflicted speaker in Ps. 22, transforming affliction into execution, specifically crucifixion. But that's not all. What Mark leaves unsaid may be just as important, namely, how Ps. 22 concludes with unbridled thanksgiving and praise from

---

10. New Testament citations are drawn from the NRSV.

11. In addition, the attempt to give Jesus "sour wine" in Mark 15:36 recalls Ps. 69:21b, "For my thirst they gave me vinegar to drink."

someone delivered by God and who now beseeches the world, no less, including the dead and the unborn, to give praise to God (vv. 21b–31 [22b–32]). For those who have ears to hear, the psalmic echoes in Mark's passion narrative point to a seamless yet surprisingly abrupt move from affliction to salvation, from anguished despair to transcendent praise. Psalm 22 runs the gamut and turns on a hairpin: v. 21 (22) is a whiplash moment that immediately transforms bitter complaint and desperate petition into powerful testimony and extravagant praise.

> Save me from the mouth of the lion!
>   From the horns of the wild oxen you have answered me! (mg.)

Mark presses Ps. 22 into service on the cross, leading to Jesus' humiliating death, but leaves unstated how the psalm might also point to Christ's resurrection. The deafening silence seems to be part of Mark's ploy.

The case of Ps. 22 and Mark 15 illustrates a wide range of scriptural usage, from direct quotation to allusion, from the obvious to the subtle. Perhaps the most subtle (and speculative) is the possibility that Mark presupposes the second half of Ps. 22 to anticipate Jesus' resurrection. At least that would be one way of reading Mark's depiction of Christ's crucifixion (and beyond) from the perspective of Psalm 22. In any case, by reciting the psalmist's cry on the cross, Jesus becomes the canonical voice of lament. In so doing, Jesus identifies himself with all who suffer, particularly those who suffer unjustly and feel abandoned by God, in the hope of deliverance by God.

"Green Grass": Psalm 23 and Mark 6:39

A particularly subtle but powerful example of a canonical connection is the possible use of Ps. 23 in the Markan narrative of the feeding of the five thousand in the desert. The narrative turns on these verses:

> [38] [Jesus] said to them, "How many loaves have you? Go and see." When they had found out, they said, "Five, and two fish." [39] Then he ordered them to get all the people to sit down in groups on the green grass. [40] So they sat down in groups of hundreds and of fifties. [41] Taking the five loaves and the two fish, he looked up to heaven, and blessed and broke the loaves, and gave them to his disciples to set before the people; and he divided the two fish among them all. [42] And all ate and were filled. (Mark 6:38–42)

There is one word that is unique in the Markan version of the feeding event that does not occur in the other Gospel accounts. It is the word "green" (*chlōros*, v. 39), referring to the fresh grass that the people are to sit on when they are fed. This added Technicolor detail could be merely ornamental, or it could be highly significant. Compare the opening lines of Ps. 23.

> YHWH is my shepherd;
>   I lack nothing.
> In meadows of fresh grass he lets me lie;
>   to waters of repose he leads me, refreshing my soul. (AT)

The psalmist paints an idyllic picture of abundant provision, set within the pastoral imagery of sheep lying on grass. Could it be that Mark, with this one word, wants the reader to recall the pastoral imagery of the Shepherd Psalm, and if so, to identify Jesus with the Shepherd (so Long 2005, 85)?[12] The answer is, I believe, yes. Not only because of one little word, but also because in an earlier verse Mark has this to say about Jesus:

> As [Jesus] went ashore, he saw a great crowd; and he had compassion for them, because they were like sheep without a shepherd; and he began to teach them many things. (6:34)

The lush grass is a setting for abundant provision and protection, and the shepherd leads the sheep there. So does Jesus, according to Mark, to feed the crowd. Jesus is the Good Shepherd—not an unprecedented identification in the New Testament (John 10:1–16), to be sure, but Mark offers a glimpse of Jesus' shepherding role in a particularly dramatic and subtle way. By allusively invoking Ps. 23, Mark adds pastoral depth to the feeding scene and at the same time envisions a world of provision and security that Jesus offers.

GENESIS CREATION ACCOUNTS

How far canonically does Gen. 1 extend? In principle to the end of the canon, as with any text. But before we get to the end, there are certain texts in the Hebrew Bible to which the first creation account of the Bible canonically relates.

Genesis 1 and Isaiah

There are two texts in Isaiah that establish a canonical connection with Genesis: Isa. 45:7 and vv. 18–19, and they do so specifically through their "disagreements" with Genesis.

> I form light and create darkness,
>   I make weal and create woe;
>   I YHWH do all these things. (Isa. 45:7)

Note that "darkness" (ḥōšek) is the same darkness with which creation began in Gen. 1:2. What might Isaiah be saying to Genesis, one could ask canonically? Whereas Gen. 1 depicts God speaking light into being, the very first act of creation (v. 3), God in Isaiah testifies to having created *both* light and darkness. Thus it seems that God's creative range in Isaiah is wider than that given in Genesis. But there is a cost involved in this broadening of creative agency. By attributing darkness as a creative act of God, Isaiah describes God as the author of both "weal" (šālôm) and "woe" (rāʿ), which can also be translated as "evil." Is God the author of such dualistic outcomes? By comparison, Gen. 1 is reluctant to take such a route. Isaiah, however, has no hesitation. And so the theological dialogue continues. At the very least, the Isaianic text highlights a "gap" in

---

12. The Septuagint translates the beginning of Ps. 23:2 as "green place" (*topon chloēs*), related but not identical to the word Mark uses.

Gen. 1, namely, the "genesis" of darkness. Where does darkness come from? What are the theological and ethical implications of attributing, or not attributing, darkness to God's creative activity?

More compatible with, yet nevertheless distinct from, Gen. 1 is the passage a few verses later in Isaiah, in which God's intention in and for creation has nothing to do with "darkness" or with "chaos," but with life.

> For thus says YHWH,
>> who creates the heavens (he is God!),
>> who forms the earth and fashions it;
>>> He established it;
> he did not create it a chaos [tōhû];
>> he formed it to be inhabited!
> "I am YHWH,
>> and there is no other.
> I did not speak in secret, in a land of darkness [ḥōšek].
>> I did not say to Jacob's offspring, 'Seek me in chaos [tōhû].'
> I YHWH speak the truth,
>> I declare what is right." (45:18–19 AT)

This creation poem divides itself evenly into two parts. The creation part (v. 18) introduces the divine declaration (v. 19). God's intention for creation is habitation, not "chaos" or "darkness," and seeking God can only take place in a well-ordered creation, one vibrant with life (cf. Jer. 4:23–26). "Seek me" in a life-sustaining creation is God's invitation to a despairing and displaced people in exile. Seeking God in chaos, on the other hand, is simply a waste.

The connection to Gen. 1 is both obvious and subtle. Isaiah deploys a word that constitutes the first half of the farrago tōhû wābōhû featured in Gen. 1:2 to describe "chaos," a cosmic mishmash devoid of structure and life. Similarly in Isa. 45, "chaos" (tōhû) is uninhabitable; it is incapable of hosting life and thus is the opposite of creation. It is also whatever inhibits "seeking" God. Taken together, darkness is part of God's creation, but as this subsequent text from Isaiah makes clear, it is *not* part of God's intent in creation. Moreover, God's intent according to Isaiah is to be *sought*, not in chaos, but in a habitable, ordered creation. This adds a new dimension, a distinctly didactic dimension perhaps, to cosmic creation in Gen. 1: God is "seekable" in creation; God speaks "truth" in creation, rather than in chaos or in secret. And as for the picture of creation that Isaiah has in mind, a creation that is fully inhabitable, the one depicted in Gen. 1 would fit the bill quite nicely: order is the prerequisite for life.

A more subtle connection is found in a distinction between the two texts that prompts one to reread Gen. 1 in the light of Isa. 45. The latter text is up front and direct about claiming God's purpose in creation: to establish order and, in so doing, inhabitability in creation. More specifically, God in and through creation, according to Isaiah, desires to be sought, as well as to be heard. Such a blatant articulation of purpose, however, is not to be found in Gen. 1. By comparison, the first account of creation in Genesis seems reluctant to declare any overarching purpose. We can certainly infer purpose from God's creation of the cosmos, as Isaiah does, but it may be worth considering why Gen. 1 does *not* explicitly declare divine intent in creation. God simply creates. Period. Is that purpose left open? One can only wonder.

Lastly from Isaiah, another text lifts up a certain quality of the divine that coheres with God's role as Creator: Isa. 40:28–31. Formally speaking, this well-known text is a disputation consisting of a divine rebuke that leads to a counterresponse, which is expressed as a doxology and salvation oracle. At first glance, this text may not seem to have much to do with Genesis, until one considers the interpretive possibilities regarding what God was "doing" on the seventh day in 2:1–3. Did God need to rest? Was God tired? Isaiah offers as answer.

> [God] does not grow tired or weary;
>   there is no fathoming his understanding.
> He gives power to the weary,
>   and for the powerless he increases might.
> Whereas youths grow tired and weary,
>   and the athletic fall exhausted,
> those who wait for YHWH shall put on strength;
>   they shall sprout pinions like eagles.
> They shall run and not grow weary;
>   they shall walk and not be fatigued. (40:28b–31 AT)

Isaiah's God does not cease or rest, unlike the God of the Sabbath. Whereas the God of Genesis models the salutary rhythm of work and rest, the God of Isaiah *unceasingly* empowers "the faint" and strengthens "the powerless" (40:29).[13] For Isaiah, creation is ongoing, bearing witness to YHWH's unrivaled claim of sovereignty. This God is the *only* God, the God of all creation. Moreover, this unstoppable, uninterruptable creator of all is YHWH, Israel's God.

Genesis 1 and John 1

Finally, in the New Testament the most obvious text canonically tied to Gen. 1 is John 1, specifically vv. 1–5, 9–14. The connections between John 1 and Gen. 1 are profound and nearly inexhaustible. The first two words in John replicate the first words in the Septuagint (Greek) translation of Gen. 1: *en archē* (in beginning). What connections do you see thereafter? Here are a few observations. By identifying the "beginning" with the *Logos*, John reaches behind the dark and watery void of Genesis to discover something so fundamental that it is able to account for all creation. Typically translated as "Word," *logos* has its home in Greek Stoic philosophy and refers to the structuring principle of the universe that makes life possible. By invoking the *Logos*, John claims a cosmic rationale for all creation. But *Logos* is more than a rational abstraction.

According to Gen. 1, God created by verbal edict. With a little help from the Stoics, John takes up this Priestly theme of creation by word, turns it into a cosmic code, and then in a surprising twist turns the *Logos* into a person. To get from cosmic principle to person, John offers the central metaphor of light, the "light of all peoples," the light that

13. See Fishbane 1985, 326; Sommer 1998, 144.

darkness cannot "overcome," "the light of the world," as Jesus later says of himself (8:12; 9:5). No wonder. Light, according to Genesis, is the first act of creation. But for John, there is more to light than its cosmic cast. The "light of the world" is also *in* the world, this light of the *Logos*.

Arguably, the center of John's cosmic prologue is found in v. 14: "The Word became flesh and made his home among us" (CEB). The second verb literally means "pitch one's tent," or "tabernacle" (*skēnoō*), which points back to the tabernacle construction in Exodus. If at the beginning of creation, according to Gen. 1, God built a cosmic temple, then John poses a crucial question that is left unaddressed in Genesis: when and how does God *enter* creation? According to Exodus, it is in and through the completion of the tabernacle (Exod. 40). According to John, it is in and through Christ. Canonically, then, John 1 establishes a narrative trajectory extending from Genesis to John, from creation to incarnation, and in so doing, John has rewritten Gen. 1 christologically.

GENESIS 2–3

With the exception of Genesis (up until 5:5) and 1 Chr. 1:1, there is nothing in the Hebrew Bible that talks of Adam and/or Eve, a rather surprising absence.[14] However, Eden, the "garden of God," is attested in scattered references in the prophetic tradition, specifically in Ezekiel and Isaiah (cf. Joel 2:3). Discussed earlier (in chap. 9) is an Eden tradition in Ezekiel that targets the king of Tyre as the villain deserving of a "fall," "cast to the ground" (Ezek. 28:11–19). Elsewhere in Ezekiel, the "trees of Eden" are singled out for their majesty, comparable to the cedars of Lebanon (31:16), all brought down with the fall of Assyria and Egypt (vv. 16b, 18). In Ezekiel, not only does the king fall, but also Eden's trees, an ecological catastrophe.

Eden's Restoration?

Nevertheless, Eden surfaces again in a salvation oracle from Ezekiel in which God promises to restore Israel's land, making it akin to "the garden of Eden" in 36:33–35. Here and elsewhere, Eden's garden is symbolic of full restoration, both urban and agricultural, following the ravages of divine judgment. So also Isaiah:

> For YHWH will comfort Zion;
>   he will comfort all her waste places,
> and will make her wilderness like Eden,
>   her desert like the garden of YHWH;
> joy and gladness will be found in her,
>   thanksgiving and the voice of song. (Isa. 51:3)

In both Ezekiel and Isaiah, the outcome of God's restoration is not equated with Eden, but rather compared to Eden in resemblance, "like Eden." While Eden itself may not be

---

14. Such silence is sometimes taken as evidence for the lateness of Gen. 2–3, but this is a tenuous argument if left to itself. The absence of evidence is not the evidence of absence.

attainable, the comparison is not meant to be a diminishment of Israel's restoration by any measure. To the contrary, the references to Eden in both prophetic passages are hyperbolically poetic. It is not that Eden can be regained, but something resembling Eden can be cultivated even on a once-devastated land, planted by God, the first cultivator, no less (Gen. 2:8). Eden thus becomes a cipher for the land's restoration, mythic or otherwise. "Paradise" is not entirely lost.[15]

Adam in the New Testament

There are a few quotes of Gen. 2–3 in the New Testament. One versatile example is Gen. 2:24, which Jesus quotes on the issue of divorce in Matt. 19:5 (//Mark 10:7–8). In Eph. 5:31, Paul uses the citation to talk of the love between Christ and the church, "a great mystery" (v. 32).

Most frequent are the NT references to "Adam," mostly from Paul, the exception being the genealogical reference in Luke 3:38. In Rom. 5:12–14, Adam is deemed the root cause of sin and, along with sin, death in the world. On the one hand, Paul reads the garden story in Gen. 2–3 as a story of how humanity became afflicted with sin and death. On the other hand, Adam is a "type" (*typos*) of the one to come, Jesus Christ. What that means is explicated in vv. 17–18. Here Adam and Christ embody a symmetry of opposites: sin and death from Adam's "trespass" versus grace, righteousness, justification, and "life for all" from Christ's "act of righteousness." The latter trumps the former. This comparison is further sharpened in 1 Cor. 15:21–22. Both Adam and Christ usher in ultimate conditions of human life: death on the one hand, and resurrection on the other. As for how this is the case, Paul draws from Gen. 2 in 1 Cor. 15:44–49.

> [44] It is sown a physical body, it is raised a spiritual body. If there is a physical body, there is also a spiritual body. [45] Thus it is written, "The first man, Adam, ***became a living being***"; the last Adam became a life-giving spirit. [46] But it is not the spiritual that is first, but the physical, and then the spiritual. [47] The first man was from the earth, a man of ***dust***; the second man is from heaven. [48] As was the man of ***dust***, so are those who are of the ***dust***; and as is the man of heaven, so are those who are of heaven. [49] Just as we have borne the ***image*** of the man of dust, we will also bear the ***image*** of the man of heaven.

In 1 Cor. 15:45, Paul draws from Gen. 2:7, quoting its ending in Greek (*psychēn zōsan*), and builds on the theme of dust (1 Cor. 15:48), signifying mortality, as it does in Gen. 3:19b. Creatively, Paul also draws from Gen. 1, specifically the language of "image" (*eikōn*) in 1 Cor. 15:49, the same word in the Septuagint for the Hebrew *ṣelem* in Gen. 1:27, "*image* of God." But for Paul, there are *two* "images" in his creative conflation of both accounts: the "image of the man of dust" (Adam) and his opposite, "the image of the man of heaven" (Christ). The latter establishes an indelible link between Christ, "the man of heaven," and God.

---

15. Phyllis Trible argues that the Song of Songs marks a reentry into Eden, since this book of love poetry between a man and a woman has as its poetic setting a lush garden (1978, 144–65).

It is clear for Paul that Adam's disobedience, his "trespass" (Rom. 5:15–18) in the garden, brought both sin and, consequently, death into the world. This is unclear in Gen. 2–3. The question whether Adam (and Eve) were created immortal remains open to debate (see chap. 10). Indeed, Paul could be read as taking both sides of the issue by emphasizing that Adam was "a man of dust," created so according to Gen. 2:7. Yet to contrast Adam with Christ, Paul must highlight what Adam has done for *all* humanity: Adam has ushered in death for all as Christ, all the more so, has brought about new life to all. As earth and heaven are reflected in Adam and Christ, respectively, so people in Christ move from "dust" to "heaven."

A canonical comparison between Paul and Genesis reveals striking differences as well as subtle connections. Through close comparison, one can moreover discern something of the rationale behind Paul's own claims about Adam. As the representative figure of humanity, Adam is viewed as both a foil and a forerunner to Christ. It is Adam who sets the stage, who introduces the tragic human condition, making way for the new condition of salvation in Christ. For Paul, the story of Adam in Genesis finds its fulfillment in Christ in the gospel, building a narrative arc that proceeds from condemnation to salvation, from death to new life for "all" humanity (Rom. 5:18).

Paul, thus, reads Adam through the lens of Christ. But how might one read in the other direction, that is, read Paul's Christology from the perspective of the Yahwist? That Adam is a "groundling" in Gen. 2–3, a creature tied to the ground and, thus, to all life fashioned "out of the ground" (Gen. 2:19), may have significant bearing on the scope of Christ's salvific work. In Rom. 5 and 1 Cor. 15, Paul focuses exclusively on Christ's impact upon the human condition. But what about Christ's significance for the "ground" itself, cursed as it is by Adam's disobedience (Gen. 3:17–19)? In Rom. 5 and 1 Cor. 15, Paul has nothing to say about the "ground," much less about creation as a whole. Could the narrative trajectory that Paul charts also move from cosmic brokenness to cosmic renewal, from creation's bondage to liberation? Indeed, Paul seems to make that move elsewhere, in Rom. 8:19–23. Let the reader decide. In any case, the canonical approach can cut both ways.

Eve in the New Testament

What about Eve? The only mention of Eve in the New Testament (other than in 2 Cor. 11:3) is in a pastoral epistle, and it is not a flattering picture.

> Let a woman learn in silence with full submission. I permit no woman to teach or to have authority over a man; she is to keep silent. For Adam was formed first, then Eve; and Adam was not deceived, but the woman was deceived and became a transgressor. (1 Tim. 2:11–14)

As justification for his view of women's subordinate status, Paul draws from Gen. 2:21–23 and 3:1–7. Paul finds the sequence of human creation to indicate hierarchy, associating the first human creature (Adam) with superiority. Moreover, Paul interprets the account of disobedience in the garden as involving only Eve, while "Adam was not deceived." Both interpretations are questionable in light of the Genesis text. In Genesis, the issue of subordination does not raise its head until the punishment in 3:16b: "he shall rule over you." Yet Paul reaches back to the moment of creation to launch his argument against a woman having "authority over a man." For him, subordination comes when the woman is created.

Paul, moreover, absolves Adam of (some) guilt by laying the blame of disobedience squarely upon Eve. Such a move seems to differ from the depiction given in Genesis, which states that the man was with the woman when she partook (Gen. 3:6–7). In Paul's view, Adam's eating of the fruit is not as culpable as Eve's. Decisive for Paul is not the disobedience but the deception, which according to him applies only to Eve. There is textual warrant for this in Genesis, slim as it may seem: while the woman confesses to God that she was "tricked" (Gen. 3:13), Adam does not. He simply states that he ate the fruit given to him by the woman (v. 12). Remaining purely on the surface of the text, Paul observes that the language of "deception" applies only to Eve. But on the deeper narrative level was not Adam deceived as well, who was beside Eve all the time? Were not both of them deceived? In any case, the Genesis text is clear that both Adam and Eve are equally culpable. A canonical reading resists the temptation to simply dismiss one passage in favor of another. Instead, it begins by asking how a certain reading of an earlier passage could have arisen as a way of hosting a genuine dialogue between them. Nevertheless, in some cases, particularly in cases of stark disagreement, a decision must be made as to which one carries greater theological weight.

Tree of Life Revisited

Lastly, it is no coincidence that the Christian canon is arranged in such a way that the book of Revelation constitutes its last book, concluding with a vision of the new creation. How does John's depiction of the new creation relate to the "old," specifically that which is depicted in Gen. 1–3?

As in Gen. 2–3, reference to the "tree of life" brackets the book of Revelation, appearing near the beginning and reappearing at the end.

> Let anyone who has an ear listen to what the Spirit is saying to the churches. To everyone who conquers, I will give permission to eat from *the tree of life* that is in the paradise of God. (Rev. 2:7)

> Blessed are those who wash their robes, so that they will have the right to *the tree of life* and may enter the city by the gates. (Rev. 22:14; cf. v. 19)

John declares that access to the tree of life has been cleared for anyone who "conquers," a motif in Revelation (see, e.g., 2:11, 17, 26, 28; 3:5, 12, 21). The language of "conquer" in Revelation functions to undercut Roman imperial language associated with Nike, the Greek goddess of victory (Roman "Victoria"). To "conquer" according to Revelation is to follow the *slain* Lamb, the crucified one (e.g., 5:12; 13:8). This twisting of rhetoric marks a subversive reversal of imperial discourse. And the reward for such "conquering" is the tree of life, which imparts not only resurrection but also "the healing of the nations."

> Then the angel showed me the river of the water of life, bright as crystal, flowing from the throne of God and of the Lamb through the middle of the street of the city. On either side of the river is **_the tree of life_** with its twelve kinds of fruit, producing its fruit each month; and the leaves of **_the tree_** are for the healing of the nations. (22:1–2)

Moreover, John sees not only one "tree of life," but many, for along the river's two banks flourishes a grove of such trees.[16] Every fruit tree now is a tree of life!

What John sees in his vision of the new creation is not the replacement of the garden with a city, but a garden *in* a city, an urban garden. In his vision Eden and Jerusalem merge, and in this urban paradise the tree of life in Genesis is cultivated into a veritable forest in Revelation. This is not without biblical precedent elsewhere, although you will not find it in Gen. 2–3. No city is mentioned there (cf. Gen. 4:17). However, the prophetic references to Eden noted above reflect the restoration of the land for a people, including the city. According to John, the new Jerusalem is not simply "like" the Eden of Genesis; it is *more* than Eden.[17]

With respect to Gen. 1, the text of Rev. 21 is quite explicit about the differences the new creation has in relation to the old. Notice the following three references:

> Then I saw a new heaven and a new earth; for the first heaven and the first earth had passed away, and the sea was no more. (v. 1)

> I saw no temple in the city, for its temple is the Lord God the Almighty and the Lamb. And the city has no need of sun or moon to shine on it, for the glory of God is its light, and its lamp is the Lamb. (vv. 22–23)

> And there will be no more night; they need no light of lamp or sun, for the Lord God will be their light, and they will reign forever and ever. (22:5)

The new creation exceeds creation in Genesis not only by what is enhanced but also by what is eliminated. Heaven and earth have become one, and as a result some things drop out, as it were: the sea, the temple, the sun and moon, night, all replaced by God's radiant, life-giving presence (21:22–23). The reason the sea is singled out is because, from John's perspective, the sea connotes chaos, specifically the chaos of imperial rebellion against God (e.g., 13:1). It is where the monsters of Rome and Babylon reside; it is the source of their international power. This "sea," therefore, has no place in the new creation (21:1). So too the night: there will no longer be darkness, for God's glory will provide uninterrupted light, the lamp of the Lamb, the crucified Christ (v. 23). And then there is death, which will also be eliminated (21:4), as the "trees of life" flourish on the river's banks (22:2).

In the new creation, there is no temple, for God's holy and wholly immanent presence renders any localized temple obsolete. Indeed, the entirety of creation, both heaven and earth, has been God's temple from the very beginning. Here the end does mirror the

---

16. Here the sg. word "tree" in Greek (*xylon*) is used collectively.
17. Blount 2009, 397.

beginning, recalling the Priestly view of creation as God's cosmic sanctuary (see chap. 8), even as the end exceeds the beginning. The glorious result is the holy habitation of the Most High on earth.

In sum, the Christian canon is bookended by creation: Gen. 1–3 at the beginning and Revelation 21–22 at the end. Creation and new creation are bound together canonically and interrelated theologically. The Revelation account draws liberally from the Genesis accounts while at the same time exceeding them. Revelation's new creation is both continuous and discontinuous with respect to creation in Genesis. The new creation is not created ex nihilo; indeed, as the Voice from the throne declares: "See, I am making all things new" (Rev. 21:5). God does not say, "I am making all new things." The work of new creation is the work of renewal. Together Genesis and Revelation ensure that God's salvific work attested throughout Scripture is cosmically significant, from beginning to end.

CONCLUSION

A canonical approach looks for connections and trajectories that extend from one biblical text to another, regardless of how literarily distant or historically separated they are. In so doing, a canonical reading involves hosting a dialogue, asking how each text contributes to the ongoing theological dialogue that unfolds in Scripture. Broadly put, reading canonically means considering the parts in light of the whole, even though "the whole" is hard to summarize, given the Bible's diversity. Hence, interpreting a text canonically entails making decisions that are theologically constructive and instructive. And through one's engagement with texts, the exegete must decide what is central and, in turn, what is peripheral. It is hard to predict the direction, let alone the destination, of the canonical dialogue, for reading texts in conversation around the "table" is bound to uncover new insights, perhaps even a few surprises.

BIBLIOGRAPHY FOR CHAPTER 13

Beale, G. K. 2014. *Handbook on the New Testament Use of the Old Testament: Exegesis and Interpretation*. Grand Rapids: Baker Academic.

Beale, G. K., and D. A. Carson, eds. 2007. *Commentary on the New Testament Use of the Old Testament*. Grand Rapids: Baker Academic.

Blount, Brian K. 2009. *Revelation: A Commentary*. NTL. Louisville, KY: Westminster John Knox Press.

Bratcher, Robert G. 1967. *Old Testament Quotations in the New Testament*. 2nd ed. London: United Bible Societies.

Brettler, Marc Zvi. 2007. "Biblical Authority: A Jewish Pluralistic View." In Brown 2007, 1–10.

Brown, William P., ed. 2007. *Engaging Biblical Authority: Perspectives on the Bible as Scripture*. Louisville, KY: Westminster John Knox Press.

Childs, Brevard S. 1979. *Introduction to the Old Testament as Scripture*. Philadelphia: Fortress Press.

———. 1993. *Biblical Theology of the Old and New Testaments: Theological Reflections on the Christian Bible*. Minneapolis: Fortress Press.

———. 2001. *Isaiah*. OTL. Louisville, KY: Westminster John Knox Press.

Fishbane, Michael. 1985. *Biblical Interpretation in Ancient Israel*. Oxford: Clarendon Press.

Levenson, Jon D. 1988. *Creation and the Persistence of Evil: The Jewish Drama of Divine Omnipotence*. San Francisco: Harper & Row.

Long, Thomas G. 2005. *The Witness of Preaching*. Louisville, KY: Westminster John Knox Press.

Moyise, Steve. 2001. *The Old Testament in the New: An Introduction*. London and New York: T&T Clark International.

Porter, Stanley E., ed. 2006. *Hearing the Old Testament in the New Testament*. Grand Rapids: Eerdmans Publishing.

Sanders, James S. 1972. *Torah and Canon*. Philadelphia: Fortress Press.

Scalise, Charles J. 1996. *From Scripture to Theology: A Canonical Journey into Hermeneutics*. Downers Grove, IL: InterVarsity Press.

Sommer, Benjamin D. 1998. *A Prophet Reads Scripture: Allusion in Isaiah 40–66*. Stanford, CA: Stanford University Press.

Soulen, R. Kendall. 1996. *The God of Israel in Christian Theology*. Minneapolis: Augsburg Fortress Press.

Trible, Phyllis. 1978. *God and the Rhetoric of Sexuality*. OBT. Philadelphia: Fortress Press.

Interlude

14

From Text to Table

Tell all the truth, but tell it slant.
Emily Dickinson[1]

We are about to shift our focus in the following chapters in a significant way—significant but by no means unprecedented. So far we have considered the more analytically oriented issues of exegesis, from the translation of the text to its design, growth, and historical background. Such efforts have been largely focused on describing the text's own contours, both internally (e.g., translation and structure) and externally (e.g., historical background and relationship to other texts). These chapters have had a largely descriptive aim, with the slight exception of the canonical approach, which is also constructive in practice. That is not to say that making critical, subjective judgments has not been crucial. On the contrary, exegetes must make decisions to the best of their judgment, using the available exegetical tools. Even at the level of analysis, the text can be read in different ways such that, for example, your translation of the text or your conclusions about the text's structure may be different from mine. Nevertheless, the biblical text has been the primary center of attention so far: how to translate it, describe its structure, understand its rhetoric, identify its precursors and parallels, discern its growth, glimpse its historical background, and identify connections with other biblical texts. We have done our best, in other words, to place ourselves "in," "around," and "behind" the text.

Now is the time to engage more directly the realities "in front of" the text, that is, engage the text from more embodied, contemporary places and perspectives, including first and foremost your own. That is why you were asked early on to develop a hermeneutical self-profile to get to know *your* place or context(s) in relation to the text. Now you will be able to reflect more self-consciously as we proceed to the next several chapters. Of course, your own contexts, from the familial to the cultural, from the religious to the personal, have been at play all this time: they have already informed the way you see and read the text "in" the text. But now you will have greater opportunity to bring your various contexts (and those of others) to bear in your interpretive work.

1. Dickinson 1976, 506.

In the previous chapters, the text's relevance to contemporary contexts was not of foremost concern. Now, however, meaning and relevance begin to merge as one moves toward what you consider to be meaning*ful* in your understanding of the text. What does the text mean *to* you and *to* the communities with which you associate, as well as to other communities with which you may not identify? Meaningful biblical interpretation is not simply a matter of translation and analysis; it is also a matter of cultural competence, and that means becoming more aware of others in their various places or locations who read the text differently than you, as well as becoming more aware of yourself and your own cultural particularities and experiences. While analytical inquiry can be done alone, more culturally critical forms of inquiry necessitate a more dialogical engagement, that is, an eagerness to engage the text in the company of others. The following chapters, in other words, are intended to enlarge the table of discourse.

What does all this mean for texts that you have explored and analyzed thus far? That is hard to predict, since the exegetical outcomes are never predictable when one reads the text in the company of others. Fresh insights are gained, new implications are drawn, critical light is cast, new relevance is found. Sometimes this involves having to read against the grain of the text, that is, reading it with a hermeneutic of suspicion (Newsom 2009, 541–47). Take, for example, the opening line within the body of the U.S. Declaration of Independence (1776):

> We hold these truths to be self-evident, that all men are created equal, that they are endowed by their Creator with certain unalienable Rights, that among these are Life, Liberty and the pursuit of Happiness.

While the document speaks approvingly of universal rights, tensions are evident when one notices that the use of "men" points to gender exclusion and that the document was written in a time of racially based slavery.[2] Who are the "men" who enjoy these "unalienable Rights"? Land owners and slaveholders. Whose interests did the Declaration of Independence serve historically? Ditto. These are critical questions.

Similarly, we can ask the biblical text, either in its ancient setting or in contemporary contexts, whether it legitimizes certain forms of power that prove to be oppressive or dehumanizing. Does the text, for example, uncritically presuppose slavery? Has it been used to relegate women to second-class status vis-à-vis men? Does the text promote violence? Another way to describe this shift is to say that we are moving from the *wonder(s) of* the text to *wondering about* the text in light of various contemporary contexts, including your own. Biblical criticism invariably requires self-criticism, critical reflection on one's own prejudgments in interpreting the text (see Bailey 1998).

By enlarging the textual dialogue with other interpreters, you will soon discover that what you like about the text—its claims and values that solicit your assent—may not have the same impact on other interpreters (and vice versa). But that is when genuine dialogue can emerge at the open table of interpretation. Biblical interpretation involves becoming

---

2. Compare this to the "Declaration of Sentiments," codified at the first women's rights convention in 1848 in Seneca Falls, New York, and authored by Elizabeth Cady Stanton: "We hold these truths to be self-evident: that all men and women are created equal; that they are endowed by their Creator with certain inalienable rights; that among these are life, liberty, and the pursuit of happiness." See http://ecssba.rutgers.edu/docs/seneca.html.

more self-conscious about yourself as an interpreter of Scripture, becoming more aware of how others interpret the text differently, and finding ways for continued conversation.

The next several chapters bring various partners and perspectives into the exegetical dialogue, representing different "places" for interpreting the biblical text. Diverse as they are, the following chapters by no means offer an exhaustive list of perspectives. The list, in fact, keeps growing. Not all of them will, I suspect, resonate with you, but each one, I submit, deserves serious attention. The "places" elucidated in these next chapters represent critically significant perspectives that my students and I have considered important in our interpretive work together over the years. But there will always be more chapters to be written.

BIBLIOGRAPHY FOR CHAPTER 14

Bailey, Randall C. 1998. "The Danger of Ignoring One's Own Cultural Bias." In *The Postcolonial Bible*, edited by R. S. Sugirtharajah, 66–90. Bible and Postcolonialism 1. Sheffield: Sheffield Academic Press.

Dickinson, Emily. 1976. "Tell All the Truth But Tell It Slant (1129)." In *The Complete Poems of Emily Dickinson*, edited by Thomas H. Johnson, 506. Boston: Back Bay Books.

Newsom, Carol A. 2009. "Reflections on Ideological Criticism and Postcritical Perspectives." In *Method Matters: Essays on the Interpretation of the Hebrew Bible in Honor of David L. Petersen*, edited by Joel M. LeMon and Kent Harold Richards, 541–59. RBS 56. Atlanta: Society of Biblical Literature.

O'Connor, Kathleen. 1998. "Cross Borders: Biblical Studies in a Trans-Cultural World." In *Teaching the Bible: The Discourse and Politics of Biblical Pedagogy*, edited by Fernando Segovia and Mary Ann Tolbert, 322–37. Maryknoll, NY: Orbis Books.

PART III

Readings in Place

15

Science

The religion that is married to science today will be a widow tomorrow. . . .
But the religion that is divorced from science will leave no offspring tomorrow.
Holmes Rolston III[1]

One important place from which to read Scripture today is science. From its methodology to its discoveries, science is undeniably a global culture in its own right. Time and again science has proved itself to be an indispensable tool for understanding the world and ourselves. Part of the appeal of science is that it works; it has been and remains spectacularly successful. The other part of its appeal is that it cultivates an insatiable curiosity to know more about the physical world in which we live. Although a distinctly modern mode of inquiry, the history of the scientific discipline actually spans several centuries, beginning most notably with Nicolaus Copernicus (1473–1543). Many scientific discoveries have been nothing short of revolutionary, significantly revising how we view the world and our place in it (Kuhn 1970). Science has upended historically commonsense views of the world, such as that the sun moves across the sky, that Earth lies at the center of the universe, that the human species is categorically distinct from all other species, and that space is static. One could go on.

Science itself is a manifold discipline. The so-called hard sciences study the physical world, from the quantum to the cosmic, to understand how it works: cosmology, astronomy, physics, chemistry, geology, biology, botany, paleontology, and neuroscience, to name a few. There are also the social sciences, from psychology to sociology and anthropology. And then there are the applied sciences such as medicine and engineering. Biblical study, given its historical focus, has relied on archaeology, a discipline that has developed scientifically over the years. In addition, anthropology and sociology have become enormously helpful to biblical interpreters intent on exploring the cultural dynamics of ancient Israel.

---

1. Rolston 2006, ix.

This chapter will focus primarily on the hard sciences, in part because they provide a critical and relevant perspective on the creation texts of Genesis, while at the same time broaching the hermeneutical issue of what constitutes truth. Hence the central question posed in this chapter is this: *How can one interpret the biblical text in the light of science without compromising either science or the wisdom of the biblical text?* Such a question is not limited to adjudicating conflicting truth claims, which all too often assume an antagonistic relationship between science and faith (see below). Rather, it asks how one can appropriate the findings of science while also recognizing their limits in biblical interpretation. The question is meant to be generative, not defensive or apologetic.

This admittedly is one of the longer chapters of the book for the simple reason that, I assume, most readers are not scientifically literate. For those who hold a degree in science, I apologize. It has been my experience that most students entering theological studies are not strong in the hard sciences. Indeed, some might regard the biological sciences in particular with suspicion. Many assume that most scientists are antireligious. This is not true (Ecklund 2010). It has also been my experience that students thoroughly familiar with science often wonder how they can cross the "divide" between their theological education and their background in science.

SCIENTIFIC METHOD

First, a few words about how science works. Science is defined by its empirical method, which consists of making observations and taking measurements, as well as formulating and testing hypotheses through experimentation. Being naturally inquisitive creatures, we pose questions about the things we perceive, and we consider possible explanations as to why things are the way they are. The best hypotheses in science lead to predictions that can be tested, including making further observations about nature. Depending on how well the tests match the predictions, the original hypothesis may require refinement, alteration, expansion, or rejection. If a particular hypothesis becomes well supported, a general theory may be developed. The virtue of the scientific mind is its openness to change course when tests falsify a hypothesis. Curiosity is a driving force, so also the acceptance of doubt and uncertainty. As the great physicist Richard Feynman states, "I think it's much more interesting to live not knowing than to have answers which might be wrong."[2]

The strongest tests in science come from carefully controlled, replicated experiments that gather empirical data. But this is not always possible in certain scientific disciplines, such as astronomy, where stellar objects, for example, cannot be "controlled" or experimented on. Indeed, astronomy and related disciplines (e.g., cosmology, astrophysics, and astrobiology) are guided by the assumption that the natural laws with which we are familiar also hold true elsewhere in the universe at large, an assumption that cannot be proved or disproved empirically (Fry 2015, 23). Of course, the claim that the world was created by God cannot be settled empirically either. Nevertheless, the presupposition

2. "BBC Interview with Feynman (Uncertainty)," https://www.youtube.com/watch?v=_MmpUWEW6Is.

that natural processes depend on natural causes is fundamental to the advancement of scientific research.[3]

WHY ENGAGE SCIENCE?

One of the challenges in theological education today is to foster greater "cultural competence": the capacity to dialogue with others of different backgrounds, perspectives, and interests in an informed and appreciative way. Being appreciatively informed by science is part of being culturally competent. According to Martin Rees, a noted British astronomer, science is "the one truly global culture" (2009). As imperialistic as that may sound, acknowledged is the fact that science constitutes a complex and globally pervasive culture, with its own discourse, methods, and interests. Hence it qualifies as an important interpretive lens for reading Scripture. We look at the world through science. Why not also the world of Scripture?

If theology, to quote Anselm of Canterbury (1033–1109), is "faith seeking understanding"[4] and science is a form of understanding seeking further understanding, then theology has nothing to fear and in fact has much to learn from science. To be sure, theology cannot advance the scientific quest to understand the underlying constituents of matter and the physical nature of causation. Science, in turn, cannot lay claim to know God and God's purposes, let alone prove or disprove God. Both disciplines represent independent fields of inquiry. But, I ask, does their independence preclude constructive dialogue? Because both seek truth, because each discipline is driven by an "ontological thirst, by the thirst to know reality as it is" (Peters 2002, xiii), theology can learn from science. If theology is about relating the world and all therein to God (cf. Ps. 24:1) but does not consider the world as known through science, then it fails.

WAYS OF RELATING SCIENCE AND THEOLOGY

There are actually various ways in which science and theology (or religion) have encountered each other. Ian G. Barbour, professor of physics and religion, describes them in a simple fourfold typology: (1) conflict, (2) independence, (3) dialogue, and (4) integration (2000, 2–4).

1. *Conflict.* As far as religion and science are concerned in the media, antagonism seems to be the most popular way of relating the two. For certain biblical literalists and atheistic scientists, religion and science are simply incompatible at best and enemies at worst. Some consider religion as simplistic and superstitious. Others see science as a threat to faith, eroding humanity's nobility as created in God's image. Conflict inevitably ensues in discussions about God and evolution, for example. There is no room for dialogue, only debate.

3. This rules out "Intelligent Design" as a scientific discipline. See K. Miller 2000, 129–64.
4. From *fides quaerens intellectum*, the original title to Anselm's *Proslogion* as referenced in his preface. See Anselm 1998, 83–87.

2. *Independence.* Alternatively, theology and science are considered independent realms of inquiry that have (and should have) nothing to do with each other. They are, in the words of the eminent biologist Stephen Jay Gould, "non-overlapping magisteria" or NOMA (Gould 1999, 5). Because of their different kinds of discourse, there is no possibility of mutual dialogue, much less collaboration. Conversely, there is no possibility of conflict either. Science asks how things work. Religion deals with matters of value and ultimate meaning. One asks "How?" The other asks "Why?" Or as Galileo famously popularized, "The intention of the Holy Ghost is to teach us how one goes to heaven, not how heaven goes," which he attributes to Cardinal Baronius (Galileo 1957, 186).

3. *Dialogue.* While this model acknowledges the differences between science and theology, it does so in such a way that fosters respectful conversation over issues worth talking about from both perspectives. Theology and science can be held as complementary disciplines that have particular points of contact or intersections. Instead of NOMA, we have TOMA, "tangentially overlapping magisteria" (W. Brown 2009). While Stephen Jay Gould is famous for his NOMA typology regarding the relationship between religion and science (see above), largely overlooked is his remark on the need to "unite the patches built by our separate magisteria into a beautiful and coherent quilt called wisdom" (1999, 178). Wisdom, one could argue, necessitates constructive dialogue.

4. *Integration.* On the other end of the spectrum is the attempt to fully integrate science and theology. This can take the form of reformulating theological tenets in the light of scientific understandings or drawing direct theological implications from the findings of science. For example, some theologians with a scientific bent regard the "finely-tuned" universe, the precisely "set" parameters by which the universe evolved to produce intelligent life, as evidence of divine providence. Others harmonize the biblical text to align itself with science, for example, by identifying the big bang with God's creation of light in Gen. 1:3. Theologically, this could include revising the theological notion of divine omnipotence in light of the contingencies of existence as observed by science (i.e., "chance" and "mutation") or lodging the "causal joint" of divine action in the indeterminate realm of quantum mechanics. Here I find theological potential but am reluctant to let science entirely determine the course of theological discussion (and vice versa). Indeed, an extreme form of this is to view science and religion as two sides of the same coin, with one (take your pick) completely overlapping or subsuming the other. Call it "completely overlapping magisteria," or COMA.

How to relate two very different forms of discourse, one theological and one empirical, one with ancient, prescientific roots and one that is thoroughly modern, is a perpetual challenge. But it is an inevitable challenge, an unavoidable one. We live in an age of science, in cultures shaped by science, and while the ways in which science and theology have engaged each other in the past are various, the possibilities for the future are manifold.

SCIENCE AND SCRIPTURE

When it comes to biblical interpretation, the situation is more focused yet more variable. In keeping with the overall approach of this handbook, dialogue is the option most favored, simply because it is the most open-ended and the results are not predetermined or forced. Dialogue is something like an experiment. And I begin by simply asking, with apologies to Karl Barth, What is it like to read the Bible in one hand and the journal *Science* or *Nature* in the other? In my own hermeneutical quest, I have found that science holds the promise of deepening the Bible's own perspectives on creation. Astronomy, geology, and biology have put to rest all *un*biblical notions that the world is simply a static given, a ready-made creation dropped from heaven. Nature, indeed the cosmos, has its own story to tell. And one needs to know it, if only to talk more competently about the story of God's creative work in the world and to counter the woefully narrow view that creation is merely the backdrop for humanity's salvation. As astrobiologist Lucas Mix openly states, "As a Christian, I think of astrobiology as a way to better understand how God created the world" (2009, 6). And why not? If Earth's story is deemed at all important for our time, then it must find a place within or at least alongside God's story (i.e., the Bible's) for all time.

Precedence for reading Scripture and creation together is deeply rooted in Christian tradition, which at times has regarded both as God's "two books," a motif that began at least with John Chrysostom (ca. 347–407 CE) and Augustine (354–430), and extends to Galileo (1564–1642).[5] Augustine, for example, refers to creation as God's "great big book, the book of created nature" (1991, 225). He goes on to say, "Look carefully at it from top to bottom, observe it, read it. . . . Observe heaven and earth in a religious spirit" (226). That "religious spirit," however, does not mean rejecting the findings of science in favor of, say, the three-tiered model of the universe given in Genesis. On the contrary, Augustine found it shameful for Christians to make empirical claims about creation by simply spouting Scripture (*Genesis Literally Interpreted* 1.19.39). It thus is a matter of exegetical duty that God's "two books" be read together, for God is the author of both. It is no coincidence, in fact, that a certain psalm begins with "The heavens are telling the glory of God; and the firmament proclaims his handiwork" (Ps. 19:1 [2]) and concludes with profound reflections on God's Torah: "The precepts of YHWH are right, rejoicing the heart; the commandment of YHWH is clear, enlightening the eyes" (v. 8 [9]). Psalm 19 binds together God's creation and God's Torah, God's World and Word, into an inseparable whole.

Critical to me as an interpreter is the exegetical payoff. Reading Scripture from the place of science highlights certain features of biblical discourse that might otherwise be overlooked. Reading Genesis through the lens of science raises questions and issues that are not commonly entertained or appreciated in standard commentaries but, I submit, prove fruitful exegetically and theologically. Moreover, exegesis itself may have something to learn from the dynamic nature of scientific investigation, which is ever open to proceeding in unanticipated directions and arriving at unanticipated conclusions. And so we return to our two familiar creation texts of the Bible, the first read through the lens of cosmology and the second through the lens of evolutionary biology. We proceed with an openness to surprise.

---

5. For a historical survey of this notion, see Hess 2002.

GENESIS 1 AND COSMIC EVOLUTION

According to best-selling author Marilynne Robinson, Gen. 1 is the Bible's closest thing
to a "scientific" account of creation: "If ancient people had consciously set out to articulate a worldview congenial to science, it is hard to imagine how, in terms available to
them, they could have done better" (1998, 39). Is Gen. 1:1–2:3 scientific? Certainly not by
any modern standards. Nevertheless, of all the extensive creation accounts of the ancient
Near East, Gen. 1 seems to be the most "naturalistic" by comparison. Compared to the
rough-and-tumble, theogonic world of the *Enuma Elish*, Gen. 1 reads like a treatise, a rig-
orous exercise in mythological reduction. By its own measure, this first creation account
of the Bible resembles more an itemized list than a flowing narrative, more a report than
a story. Creation as depicted in Gen. 1 methodically recounts the formation of structure
and ultimately life, with each "day" building on the previous one. Genesis depicts the
cosmos as dynamic and differentiated.

I am not interested, however, in demonstrating how "proto-scientific" Gen. 1 is. Many
of the claims made by Genesis simply cannot be reconciled with modern science (see
below). What I want to do, however, is read Genesis *through the lens* or *from the place* of
science and see what happens. The distinction is not subtle. Reading Genesis *as* science
treats the text as scientific such that its claims about the natural world are forced to either
"prove" or "disprove" the claims of modern science. This kind of reading, relying on a
rigid view of biblical authority, collapses the dialogical space between the text and its
reader. Call it hermeneutical reductionism. In sharp distinction, reading Genesis through
the lens of science acknowledges that science resides "in front of" the text, in the reader
who is embedded in a culture of science. Such an approach is conducted in the spirit of
hermeneutical openness.

Cosmic Evolution

In reading the biblical text through the lens of science, it is important at the outset to
notice both the collisions and possible consonances evident between the claims made by
the biblical text and those made by science. Consider below the milestones identified by
science regarding cosmic, geological, and biological evolution. The temporal figures are
approximate and subject to change. Particularly important is the sequence of events.

1.	Big bang (beginning of inflation)	$t = 10^{-43}$ seconds (13.81 billion years ago)
2.	Fusion stops; nuclei form	3 minutes
3.	Formation of atoms	380,000 years
4.	Onset of darkness	1 million years
5.	First stars	400–600 million years
6.	Sun	8.7 billion years (5 billion years ago)
7.	Earth	4.55 billion years ago
8.	Microbial life on Earth	3.85 billion years ago
9.	Photosynthesis via cyanobacteria	2.7 billion years ago
10.	Multicellular organisms	1.7 billion years ago
11.	Cambrian explosion (invertebrates)	540 million years ago

12.	First (jawless) fishes	510 million years ago
13.	Land colonized by algae and insects	500 million years ago
14.	Plants with seeds, first forests	408 million years ago
15.	Animals colonizing the land	370 million years ago
16.	Trees, ferns, reptiles	345 million years ago
17.	Dinosaurs, mammals	230 million years ago
18.	Extinction of dinosaurs	65 million years ago
19.	*Homo sapiens*	200,000 years ago

Notice that the twenty-four-hour day is nowhere a factor in the astronomical and geological scale of evolution. Rather, the temporal scale of cosmic evolution swings wildly from mere fractions of a second to millions and billions of years.

Consider, now, the creational milestones identified in Gen. 1 in order of their cosmic sequence.

1.	Light	Day 1
2.	Firmament	Day 2
3.	Oceans and Land	Day 3
4.	Plants	Day 3
5.	Sun, Stars, and Planets	Day 4
6.	Sea and Aviary Life	Day 5
7.	Land Animals	Day 6
8.	Human Beings	Day 6

On the one hand, the earth and the creation of plants occur *prior to* the sun, impossible scientifically.[6] On the other hand, human beings are identified as the latest species of creation, a claim that is consonant with science. On the one hand, the "firmament" according to Gen. 1 is a hard metallic-like shield (*rāqîʿa*, 1:7) that prevents the cosmic "waters above" from inundating the land (cf. Gen. 7:11b). Scientifically speaking, however, there is no such firmament, nor is interstellar space filled with water. On the other hand, the atmosphere that blankets our planet does shield its inhabitants from solar ultraviolet rays, and water is actually quite prevalent in our solar system and beyond. One could go on oscillating between "on the one hand" and "on the other hand." Collisions and consonances are, as one might expect, deeply intertwined throughout the Genesis narrative in dialogue with science.

One perennial hermeneutical issue is how one should understand the word "day" in Gen. 1. The temptation is to count the biblically enumerated "days" as longer than the normal span of twenty-four hours. But by harmonizing the text with cosmic evolution as reconstructed by science, one would quickly find the chronological value for each "day" in Genesis to vary widely, some measured in billions of years, others in millions, still others in milliseconds or shorter, an utterly inconsistent use of "day." Symbolic days with wildly divergent temporal values, I suspect, are not what the Priestly author had in mind. Moreover, the alternation between night and day, darkness and light, evening and

6. For a solar system to form, the star comes first, since it is by its gravitational force that the process of planet formation from interstellar dust begins.

morning, seems to be quite regularized from the beginning after the separation of light from the darkness in Genesis. A hermeneutic of harmonization, moreover, cannot resolve the obvious collision between Genesis and science over the sequence of events. The scientific witness offers a far different understanding of the chronological order of cosmic evolution. From a scientific standpoint, one can credit the biblical author for imagining a distinction between primordial light on Day 1 and stellar light on Day 4 (see below), as well as discerning an overarching movement from biological simplicity to complexity. But the scientific consonances stop there. It is precisely the *incompatibility* between science and Genesis that forces an alternative interpretive approach to understanding the time frame enumerated in Gen. 1, as we shall see.

To get there, I want first to address four questions for dialogue between science and Genesis: (1) What is the cosmos made out of? (2) What happened in the "beginning"? (3) How did the cosmos evolve? (4) What is unique about humanity? For each question, we will explore how science can suggest ways of rereading or reimagining certain aspects of Genesis. If science teaches us anything, it is to be keen observers of the world. For exegetes, that would also include the world of the text.

Cosmic Stuff

The cosmos as depicted in Gen. 1 bears little resemblance to the physical cosmos observed by scientists today. Cosmologists have discovered an expanding universe populated by at least a hundred billion galaxies, each of which contains at least a hundred billion stars, many hosting planetary systems of their own. By contrast, the world according to Genesis is a three-tiered universe or "Astrodome": the waters above are held aloft by a firmament or dome, and the waters below are separated by land. The stars interspersed upon the celestial vault somehow act as conduits of primordial light created on the first day. In between the firmament and the waters below lies a narrow band of space, within which terrestrial life flourishes.

We know better from science, which has much to say about what is out there "above" us. The vastness of the cosmos is not filled with water poised to inundate us from above if the firmament is ever breached (as told in the biblical account of the flood). Nevertheless, the heavens are not entirely composed of some alien element either. There is, in fact, empirical evidence of abundant water in the universe, as found, for example, in comets and on other planets.[7] The Oort cloud, a spherical cloud of comets that surrounds the solar system, consists mostly of frozen water, ammonia, and methane. In addition, interstellar clouds, wherein stars are born, contain vast amounts of carbon, hydrogen, and oxygen in the form of CO_2 and, yes, H_2O (Hazen 2005, 122). However alien outer space might appear, as it did to the ancients and as it does to our modern eyes, both science and the Bible affirm surprisingly familiar elements. On the atomic level, the four most common chemically active elements in the universe just happen also to be the most common elements of life on Earth: hydrogen, oxygen, carbon, and nitrogen.

---

7. Comets are typically composed half of water. Europa, a moon of Jupiter, actually has more liquid water than Earth, making it a prime candidate in the search for exoplanetary life.

From the purview of Genesis the universe looks a lot simpler than what the astronomical sciences observe. The ancients saw the world beyond the "firmament" as the great unknown: it was filled with the "waters above," and above the waters was the domain of cosmic light and the realm of the divine. For astronomers, what is "up" there is also "down" there. There are stars "above" us, but equally so stars "below" us. Directions do not apply on the cosmic scale (Wallace 2016, vii–viii). But like modern cosmologists, the biblical authors recognized that the observable world was only a small part of what was "out there," the realm of transcendence. For modern cosmologists, all that can be seen is but a small slice of cosmic stuff. As astrophysicist Peter Coles puts it, "Ordinary matter . . . may be but a small contaminating stain on the vast bulk of cosmic material whose nature is yet to be determined" (2001, 81). The periodic table with all of its elements (currently at a count of 118) represents only a slice of reality. The cosmos remains, for the most part, a mystery.

In the Beginning: "Chaos" and Light

The big-bang model of the universe's inception is sometimes invoked as a scientific parallel to Gen. 1:1–3. Ironically, when the big bang was first proposed, it met stiff resistance from the famous astronomer Fred Hoyle, who actually coined the phrase as a disparaging remark. Hoyle instead championed the "steady-state" theory in part because the big bang, in his opinion, found too great a "conformity to Judeo-Christian theologians" (Hoyle 1982, 2–3). Regardless of any alleged "conformity," the big bang continues to carry the day in science. Nevertheless, caution is in order. First are some common misconceptions regarding this cosmological model. The theory of the big bang does not explain the *origin* of the cosmos but accounts only for its *evolution* beginning a fraction of a second *after* time equals zero ($t = 10^{-43}$ seconds), prior to which the laws of physics, specifically general relativity, break down. Similarly, Gen. 1:1–2 begins not at the absolute beginning of creation (see chap. 4).

"In the beginning, at the Big Bang singularity, everywhere and everything was in the same place" (Coles 2001, 44). This statement counters another widely held misconception, namely, that the universe began as a point located in space, from which everything expanded. But there was no point *in* space, no center of the universe, for space itself was contained, reduced, as it were, almost infinitesimally at the moment of the "bang." Hence, there is no place to which one can point that marks the center of the universe, just as there is no center described in Gen. 1:2 with the omnipresent waters.

Both the ancient narrator of Genesis and the modern cosmologist find some common ground in the notion that creation began in extreme conditions. For science, the cosmos began in a condition of incredible density, uniformity, and intensity. Physicists describe this initial condition as a situation of inconceivable intensity in which the temperature remained above a million billion degrees Kelvin (10^{15}), with wild fluctuations of energy so severe that all known particles assumed zero mass, a state of formless chaos. The universe may have existed in a state of space-time "singularity," as some physicists describe it, a state thoroughly "jittery and turbulent" on the quantum level (Greene 2004, 306). Something akin to *tōhû wābōhû*?

In this state of singularity all the known forces were unified: gravity, electromagnetic force, strong nuclear force, and weak nuclear force. It was a "perfect unity" (Kaku 2005, 84) until the bang—an "explosion" occasioned perhaps by a false vacuum state or gravitational repulsion. This state of negative pressure expanded space by a factor of at least 10^{30}, lasting for the briefest of moments. Such was the universe's most dramatic expansion: the smallest suddenly writ large, setting within the twinkling of an eye the cosmic pattern for variety amid uniformity. Such marked the earliest stage of cosmic evolution. Genesis 1:2, one could read, also describes a state of colossal potential, of cosmic readiness for creation: God's breath suspended above the dark waters, pent-up creative energy poised to burst forth. Both Genesis and science point to a generative moment of astronomical or, I can't resist, biblical proportions.

"The most obvious and fundamental medium of our connection to the universe is light," according to physicist Lee Smolin (1997, 27). Light, not coincidentally, is God's first and fundamental act of creation in Genesis. Characterized by a diffuse sea of photons, this first epoch of light dramatically began with the bang, which "flooded the infant universe" with "light brilliant beyond description" (Frank 2006, 31). In this "smooth, hot, dense soup of exotic high-energy particles," matter and radiation were nearly indistinguishable ("coupled"), and any photon could travel only for a small distance before being absorbed and reemitted. The visual result was a glowing fog in all directions as bright as the sun, brilliant yet opaque.

During this time, fundamental atomic particles began to emerge, bringing form from formless plasma. Within the first three minutes, the nuclei of helium and lithium appeared. When the temperature dropped below 3,000 degrees Kelvin after 380,000 years, electrons and protons combined to form neutral hydrogen, the most abundant element in the universe. Matter was no longer composed of highly charged plasma but of neutral atoms. Consequently matter and light parted ways: photons could now travel unimpeded, their wavelengths stretching along with the expanding universe. Born was the cosmic microwave background (CMB), which remains today as the big bang's cosmic fingerprint. The universe became transparent.

But then darkness returned less than one million years after the big bang. Astronomers refer to this new era as the Dark Ages, persisting close to a billion years, occasioned by the growing dominance of neutral hydrogen gas throughout the universe. Although neutral hydrogen gas could not absorb cosmic background photons, it efficiently absorbed visual and ultraviolet (UV) light (Frank 2006, 32). Visible light thus became "reshackled." Hence, the universe came to appear dark and "extraordinarily smooth." "The Dark Ages mark[ed] an era of transitions, not only from [darkness] to light, but also from formlessness to form" (32).

Under the cover of darkness, gravity began to pull matter together. What began as tiny perturbations or inhomogeneities from the big bang grew larger and denser. Due to the persistent force of gravity, the first stars began to appear 400 to 600 million years after the big bang, producing a torrent of ultraviolet photons that ionized the surrounding hydrogen gas by stripping the neutral hydrogen atoms of their electrons. The Dark Ages finally came to an end as more and more stars and galaxies ionized most of the universe. The result: a new era of light commenced. The first billion years of the universe, in short, proceeded from diffused light to total darkness to focused light emitted by stars. The "fourth day" in Genesis?

Like science, Genesis acknowledges that the creation of primordial light is temporally distinguishable from the light emitted by the stars. But that is as far as the similarity goes. From the biblical perspective, the realm of primordial light lies inaccessibly beyond the firmament; it is transcendent light. Nevertheless, it is this light that is transmitted by the astral bodies that God set in the firmament. "There was light," but only thereafter came the stars, three "days" later according to Genesis, or half a billion years according to astrophysicists.

Creation as Process

At the broadest level, both Gen. 1 and modern cosmology affirm that the universe was not a onetime event. It was, and continues to be, a process that developed from simplicity to complexity, from uniformity to diversity, from "singularity" to manifold abundance. Creation is a cosmic process, an evolution of 13.81 billion years of expansion and formation, of stars living and dying, setting the stage for new cosmic life. More down to earth, scientists have reconstructed nearly three billion years of biological evolution, from unicellular to human life. The ancient sages, of course, had no inkling of such a cosmic span of time. But what they did share with science is an awareness that the universe took time to develop, that it began with an initial defining event characterized by an effusion of energy, the onset of time, the structuring of space, and eventually the emergence of life.

In Gen. 1 the emphasis on life "filling" every domain offers ancient testimony to creation's fecundity and resilience. Such also is the testimony of evolution. "Life has been expansionist from the beginning" (Margulis and Sagan 2005, 240). The ancients knew full well the power of reproduction and succession. Genesis 1 acknowledges the (re)generative power of life in trees and animals alike. To the evolutionary biologist, the "goal" of every living species is the transmission of genetic identity that enables the fitness of both the organism and the species to its environment. There is no fittest kind of organism, only an organism that is fit for its particular niche. To "fill," in other words, is to fit. Evolution is not about the "survival of the fittest" (coined by Herbert Spencer, not Charles Darwin) but about the survival of the fit enough.

According to Genesis, all species have their "fit" in certain domains: water, land, and air. Fins and wings, gills and lungs, legs and tails: all have their functions within their respective domains. Life in all its variety corresponds to its various domains. But as better adapted species emerge, others are forced into a corner. Death follows life. Unacknowledged in Gen. 1 is the dark side of evolution's creative force. "Life today was earned at the cost of the death of almost all that went before," states geneticist Steve Jones. Extinction "is a crucial part of the evolutionary machine and is as inevitable as is the origin of species" (2001, 92). In addition, natural history testifies to several cataclysmic extinctions, the most recent one caused by a meteor impact in the northern Yucatan Peninsula about 66 million years ago, wiping out nearly every land animal bigger than a bread box and destroying almost all surface marine life. Thus began a new stage in evolution, the Cenozoic Era, or the Age of Mammals. The dinosaurs' extinction left an ecological window that allowed mammals to evolve from former "dino-hors d'oeuvres,"[8] such as tree shrews, to the great variety of mammal forms found today, including human beings.

In Genesis, God enlists the natural elements such as the earth and the waters to participate freely in the creative process. The creation narrative, moreover, acknowledges the continuing struggle of life (1:26, 28). To "fill" the earth involves, from a Darwinian perspective, competition. "Subduing" the earth, according to Genesis, is required for the flourishing of human life (1:28). Indeed, biologically speaking the commission to "subdue" extends to *all* species for their survival. And yet life does not thrive by competition alone. Life depends on sustaining interdependent relations through cooperation and collectivity. Networking is also critical in biological evolution (Margulis and Sagan 1997, 27).

In its own way Gen. 1 depicts a "progression" of life from simple to complex forms: vegetation sprouts forth on Day 3, aquatic and aviary life emerges on Day 5, and on the sixth day land animals and human beings are created. The chronological order, however, is not biologically accurate: life originated in the sea, not from plants on land. That all life, from bacteria to *Homo sapiens*, is composed mostly of water is itself sufficient testimony of our watery origins. To the Priestly narrator's credit, sea life is presented the "day" before terrestrial life. Plants, however, began to fill the earth millions of years only *after* life in the sea had its start. Day 6 would have been the natural "period" for the sprouting of vegetation, not Day 3.

From a biological standpoint, the development of life is no linear progression. Complexity, in fact, does not necessarily reflect improvement or progress. "Some lineages get more complicated, some simpler, and much of life has to struggle to stay in the same place" (Jones 2001, 229). Nevertheless, complexity remains a useful way of charting the broad arc of evolution's work at least from microbe to human being. Natural selection alone cannot generate complexity and innovation (Margulis and Sagan 1995, 9). Complexity emerges, rather, from the dynamic interaction between mutation and necessity (see Morowitz 2002). The fact that genetic copies are never perfect is key. "The capacity to blunder slightly is the real marvel of DNA. Without this special attribute, we would still be anaerobic bacteria and there would be no music."[9] Imperfection is the basis of biological innovation and diversity.

Central to the Genesis narrative is the repeated utterance of God's "word." Here too science offers a rich analogy. The divine word serves to enlist and unleash the elemental powers of creation. One could imagine God's words including the laws of physics, which direct the evolution of cosmic structure and eventually life. The divine word is not only formative in the process of creation; it is also informative in defining the roles and activities of other agencies. Information, not coincidentally, is increasingly recognized for its formative role in biology. Coded in DNA, information exhibits its own agency. Like language, DNA transmits information, specifically a message containing four different modules or nucleotides (A, C, T, G).[10] Like letters in a written language,

8. Tyson and Goldsmith 2004, plate 38.
9. Attributed to Lewis Thomas, via Impey 2007, 175.
10. The letters stand for the four types of nucleotide and their nitrogenous bases: adenine, cytosine, thymine, and guanine.

different sequences of DNA modules transmit different information. The interpretation or decoding of such information lies in certain biochemical mechanisms that translate the sequence of DNA nucleotides into amino acids to form proteins. It is these proteins that ultimately determine what an organism is and does. As Holmes Rolston points out, the genetic code is more than causal: it is purposive (2006, xix). The process of transmission leads to "the achievement of increasing order, maintained out of the disorder" (xvii). One could say the same, perhaps, for God's commands in Genesis.

Human Uniqueness

Both the biologist and the biblical sage agree that humanity is a latecomer. Anatomically modern humans emerged only around 200,000 years ago. If Earth's history (ca. 4.6 billion years) were compressed into a single hour, the first cells would have appeared just after 17 minutes, but the first humans would have emerged at the last one-tenth of the last second of that hour. Or if you are a bibliophile, then in a 1,000-page book, with each page representing 4.5 million years, the age of the dinosaurs would begin on page 728, and all of recorded human history would fit comfortably on the last line of the last page. We are an endnote, but likely not the final endnote. The "book" of creation continues to be written.

All members of the human species are 99.5 percent identical at the DNA level. Of course, there is much more to the human species than its uniformity. Biologically, it is the size of the brain relative to the body that makes human beings distinctive in the animal world. The hominin brain has doubled in size the past two million years. Human beings exhibit critical acumen far beyond the capacities of their primate ancestors and "cousins." While our protein molecules are only 3 percent different from those in chimpanzees, our cranial cortex is three times larger. For all that is similar between humans and chimps on the genetic, chromosomal, cellular, and neuro-anatomical levels, "the developmental modifications" that gave rise to human cognition and culture "culminated in a massive singularity," observes geneticist J. Craig Venter (2001, 1346–48). Holmes Rolston III aptly calls it the third "big bang" (2010, 87–124).

The human brain is of such complexity that quantifying it reaches astronomical proportions. One estimate is 10^{13} neurons, each equipped with several thousand synapses. Such a lively network of informational exchange results, in principle, in an explosion of "more possible thoughts than there are atoms in the universe" (Rolston 2006, xxv)—not that this is ever achieved on a regular basis. But for all that is qualitatively and remarkably distinct about its capacities, the human brain did not suddenly appear fully formed. It emerged within the last six million years, when the evolutionary lineages that led to modern humans and chimpanzees diverged. The human brain seems to have reached its current development within the last 50,000 years, as evidenced in the spectacular cave art of Western Europe, dated as early as 36,600 BCE. During this time, several lines of cognitive and cultural development converged, including spoken language, symbolic thinking, and religious practice (Mithen 1996, 70–72, 153–84).

In the light of evolutionary science, the designation of humanity as "made in the image of God" in Gen. 1 encompasses all the cognitive, emotive, and cultural aspects that constitute human identity. No single trait, thus, can be considered definitive for human uniqueness (Van Huyssteen 2006, 106). Moreover, one should not regard the *imago* as an individual matter at all. Human beings were created, according to Gen. 1, as a collective plurality, and out of this plurality arose culture. The individual human brain, with all of its networking neurons, cannot hold a candle to the "collective of human brains and their psychological processes that make up human culture" (Plotkin 1998, 222). However it is to be defined, culture is something more complex than the simple sum of human individuals. It "seems to involve the creation of something whole, something cohesive, and possibly something which seems to be greater than its constituent parts" (223). Similarly, the *imago* in Gen. 1 is greater than the human mind; it encompasses humanity collectively and thus culturally.

The various capacities that constitute human uniqueness, individual and cultural, artistic and religious, scientific and poetic, all converge for a specific purpose in Genesis: human beings reflect the manifold character of divinity required for "ruling" over creation (1:26, 28). In Gen. 1 the functional side of the *imago Dei* is expressed in humanity's exercise of power in and over creation. Only humans are given the responsibility of dominion. In the words of biologist Edward O. Wilson, "We are the first species to become a geophysical force, altering Earth's climate, a role previously reserved for tectonics, sun flares, and glacial cycles" (1998, 303), as well as, one should add, cataclysmic meteorites. On the evolutionary scale, humanity has clearly achieved such dominance, changing the very face of the planet. The world has become humanity's global niche; because of this, humanity has entered into what some consider a new geological era, the so-called Anthropocene epoch. It is deeply ironic that the most intelligent, gifted, powerful creature on the planet, no less than God's very "image," is now endangering the planet. Perhaps the *imago Dei* is not meant to champion our superiority so much as lift up our special purpose and responsibility on behalf of creation (see chap. 16).

THE POWER OF SEVEN

And so we return to the "problem" of the seven "days" of creation, that is, how to interpret it in the light of science. Again, "days" taken symbolically with wildly divergent time spans are not what the text seems to indicate. Given this collision between text and science, the theological question presents itself: *Why* is creation ordered according to seven days? In chap. 8, we saw that the seven days in Genesis serve to demarcate the architecture of the temple/tabernacle, thus configuring the universe as God's cosmic temple. If that was not astounding enough, there is also the anthropological side to the seven-day equation. The order of God's creation in Genesis models the weekly rhythm of work and rest. As the Sabbath commandment in Exodus states: "Six days you shall labor and do all your work. But the seventh day is a sabbath to YHWH your God; you shall not do any work" (Exod. 20:9). Perhaps the orderly unfolding of creation by God is, in the end, meant to shape human conduct. That is to say, the creative process described in Genesis bears a distinctly liturgical rhythm that models human activity. God's prescriptive blessing for humanity is a Sabbath-tempered "dominion." The Sabbath is not an afterthought but the grand conclusion of creation. The seven-day schema of creation in Genesis serves to regularize human activity, in imitation of God (*imitatio Dei*), in order to ensure creation's flourishing. An honest engagement with science, in fact, highlights this theological conviction. In sum, the world created in *seven* days is not a scientific report. Rather, it is a model for human flourishing and a mandate for human responsibility .

In our discussion of Genesis thus far, I have tried to model something of a respectful back-and-forth dialogue between scientific understandings of the natural world and various perspectives conveyed in Gen. 1, identifying points of difference as well as contact or resonance. The process, I'm convinced, has led to a deeper understanding of the text that at the same time has generated creative (re)interpretations. What has proved to be fruitful, for example, is the construction of analogies (e.g., "information" in relation to divine word) by which to reread the Genesis text. Moreover, the questions and issues posed by science have helped to frame new questions to pose to Genesis. Finally, points of divergence (or "collisions") have led to highlighting more intently the theological and ethical implications of Genesis. More surprising results are in store as we engage the Yahwist's creation account in dialogue with science.

GENESIS 2–3 AND HUMAN EVOLUTION

The garden of Eden story (Gen. 2:4b–3:24) has been the center of exegetical controversy ever since Darwin's *On the Origin of Species* was published in 1859 and *The Descent of Man* in 1871. As a historical case in point, Dr. James Woodrow, professor of chemistry and uncle of Woodrow Wilson, was appointed the "Perkins Professor of Natural Science in Connection with Revelation" at Columbia Theological Seminary, South Carolina, in 1861, an appointment that was clearly ahead of its time. In 1883 Dr. Woodrow was asked to "set forth his views upon evolution in order that the church might have the benefit of his opinions" (LaMotte 1937, 189). In a public address, Woodrow suggested that Adam was created out of the organic layer of the ground and that it happened incrementally over a long period of time. That was enough to get him dismissed from the seminary in 1886. Although Woodrow's dismissal was prompted by a number of factors, from personality clashes among the faculty to the seminary's fiscal crisis, it was the perceived threat of Darwinism to Christian faith that carried the day.[11]

Some things have not changed. Variations of the Scopes Trial continue to be played out today,[12] polarizing communities and fostering a conceptual apartheid that keeps faith and science not simply at arm's length but also at odds with each other. The central question for us, similar to the case of Gen. 1, is this: *How can one interpret the garden story of Gen. 2–3 in the light of human evolution without on the one hand debating science and on the other hand undermining the wisdom of the biblical story?* More generally, *What new light can science shed on this biblical account of human origin?* We begin again with an expectancy for surprise.

11. For a detailed recounting of Woodrow's dismissal, see J. Miller 2009.
12. Formally known as "The State of Tennessee v. John Thomas Scopes," the trial took place in 1925 in Dayton, Tennessee; John Scopes, a high school teacher, was accused of violating Tennessee's Butler Act, which made it illegal to teach human evolution in a state-funded school.

Human Origins

The Yahwist's account depicts all life fashioned from the "ground," human, animal, and plants. The ʾādām created from the "dust of the ʾădāmâ" provides a wordplay that casts ʾādām as a "groundling," a creature related to the ground yet sharing in the divine breath that animates him as a "living being" (Gen. 2:7). The evolutionary account from science provides a much more complicated picture. One collision between the biblical and evolutionary account is the order of appearance. In Gen. 2, the ʾādām was created *before* the animals (2:7, 19). Biologically, however, humanity was "created" *from* the animals. The fact that all organisms we know share the same kind of genetic coding (DNA), with only slight variations, is itself testimony that life on Earth descended from a common group of primitive bacterium-like cells. These rudimentary cells eventually evolved from the simple prokaryotic variety to the more complex eukaryotic kind, which features a tightly organized nucleus contained within a porous membrane. The next major evolutionary advance was the emergence of multicellular life, manifest eventually in such forms as crustaceans and mollusks, each bearing sense organs and a central nervous system. From them the more advanced life-forms eventually emerged, including humanity (*Homo sapiens*), as the spread of life in general continued to fill and fashion the various niches of the biosphere. In a figurative sense, humanity, as with all life, came from below.

By claiming such a bottom-up beginning, both the ancient narrator of Genesis and the evolutionary biologist of today acknowledge the interconnectedness of life. The ʾādām is an animal, and the other animals that God creates are also created from the ground. From God's perspective, the ʾādām and the other animals all share the same substance. From the scientific perspective, the basic biochemical and genetic unity of life points to a single biological origin for all known living beings. Gene counts between human beings and much simpler organisms, such as "worms, flies, and simple plants," all fall in the same range, "around 20,000" (Collins 2006, 125). Among primates, humans (*Homo sapiens*) and chimpanzees (*Pan troglodytes*) are 96 percent identical at the DNA level (137), making chimps humanity's closest nonhuman relatives. While the human has twenty-three pairs of chromosomes, the chimpanzee (along with the gorilla and the orangutan) has twenty-four. The difference lies in the fusion of two ancestral chromosomes shared by chimpanzees resulting in Chromosome 2 for *Homo sapiens*, a simple genetic fusion that made all the difference in our evolutionary development.

Fusion also pertains to humanity's evolution in another way. DNA research suggests a picture of human origins more detailed than what the fossil record reveals. The ancestors of human beings and those of chimpanzees parted ways some 6–7 million years ago, but it was by no means a clean break.[13] There was extensive interbreeding for over a million years before they followed their separate paths for good. In addition, many human beings share a bit of the Neanderthal genome, indicating interbreeding across species, at least five "encounters," over the past 60,000 years.[14] Our origin, thus, was indeed

13. It is a misconception that humans descended from chimpanzees. Rather, both descended from a common ancestor, from which one "line" led to humans and the other line to chimps. For the genetic data, see The Chimpanzee Sequencing and Analysis Consortium 2005.

14. Vernot and Akey 2014; Gibbons 2016. This applies only to humans of European, Asian, and Melanesian descent, not to those of exclusive African descent.

messy, or more precisely stated, full of divergences and convergences (Cole-Turner 2016, 124–25).

The genetic messiness between humans and other primates extends into the social and perhaps even the moral realm. Chimpanzees exhibit a remarkable range of behaviors and skills. They employ and build tools, hunt in groups, engage in violence (including a primitive form of warfare), form alliances, and reconcile after quarrels (Ehrlich 2002, 70). They are by nature social creatures and appear to exhibit empathy, self-awareness, cooperation, planning, and learning. The links between humans and chimps include far more than just expressive faces and opposable thumbs. Frans de Waal of the Yerkes Primate Research Center argues that the antecedents of human morality can be found in nonhuman primate behavior.[15] Consolation, for example, is universal among the great apes (2006a, 33–36). De Waal has observed several common forms of moral behavior among certain primates: cognitive empathy (empathy combined with appraisal of the other's situation), reciprocity, and fairness (21–56). They are, in his words, "moral sentiments" (2006b, 168). With regard to empathy, bonobos exhibit more affinity to human beings than chimps.[16] De Waal is convinced that the evolutionary origin of the ape's ability to take another's perspective is to be sought not in social competition but in the need for cooperation and community concern, the results of group living and social pressure (de Waal 2006c, 72).

To sum up thus far: while all animals are not human, all humans are animals, biologically speaking. The Yahwist would confirm this: the ʾādām was created an animal, a groundling, and remains so even after his painful transition into becoming fully human, as told in Gen. 3. He is still an ʾādām, the quintessential animal. For both the biologist and the Yahwist, the primordial past points to what humanity shares with all of life.

The Emergent Human

In Gen. 2 there are only two kinds of life (in addition to fruit trees): animal and divine. By the end of Gen. 3, however, there are three: animal, divine, and human. Something dramatically changed when the couple's eyes were "opened." Evolutionarily speaking, the transition occurs no less dramatically in the grand scheme of life's history on Earth.

The evolution of hominins,[17] including the various species of the *Homo* genus,[18] continues to be fleshed out by paleoanthropologists and geneticists. We know much more now than what was known forty years ago when "Lucy" was discovered (1974), and the story of our evolutionary heritage continues to be rewritten as new fossils are discovered and DNA testing becomes more precise. While many gaps remain, some things we do know.[19] Since the time of Darwin's publications, many missing links have been

15. For a thorough survey of his observations and analysis, see de Waal 1996. A recent engagement on the philosophical and moral issues can be found in his discussion with a panel of critics in Macedo and Ober 2006.

16. In DNA comparisons, humans and bonobos "share a microsatellite related to sociality that is absent in the chimpanzee" (de Waal 2006c, 73).

17. "Hominin" includes modern humans and our immediate ancestors, including *Ardipithecus* (see below). The term "hominid" refers to all the great apes, including their ancestors.

18. Genus refers to the broad classification that includes more than one species. The designation *Homo* includes the genus, always capitalized, followed by the species category.

19. For an engaging interactive presentation on human origins, I recommend the Smithsonian National Museum of Natural History's Web site on human origins: http://humanorigins.si.edu/.

discovered that begin to fill out humanity's ancestral lineage, which now resembles more a sprawling bush than a towering tree or ladder. It began with the discovery of the fossilized remains of a Neanderthal[20] in 1856 and Eugène Duboi's discovery of the "ape-man" (*Pithecanthropus*) in 1891. Other major finds include Raymond Dart's discovery in 1924 of a baboon-sized fossil skull at a quarry near Taung, north of Johannesburg, which he named *Australopithecus africanus* ("the southern ape from Africa" of 3.2 to 2.5 million years ago) but is known colloquially as the "Taung child." Five years later, fossil remains were found in China's Zhoukoudian Cave, eventually classified as *Homo erectus* (770,000 years ago). Perhaps most famous was the discovery of "Lucy" in 1974 at Hadar, Ethiopia, nicknamed after the Beatles' song but classified *Australopithecus afarensis* "southern ape from Afar" and dated to about 3.5 million years ago.

Lucy's discovery shocked the anthropological world because she was bipedal yet lacked a brain size anywhere near that of a human, about one-third of the human brain. It was thought that bipedalism was based on large brain size, which we now know developed much later. Many discoveries since then have increased the number of branches on the phylogenetic tree. One of the most recent findings is the discovery of the so-called hobbit species (*Homo floresiensis*), discovered in a cave on Flores, an island east of Bali. The skeletal remains indicate a human species of 18,000 years ago that grew no larger than a three-year-old modern child and were thought to belong to the ancestral line of *Homo erectus* (P. Brown 2007) but now is considered to be a separate species descended from a hominin ancestor that branched off before the origin of the common ancestor of Neanderthals and modern humans (Tocheri 2007).

Another find is *Ardipithecus ramidus*, "Ardi" for short, whose fossil remains were discovered in Ethiopia in 1994 and are dated to 4.4 million years ago (mya). Her genus may have reached as far back as 5.8 mya (Gibbons 2009). *Ardi* provides one of our closest snapshots of the "last common ancestor" of both humans and chimpanzees, and she is distinctly unchimpanzee like! *Ardi* was able to walk upright (without having to use knuckles), albeit awkwardly. She was more human than chimpanzee. Moreover, the faunal remains indicate that she lived in a wooded environment, indicating that bipedalism evolved prior to when environments became more open and grassy. An even more recent discovery in South Africa is *Homo naledi* ("star" in the Sotho language), which at this point in time cannot be dated. Its body structure bears a remarkable mix of primitive and modern qualities, making it a human species unlike any other early human species we know. On the one hand, *Homo naledi* features a braincase one-third the size of modern *Homo sapiens* and extremely curved fingers, demonstrating climbing capability (Gibbons 2015). On the other hand, the feet of this species are remarkably human by modern standards, suited for upright long-distance walking and running, and its wrists seem adapted for tool use.

The evolving picture of human evolution is turning out to be complicated: divergences, convergences, and extinctions all characterize the human lineage. As more remains are discovered, the picture will no doubt become even more variegated. But if we place the modern *Homo sapiens* at the top branch of this expansive "bush," then "standing" at the trunk is the bipedal primate, which made its appearance as early as 5.8 million years

---

20. So named by its discovery in the Neander Valley, near Düsseldorf.

ago (*Ardipithecus*). The ability to walk upright has traditionally been seen as the prime diagnostic feature of hominins from *Australopithecus* to *Homo*. That can no longer be held with the discovery of *Ardipithecus*. Still, bipedality eventually gave rise to distinctly human capabilities, including language, art, and music (Mithen 2006, 144–58). Physical uprightness required the lowering of the larynx, thereby broadening the voice's pitch and enhancing its diversity of sounds.

Among the various hominins, *Homo erectus* (1.89 mya–143,000 ya) was likely the first of our ancestors to lose most of their body fur, an evolutionary advantage for life in the African savannah, hence the "first truly 'naked ape'" (Ehrlich 2002, 92). It was also the first to emigrate out of Africa, settling parts of Eurasia, including China and Indonesia, and consequently the first to wear clothing,[21] presumably from animal skins, for protection from the cold. The species is often associated with the use of hand axes, the first major innovation in stone tool technology. The question of whether *Homo sapiens* is a direct descendant of *Homo erectus* remains debated. Recent findings in Java, in any case, suggest a separate line of *Homo erectus* that became an evolutionary dead end (Baba 2003).

By analyzing mitochondrial DNA, which is passed only from mother to offspring, molecular biologists have ascertained that the earliest version of human beings ("archaic *Homo sapiens*") evolved in Africa around 600,000 years ago and that *Homo neanderthalensis* emerged as a separate species, beginning around 400,000 years ago. Compared to modern *Homo sapiens*, Neanderthals carried a larger but lower skull (Ehrlich 2002, 97). As such, they lacked the frontal lobes of the neocortex, where highly cognitive thinking is lodged. Nevertheless, this species launched a new technological era marked by a greater refinement of stone tools. In addition, Neanderthals may have been the first to bury their dead, perhaps with accompanying ceremony and symbolic offerings (Wood 2005, 98). Use of language and art remains a matter of debate. Steven Mithen argues that Neanderthals performed music and dance but did not exhibit linguistic abilities comparable to those of *Homo sapiens* (2006, 228). Their extinction about 40,000 years ago remains a mystery. Although more robust physically, Neanderthals were evidently no match for *Homo sapiens* in the competition for resources when the latter began to settle Europe, even as interbreeding occurred.

Mitochondrial DNA analysis traces the ancestry of modern *Homo sapiens* back to a single African population that lived around 200,000 years ago, to what was once called the "mitochondrial Eve," or African Eve—allegedly one woman from whom all modern humans are descended. Recent analyses, however, point to a discrete group of *Homo sapiens* in southeastern Africa, numbering perhaps around 10,000 (Wood 2005, 105–6). For the past two million years Africa seems "to have been the source of 'pulses' of hominin evolutionary novelty" (Wood 2005, 108). From what we know of our genomic history, Africa was our "Eden."

As with previous hominins, our species did not linger: the emergence of *Homo sapiens* out of East Africa 75,000–50,000 years ago led to an extensive spread throughout Africa and Eurasia, rapidly replacing their predecessors. By 40,000 years ago, Australia and New

21. As Ehrlich points out, archaeological evidence of sewed skins dates to around 20,000 years ago, but "crude clothing" was a necessity once hominins ventured into colder environments (2002, 95).

Guinea were colonized. It was also throughout this time that Upper Paleolithic technology developed, prompting what some have called the "most rapid and radical cultural change ever recorded in the [hominin] line" (Ehrlich 2002, 104). Sewing implements were invented, and full-blown art flourished, yielding magnificent cave paintings, statuettes, and jewelry.[22] Burials were accompanied by elaborate artifacts, indicating religious ritual and belief in an afterlife. While theories range from greater competition for resources to neurological transformations of the brain, the specific reasons behind this cultural development remain unknown. Most recent discoveries, particularly that of prehistoric art, suggest that this "radical cultural change" was not so much a sudden explosion as it was a graduated launch that began perhaps as far back as 100,000 years ago (Cole-Turner 2016, 100–105).[23]

Hominin evolution passed through 700,000 years of turbulent environmental change. Such instability forced greater mobility and versatility upon early humans as they adapted to a wide range of environmental conditions. According to Richard Potts, versatility was modern humanity's hallmark: "the capacity . . . to buffer survival risks and resource uncertainty" (2005, 261–63). From 700,000 to 50,000 years ago, brain size increased, stone tools diversified, and social interactions intensified. Around 400,000 years ago, hearths and shelters began to proliferate. Humanity was gradually filling and constructing its global niche.

Mindful Evolution

As cognitive capacities increased among hominins over time, enter the mind on the evolutionary stage. But first comes the brain. Its expansion is "the reason why human beings instead of baboons or chimpanzees burst out of Africa, occupied the entire planet, and shaped Earth to their own uses" (Ehrlich 2002, 109). Most distinctive about the brain is the large cerebral cortex or neocortex, the brain's outer shell, "perhaps the most complex entity known to science" (Gazzaniga 2008, 9). In the cerebral cortex the "higher" cognitive functions occur, including the development of language, tool manufacture and use, social skills, and memory capacity.

However defined, the mind is inseparably linked to consciousness: the reflective awareness of one's own self. Self-conscious activity includes the ability to exercise moral judgment and creative imagination, the work of "evaluating that which moves one to action" (Murphy 2006, 99). The ability to step outside ourselves and critically examine our presuppositions, practices, and motives and to act accordingly is a capacity that makes us cognitively distinct from the nonhuman animal world. Whatever it is precisely, the mind is a function of the highest cultural order, enabling a sense of self-transcendence. Moreover, human "consciousness"—specifically its origin and explanation—remains a mystery. David Chalmers, for example, argues that consciousness can never be explained

---

22. Such as the stunning Chauvet Cave paintings in southern France, now dated to ca. 36,600 years old through radiocarbon dating. But the actual origin of art extends much farther back in time (see below).
23. One recent proposal argues that symbolic art began over 100,000 years ago, as evidenced in the "cross-hatched patterns" found on pieces of red ochre discovered at Blombos Cave in South Africa (Balter 2009a). Others suggest that certain modified stones ostensibly resembling human figures indicate a date as early as 300,000 years ago (Balter 2009b).

completely by neuroscience, since subjective experience cannot be reduced to physical processes (2002). Such is the "hard problem" of consciousness. This is not to deny that consciousness arises from the brain, but the link between the brain and the mind remains "perplexing" (93).[24] But explainable or not, the mind as an emergent, evolved property cannot be gainsaid.

For all that must be kept in mind regarding what distinguishes humans from nonhuman animals, the cognitive difference remains one of degree rather than in kind. It is the *degree* to which human beings are self-conscious that makes us unique and marks a "phase shift" in hominid evolution (Gazzaniga 2008, 302). Acknowledging this biological, specifically neurological, common ground yields a distinctly ethical payoff: "Assuming various degrees of animal consciousness spares us the hubris of seeing ourselves as the sole possessors of consciousness" (Ehrlich 2002, 112–13), as well as, one should add, the sole possessors of dignity. "Our dignity arises within nature, not against it" (Midgley 1995, 196). Our dignity as human beings should not feel threatened by "our continuity with the animal world" (196). The Yahwist would agree. We are all by nature groundlings.

In sum, human evolution is anything but a straight line, certainly no towering tree growing ever upward and onward. To the contrary, the human evolutionary picture is filled with branches extending in all different directions, some of them even crisscrossing, but all of them ending up dead, except for one. *Homo sapiens* is the only surviving hominin species today, but that was not the case up until around 40,000 years ago. Multiple species coexisted when *Homo sapiens* emerged. Moreover, the branching out of discrete lineages was not always discreet. It was messy. Divergences emerged amid convergences (i.e., interbreeding). The story of human evolution is full of twists and turns. The "line" of human evolution, in other words, is by no means singular; it is full of offshoots, crossovers, and detours. The human family tree is a tangled bush, and *Homo sapiens* is a semimixed species. Perhaps there is something experimental about evolution as different physical traits were embodied in different species in different environments, all before *Homo sapiens* came to be the sole representative of the genus. Look again at Gen. 2, and you may find God "experimenting" as well, creating from the soil, establishing boundaries, providing companionship, implementing Plan A, and resorting to Plan B. Call it God's "Anthropos Project."

What about the Fall?

Evolutionary science has yet to demonstrate anything resembling the "fall." There is no paleontological evidence to indicate that hominins once existed in blissfully peaceful relations and that snakes, for that matter, once walked upright and talked. This constitutes a significant collision between science and the traditional interpretation of the biblical fall. By itself, the Yahwist's tale offers profound reflections concerning the origin of human sin, about how human violence begets violence, leading up to God's grief-stricken resolve to "blot out" all life on the land by flood (Gen. 6:7). But the garden story has been traditionally read as an etiology for all pain and suffering in the world, from animal predation

---

24. Chalmers argues that because conscious experience is "irreducible to anything more basic," it qualifies as a "fundamental feature" (2002, 96).

to earthquakes, all the result of the primal couple's disobedience. Humanity's fall from paradise, it is claimed, brought about nature's fall from perfection. Yet the biblical story itself is much more limited in scope. Its primary focus is on the human family, not the family of life.

A scientific understanding of evolution challenges all sweeping interpretations to broaden the purview of the "fall" beyond the human family. Savage competition, untold suffering, ravaging disease, and extinction were all endemic to the natural order long before humans or hominins ever arrived on the scene. Nature was very much "red in tooth and claw," to quote Tennyson, prior to the advent of human beings. Think of the *Tyrannosaurus rex* rampaging the land some 80 million years ago or the saber-toothed tiger (*Smilodon fatalis*) of 2.5 million years, whose teeth were perfectly adapted to ripping open the throats of its prey. At no time in evolutionary history did the lion ever eat straw "like the ox" or the leopard lie "down with the kid" (cf. Isa. 11:6–7). To attribute predation and suffering to human disobedience is scientifically unfounded. There is no evidence whatsoever, and all evidence to the contrary, for nature to have "fallen" from an original harmonious perfection. Instead, the evolution of life has from the very beginning operated under death, predation, extinction, and competition while, at the same time, giving rise to diversity, complexity, beauty, and the self-consciousness to perceive it all.

Nevertheless, nature has suffered considerably as a result of the emergent *Homo*. Humanity has been a "plague mammal . . . with a long track record for transforming, and impoverishing, a range of ecosystems" (Southgate 2008, 100). Currently at around 7.5 billion in number and expected to reach around 10 billion by 2056, humans have become the most invasive species on Earth. But numbers alone do not tell the whole story. Ever since we learned how to hunt, extinction upon extinction of animal species has occurred, beginning around 13,000 years ago and now at an alarmingly rapid rate due to habitat destruction and climate change. Within the first few thousand years of the arrival of humans into North America, 70 percent of large mammalian species were pushed to extinction (Boulter 2003, 9). E. O. Wilson estimates that the rate of species extinction is "now 100 times the rate at which new species are being born," an unprecedented figure since the end of the Cretaceous Period 66 million years ago (2006, 117). If left unabated, anthropogenic degradation of the biosphere could destroy "half the species of plants and animals on Earth by the end of the century" (117).

So yes, the ancient tale of human disobedience, of the urge to snatch divinity and transgress limits, beginning with plucking fruit from a forbidden tree, can be read to highlight the irreversible damage to creation wrought by human hands. As a consequence of humanity's rise to power, countless species have suffered their own fall into extinction. And as a "plague mammal," humanity continues to be, as it always has been, plagued by sin, which according to the Yahwist is most evident in the human will to power to the point of violence and in the failure to take responsibility to "serve and preserve" the earth (Gen. 2:15).[25] From the biosphere's perspective, our birth was by no means benign. So also from the Yahwist's.

---

25. See Gen. 4:8–11, 23–24; 6:11–13.

Opened Eyes

As an interpretive lens, science highlights the developmental dimensions of the garden story, as well as the "messiness" of the narrative's plot. With its evolving characters, the Yahwist's tale builds to its climactic episode of disobedience. The couple's partaking from the tree of knowledge renders them self-reflectively conscious. This tree elicits the capacity to discriminate between what is "good" and what is "bad," presupposing rational, deliberate choice. And with that comes the capacity of self-awareness. The man and the woman recognize themselves in a mirror, as even chimpanzees and elephants do, but a mirror that reflects something entirely new about themselves. They see themselves as "naked" and thus as distinctly human. Such awareness in and of itself reflects the human capacity for self-consciousness. Nakedness, after all, is an anthropological distinction. Other animals are not naked (even if we do dress up our pets). Only humanity is the *naked* ape.

The turning point that led to consciousness had been building all along within the narrative. The groundling was placed in the garden and given a job, for which no moral assembly was required, only the specialized knowledge of garden care. At this point human identity remained at a "nascent stage" (Lapsley 2005, 14). The attainment of moral agency was yet to happen. It began when the groundling was given an imperative, one that conjoined freedom and restriction with a well-defined consequence: death. The prohibition ushered in a new stage of human development: choice becomes a meaningful factor for the first time in the narrative. Disobedience is now a possibility. Nevertheless, the choice to obey is not grounded "in a larger vision of the good" (14). The ʾādām remains, as it were, a child faced with a parental command accompanied by the threat of punishment. The next stage in the couple's development is occasioned by the cognitive dissonance introduced by the snake's countertestimony and the tree's desirability for acquiring wisdom. Disobedience emerges out of a conflictive mix of desire and dilemma. By partaking from the tree, they gain a level of self-consciousness, an awareness of their vulnerability and of their newly acquired ability to make decisions on their own. In choosing to become fully divine, they become, paradoxically, fully human, with all the costs, challenges, and complexities of becoming so.

So who were "Adam and Eve"? The ancient narrative shows them to be a work in progress, covering an astonishingly wide spectrum of human development in such a short narrative span. Both the ancient narrative and the evolutionary account expand our narrow view of what constitutes "being human." Borrowing from Gen. 1, one can seriously ask whether the "image of God" pertains only to modern *Homo sapiens*. Why not *Homo neanderthalensis* or *Homo erectus*? Why not include *Ardi* as well as Adam? One can only wonder. In any case, Adam and Eve need not represent simply the first hominin group who acted "religiously" some 40,000 years ago. The Yahwist's view is not so narrow in scope. Read through the lens of human evolution, the primal couple in the garden points toward the hominin developing through various challenging transitions: from specialized knowledge to moral consciousness, from gathering food to cultivating the land, from naked to clothed, from forest to open land. This short story is a wonder of "evolutionary" conflation. While the Yahwist never read Darwin, the garden story, in its own way, is a story of human development. Call it "Process Anthropology."

BIBLIOGRAPHY FOR CHAPTER 15

Anselm. 1998. *Anselm of Canterbury: The Major Works.* Edited by Brian Davies and G. R. Evans. Oxford World's Classics. Oxford: Oxford University Press.

Augustine of Hippo. 1991. "Sermon 68." In *The Works of Saint Augustine: A Translation for the 21st Century,* vol. III/3, *Sermons 51–94,* translated by Edmund Hill, 222–34. Augustinian Heritage Institute. Brooklyn: New York City Press.

Ayala, Francisco J. 1974. "The Concept of Biological Progress." In *Studies in the Philosophy of Biology: Reduction and Related Problems,* edited by Francisco Jose Ayala and Theodosius Dobzhansky, 339–55. Berkeley: University of California Press.

———. 2007. *Darwin's Gift to Science and Religion.* Washington, DC: Joseph Henry Press.

Baba, Hisao, et al. 2003. "*Homo erectus* Calvarium from the Pleistocene of Java." *Science* 299 (Feb. 28): 1384–88.

Baker, Catherine. 2006. *The Evolution Dialogues: Science, Christianity, and the Quest for Understanding.* Edited by James B. Miller. Washington, DC: AAAS.

Balter, Michael. 2009a. "Early Start for Human Art? Ochre May Revise Timeline." *Science* 323 (Jan. 30): 569.

———. 2009b. "On the Origin of Art and Symbolism." *Science* 323 (Feb. 9): 709–11.

Barbour, Ian G. 2000. *When Science Meets Religion: Enemies, Strangers, or Partners?* New York: HarperSanFrancisco.

Boulter, Michael. 2003. *Extinction: Evolution and the End of Man.* London: HarperCollins.

Brown, Peter, et al. 2007 "A New Small-Bodied Hominin from the Late Pleistocene of Flores, Indonesia." *Nature* 431 (Oct. 28): 1055–61.

Brown, William P. 2009. "From NOMA to TOMA: Bible, Science, and Wisdom." *SciTech* 18, no. 2:1, 4. Published by the Presbyterian Association on Science, Technology, and the Christian Faith (PASTCF).

———. 2010. *The Seven Pillars of Creation: The Bible, Science, and the Ecology of Wonder.* New York: Oxford University Press.

Chalmers, David J. 2002. "The Puzzle of Conscious Experience." *Scientific American* 280 (Apr. 1): 91–100.

The Chimpanzee Sequencing and Analysis Consortium. 2005. "Initial Sequence of the Chimpanzee Genome and Comparison with the Human Genome." *Nature* 437 (Sept. 1): 69–87.

Cole-Turner, Ron. 2016. *The End of Adam and Eve: Theology and the Science of Human Origins.* Pittsburgh, PA: TheologyPlus Publishing.

Coles, Peter. 2001. *Cosmology: A Very Short Introduction.* Oxford: Oxford University Press.

Collins, Francis S. 2006. *The Language of God: A Scientist Presents Evidence for Belief.* New York: Free Press.

Cunningham, Mary Kathleen. 2007. *God and Evolution: A Reader.* London: Routledge.

Darwin, Charles. 2006a. *On the Origin of Species by Means of Natural Selection.* In *From So Simple a Beginning: The Four Great Books of Charles Darwin,* edited by Edward O. Wilson, 441–760. New York: W. W. Norton.

———. 2006b. *The Descent of Man, and Selection in Relation to Sex.* In *From So Simple a Beginning: The Four Great Books of Charles Darwin,* edited by Edward O. Wilson, 767–1248. New York: W. W. Norton.

Ecklund, Elaine Howard. 2010. *Science vs. Religion: What Scientists Really Think.* New York: Oxford University Press.

Ehrlich, Paul. 2002. *Human Natures: Genes, Culture, and the Human Prospect.* New York: Penguin Books.

Frank, Adam. 2006. "The First Billion Years." *Astronomy* 34, no. 6 (June): 30–35.

Fry, Iris. 2015. "The Philosophy of Astrobiology: The Copernican and Darwinian Presuppositions." In *The Impact of Discovering Life beyond Earth,* edited by Steven J. Dick, 23–37. Cambridge: Cambridge University Press.

Galileo. 1957. "Letter to the Grand Duchess Christina." In *The Discoveries and Opinions of Galileo*, translated by Stillman Drake, 175–216. New York: Anchor Books.

Gazzaniga, Michael S. 2008. *Human: The Science behind What Makes Us Unique*. New York: HarperCollins.

Gibbons, Ann. 2009. "A New Kind of Ancestor: *Ardipithecus* Unveiled." *Science* 326, issue 5949 (Oct. 2): 36–40.

———. 2015. "New Human Species Discovered." *Science* 349, issue 6253 (Sept. 11): 1149–50.

———. 2016. "Five Matings for Moderns, Neanderthals." *Science* 351, issue 6279 (Mar. 18): 2150–51.

Gilkey, Langdon. 1959. *Maker of Heaven and Earth: A Study of the Christian Doctrine of Creation*. Garden City, NY: Doubleday.

Goodenough, Ursula. 1998. *The Sacred Depths of Nature*. Oxford: Oxford University Press.

Gould, Stephen Jay. 1999. *Rocks of Ages: Science and Religion in the Fullness of Life*. New York: Ballantine.

Greene, Brian R. 2004. *The Fabric of the Cosmos: Space, Time, and the Texture of Reality*. New York: Vintage Books.

Haught, John F. 2008. *God and the New Atheism: A Critical Response to Dawkins, Harris, and Hitchens*. Louisville, KY: Westminster John Knox Press.

———. 2010. *Making Sense of Evolution: Darwin, God, and the Drama of Life*. Louisville, KY: Westminster John Knox Press.

Hazen, Robert M. 2005. *Genesis: The Scientific Quest for Life's Origin*. Washington, DC: Joseph Henry Press.

Hess, Peter J. 2002. "'God's Two Books': Revelation, Theology, and Natural Science in the Christian West." In *Interdisciplinary Perspectives on Cosmology and Biological Evolution*, edited by Hilary D. Regan and Mark William Worthing, 19–51. Australian Theological Forum Science and Theology Series 2. Hindmarsh, Australia: Australian Theological Forum.

Hoyle, Fred. 1982. *Facts and Dogmas in Cosmology and Elsewhere*. Cambridge: Cambridge University Press.

Impey, Chris. 2007. *The Living Cosmos: Our Search for Life in the Universe*. New York: Random House.

Johnson, Elizabeth A. 2014. *Ask the Beasts: Darwin and the God of Love*. London: Bloomsbury/Continuum.

Jones, Steve. 2001. *Darwin's Ghost: The Origin of Species Updated*. New York: Ballantine.

Kaku, Michio. 2005. *Parallel Worlds: A Journey through Creation, Higher Dimensions, and the Future of the Cosmos*. New York: Anchor Books.

Kuhn, Thomas S. 1970. *The Structure of Scientific Revolutions*. Chicago: University of Chicago Press.

LaMotte, Louis C. 1937. *Colored Light: The Story of the Influence of Columbia Theological Seminary, 1828–1936*. Richmond, VA: Presbyterian Committee.

Lapsley, Jacqueline E. 2005. *Whispering the Word: Hearing Women's Stories in the Old Testament*. Louisville, KY: Westminster John Knox Press.

Macedo, Stephen, and Josiah Ober, eds. 2006. *Primates and Philosophers: How Morality Evolved*. Princeton, NJ: Princeton University Press.

Margulis, Lynn, and Dorion Sagan. 1997. *Microcosmos: Four Billion Years of Evolution from Our Microbial Ancestors*. Berkeley: University of California Press.

———. 1995. *What Is Life?* Berkeley: University of California Press.

McLeish, Tom. 2014. *Faith and Wisdom in Science*. Oxford: Oxford University Press.

Midgley, Mary. 1994. *The Ethical Primate: Humans, Freedom, and Morality*. London: Routledge.

———. 1995. *Beast and Man: The Roots of Human Nature*. 2nd ed. London: Routledge.

Miller, James B. 2009. "Evincing the Harmony: Confronting the Challenge of Science for the Church." *SciTech* 18, no. 4 (November): 1, 7–10. Published by the Presbyterian Association on Science, Technology, and the Christian Faith (PASTCF).

Miller, Kenneth R. 2000. *Finding Darwin's God: A Scientist's Search for Common Ground between God and Evolution*. New York: Harper.

Mithen, Steven. 1996. *The Prehistory of the Mind: A Search for the Origins of Art, Religion, and Science*. London: Thames & Hudson.

―――. 2006. *The Singing Neanderthals: The Origins of Music, Language, Mind, and Body*. Cambridge, MA: Harvard University Press.

Mix, Lucas John. 2009. *Life in Space: Astrobiology for Everyone*. Cambridge, MA: Harvard University Press.

Morowitz, Harold J. 2002. *The Emergence of Everything: How the World Became Complex*. Oxford: Oxford University Press.

Murphy, Nancey. 2006. *Bodies and Souls, or Spirited Bodies?* Current Issues in Theology. Cambridge: Cambridge University Press.

Peters, Ted. 2001. "From Conflict to Consonance: Ending the Warfare between Science and Faith." *Currents in Theology and Mission* 28, nos. 3–4 (June/August): 238–47.

―――. 2002. "Introduction: What Is to Come." In *Resurrection: Theological and Scientific Assessments*, edited by Ted Peters, Robert J. Russell, and Michael Welker, viii–xvii. Grand Rapids: Eerdmans Publishing.

Plotkin, Henry. 1998. *Evolution in Mind: An Introduction to Evolutionary Psychology*. Cambridge, MA: Harvard University Press.

Polkinghorne, John. 1998. *Belief in God in an Age of Science*. Terry Lecture Series. New Haven: Yale University Press.

Potts, Richard. 2005. "Sociality and the Concept of Culture in Human Origins." In *The Origins and Nature of Sociality*, edited by Robert W. Sussman and Audrey R. Chapman, 249–69. New York: Aldine de Gruyter.

Rees, Martin. 2009. "Pondering Astronomy in 2009." *Science* 323 (Jan. 16): 309.

Robinson, Marilynne. 1998. *The Death of Adam: Essays on Modern Thought*. Boston: Houghton Mifflin.

Rolston, Holmes, III. 2006. *Science and Religion: A Critical Survey*. 2nd ed. Philadelphia and London: Templeton Foundation Press.

―――. 2010. *The Three Big Bangs: Matter-Energy, Life, and Mind*. New York: Columbia University Press.

Ruse, Michael. 2001. *Can a Darwinian Be a Christian? The Relationship between Science and Religion*. Cambridge: Cambridge University Press.

Russell, Robert John. 2008. *Cosmology: From Alpha to Omega; The Creative Mutual Interaction of Theology and Science*. Theology and the Sciences. Minneapolis: Fortress Press.

Smithsonian National Museum of Natural History. 2016. *Human Origins: What Does It Mean to Be Human?* http://humanorigins.si.edu/.

Smolin, Lee. 1997. *The Life of the Cosmos*. London: Phoenix Paperback.

Southgate, Christopher. 2008. *The Groaning of Creation: God, Evolution, and the Problem of Evil*. Louisville, KY: Westminster John Knox Press.

Taylor, Barbara Brown. 2000. *The Luminous Web: Essays on Science and Religion*. Cambridge: Cowley.

Tocheri, Matthew, et al. 2007. "The Primitive Wrist of *Homo floresiensis* and Its Implications for Hominin Evolution." *Science* 317 (2007): 1743–45.

Tyson, Neil DeGrasse, and Donald Goldsmith. 2004. *Origins: Fourteen Billion Years of Cosmic Evolution*. New York: W. W. Norton.

Van Huyssteen, J. Wentzel. 2006. *Alone in the World? Human Uniqueness in Science and Theology*. The Gifford Lectures. Grand Rapids: Eerdmans Publishing.

Van Huyssteen, J. Wentzel, and Niels Henrik Gregersen, eds. 1998. *Rethinking Theology and Science: Six Models for Current Dialogue*. Grand Rapids: Eerdmans Publishing.

Venter, J. Craig, et al. 2001. "The Sequence of the Human Genome." *Science* 291, issue 5507 (Feb. 16): 1304–51.

Vernot, Benjamin, and Joshua M. Akey. 2014. "Resurrecting Surviving Neandertal Lineages from Modern Human Genomes." *Science* 343, issue 6174 (Feb. 28): 1017–21.

Waal, Frans de. 1996. *Good Natured: The Origins of Right and Wrong in Humans and Other Animals*. Cambridge, MA: Harvard University Press.

―――. 2006a. "Morally Evolved: Primate Social Instincts, Human Morality, and the Rise and Fall of 'Veneer Theory.'" In Macedo and Ober 2006, 1–58.

———. 2006b. "The Tower of Morality." In Macedo and Ober 2006, 161–82.

———. 2006c. "Appendix A: Anthropomorphism and Anthropodenial." In Macedo and Ober 2006, 59–67.

Wallace, Paul. 2016. *Stars beneath Us: Finding God in the Evolving Cosmos*. Minneapolis: Fortress Press.

Wilson, E. O. 1998. *Consilience: The Unity of Knowledge*. New York: Vintage Books.

———. 2006. *The Creation: An Appeal to Save Life on Earth*. New York: W. W. Norton.

Wood, Bernard. 2005. *Human Evolution: A Very Short Introduction*. Oxford: Oxford University Press.

16

Ecology

My friend, we have reduced the forest to a wasteland.
How shall we answer Enlil in Nippur?

Enkidu[1]

The earth is changing, from its climate to its land and oceans. It always has been. But the past several decades alone have witnessed an unprecedented rise in industrial heat-trapping gases, particularly carbon dioxide (CO_2) and methane (NH_4), extreme weather patterns, acidification of the oceans, sea levels, bleached coral reefs, polluted streams and fields, collapsed fisheries, and species extinction from habitat destruction and climate change.

With these crises mounting in magnitude, recommended public policy has dramatically changed over the past several years. The shift in language, for example, by the Intergovernmental Panel on Climate Change (IPCC) is notable: the focus is no longer on the prevention or avoidance of climate catastrophe but now on "adaptation and mitigation."[2] Unprecedented environmental degradation attributable to human activity is now an indelible part of our global context, with the developing nations and the poor suffering the brunt of the damage. Along with the changing state of the planet,[3] our periodization of time is also changing. Some have proposed a name for this new geological age, the Anthropocene period, or "human" epoch, whose beginning can be traced to the Industrial Revolution, about 250 years ago.[4] Although it lacks official designation among geologists, the proposal to rename the present age is a startling testimony to the

---

1. From a recently discovered fragment that helps complete the Standard Babylonian version of the Gilgamesh Epic. Enkidu is Gilgamesh's partner in vanquishing the guardian of the Cedar Forest, but their victory over Humbaba is subsequently lamented. See Al-Rawi and George 2014, 74. The quotation, along with its reconstruction, is from Tablet V, line 303.
2. See "Climate Change 2014 Synthesis Report Summary for Policymakers," esp. 17–31, http://www.ipcc.ch/pdf/assessment-report/ar5/syr/AR5_SYR_FINAL_SPM.pdf.
3. Or as Bill McKibben has written, "Eaarth," to signify the new state of the planet (2010).
4. See, e.g., Clark 2015; Hamilton, Bonneuil, and Gemenne 2015.

world-changing power of our species. Some also foresee Earth moving into a sixth major extinction.[5]

What, then, does it mean to interpret the Bible in the Anthropocene age, in the light of mounting environmental catastrophes, all caused, directly or indirectly, by human activity? Can the Bible be read in ways that foster ecological wisdom? One might think otherwise, since the biblical authors could not have imagined the technological prowess and consumptive habits that threaten the planet today. Indeed, some have claimed the Bible itself to be part of the problem.

THE CHALLENGE

The dialogue between the Bible and ecology began in earnest with an arresting essay by Lynn White Jr. in 1967 titled "The Historical Roots of Our Ecological Crisis." White (1907–87) was professor of medieval history, specifically medieval technology, at Princeton University and the University of California. He was also the son of a Presbyterian minister and held, in addition to his PhD from Harvard, an MA from Union Theological Seminary in New York. In his essay, White observed that "Human ecology is deeply conditioned by beliefs about our nature and destiny—that is, by religion" (1967, 1205). Ecology, in other words, is not only a matter of scientific study. It is also concerns how human beings see themselves in relation to the world, with religion playing a formative role. The problem, as identified by White, is that one particular form of religion, western Christianity, has fostered a worldview that pits humanity against nature, that regards the natural world only "for man's benefit and rule" (1205). The verdict:

> Especially in its Western form, Christianity is the most anthropocentric religion the world has seen. . . . Man shares, in great measure, God's transcendence of nature. Christianity . . . not only established a dualism of man and nature but also insisted that it is God's will that man exploit nature for his proper ends. (1205)

White lays the blame on Gen. 1, which in his mind gives license to exploit the earth without limit. Made in God's image, humankind shares no part of nature (1205). In short, the Bible is not only unhelpful in developing an ecological sensibility; it is also downright destructive, allowing ecocide in the name of human dominion. Yet White does not give up on Christianity entirely. He offers an alternative Christian view to his assessment of western Christianity by commending the example of Francis of Assisi, who modeled humility and solidarity with all of nature, as the patron saint of ecologists (1207).[6]

Biblical scholars have been responding to White's sweeping condemnations ever since. But White is surely to be commended for laying out the issues so pointedly and for

5. The five major extinctions are (1) *Ordovician–Silurian* extinction (450–440 mya); (2) *Late Devonian* extinction (375–360 mya); (3) *Permian–Triassic* extinction (252 mya); (4) *Triassic–Jurassic* extinction (201.3 mya); and (5) *Cretaceous–Paleogene* extinction (66 mya).

6. Not coincidentally, Pope Francis's encyclical letter *Laudato Si'* (2015) quotes the first line of Saint Francis's canticle in its title. Its subtitle is "On Care for Our Common Home."

prompting, almost single-handedly, the dramatic rise of ecological concern among Christians and Jews. But simply defending the Bible in the face of White's criticism, as many have done, has proved insufficient.[7] White's reading of Genesis, whether it can be attributed directly to Genesis or to bad interpretations of Genesis, remains dominant among Western readers. Moreover, the environmental crises encountered in the late 1960s have only multiplied at an alarming rate.

ENVIRONMENTAL ETHICS AND HERMENEUTICS

Thus we return to the hermeneutical challenge mentioned at the outset, cast most generally: *How do we read the Bible from a place of ecological concern? Can the Bible, beginning with Genesis, be read in ways that foster ecological wisdom? Is it possible to develop an ecological orientation from Scripture that promotes, rather than ignores or undercuts, environmental ethics?* The last question requires some familiarity with what environmental ethics is about.

Environmental Ethics

As a discipline, environmental ethics was unknown until the mid-1970s (Rolston 2012, 19), when it quickly developed amid the growing awareness of the damaging effects of water and air pollution. The alarm raised by scientists, for example, over the depletion of ozone in the upper atmosphere led to the Montreal Protocol in 1987, which banned the use of chlorofluorocarbons (CFCs), among other substances. The Protocol continues to be hailed as an exceptional example of international cooperation and political will.

Major figures of the environmental movement in the United States include Aldo Leopold on soil conservation,[8] Rachel Carson on pesticide control,[9] and John Muir on wilderness preservation.[10] Today environmentalists work on a number of issues and fronts: energy and water conservation, animal welfare, transitioning toward renewable energy (e.g., sun, wind, geothermal), clean water, justice on behalf of minorities and the poor, organic agriculture, wilderness preservation, and preserving endangered species, to name only a few. Overall, environmental ethics adopts a more biocentric orientation toward the planet by fostering respect for all life, both individual and species specific, as well as the

7. See, e.g., Richard Bauckham's historical analysis of the "dominion" interpretation, which attributes the misreading of Gen. 1 to Greek philosophy and Renaissance interpretation (2011, 14–62).

8. Aldo Leopold (1887–1948) articulated the ethic that inspired the modern environmental movement: "A thing is right when it tends to preserve the integrity, stability, and beauty of the biotic community. It is wrong when it tends otherwise" (1968, 224–25). For Leopold, the "land" is communal, since it includes the soil, its water systems, vegetation, and animals. Such a communally based environmental ethic "changes the role of *Homo sapiens* from conqueror of the land community to plain member and citizen of it" (204).

9. Rachel Carson's groundbreaking study *Silent Spring* (1962) documented the detrimental effects of indiscriminate pesticide use to wildlife. Eliciting great public outcry, its publication resulted in the creation of the Environmental Protection Agency (EPA) in 1970 and a nationwide ban on the use of DDT in 1972.

10. The naturalist John Muir (1838–1914) is known for the accounts of his adventures hiking in the Sierra Nevada Mountains. He was instrumental in saving Yosemite National Park, Sequoia National Park, and many other wilderness areas. He founded the Sierra Club, one of the most powerful conservation organizations today.

delicate ecosystems that sustain them. The word "ecology" refers to the "household" of our planet, derived from the Greek *oikos*, adopting a broad systemic focus on what sustains life. Any environmental ethic values life's diversity and interconnectedness and proposes ways to lessen our ecological "footprint" on the planet.[11] It is said that environmental ethics is "the most altruistic form of ethics" (Rolston 2012, 60).

Environmental Hermeneutics

While it does not yield a discrete environmental ethic, the Bible can potentially lift up the importance of, and need for, an environmental ethic. An ecologically oriented reading strategy focuses critically on certain features of the biblical text that could promote (or discourage) an environmental ethic. *How, for example, are the land, water, and sky described in the text? How biocentric is the text's orientation toward creation?* Or conversely, *how anthropocentric is it? What is humanity's relationship to the rest of creation?*

As environmental concerns have played an increasingly significant role in biblical interpretation, particularly after Lynn White's landmark essay, two major approaches so far have developed. One approach is what David Horrell calls the "recovery strategy," which aims at recovering or retrieving the Bible's ecological wisdom, "a wisdom that has been hidden and obscured by interpreters who failed to see or attend to such dimensions of the text" (Horrell 2010, 11). Such a strategy holds the Bible as an unambiguously constructive source of ecological wisdom and aims at clarifying certain problematic texts, such as Gen. 1:26–28, with its language of dominion. The problem is that such a strategy ends up being unnecessarily defensive for the more problematic texts (see below).

Another approach is the "strategy of resistance," which acknowledges that the Bible, at least in certain places, "inculcates a damaging form of anthropocentrism" (Horrell 2010, 13) and, I add, a damaging form of dualism. It begins with a hermeneutic of suspicion that identifies and rejects (resists) those biblical texts that are shown to be problematic. The most systematic form of this strategy can be found in the multi-volume Earth Bible series, which presently offers the most extensive attempt to engage the Bible ecologically. The strength of this approach is found in its systematic focus on reading the Bible "from the perspective of Earth," guided by six "ecojustice" principles meant to guide interpreters in reading any biblical text. They are as follows (Habel 2008, 2):

1. The Principle of Intrinsic Worth
   The universe, Earth, and all its components have intrinsic worth/value.
2. The Principle of Interconnectedness
   Earth is a community of interconnected living things that are mutually dependent on each other for life and survival.
3. The Principle of Voice
   Earth is a subject capable of raising its voice in celebration and against injustice.
4. The Principle of Purpose
   The universe, Earth, and all its components are part of a dynamic cosmic design, within which each piece has a place in the overall goal of that design.

---

11. The "ecological footprint" is a measure of the amount of biologically productive land and sea area that is necessary to sustain our consumptive habits.

5. The Principle of Custodianship
   Earth is a balanced and diverse domain requiring responsible custodians who function as partners with, rather than rulers over, Earth to sustain its balance and diversity.
6. The Principle of Resistance
   Earth and its components not only suffer from human injustices but actively resist them in the struggle for justice.

By way of categorization, three of these principles ascribe subjectivity to nature: Earth has intrinsic worth (1), has voice (3), and suffers and engages in resistance (6). The task of the exegete, therefore, is to retrieve Earth's voice and to hear it as a subject that suffers from and resists "human injustices." The remaining principles highlight nature's interconnectedness (2), purpose (4), balance and diversity (5), thereby warranting "custodial" care by its human "partners." All of these principles, it should be noted, are cast nontheologically (Tucker 2009, 360).

In addition to the six ecojustice principles, Habel has delineated three hermeneutical steps to guide the interpretive process, modeled on feminist criticism: (1) suspicion, (2) identification, and (3) retrieval (2008, 3–8). The first step acknowledges the "probable anthropocentric bias" of the biblical text (2008, 8). "Identification" encourages readers to identify with Earth by confessing our "kinship with the Earth." The final step, "retrieval," involves hearing and articulating nonhuman voices, collectively Earth, in the text as subjects rather than as objects.

Although "retrieval" is the end point of the interpretive task in the Earth Bible program, it is not reached simply by clarifying the biblical text. The Earth Bible approach ultimately falls on the side of suspicion and resistance: every text is measured against the six principles, and while some texts are found to be better than others, all biblical texts are deemed not fully liberative, because Earth is never fully voiced in the text. In other words, both exposing and resisting "anti-Earth perspectives" *in* the Bible are paramount.

I propose a mediating approach, one that is not so hard-nosed suspicious, yet not so apologetically naive. I begin with reading two indisputably "greener" biblical texts to explore why they should be considered ecologically constructive. I am asking, in effect, about their valuation of creation. Following that, I will reread the creation accounts in Genesis in light of these two eco-friendly texts.

Job 38–41 and Psalm 104

Are there biblical texts that come close to articulating an inclusive biocentric perspective? A favorite of ecologically oriented exegetes is God's answer in the book of Job, in chaps. 38–41 (see, e.g., McKibben 2005). In this climactic episode, God confronts Job by showing him the vastness and vitality of all creation, from top to bottom, end to end, and everything in between. In so doing, God brings the margins of creation to the center of Job's purview, including various wild creatures, from lions to Leviathan. God seems to swell with pride in showing off these creatures, describing them in great detail to Job, giving them each their poetic due and dignity.

Nowhere in God's answer to Job is humanity lifted up as an agent of dominion. Indeed, hardly any reference is made to human beings at all, except for the allusion to Job vis-à-vis Behemoth:

> [15] Behold Behemoth, which I made with you [*ʿimmāk*]![12]
>   It eats grass like an ox.
> [16] Behold the strength in its loins,
>   and its power in the muscles of its belly. . . .
> [19] It is the first [*rēʾšît*] of God's works;
>   [Only] the one who made it can approach it with sword.[13]
> [20] Indeed, the mountains yield food for it,
>   where every wild animal plays. (Job 40:15–16, 19–20 AT)

Behemoth is the "first (or chief) of God's works" (v. 19). Not humankind, not Job, but a mythically fierce beast. Among the animals of the wild, both whimsical and monstrous, both dangerous and dependent, Job himself seems to have no place. But he does occupy one brief reference in v. 15: God created Behemoth "with" Job. Whatever that means exactly, Job is at least acknowledged by God to be as much a part of creation as Behemoth. Job and Behemoth, in other words, share in common the bond of creaturehood.

The climax of this created order is found not in humanity but in Leviathan, a creature without fear and equal (41:33 [25 MT]), "king over all the sons of pride" (v. 34 [26] AT), the quintessential figure of chaos (cf. Ps. 74:14; Isa. 27:1). The difference could not be more stark between Job 38–41 and Gen. 1: humanity is dethroned in Job, replaced by Leviathan. Absent is any talk of *human* dominion. God's answer upends Job's worldview (and that of Genesis), which consigned such creatures to the margins. As often noticed, Job (along with humanity) is "decentered." Creation apart from humanity has intrinsic value; it is the object of God's unbridled boasting to Job—a testimony to God's creative power, on the one hand, and creation's inalienable dignity, on the other.

Another biblical passage that does much the same thing is Ps. 104, a psalm of creation that celebrates the diversity of God's creatures: "YHWH, how manifold are your works! In wisdom you have made them all; the earth is full of your creatures" (v. 24). The psalmist references a host of animals: onagers, birds, cattle, cedars and trees, stork, wild goats, coneys, lions, and, yes, Leviathan, all in praise of God for God's wise handiwork. As for human beings, they have a place but no dominant role in relation to the other creatures. While "cattle" are mentioned (v. 14a), it is not to highlight their use for human consumption or servitude. Instead, they are consumers of "grass" as much as human beings are consumers of plants. The cedars of Lebanon are praised not for their quality of lumber but for their majestic stature as the "trees of YHWH" (v. 16). Indeed, the only difference between lions and human beings is that the lions take the night shift in order to secure their living while humans go out during the day to do the same (vv. 19–23). Overall, the psalmist celebrates the habitability of the earth and the diversity of its inhabitants, with each species

---

12. Literal reading. NRSV has "just as I made you"; NJPS has "made as I did you." This may be the basic sense, but the sole use of the preposition (*ʿim*) in the MT can also suggest connection, even companionship (cf. Gen. 3:12).
13. Literally, "can bring near his sword."

rightfully occupying its own space or niche. The God of Ps. 104 is the consummate bio-phile, the creator who takes delight in all creatures, providing for them (vv. 27–31).

In both Job and the psalm, creation is portrayed in more biocentric than anthropo-centric terms. Humanity does not take center stage in either passage. Far from it, in their rich descriptions of the natural world, Job and the psalm place God at the center, God the provider of all life. The final explicit reference to humanity in Ps. 104 is at the very end, yet not as the climax of creation but as its liability: "Let sinners be consumed from the earth, and let the wicked be no more" (v. 35). Who are the wicked? The psalmist does not say, but if the wicked have any connection to what the psalmist has lovingly detailed earlier, then they are the ones who pose a threat to creation, not Leviathan, as construed elsewhere in biblical tradition (v. 26; cf. Ps. 74:14; Isa. 27:1)

These texts stand out as being two of the "greener" texts of the Bible. Both celebrate the diversity of biological life, acknowledging the worth of each creature in creation. At the same time, Job 38–41 and Ps. 104 level out the differences that set humanity apart from the rest of creation. In both passages, humanity is merely one species among many.

How do the Genesis texts measure up? Before we turn to them, it is good to step back and identify the main issues that have emerged from our discussion of Job and Ps. 104 thus far. I prefer not to identify strict principles but rather to lift up certain "orienting issues" that can focus our attention on various aspects of the text that could be germane, positively or negatively, to contemporary ecological concerns.

1. Creation's worth
2. Creation's diversity
3. Creation's interdependence
4. Humanity's relationship to the rest of creation
5. God's relationship to creation

GENESIS 1

While Job and Psalm 104 are helpful for raising environmental concerns, particularly the value of biodiversity and humanity's relationship to creation, an ecological approach to Scripture must address Gen. 1. Given its canonical position, this creation account assumes pride of place in the Bible. It is also, as noted above, a flashpoint of ecological contention. Using our five orienting issues, we begin our ecological exploration of Gen. 1.

Creation's Worth

The one discriminating term of value expressed in Gen. 1 is found in the repeated for-mula of God's approbation, "good" (1:4, 10, 12, 18, 21, 25, 31). Light, the formation of land and seas, vegetation, the lights (including sun and moon), sea creatures, and land creatures are all specifically identified as good. But lest there be any moral distinctions among God's various creations, the final approbation is extended to all creation (1:31). Two key questions are posed by an ecologically focused interpretation: (1) Is "goodness" intrinsic to creation? (2) What is the meaning and scope of creation's "goodness"?

Although the first question may not be answerable to the ethicist's satisfaction, it is worth exploring exegetically. Does God declare creation "good" because God recognizes it as good? Or is creation "good" because God pronounced it so? Another way to put it, does creation's goodness exist apart from God's approval? The obvious response may seem to be negative, but the text does not offer a simple answer. "And God saw that it was good" is not "And God made it good." The formula is rooted in divine perception ("God saw"), signaling the satisfactory completion of something created, whether it is light or the "great sea monsters." Hence, the goodness of creation is, first and foremost, something acknowledged by God, and it is no coincidence that some of these creative acts of God are described as acts of creation itself.

For example, God commanded the earth to "put forth vegetation" (Gen. 1:11), and the earth did so (v. 12a). "And God saw that it was good" (v. 12b). Goodness here is the product of the earth's creative capacity to yield vegetation. And so the status of "goodness" is not necessarily an either-or matter in Gen. 1. Creation's goodness is, to be sure, dependent upon God, since God brought about creation, but goodness is also deemed inherent in creation as indicated in God's repeated acknowledgment. Perhaps the question poses too fine a distinction. The pressing issue is really whether creation's "goodness" is dependent upon *humankind*. Notice that the term "good" is applied to creation six times *before* the creation of human beings, and the seventh time goodness is pronounced on creation as a whole ("everything," v. 31).

What of the content and scope of creation's "goodness"? Its semantic scope may span a range of nuance, but the question directs our attention to the aspects of creation that the account itself holds as good or valuable. What qualities, aspects, or dimensions of creation does the text itself identify as "good"? Structure and order, for one. The completed creation is a bona fide cosmos, an ordered, harmonious, aesthetic whole, the opposite of *tōhû wābōhû* (cf. Isa. 45:18). Creation's structured integrity is presented as having enduring value, particularly in the final, supreme instance of God's approval (Gen. 1:31).

But there is something more. As noted in chap. 8, the chronological structure of Gen. 1 reflects something of the architecture of the tabernacle/temple, in which case its axiological center of gravity shifts from the good to the sacred. As a cosmic temple in time, creation according to Gen. 1 is more than "good": it is holy! Shaped by its structure, creation's integrity reflects the shape of sacred space. The distinction between "goodness" and "holiness" is a fine, if not permeable, line in Gen. 1. "Goodness" in Gen. 1 also connotes the plenitude of life, both animal and botanical. The plants, moreover, make possible the sustenance of life on the land. In other words, a habitable, sustainable creation is a key goal of creation in Genesis. As for creation's sustainability, seeds and sex are the means by which life is furthered. Such "goodness" has paramount ecological worth.

Creation's Diversity

Ten times in Gen. 1 the little word "kind" (*mîn*) is deployed to highlight the diversity of creation, from the botanical to the biological: seeds, trees, aquatic and aviary creatures, and land animals. The term, however, is not used for humankind, since humankind's diversity is not biological but, as will be accounted for later in the Genesis narrative, cultural (cf. Gen. 10:1–31; 11:1–9). Diversity is situated within discrete domains: land, seas/oceans, and sky. Botanically, a distinction is made between fruit-producing trees and non-fruit-yielding plants, both of which bear seeds (1:11, 12). Life in the sea consists of "great sea monsters" and swarming creatures (v. 21). Life on land consists of "cattle," "creeping things," and "wild animals" (vv. 24–25). Aviary creatures are not distinguished in the text, such as between birds of prey and flying insects. Still, they are of "every kind" (v. 21). As for human beings, a fundamental distinction is introduced: "male and female" (zākār ûněqēbâ, v. 27c). Such gendered differentiation is deemed critical to humankind's creation "in the image of God" (v. 26a, 27ab). So, yes, diversity is a dominant theme in Gen. 1. It too is a distinguishing feature of creation.

Creation's Interdependence

The domains of creation, as established in the first three days, remain discrete: seas/oceans, land, and sky. Their clear delineations are integral to the larger picture of creation's integrity, as we have seen, and they reflect a certain mode of divine action during the first three days of creation, namely, separation. Light and darkness are separated (v. 4), a firmament separates the waters above from the waters below (vv. 6–7), the waters below collect themselves so that the land can appear (vv. 9–10), and the celestial bodies serve to "separate" day from night and the light from the darkness (vv. 14, 18).

Separation thus seems to be a more prominent theme than interdependence. Boundaries are critical to the Priestly view of creation. Nevertheless, a creative interdependence is also emphasized in the text, as evident with the domains themselves serving as creative agents. Plants and land animals are made possible through the earth's creative agency: "Let the earth . . ." (vv. 11, 24). So also come the sea creatures through the agency of the waters (vv. 20, 21b). These domains—at least earth and the waters—serve as creative, empowering environments for life according to its various "kinds." Genesis 1, thus, testifies to life's genetic relationship to the abiotic aspects of its environments, with the biological arising from the inorganic. The earth and the waters are more than life-sustaining domains: they are also life-generating realms. Moreover, these creative environments are deeply connected to divine creativity: through the rhetoric of divine command, God works collaboratively with the earth and the waters to fashion life.

Finally, the dependence of biological life on botanical life is vividly clear. "See, I have given you every plant yielding seed . . . and every tree with seed in its fruit; you shall have them for food" (1:29). However, it is ecologically critical to recognize that the abundance of botanical sustenance is devoted not just to human consumption; it is given to all other animals as well (v. 30). Such is the primordial diet according to Genesis: vegetarian. Meat eating does not figure into the picture of these first two chapters.

Creation's Relation to Humanity

To state the obvious, creation in "the image of God" is uniquely applied to humankind in Genesis, and it sets the condition for their purpose in exercising dominion over creation:

> Then God said, "Let us make humankind in our image, after our likeness, so that they may **rule** [wĕyirdû] over the fish of the sea, and over the winged creatures in the heavens, over the domestic animals, over all the land, and over everything that crawls on the land." (1:26 AT)

The charge given after humankind's creation is even more sharp:

> And God blessed them, and God said to them, "Be fruitful and multiply; fill the earth and **subdue it** [wĕkibšūhā] and **rule** [ûrĕdû] over the fish of the sea and over the winged creatures in the heavens and over every creature that crawls on the ground." (1:28 AT)

The repeated verb for "rule" (*rdh*) or "have dominion" evokes a distinctly royal setting, establishing the analogy: as a king rules over his subjects, so human beings rule over all other creatures. As often noted, the royal rhetoric of dominion is applied to *all* human beings. What is the nature of such universal dominion? Does it give humanity the license to exploit creation? As a word study points out, the verb *rdh* ("rule") can go either way: oppressive or beneficial. The prophet Ezekiel, for example, qualifies the kind of "rule" that he finds oppressive.

> You have not strengthened the weak, you have not healed the sick, you have not bound up the injured, you have not returned the strayed, you have not sought the lost, but with **violence** [ḥozqâ] and **cruelty** [perek] **you have ruled them** [rĕdîtem]. (34:4 AT)

The qualifiers make painfully clear what kind of rule the prophet condemns: dominion that is specifically violent and cruel. The fact that qualifiers in the prophet's condemnation are needed demonstrates that the verb can also be used to designate nonoppressive dominion, as in the case of Ps. 72, which lists the qualities that make for a good king. The psalm profiles the just king as one who establishes justice for the poor and eliminates the oppressor (v. 4), who delivers the needy and cares for the lowly (vv. 12–14). Such dominion does precisely what a "cruel" dominion does not: it delivers "from oppression and violence" (v. 14). In contrast to Ezekiel's indictment against the wicked rulers, called "shepherds," the psalmist lauds and exhorts the *just* king. This is what dominion should look like, a dominion that cares for the vulnerable.

To talk of a *just* "dominion" in Gen. 1, one could extrapolate from Ps. 72 to infer that humankind's rule in Genesis, far from being tyrannical, is meant to take care of creation, protecting, for example, those who suffer the brunt of environmental injustice, from poor people to endangered species, as well as dismantling economic structures and policies that damage the environment. Indeed, one could lift up the figure of Noah as the paradigmatic example of exercising good "dominion" when he implemented God's first "endangered species act" (Gen. 6:13–22; 7:1–5).

Some call the kind of human dominion mandated in Gen. 1 "stewardship," arguing that stewardship is an appropriate dynamic translation for 1:26, 28. Humankind is gifted with the task of "managing" creation such that all life can flourish. Both stewardship and "dominion" appropriately acknowledge humanity's capability to change the face of the earth, for good or for ill. In that sense, the mandate to exercise dominion over creation is an invitation to enter responsibly into the Anthropocene epoch. But as an environmental ethical model, "stewardship" has its limitations. It is, admittedly, a hierarchical notion that places human beings over and apart from the rest of creation. A strictly "stewardship" approach to creation care does not take into account the interconnectional nature of creation, particularly humanity's connection with the rest of life. "Stewardship," moreover, is a concept that comes from the financial world, and the last thing the world needs is more commodification of its resources for consumption. At best, stewardship covers only one side of what it means to embody sustainable practices for the sake of creation. Where, for example, does self-restraint figure in the practice of "stewarding" creation? What about humility? By itself, stewardship can create the illusion that humanity is separate from creation. The ecological crisis calls human beings to be more than managers, more than kings (and queens) over creation. It calls for partnership.

The critique of the stewardship model as incomplete applies well to Gen. 1, with its call to "rule" over creation. But more problematic is the call to "subdue" the earth (v. 28). A term of aggression, the verb in Hebrew even sounds harsh: God calls humanity to *kābaš* the earth! Outside of Genesis, the verb can connote military conquest, as in Zech. 9:15 and Num. 32:29. In Jer. 34:11, *kābaš* refers to forced subjugation into slavery. It is impossible to soften its tone, even here in Genesis. Of course, it would be an overstatement to claim that this passage envisions creation as humanity's *enemy* to be conquered. Creation is not chaos, warranting conquest either by God or by human beings. Nevertheless, "subdue" carries the dominion motif into the battlefield. Human beings are seemingly called to be "warrior kings," exercising dominion *and* subjugation. In contrast, Noah did not "subdue" creation by building the ark: he saved it.

What this passage meant to an agrarian society need not imply outright war with creation. For the farmer who had to toil painfully to turn rocky, heavily forested land into arable fields, as was the case in the hill country of ancient Palestine, this passage spoke volumes. Backbreaking effort to "tame" the land, to make it productive for human subsistence, was no "peaceful" matter. The land's rocky soil was resistant and thus had to be forced into productivity. Perhaps this was how the passage was understood by ancient agriculturalists. The passage reinscribes farming as a royal, militant enterprise. Every farmer was "king" over his land.

But the problem remains for a capitalistic society built on industry, expanding consumption, and the extraction of resources. Genesis 1:26–28 seems out of character within the larger context of a well-ordered creation. There is nothing previous to the sixth day that hints at creation requiring subjugation. The creator God is no conquering hero, because creation is no chaos. The "breath" of God "hovering over the surface of Deep" (Gen. 1:2 AT; cf. Deut. 32:11) is a scene of intimacy rather than enmity. There is no absolute dualism between chaos and order in Gen. 1, contrary to certain ancient Near Eastern testimonies. By divine command, the waters and the earth act willingly to produce what they are prompted to produce: life in all its "kinds." The task given to humanity, thus, comes as something of a surprise. Genesis 1:26–30 "poses a conflict of orientation within the Earth story that remains unresolved" (Habel 2000, 35). If one takes Earth as the "dominant subject" in Gen. 1, then vv. 26–30 come as a disruption, a disruption not caused by the creation of humanity per se but rather by humanity's specified role over creation.

Or put it this way: with humanity created in God's image, humanity is expected to "reflect" God in and for creation. And what God has done in creation is, one might say, nonviolent. Yet humanity's specified task in Genesis *is* in part violent: subdue the earth! It is as if the chaos-combat motif (*Chaoskampf*), so widespread in other ANE traditions, including biblical (e.g., Pss. 74, 89, and Isa. 27:1), has found a foothold in Gen. 1: subjugation taken up not by God but by humanity, God's representative on earth. Humanity's role, in sum, stands in ecological tension with the larger account of creation and its integrity.

By stepping back for a moment, you may have discerned that I am using Gen. 1 as a whole to question the point of the passage under question (vv. 26–28), or to put it more sharply, to let the larger passage critique the smaller. In any case, an ecological lens highlights a tension that through any other lens or approach might not seem so prominent. Is there resolution? The tension could be relieved, to an extent, by taking the mandate to "subdue the earth" less prescriptively and more descriptively or etiologically. This, I admit, may not be the "intent" of the text, since the language of subjugation in v. 28 is cast as a command. But even commands, particularly primordial commands, have their explanatory role. This is what human beings do, according to the Priestly tradition; they exercise dominion over creation. Dominion is in their power, and it is their intent to exercise it. The ecological crisis, as Lynn White so forcefully pointed out, is a testimony to human beings "subduing" the earth without thought or care of the consequences, both immediate and long range. And so it has been, but does it have to be thus from here on out? For a credible ecological ethic to be constructed from Gen. 1, one would need to change merely one word: from "subdue" to "sustain" in v. 28. That would change the course of "dominion" in the most dramatic of ways (cf. Isa. 11:5–9). Genesis 1, thus, is a most ambivalent text.

Nevertheless, the first creation account also offers one of the most constructive contributions to an ecological perspective, and that is the seventh day (Gen. 2:1–3). While humanity may be the climax of God's active work of creation, the Sabbath day marks the culmination of the creation account itself: God ceases creating because creation is now deemed complete and completely "good" (1:31), and so this final day is sanctified as a day of cessation or rest (*šbt*). Indeed, the concluding theme of Sabbath shows that Gen. 1 is more theocentric than anthropocentric in its orientation (Bauckham 2011, 5). Still, the anthropological implications are profound: with the seventh day a rhythm is established that is meant to limit human activity, as confirmed in the Sabbath command (Exod. 20:8–11; Deut. 5:12–15). Human work, including the exercise of dominion, is to be suspended on a regular basis. Human restraint is built into the order of creation for the sake of creation, including humanity. Indeed, the Deuteronomic version of the Sabbath command casts the day as a liberation from servitude and slavery (Deut. 5:14–15). By extension, the liberation of creation is in view (cf. Rom. 8:21).

God's Relationship to Creation

It is sometimes said that God is an environmentalist for the simple reason that God created the environment. God in Gen. 1 is indisputably the creator of all things environmental, "maker of heaven and earth" (cf. Gen. 14:19, 22). The "all" includes everything from "creeping things" to "great sea monsters" to human beings. God in Gen. 1 is intimately involved in the creation of structure and the formation of life. God commands and acts, as well as commands and enlists creation to act. Collaborating with the earth and the waters in the creation of life, God in Genesis creates a creating cosmos.

Creating the cosmos according to Genesis was not an instantaneous affair or a matter of divine whim. Time and effort, thought and care on the part of God were required, even if creation itself took only six "days." The methodical work of creation indicates how deeply God is invested in creation. That investment might involve love or delight, but such words are not deployed in the Priestly account. Instead, only the language of approbation ("good") is used, indicating God's satisfaction with the way creation turns out, step by step, day by day.

Creation's relationship to God is not a simple matter of dependence. While creation remains fundamentally dependent upon God, God has also established creation to be self-sustaining. That is to say, creation does not require divine intervention at every moment in order to sustain it. To the contrary, God has established creation to continue without continuous intervention. Sabbath marks both creation's completion and its freedom, a freedom that, yes, ultimately threatens to destroy creation, as the flood narrative attests (see Gen. 6:12–13), requiring a new beginning. God in Gen. 1 proves to be no micromanager.

Finally, creation figured as God's cosmic temple indicates a deeper level of relationship. While God remains independent of creation, transcendentally so, creation belongs to God, wholly so. Such is the double nature of holiness (Hundley 2013, 752–53). On the one hand, holiness connotes separation, such as God's separation from the created order, established on the seventh day. On the other hand, holiness reflects a special relationship to God. Creation belongs to God in the same way that special objects are made holy by virtue of their relationship to the divine. It is this second aspect of holiness that pertains to creation as a whole in Gen. 1 (cf. Ps. 24:1). In God, creation's holiness and wholeness are bound together. As creation is God's holy sanctuary, respect for creation is tantamount to reverence of God, the creator of all.

GENESIS 2–3

A very different creation account, the garden story, yields its own ecological highs and lows. Its setting is that of a garden, but not what we would naturally think of as a garden. Eden's garden does not consist of lined rows of vegetables. No, the garden is a grove, a forest of fruit trees (2:9), with two trees in particular.

A forest has its own allure in the human mind; it is place of wonder and awe. As environmentalist ethicist Holmes Rolston writes,

> We come to see forests . . . as a characteristic expression of the creative process.
> . . . The forest is both presence and symbol of forces in natural systems that transcend human powers and human utility. Like the sea or the sky, the forest is a kind of archetype of the foundations of the world. (2012, 51)

It is noteworthy that this Eden forest is planted by God, not by human hands (2:8). Hence, it is wild, an "archetype" of fundamental, natural creativity. How fitting. And yet this forest is also edible; certain trees within it bear fruit for human flourishing. The Yahwist account of creation begins with a forest and the human gatherers within it.

Creation's Worth

The trees are described as visually pleasant and delectably edible (2:9). The tree of knowledge is singled out as a "delight to the eyes" and desirable for wisdom (3:6). The other tree, the tree of life, confers immortality (3:22). However, the garden with only the *ʾādām* in it is considered "not good" by God (2:18). So God creates a community with the intent of providing companionship for the *ʾādām*, specifically a partner who can "help" out. The animals of the *ʾădāmâ* are named, but a particular companion is not found. This experiment, however, is not an utter failure; otherwise the animals would have been discarded or cast out from the garden. They remain as part of the growing garden community. Plan B, however, succeeds: a "woman" created out of the "man."

The garden is thus complete. Its "goodness" is achieved progressively by God, with particular lacks identified and fulfilled from the outset: the barren stretch of land is now an oasis, a well-watered grove populated by living beings, including two caretakers. A fully functioning ecosystem is the outcome, marked by sufficient provision and community, companionship and caretaking. Whether creation's goodness is logically "intrinsic" or not remains unaddressed. In any case, the garden's goodness is the result of successive acts of creation by God with the end result of material abundance and mutual community, all sustainable through the efforts of the primal couple. The garden's worth is perhaps best confirmed by God's own presence in the Garden (3:8). The narrative suggests that God's stroll was customary during the comfortably "breezy" (*lĕrûaḥ*) part of the day, likely late afternoon or early evening (cf. Gen 24:63). Indeed, God's immediate presence not only confirms the garden's goodness but also renders it intimately sacred, an arboreal sanctum.

Creation's Diversity

The garden community consists of the *ʾādām*/man, the woman, and a host of animals, including the serpent, all set in a grove of fruit trees. Serving as a taxonomist of sorts, the *ʾādām* names the animals in his search for a companion, distinguishing them between domestic and wild (2:19–20). No further specificity is given to the animals in the account, except in the case of the serpent, which is later distinguished as being the craftiest of the animals (3:1). Although zoological diversity is assumed in the narrative, there is no strong interest in it from the Yahwist's perspective, as one finds, for example, in Ps. 104 and Job 38–41.

Creation's Interdependence

The garden is a fully functioning and interconnected ecosystem. As the *ʾādām* is created from the *ʾădāmâ*, so also the other animals. There is no hierarchical distinction between lesser or lower beings. They all share "common ground" (Newsom 2000, 65–66), except that the ʾādām is given the unique task of "serving" and "preserving" the garden (2:15). What this entails, however, is not tilling, as some translations suggest (e.g., NRSV, NJPS), but rather, one can imagine, pruning, raking, and gathering, all for the upkeep of an orchard and the nourishment of the man and the woman. Indeed, as much as the ʾādām is dependent upon the orchard's productivity, so the orchard's productivity is dependent upon the ʾādām's upkeep.

Creation's Relationship to Humankind

The unfolding plot of the narrative revolves around the changing relationship between the human beings and the garden, specifically the ground. In the beginning, the ʾādām ("groundling") and the ʾădāmâ ("ground") are symbiotically related. The ʾādām "serves" the ʾădāmâ; the ʾădāmâ is productive for the ʾādām. At the end, the ʾădāmâ is cursed, made resistant to the ʾādām's efforts cultivate it. This dramatic change of affairs hinges on a single act of human disobedience, which one could read as an ecological crime, a case of illicit consumption. But perhaps the real "tragedy" is what follows: the gaining of power to discriminate, to judge between what is good and what is bad, *from a strictly human vantage point*. To borrow from Protagoras, "man" has become "the measure of all things"(Plato, *Theaetetus* 152a).

Thus anthropocentrism is born (Newsom 2000, 69). The tree has conferred the power to evaluate and choose out of self-centered interest (Callicott 1991, 123–24). Consequently, a rift erupts between the couple and the rest of the animal world; their common ground is broken. Whereas the ʾādām was once an animal among other animals, all groundlings by virtue of their creation, he is now, along with the woman, distinct, having reached a unique level of self-reflective awareness. Such self-consciousness enables the man and the woman to perceive their state of nakedness. Anthropologically speaking, the perception of nakedness is a marker of humanity. The human couple is now categorically different from the rest of creation. The man and the woman have become fully human, with all the rights, privileges, responsibilities, and challenges that pertain to being human. Those challenges are unpacked in the punishments that follow.

Enmity and violence now characterize the relationship between the woman and the serpent (3:15). The increased pain of childbirth testifies to the physiological challenges involved in human birth distinct from the birth of other animals. The woman's birth canal must accommodate the child's larger braincase. What distinguishes us from other animals, in part, is the pain of childbirth, the Yahwist claims (Newsom 2000, 70).

As for the ʾādām, enmity now characterizes his relationship to the ground, "cursed" as it is (3:17). Now the man must make the ground productive for human survival through great "toil" (ʿiṣṣābôn), no less. His painful labor recalls the woman's painful labor (ʿiṣṣābôn) in giving new life (3:16). The cursed ground is the consequence of the ʾādām's ecological crime, the result of his overconsumption, one might say, and consequently the land is now depleted of its effortless fecundity. "Thorns and thistles" plague the land. The ʾādām's service has become a matter of painful servitude, and the land now suffers under the coercive weight of his efforts.

The garden story begins with the outworking of God's intent for humanity to exist in harmony with the rest of creation, but that was not the outcome. The primal couple is expelled from the garden to begin a life of agricultural labor, a deeply ambivalent transition from one ecological setting to another, from an edible forest to a resistant land, from naturally growing fruit trees to the "plants of the field" (3:18), from gathering to farming. By a willful act of human disobedience, the ground is consequently "cursed," taking on, as it were, the consequences of human sin. The ecological damage is done, and it continues to be done. Genesis 2–3, it turns out, is a profoundly meaningful parable of ecological crisis and promise. The 'ādām's commission to "serve" and "preserve" (2:15) is one that remains powerfully pertinent: humanity created as the "servant" of God's creation—a "dominion" of service on behalf of creation. Humility from the humus.

God's Relationship to Creation

In contrast to Gen. 1, the garden story reveals an intimate portrayal of God's relationship to creation. God in Gen. 3 strolls through creation during a comfortable time of the day, as apparently was God's custom. God thus enjoys the garden and its community, reveling in fellowship particularly with the primal couple. As the simple narrative unfolds, God is found to be intimately involved in making good from what is "not good" or deficient, particularly when it comes to creating community, a task performed experimentally in the best sense of the term.

In the garden story God is a hands-on deity who works with the soil, planting a grove and forming bodies, animating them with God's own breath. God gets dirty with creation in the role of farmer, potter, and surgeon. There is joy in the toil in the soil. And, one can imagine, there is pain in the rupture of relationship, although the Yahwist, typical of biblical narrators, does not let on too much about God's emotions. Instead, God turns into judge and evictor. The variety of roles that God plays in Gen. 2–3 suggests that God is a versatile responder to creation's various needs. God is ever responsive to the situation that arises, and the range of response is wide. At every step God responds and provides, whether it is water for the parched ground, a tiller for the soil, a companion for the groundling, or clothes for the evicted.

BIBLIOGRAPHY FOR CHAPTER 16

Al-Rawi, F. N. H., and Andrew George. 2014. "Back to the Cedar Forest: The Beginning and End of Tablet V of the Standard Babylonian Epic of Gilgameš." *JCS* 66:69–90.

Bauckham, Richard. 2010. *The Bible and Ecology: Rediscovering the Community of Creation*. Waco, TX: Baylor University Press.

———. 2011. *Living with Other Creatures: Green Exegesis and Theology*. Waco, TX: Baylor University Press.

Berry, Thomas. 2009. *The Sacred Universe: Earth, Spirituality, and Religion in the Twenty-First Century*. New York: Columbia University Press.

Berry, Thomas, with Mary Evelyn Tucker and John Grim. 2014. *Selected Writings on the Earth Community*. Moder Spiritual Masters Series. Maryknoll, NY: Orbis Books.

Brown, William P. 2010. *The Seven Pillars of Creation: The Bible, Science, and the Ecology of Wonder*. Oxford: Oxford University Press.

Callicott, J. B. 1991. "Genesis and John Muir." In *Covenant for a New Creation: Ethics, Religion, and Public Policy*, edited by C. S. Robb and C. J. Casebolt, 107–40. Maryknoll, NY: Orbis Books.

Carson, Rachel. 2002 [1962]. *Silent Spring*. 40th anniversary ed. Boston: Houghton Mifflin.

Clark, Timothy. 2015. *Ecocriticism on the Edge: The Anthropocene as a Threshold Concept*. London and New York: Bloomsbury.

Conradie, Ernst M. 2004. "Towards an Ecological Biblical Hermeneutics: A Review Essay on the Earth Bible Project." *Scriptura* 85:123–35.

———. 2010 "What on Earth Is an Ecological Hermeneutics? Some Broad Parameters." In *Ecological Hermeneutics: Biblical, Historical and Theological Perspectives*, edited by David G. Horrell, Cherryl Hunt, and Christopher Southgate, 295–313. London and New York: T&T Clark.

Davis, Ellen F. 2009. *Scripture, Culture, and Agriculture: An Agrarian Reading of the Bible*. Cambridge: Cambridge University Press.

Francis, Pope. 2015. *Laudato Si'*. Encyclical Letter. http://w2.vatican.va/content/francesco/en/encyclicals/documents/papa-francesco_20150524_enciclica-laudato-si.html.

Habel, Norman C. 2000. "Geophany: The Earth Story in Genesis 1." In *The Earth Story in Genesis*, edited by Norman C. Habel and Shirley Wurst, 34–48. Sheffield: Sheffield Academic Press.

———. 2008. "Introducing Ecological Hermeneutics." In *Exploring Ecological Hermeneutics*, edited by Norman C. Habel and Peter Trudinger, 1–8. SBLSS 46. Atlanta: Society of Biblical Literature.

———. 2013. "Ecological Criticism." In *New Meanings for Ancient Texts*, edited by Steven L. McKenzie and John Kaltner, 39–58. Louisville, KY: Westminster John Knox Press.

Hamilton, Clive, Christophe Bonneuil, and François Gemenne, eds. 2015. *The Anthropocene and the Global Environmental Crisis: Rethinking Modernity in a New Epoch*. Routledge Environmental Studies. London and New York: Routledge.

Hiebert, Theodore. 1996. *The Yahwist's Landscape: Nature and Religion in Early Israel*. Minneapolis: Fortress Press.

———. 2011. "Reclaiming the World: Biblical Resources for the Ecological Crisis." *Interpretation* 65 (October): 341–52.

Hillel, Daniel. 2006. *The Natural History of the Bible: An Environmental Exploration of the Hebrew Scriptures*. New York: Columbia University Press.

Horrell, David G. 2010. *The Bible and the Environment: Towards a Critical Ecological Biblical Theology*. Biblical Challenges in the Contemporary World. London: Equinox.

Horrell, David G., Cherryl Hunt, and Christopher Southgate. 2010. *Greening Paul: Rereading the Apostle in a Time of Ecological Crisis*. Waco, TX: Baylor University Press.

Hundley, Michael B. 2013. "Sacred Spaces, Objects, Offerings, and People in the Priestly Texts: A Reappraisal." *JBL* 132, no. 4:749–67.

Leopold, Aldo. 1968 [1949]. *A Sand County Almanac and Sketches Here and There*. Oxford: Oxford University Press.

McKibben, Bill. 2005. *The Comforting Whirlwind: God, Job, and the Scale of Creation*. Cambridge, MA: Cowley Publications.

———. 2010. *Eaarth: Making a Life on a Tough, New Planet*. New York: St. Martin's Griffin.

Newsom, Carol A. 2000. "Common Ground: An Ecological Reading of Genesis 2–3." In *The Earth Story in Genesis*, edited by Norman C. Habel and Shirley Wurst, 60–72. Sheffield: Sheffield Academic Press.

Rolston, Holmes, III. 2012. *A New Environmental Ethics: The Next Millennium for Life on Earth*. New York and London: Routledge.

Tucker, Gene M. 2009. "Ecological Approaches: The Bible and the Land." In *Method Matters: Essays on the Interpretation of the Hebrew Bible in Honor of David L. Petersen*, edited by Joel M. LeMon and Kent Harold Richards, 349–67. RBS 56. Atlanta: Society of Biblical Literature.

White, Lynn, Jr. 1967. "The Historical Roots of Our Ecological Crisis." *Science* 155:1203–7.

17

Gender I

Feminist

> One is not born, but rather becomes, a woman.
> *Simone de Beauvoir*[1]

> If God is male, then the male is God.
> *Mary Daly*[2]

However we define it, gender is an integral part of what makes us "fearfully and wonderfully made" (Ps. 139:14), whether it's the wonder of our bodies, the cultural forces that construct our social "identities," or the not-so-scripted ways we interact with each other. The category of gender includes everything from biological sex and cultural expectations to how power becomes embodied and is distributed. All of us are shaped in part by gender expectations: woman, man, masculine, feminine, androgynous, intersex, gay, straight, transgendered, fluid. Most generally, gender has to do with how we live and move and have our embodied being in community. We begin in this chapter with the label "female" or "femininity." In the history of biblical criticism, the issue of gender, broad as it is, was first broached by feminist interpreters. The next chapter (18) includes other forms of gender-based criticism, particularly those that more overtly address issues of race, class, and sexual orientation. Gender criticism is complicated and wide ranging; it addresses the problem of "identity" in its various complexities and nuances, from the biological to the political and the theological.

FEMINIST CRITICISM

Textually, feminist criticism begins with exploring how women are characterized within the world of the biblical text, what is said about them and by them, and what is done to them. But that is not all. By questioning the patriarchal "normativity" of the Bible,

---

1. De Beauvoir 1997, 295.
2. Daly 1973, 9.

feminist criticism can take on an advocacy position, since many of its practitioners share a commitment to the equality of women vis-à-vis men. As a discipline with a rich history, feminist criticism was developed predominantly by white women in North America and Europe. Women of color, while finding many points of contact with (white) feminists, have developed alternative hermeneutical perspectives and reading strategies, as we shall see in the next chapter.

Hebrew Bible scholar Kathleen O'Connor writes movingly about how the feminist movement came to her and her contemporaries as an "electrifying summons" in the latter half of the twentieth century:

> It seemed like the voice of the Spirit beckoning our spirits to rise and directing us to think and live differently. From the beginning the movement was a call to conversion. Feminist ideas broke in upon us all as a troubling disruption of the way things were and as an exhilarating revelation of how they might be. (2006, 3)

Such a "call to conversion," she states more broadly, is a call to "see the world through the eyes of others so that God [can] be found among us all" (20), a call that extends to women and men.

The feminist movement of the 1960s came with the deepening recognition that women around the world, including North America, suffered under oppressive conditions established and maintained by men. "It seemed as if a multi-armed octopus kept us in our place with a set of tentacles that were economic, legal, spiritual, sexual, psychological, and theological" (O'Connor 2006, 5). That "octopus," to give it a word, is sexism, a prevailing gender bias that manifests itself in countless ways, both overt and covert, psychologically and institutionally. Sexism is a way of thinking, acting, and living that benefits one sex to the detriment of the other, as in the treatment of women as second-class citizens.

While many definitions of feminism have been put forth, Phyllis Bird's definition is as good as any. Feminism is

> a critical and constructive stance that claims for women the full humanity accorded to men, insisting that women be represented equally in all attempts to describe and comprehend human nature and that they be full participants in the assignment and regulation of social roles, rights, and responsibilities. (Bird 1999, 124).

As a complement to Bird's definition, Pamela Thimmes highlights more sharply the political dimension: feminism is "a liberation movement that not only critiques the oppressive structures of society but, by its various voices and approaches, works for transformation" (1999, 134–35). Each in her own way, Bird and Thimmes stress the "critical and constructive" sides of a feminist criticism, the deconstructive and the transformative.

Behind each (and every) definition of feminism is a word that, although unstated in the definitions above, is crucial: power. Gender is a matter of power, specifically power that is either shared equally by all or exercised by one gender over another. Biology is only part of the story. Yes, women and men are biologically different, but physical differences do not account for the inequity of power that underscores the roles and expectations assigned to men and women (Lawrence 2009, 334). Instead, cultural and societal norms are the primary determining factors. Like race (see chap. 20 below), gender is largely a social construction. "People are born male or female, but they become men and women" by virtue of cultural constructions (Fewell 1999, 273). Such constructions result in hierarchies that institutionalize social inequities and imbalances of power. Feminist African American author bell hooks observes that "like women, men have been socialized to passively accept sexist ideology. . . . Men are not exploited or oppressed by sexism, but there are ways in which they suffer as a result of it. . . . They benefit from patriarchy and yet are also hurt by it" (1984, 72). This includes, to which I speak personally, loss of mutual relationships, embodying masculine stereotypes, and feeling shame over my complicity in the systemic mistreatment of women. The critical analysis of culture provided by feminism applies to both women and men as they work together for gender equality.

Feminist Biblical Interpretation

As ecological criticism of the Bible questions the *anthropocentric* worldview of biblical texts, so feminist criticism exposes and critiques the Bible's *androcentric*, or male-centered, perspective. The impetus of feminist biblical criticism in the United States can be traced back to *The Woman's Bible*, written by Elizabeth Cady Stanton and the "Revising Committee" (1895), whose aim was "to revise only those texts and chapters directly referring to women and those also in which women are made prominent by exclusion" (Stanton 1993, 5).[3] This was not so much an exercise in rewriting texts as it was rejecting them outright, with the notable exception of Gen. 1:26–28 (see below). On the other hand, Stanton concedes, "the Bible cannot be accepted or rejected as a whole," because its traditions "differ widely from each other" (13). Yes, indeed. Nevertheless, Stanton roundly condemned the Bible's widespread use as a tool of oppression against women in the United States, and rightly so.

Because of the vehement reactions against Stanton after its publication, *The Woman's Bible* was nearly forgotten until it was reprinted in 1974. Since the 1970s, a variety of feminist approaches to biblical interpretation developed, beginning with the groundbreaking works of Phyllis Trible in Hebrew Bible, Rosemary Radford Ruether in theology, and Elisabeth Schüssler Fiorenza in New Testament. In her 1985 essay, Carolyn Osiek identified five major hermeneutical positions that feminist biblical critics had developed:

1. The *rejectionist* involves rejecting the Bible partially or entirely.
2. The *loyalist* affirms the integrity of the biblical text as authoritative and liberative.
3. The *revisionist* takes a middle position by seeking to find glimmers of good news in otherwise hopelessly androcentric texts.
4. The *sublimationist* focuses on feminine imagery and symbolism but sometimes at the cost of ignoring the political and social dimensions and consequences of the text.
5. The *liberationist* approach affirms the Bible's central message of human liberation as a way of critiquing texts that do not promote the full equality of women.[4]

---

3. *The Woman's Bible* was not the only work produced at this early stage of feminist criticism. For a helpful overview of the "forerunners" of feminist interpretation, see Junior 2015, 19–38.

4. For further discussion and assessment, see Brayford 2009, 314–17; McKay 1997.

While conceptually helpful, such delineations can easily serve to pigeonhole feminist scholars in their multifaceted work. The positions need not be mutually exclusive, except obviously the first two. Today the variety of positions has increased. One should add a *historicist* position, an approach interested in reconstructing the sociohistorical, socio-economic, and sociopolitical conditions of life for women—their material realities in antiquity, which takes us into social-scientific study (e.g., Meyers 1988; 2013; Pressler 1993; Yoder 2001). In addition, feminist biblical interpretation has diversified to include evangelical, mainstream, progressive, and postreligious feminists, all articulating different positions and points of departure (Newsom 2012, 22). Feminist criticism, moreover, is no longer the purview of only white women in developed countries. Issues of class, ethnicity, culture, nationality, for example, are also integral factors in contemporary feminist exege-sis, what is sometimes called "third-wave" feminism.[5] African American women (wom-anist), Latina women (*mujerista*), and Asian women have explored the fruits of feminist criticism within their own cultural contexts (see chap. 18).

Gender Observations about Language and Culture

Feminist criticism, and more broadly gender analysis, is more an interpretive lens than a well-defined method. It begins with a set of guiding questions, such as these:

> How is gender inscribed or prescribed in the text?
> How and why are male and female characters portrayed as they are?
> What is the status of women in the text?
> Does the text present an ideal reality or a more realistic reflection of the social world of women and men?
> Does the text reinforce domination of men over women, or does it (potentially) subvert patriarchal norms and habits?
> More generally, whose interests are being served by the text?

We can begin with some brief observations about language. Hebrew is a highly gen-dered language, grammatically binary. There is no "neuter" in Hebrew as there is in Greek or German. Every noun in Hebrew is either masculine or feminine, and most nouns (but not all) are spelled to indicate gender. While it is important to distinguish at least provisionally between *grammatical* gender and *socially constructed* gender,[6] it can-not be denied that language both reflects and shapes the way reality is perceived. Words

---

5. The feminist movement is frequently described in terms of three "waves." The first "wave" began in 1848 with Elizabeth Cady Stanton and Lucretia Mott assembling a convention at Seneca Falls, New York, to discuss women's rights. This "wave" concluded with the passage of the Nineteenth Amendment to the U.S. Constitu-tion, giving women the right to vote in the United States. The second "wave" began in 1963 with the publication of Betty Friedan's *Feminine Mystique* and the Equal Pay Act, as well as with the founding of the National Organi-zation for Women (NOW) three years later. It concluded with the failure to ratify the Equal Rights Amendment (ERA) in 1982 by a sufficient number of states. "Third-wave" feminism, with its attention to diversity as well as race, gender, class, and sexuality, began with Rebecca Walker's 1992 essay titled "Becoming the Third Wave," which responded to the mistreatment of University of Oklahoma law professor Anita Hill during the Senate Judi-ciary Committee confirmation hearings of Clarence Thomas as an associate justice to the U.S. Supreme Court. For an analysis and critique of this linear way of categorizing feminism historically, see Junior 2015, 3–10.

6. Of course, even "grammatically" constructed gender has its cultural roots.

for "ground" (ʾădāmâ) and "earth" (ʾereṣ) are feminine in Hebrew, whereas the word for "human" (ʾādām) is grammatically masculine. More than grammar is at stake here, as we shall see. Furthermore, the Bible's *grammatical* references to God are consistently masculine, even if a feminine metaphor is occasionally used for God.

Like all cultures of the ancient Near East, Israel was a patriarchal society.[7] Its norms of conduct were shaped by the social values of honor and shame, with men more closely associated with honor and woman more susceptible to shame (Brayford 2009, 318).[8] Among men, the gaining of honor was something of a zero-sum game: honor could be gained by one man at the expense of another man, and shame was the result for the latter. Women, on the other hand, were assigned the status of shame as a matter of course, indicating the necessity of "sexual modesty and propriety" (318). The greatest shame for men in the ancient world was to lose their masculinity and be figured as a woman (see, e.g., Jer. 13:26–27). One narrative example of masculine shame is found in the story of David sending envoys to offer condolences to Hanun, the Ammonite king, whose father had just died. But driven by suspicion of David's true motives, Hanun "seized David's envoys, shaved off half the beard of each, cut off their garments in the middle at their hips, and sent them away" (2 Sam. 10:4). The men "were greatly ashamed" (10:5), and so David tells them to stay in Jericho until their beards have fully grown back. The feminization of masculinity was considered a dishonoring mark of weakness: "On that day the Egyptians will be like women, and tremble with fear before the hand that YHWH of hosts raises against them" (Isa. 19:16).

As for women, whether Job's wife (Job 2:10), the figure of the strange woman whose "feet do not stay at home" (Prov. 7:11), the woman who is "covered with shame" (Prov. 11:16a), or "an unloved woman . . . [who] gets a husband" and the "earth trembles" (30:21, 23)—shame was a constant companion. Nevertheless, the patriarchal world of the Bible was shaped by more than honor codes. Women were kept in their place socially and legally, matched by a division of labor that confined most women to the household. The laws in the Book of the Covenant (Exod. 20:19–23:33) and in Deuteronomy legitimate male dominance over women (Anderson 2005, 81–98). Inheritance laws, for example, favored sons over daughters. While sons received their father's inheritance, the daughters' financial well-being depended on marriage. Zelophehad's daughters had to take their case to Moses in order to receive their father's inheritance because their father had no sons, a case successfully resolved in their favor (Num. 27:1–11; Josh. 17:3–4). But in the case of sons and daughters, the principal heirs were the sons born to the father by his wife or wives (yet see the exception in Job 42:15).

Take also the case of adultery, whose definition in the Hebrew Bible does not hold men and woman equally accountable. While men could have more than one wife, women could not have more than one husband (Deut. 21:15; cf. Isa. 4:1). More to the point, raping a woman who was unmarried or not engaged did not, in fact, constitute adultery for

---

7. The term has been contested by one female scholar, Carol Meyers, but her focus is primarily directed toward the power dynamics of the household rather than toward the larger legal system (Meyers 2013, 183–99). See below.

8. Susan Brayford perceptively analyzes the story of Sarah's laugh in Gen. 18 with this social dynamic (2009, 318–28).

the married man (Exod. 22:16–17; Deut. 22:28–29). Only if the woman was married or betrothed was such an act considered adulterous, a capital offense for both the man and the woman (Deut. 22:22–26). In the situation of rape, moreover, an unmarried woman had to marry her rapist (v. 29). Was it merely a matter of hospitality that the patriarch Lot offered his two daughters to the "men of Sodom" who demanded to "know" his angelic guests (Gen. 19:8)? And then there is the "text of terror" in Judges that recounts the gang rape and death of the Levite's concubine, who was willingly offered by the man and whose body he dismembers (Judg. 19:22–30; see Trible 1984, 65–82). No wonder the Bible has been used, and continues to be used, to justify subordination and violence against women.[9]

These examples alone illustrate the inequities of power and status that characterized men and women in ancient Israel. There are, to be sure, notable exceptions. Deborah is a judge who commands men for impending battle (Judg. 4); Jael is a warrior who slays a general (Judg. 5); Huldah is a prophetess consulted by King Josiah (2 Kgs. 22). Some women in the Bible do unorthodox things: Hagar is the only woman in the Bible to name God (Gen. 16:13), and Zipporah performs circumcision (Exod. 4:24–26).[10] More ambiguous is the "woman of strength" profiled in Prov. 31:10–31, who is described in certain instances as warrior-like yet remains relegated primarily to the domestic realm, much to the economic benefit and honor of her husband, who sits with the elders at the city gate.

There is a relative scarcity of female characters in the Bible who could be lifted up as "models of faith" for women (and men). Many women mentioned in the Bible are, in fact, nameless. Moreover, the literature of the Bible was written and edited primarily, if not exclusively, by males. Consider the possible exception of Ps. 131.

> *A Song of Ascents. Of David.*
> [1] YHWH, my heart is not held high,
>   and my eyes are not raised up.
> I do not occupy myself with things too great
>   and wonderful for me.
> [2] Instead, I have calmed and quieted my soul,
>   like a weaned child upon its mother.
>   Like a weaned child upon me, so is my soul.
> [3] Hope, O Israel, in YHWH,
>   now and forevermore. (AT)

Some have identified the author of this brief prayer of trust as a woman, and one can easily see why. Maternal imagery runs deep in the final verses, and the first two verses embody self-effacing humility. But it is impossible to distinguish whether the text was written *by* a woman or attributed *to* a woman. Moreover, as Melody Knowles observes, "one might also argue that in its valorization of humility, docility, and childlikeness, Psalm 131 could have been written by someone, either a man or a woman, intent on teaching women such behavior, creating a psalm *for* women to re-inscribe patriarchal ideals" (2014, 430). One should also observe that the psalm is ascribed, albeit much later, to David.

---

9. For a study of rape in the Hebrew Bible, see Scholz 2010.
10. As noted by Lawrence 2009, 335.

These are only a few of the concerns and challenges encountered in reading the Bible through a feminist lens. Are they insurmountable challenges? That remains to be seen, since different outcomes have been chosen by different readers, all sharing a core commitment to the equal treatment of women. All in all, regardless of the results, a feminist reading strategy or approach inevitably begins by examining how power is configured in the biblical text with respect to gender. By way of illustration, we return to the two creation accounts of Genesis.

GENESIS 1:1–2:3

As for specific texts in Genesis, we begin where *The Woman's Bible* begins, with the account of humanity's creation in the first chapter of Genesis (1:26–28). Of particular interest is v. 27, where "male and female" are referenced in connection with the "image of God." Here is the verse in its context.

> [26] Then God said, "Let us make humanity in our image, after our likeness, so that they may rule over the fish of the sea, and over the winged creatures in the heavens, over the domestic animals, over all the land, and over everything that crawls on the land."
>
> [27] So God created the human being [*hāʾādām*] in his image,
>   in the image of God he created "him" [*ʾōtô*],
>   **male** and **female** he created them [*ʾōtām*].
>
> [28] And God blessed them, and God said to them, "Be fruitful and multiply; fill the earth and subdue it and rule over the fish of the sea and over the winged creatures in the heavens and over every creature that crawls on the ground." (AT)

What is the status of "male and female" in v. 27b? To be sure, nothing is said of any division of labor or role, let alone power inequity or hierarchy, between "male and female." In fact, gender as socially constructed is not the primary issue in this verse. The language of "male and female" (*zākār ûněqēbâ*) is not the same as "man" and "woman" (*ʾîš* and *ʾiššâ*), as in Gen. 2:23–24. Its domain is more biologically oriented. This is confirmed in Gen. 6:19 regarding the animals to be brought into the ark: "two of every kind, . . . male and female." The dual designation refers to the procreative capacity of animal life, nonhuman and, in the case of Gen. 1, human. Verse 27b thus provides an appropriate segue to God's blessing of procreation immediately following in v. 28 (see Bird 1994, 142–43, 149).

Of more critical interest is the relationship between biologically defined sex in v. 27b and the "image of God" preceding it. But a prior question arises: what is the scope of "humankind" here? Notice the parallelism in the translation rendered in literal Hebrew word order:

> So God created humankind [*hāʾādām*] in his image,
>   in the image of God he created "him" [*ʾōtô*];
>   male and female he created them [*ʾōtām*].

As discussed in chap. 6, lines 1 and 2 are somewhat concentrically arranged (**ABC /
C'A'B'**) in which the term "image" (in **C** and **C'**) constitutes the center. Reading the
first two lines together without the third line could suggest that God created the *ʾādām*
as male. Grammatically speaking, *ʾādām* is masculine, as seen also in the suffixed direct
object at the end of the second line: "him." But with the addition of the third line, "male
and female," the question of the *ʾādām*'s gender is clarified: it is biologically "inclusive,"
albeit from a binary perspective. In addition to the so-called democratization of God's
"image" (see chap. 10), there is also the *imago*'s biological diversification. Hence "him"
(translated grammatically) should at least be placed in quotation marks, or perhaps be
pluralized as "them" (so NRSV), although doing so obscures the grammatical progression
from singular to plural in the Hebrew, climactically realized in the last line (*ʾōtām*).

The upshot is that *hāʾādām* (humankind) is biologically inclusive in v. 27a. The theological crux is the nature of the correspondence between v. 27aβ and v. 27b: "In the image
of God he created 'him'; male and female he created them." The poetic parallelism is
unmistakable: "in the image of God" corresponds to "male and female," as much as "him"
(*ʾōtô*) correlates with "them" (*ʾōtām*). But does such poetic correspondence yield a theological correspondence? To put it another way, does humankind in its gendered differentiation reflect something of the divine? Or to put it bluntly, is God in some sense *both*
male and female? Some find such an idea "repugnant" in the eyes of the Priestly author,
who allegedly eschews anthropomorphic imagery (Bird 1994, 142).

Perhaps, but the issue can also take a more constructive turn, relating to our discussion
of feminist criticism. The poetic, if not theological, correspondence between "image of
God" and "male and female" points our attention to the masculine *and* feminine images
used for God throughout the Hebrew Bible. Though by no means equal in weight to
the preponderance of masculine imagery, feminine divine imagery is in fact deployed in
highly suggestive ways in biblical tradition. Take, for example, two passages from Isaiah:

> As a mother comforts her child,
>   so I will comfort you;
>   you shall be comforted in Jerusalem. (66:13)

> For a long time I have held my peace,
>   I have kept still and restrained myself;
>   now I will cry out like a woman in labor,
>   I will gasp and pant. (42:14)

Maternal imagery is found in both passages, but for different purposes. In the first passage, God extends maternal comfort to Israel after the exile, comfort that constitutes a
new community, a restored Jerusalem. Here God is in the business of "procreating" a new
people. In the second, written during the time of Babylonian exile, feminine imagery is
deployed as part of the warrior imagery used to describe God in battle, as the previous
verse vividly describes:

> YHWH goes forth like a soldier,
>   like a warrior he stirs up his fury;
>   he cries out, he shouts aloud,
>   he shows himself mighty against his foes. (42:13)

Though YHWH is mentioned in the third person as a "soldier," God speaks in the first person as a "woman in labor" in v. 14. YHWH fights like a woman.

Not infrequently, God is said to be "compassionate" (raḥûm) and to extend "compassion" (raḥămîm), words that are etymologically associated with "womb" (reḥem; see Trible 1978, 33–59).[11] In a Proverbs text, personified Wisdom talks proudly of her birth from God's womb (Prov. 8:24–25). In addition, Jacob's blessing of Joseph is replete with feminine imagery:

> By the God of your father, who will help you,
>> by Šadday who will bless you
>> with blessings of heaven above,
> blessings of Deep that lies beneath,
>> blessings of Breasts [šādayim] and Womb [rāḥam]. (Gen. 49:25)

This poetic blessing moves from paternal ("your father") to feminine imagery. Indeed, the concluding words could constitute a divine epithet or title for God. Notice the phonetic similarity between Šadday (typically but inaccurately translated "Almighty") and "Breasts" (šādayim).

While Gen. 1:27 does not impute procreative capacity to YHWH, it can still say something about God's differentiated identity metaphorically. Literarily, God is both masculine-*like* and feminine-*like*. Literally, God is beyond male and female, neither male nor female. Anthropologically, God grants male and female equal status in relation to the divine, in God's "image." Perhaps one could supplement the poetic tricolon by pluralizing the *imago* language to fully realize its rhetorical movement:

> God created humankind [hāʾādām] in God's image,
>> in God's image God created "him" [ʾōtô];
> male and female God created them [ʾōtām];
>> *in God's own images God created them.*

This is not to claim that the Priestly author intended this. On the contrary, in this verse the language of "image" remains correlated to the more abstract level of humanity. To be human is to be made in God's image, and that applies equally to "male and female." No one gender to the exclusion of the other, let alone one individual, can fully represent or reflect God, any more than one gender can represent the fullness of humanity. Nevertheless, the claim made by my additional line takes us one step further: it is a theologically *constructive* conclusion to the rhetorical movement of the passage. As the grammatical object of the verb becomes pluralized, so why not also the predicate: from "image" to "images"? That is to say, male and female are themselves God's "images," reflecting God equally. Being female is being God's image as much as being male is. Equal, but different. Because the two genders are different, they do not embody God's image in the same way. Thus, with the inclusion of humanity's gender specificity, God's image is itself differentiated, as we've seen metaphorically elsewhere in biblical tradition. God's image is both gender specific and gender inclusive.

---

11. E.g., Pss. 22:9–10 (10–11 MT); 103:13; Isa. 46:3–4; Jer. 1:5; Job 31:13–15.

More could be said about the creation of humankind in Gen. 1. How, in addition to the language of procreation, "fruitful and multiply," does "dominion" apply to the gender specificity of God's image in humanity? Does it apply equally to "male and female," or is it predominantly a masculine-bound role? The militaristic language of "subdue," an extension of dominion, seems to favor the latter in a patriarchal culture. Regardless, to even ask the question points to the larger issue of whether the "male and female" language in Gen. 1:27b is strictly biological in scope. Is it even possible to keep the biological entirely separate from the "psychosocial," to use Phyllis Bird's distinction (1994, 169)? Can the procreative be categorically distinguished from gender-based "identity" roles? To presuppose that to be "female" at the origin of creation is to be procreative is to claim a totalizing role for women that many would not and cannot accept. To be male or female is to be more than procreative beings. And here is where the second story of creation begins with its own gendered consciousness.

GENESIS 2–3

The Yahwist account of creation provides a very different view of gender. Biology is not a primary concern, although it is certainly assumed in the course of the narrative. Instead, the social dimensions of gender are explored dramatically and in the end, if not from the outset, patriarchally. Stanton's verdict of the second account, in comparison to the first, leaves no room for ambiguity: "There is something sublime in bringing order out of chaos; light out of darkness; giving each planet its place in the solar system; oceans and lands their limits; wholly inconsistent with a petty surgical operation" (1993, 20). Stanton goes on to state that while the "first account dignifies woman as an important factor in creation, equal in power and glory with man," "the second makes her a mere afterthought" (20). Is that true?

Centuries upon centuries of interpretation, beginning with Paul (1 Tim. 2:13–14; see chap. 13), have roundly condemned Eve in the story. She is a temptress, a seductress who commits the unpardonable sin of eating the forbidden apple and deceiving Adam to partake. Because she is created after Adam, she is inferior, and because she has sinned, she must be kept subordinate. She is created to be Adam's "helpmate" but turns out to be gullible and untrustworthy. Consequently, she is worthy of greater condemnation. So it seems in view of the weight of interpretive tradition. But viewed simply from a literary standpoint, Eve is given more fair play. Her speaking role is significantly larger than that of her male companion (Meyers 2013, 59). Also, there is no apple.

But let us begin where the story begins gender-wise: the ʾādām. Grammatically masculine, as his title indicates, is "he" a man from the outset? That is entirely debatable. Note again that in Gen. 1:27 the ʾādām refers to humanity and is gender-inclusive. The same term, including the definite article, is used in Gen. 2:7: "when YHWH God formed the ʾādām from the dust of the ground . . ." How does one picture the quintessential, primordial human being, *the* human being before "he" is a particular "man" (ʾîš) in 2:22–23? Can one imagine a sexless human being? That is, at least for me, difficult, given my gender, biologically and culturally, for my mind quickly gravitates toward the white male figure of

Leonardo da Vinci's "anatomical man" (ca. 1500), an iconic image whose hold in Western culture remains powerful.

But what was the Yahwist's image of the ʾādām? Nothing specific is given in the text except that this human creature is intimately related to the ʾădāmâ, the "ground." "He" is first and foremost, primarily and primordially, a groundling. The ʾādām's tie to the earth comes before "his" tie to the "woman," who is created after and from him. Yet one must also notice that the ʾădāmâ, the ground, is feminine, the source of all life, vegetable and animal, human and nonhuman, the ground of creaturely being. Between "groundling" and "ground," there is already a foreshadowing, an anticipated relationship of mutual intimacy that will later characterize "man" and "woman." Gender inscribes the world from the beginning. The ʾādām's service to the ʾădāmâ (2:15) is met with the ʾădāmâ's responsiveness in producing life. Consummation and procreation are set within an agrarian context.

The narrative buildup to the woman's creation begins with God's declaration of a deficient creation: "not good." So God resolves to make for the ʾādām a "copartner" (2:18). Immediately a red flag is raised: does this make the woman inferior to the man? The term ʿēzer (helper), as is often recognized, frequently applies elsewhere to God or anyone who can bring about deliverance.[12] Indeed, those who have "no helper" are typically those who are experiencing distress or suffering from some form of deprivation, such as poverty or social isolation, requiring drastic measures (Job 29:12; Pss. 72:12; 107:12; Isa. 63:5; Dan. 11:34). Thus the term itself need not imply inferiority or subordination. Moreover, the following prepositional phrase kĕnegdô literally means "in front of him" or "opposite him," implying a sense of mutual correspondence (Gen. 2:18). If there was any doubt about "helper," the prepositional phrase undercuts any potential sense of subordination. This "helper" is no lowly assistant, but a partner, or better a counterpart (Meyers 2013, 73–74). She is the one fully capable of helping the ʾādām, even rescuing him!

So what precisely does the ʾādām need help with? Opinions vary. Some have proposed help with work in the garden; others have argued procreation. Neither suggestion, however, takes into account God's own rationale for creating the woman. "It is not good that the ʾādām be alone," God observes (2:18). Hence, whatever else such "help" may involve, this new partner is to assuage the ʾādām's loneliness in the garden, to rescue him from social isolation. Companionship is the most fundamental issue at stake given the ʾādām's condition as perceived by God. This is confirmed by the ʾādām's reply to God's interrogation about his disobedience: "The woman whom you gave *to be with* me . . ." (3:12). The preposition "with," in this case connoting companionship, says it all. Nevertheless, this new creation is *for* the ʾādām, implying an asymmetrical relationship. Does the qualifying phrase kĕnegdô, which signifies correspondence of some sort, mitigate such an androcentric perspective? Only if one can draw from such "correspondence" a sense of mutual equality and full partnership. Perhaps.

God's "Plan A" involves creating more groundlings. God leaves it to the ʾādām to make the choice regarding companionship, and in the process "he" names the animals (2:20). Does the act of naming imply subordination? Possibly. Much lies in a name, to be sure,

12. E.g., 2 Kgs. 14:26; Job 29:12; Pss. 30:10 [11]; 54:4 [6]; 72:12; 121:1–2.

but most fundamental in the narrative is the issue of recognition. The ʾādām is looking for someone who corresponds to "him" and, consequently, can deliver him from his state of loneliness. In the act of naming, the ʾādām identifies each and every animal in relation to him, and it turns out that not one of them qualifies to fulfill what God intended for the ʾādām. Perhaps by naming the animals the ʾādām is asserting himself above them. However, no hierarchy in the garden is acknowledged in Gen. 2 other than possibly here. At the very least, the ʾādām taxonomically clarifies what the animals can*not* do for him.

"Plan B" results in the creation of the "woman" and, in turn, the "man." It is not until v. 23, when the ʾādām names the woman, who was "taken from" him, that the word "man" (ʾîš) makes its first appearance.

> Then the ʾādām said,
>   "This at last is bone of my bones and flesh of my flesh;
>   this one shall be called 'Woman' [ʾiššâ],
>   for out of 'Man' [ʾîš] this one was taken." (2:23)

Everything has changed. In the naming of the woman, the ʾādām has also named himself and in so doing receives a new identity. He is now a distinctly *masculine* groundling, made possibly only by the creation of his feminine partner, the woman. Man and woman, ʾîš and ʾiššâ. A certain parallel is established with the ʾādām and the ʾădāmâ, a grammatical mutuality between the masculine and the feminine. But with "man" and "woman," a gendered mutuality now emerges. As the feminine "ground" or earth is the source and sustenance of life, so, as the text will later reveal, the woman (named "Eve") is the "mother of all living" (3:20). In fact, put so broadly without reference specifically to *human* "living" in this verse, Eve and Earth are now tightly correlated. They share the same gender and procreative power (cf. Gen. 1:11–12).

As for the pairing of ʾîš and ʾiššâ, of "man" and "woman," the linguistic affinity translates well into gendered mutuality. The ʾādām has identified his partner by recognizing his common substance with her and in the process has identified himself in a new way. He is a "man" in addition to being a groundling. One does not displace the other: he is both. Although the ʾādām may not have been utterly androgynous before the creation of the woman, "his" gender identity does become more complete as a consequence.[13]

As for the woman, her creation involves being "taken from" the man. In one sense, the woman is derived from the man. But does her derivation make her secondary? The syntax of 2:23 itself does not suggest this; there is no language of subordination in this verse. Instead, physical derivation serves as the rationale for the common substance the man and woman both share: "flesh" and "bone" constitute the common ground the woman shares with the man, and it is explained by the one being "built" from and "taken from" the other (vv. 22–23). Admittedly, one could argue in either direction hierarchically: the "man" is primary because he was created first, or the "woman" is primary because she is God's crowning, culminating achievement. But the text proceeds in neither direction. It simply affirms their common substance.

---

13. Meyers, for example, describes the ʾādām as androgynous but "more male than female" (2013, 43). See also Trible's revisiting of her earlier work in 2003.

Yet there is more to say gender-wise that is often missed. The language of being "taken from" (*lqḥ* + *mn*) is profoundly suggestive from the man's point of reference in v. 23. God creates the woman by "taking from" the *ʾādām*. Thus the *ʾādām* has to lose something of himself for the woman to be created, whether it is his "rib" (doubtful) or something much larger, such as his entire "side" (see chap. 7 above). Whatever it is, the man must give up something of himself in order for the woman to be created, in order for a mutual relationship to be established. The man has to give up, in short, and he does not do so consciously or on his own accord but solely through God's initiative. He is "forced" by God in order to bring about a true partnership. Whether willingly or unwillingly, the *ʾādām* has to give up something of self to become fully a man,[14] and to do so for someone equal yet different. His loss is relationally his gain.

The penultimate verse of Gen. 2, which seemingly provides an etiology of marriage, declares what else the man must give up in order to consummate his relationship with the woman. "Therefore a man leaves his father and his mother and clings to his wife, and they become one flesh" (2:24). From a patriarchal standpoint, it is remarkable that it is the man who leaves (or "abandons") his parents to join his wife in order to become "one flesh." In ancient Israel, the married women typically lived with the husband's family, where his inheritance of land was lodged. In other words, it is the woman who would typically have to leave her parents to join her husband and *his* family, as illustrated in the ancestral narratives of Sarah, Rebekah, Leah, and Rachel. For whatever reason, this verse inverts the act: it is the man who does the leaving, severing ties with his parents. From a patriarchal perspective, it makes little sense, for it presupposes a more matriarchal setting. Perhaps this "etiology" was added to redress the patriarchal imbalance. Nothing also is said about the man giving the woman's father a gift to seal the betrothal. Perhaps the verse, then, is more a bold statement about the power of sexual attraction. Sexual attraction is so powerful that the man *would even* abandon his own parents (and his inheritance?), if need be, for the sake of love. If this is the sense of v. 24, then the verse would not be an etiology of marriage so much as a bold claim about the power of sexual attraction. Love can even upend patriarchal convention! Indeed, a comparable claim is made in the Song of Songs, in which not the father's but the mother's household constitutes a central setting for the drama of love poetry (Song 3:4; 8:2; cf. Gen. 24:67). If Gen. 2:24 is an etiology, then it is an etiology of sexual union, not marriage at least as patriarchally conceived.

In any event, there is no talk of possession or subordination of the woman in 2:24. Far from it! The man comes to the woman; she draws him to her in order to reenact the original union (Trible 1978, 104; cf. Song 3:4; 8:2). Indeed, a sort of balance is achieved between the man's union in Gen. 2:24 and the woman's creation in vv. 22–23. As the woman was "taken from" the man in her creation, so the man is taken from his family in order to consummate their relationship. The purpose is not for procreation, first and foremost, but for sexual union. They were created for each other, to complete each other. "Their union in 'one flesh' is a reunion" (Bird 1994, 48n89).

The narrative turns tragic in Gen. 3. And it is here that mutuality and equality give way to alienation and subordination, inviting critical scrutiny. The act of disobedience begins

---

14. For further exploration of the story from a masculine point of view, see Olson 2006, 73–80.

with the woman: after determining that the tree is desirable for gaining the power of wise discrimination, she acts on her own volition. At this juncture her husband is only a passive presence. But equally notable, he is also not absent from the scene. Through it all, he is "with her" (3:6b), a remark that is absent from many English translations, allowing for the possibility of absolving the man and blaming only the woman (see chap. 4 above). But the text does not leave the man off the hook. His crime, according to God, is that he "listened to the voice of [his] wife," that is, he obeyed her (v. 17), the cardinal androcentric sin! On the one hand, one can admire the woman who takes initiative and acts independently for her own good. On the other hand, the narrative roundly condemns her for doing just that and equally condemns the man for his compliance.

Why is the woman the one to first take hold of the fruit? Patriarchy is one answer, whereby women served as "natural" targets for blame when something went wrong, as in the classic myth of Pandora's box (Phipps 1988). However, the narrative is trying to reach behind (or more literally before) the ethos of patriarchy in order to explain its emergence. Perhaps because women in ancient times were the ones involved in food preparation. Or because the feminine is more closely associated with wisdom than the masculine (see Prov. 1, 4, 8). One wonders. In any case, the tree of knowledge is *her* tree to partake from.

The couple's entangled unity is demonstrated in the consequences of eating the fruit of disobedience. Only after *both* partake of the fruit is it said that their eyes "were opened" (3:7). They now see themselves as "naked," both of them. With such self-awareness, they take matters into their own hands. While the awareness of "nakedness" serves anthropologically to distinguish the human couple from the other animals (see chap. 15 above), the awareness also has its gender-related implications. Compare the command in Lev. 18:7: "You shall not uncover the nakedness of your father, which is your mother's nakedness; she is your mother, you shall not uncover her nakedness." In this prohibition against intergenerational incest, the father's "nakedness" actually designates the mother, his wife. Each is the other's nakedness, although such designation is not mutually shared across genders in Leviticus: while the husband's nakedness refers to his wife's, nothing is said conversely, reflecting a one-sided, androcentric perspective (see Lev. 18:14, 16). But in Genesis both the man and the woman are recognized as naked, mutually naked and thus mutually ashamed. Their newly recognized awareness does not signal the birth of sex, but rather the birth of shame in and beyond sex. As companionship and intimacy were equally shared by the two human beings, so now also shame.

More consequences follow, tragically so. Fear has entered the vocabulary of human response (3:10) as well as blame, if not betrayal (v. 12). The punishments follow:

> To the woman he said,
> "I will greatly increase your pain [ʿiṣṣābôn] in pregnancy;[15]
>   in pain you shall bear children.
> Yet your husband is the object of your desire;
>   he shall rule over you [yimšol-bāk]." (3:16 AT)

---

15. Literally, "your pain and your pregnancy," but this is likely a hendiadys to be translated together, as suggested by the following parallel phrase (contra Meyers 2013, 81–102).

With this divine declaration, the harmony is broken. Indeed, it already has been with the man blaming the woman in v. 12. Her partner has now become her betrayer. And subordination is the punishment: the husband shall "rule over" the wife. In fact, one common word for "husband" in Hebrew is *ba'al*, which can also mean "lord" or "owner."[16]

As the woman is cursed with painful pregnancy, the man is cursed with painful labor, as befits the groundling that he is.

> And to *'ādām* [God] said,
> > "Because you heeded your wife,
> > > and ate from the tree about which I commanded you,
> > > > 'Do not eat from it,'
> > the ground is cursed on your account;
> > > in pain ['*iṣṣābôn*] you shall eat from it all the days of your life." (3:17 AT)

The man and the woman share in common the pain of labor, divided now by their gendered roles: childbearing and farming. The text itself does not discriminate which is the more painful. However, one can imagine the Yahwist (likely a male author) deliberately elevating the "pain" of farming to the level of pain experienced by women in childbirth, an experience that in ancient times frequently led to death. Suffice it to say that 3:16 was often cited after the discovery and use of anesthesia to justify the suffering of women during labor without the benefit of pain-reducing medication. Air-conditioned tractors, however, have never met such resistance from a "biblical" point of view.

Once the judgments are given and God clothes the couple, the conclusion of the narrative focuses exclusively on the *'ādām* and his expulsion from the garden (3:22–24). The expulsion, in contrast to the judgments given earlier, is not itself a punishment but instead a preventative. God expels the *'ādām* in order to squelch any opportunity for immortality. Striking here is the narrative's singular focus on the *'ādām*. It is as if the woman has disappeared. Whereas the gap-filled logic of the narrative assumes that both are expelled, the exclusive focus on the *'ādām* suggests that the division of genders in the garden corresponds to the division of trees in the garden. While the woman is associated with the tree of knowledge, the *'ādām*/man is associated with the tree of life, which grants immortality, in other words, divine power. Wisdom and power, woman and man, *'ădāmâ* and *'ādām*: Eden comes to be a thoroughly gendered garden.

BIBLIOGRAPHY FOR CHAPTER 17

Anderson, Cheryl B. 2005. *Women, Ideology, and Violence: Critical Theory and the Construction of Gender in the Book of the Covenant and Deuteronomic Law*. JSOTSup 394. New York: T&T Clark.

Beauvoir, Simone de. 1997. *The Second Sex*. Translated by H. M. Parshley. London: Vintage.

Bellis, Alice Ogden. 1994. *Helpmates, Harlots, Heroes: Women's Stories in the Hebrew Bible*. Louisville, KY: Westminster John Knox Press.

Bird, Phyllis. 1994. *Feminism and the Bible: A Critical and Constructive Encounter*. The 1993 J. J. Thiessen Lectures. Winnipeg, MB: CMBC Publications.

---

16. E.g., Gen. 20:3; Exod. 21:3, 22, 28, 29; 21:3; Deut. 22:22; 24:4; Prov. 12:4; 31:11; cf. Hos. 2:16 (18 MT).

———. 1997. *Missing Persons and Mistaken Identities: Women and Gender in Ancient Israel*. OBT. Minneapolis: Fortress Press.

———. 1999. "What Makes a Feminist Reading Feminist? A Qualified Answer." In *Escaping Eden: New Feminist Perspectives on the Bible*, edited by Harold Washington, Susan Graham, and Pamela Thimmes, 124–31. New York: New York University Press.

Brayford, Susan. 2009. "Feminist Criticism: Sarah Laughs Last." In *Method Matters: Essays on the Interpretation of the Hebrew Bible in Honor of David L. Petersen*, edited by Joel M. LeMon and Kent Harold Richards, 311–31. RBS 56. Atlanta: Society of Biblical Literature.

Brenner, Athalya, and Carole Fontaine, eds. 1997. *A Feminist Companion to Reading the Bible: Approaches, Methods, and Strategies*. Sheffield: Sheffield Academic Press.

Brenner-Idan, Athalya. 2015. *The Israelite Woman: Social Role and Literary Type in Biblical Narrative*. 2nd ed. London: Bloomsbury.

Daly, Mary. 1973. *Beyond God the Father: Toward a Philosophy of Women's Liberation*. Boston: Beacon Press.

Day, Peggy L., ed. 1989. *Gender and Difference in Ancient Israel*. Minneapolis: Augsburg Fortress Press.

Fewell, Danna Nolan. 1999. "Reading the Bible Ideologically: Feminist Criticism." In *To Each Its Own Meaning: An Introduction to Biblical Criticisms and Their Application*, edited by Steven L. McKenzie and Stephen R. Haynes, 268–82. Rev. and expanded ed. Louisville, KY: Westminster John Knox Press.

hooks, bell. 1984. *Feminist Theory from Margin to Center*. Boston: South End.

Junior, Nyasha. 2015. *An Introduction to Womanist Biblical Interpretation*. Louisville, KY: Westminster John Knox Press.

Knowles, Melody. 2014. "Feminist Interpretation of the Psalms." In *The Oxford Handbook of the Psalms*, edited by William P. Brown, 424–36. Oxford: Oxford University Press.

Lapsley, Jacqueline. 2005. *Whispering the Word: Strategies for Reading Women's Stories in the Old Testament Theologically*. Louisville, KY: Westminster John Knox Press.

Lawrence, Beatrice. 2009. "Gender Analysis: Gender and Method in Biblical Studies." In *Method Matters: Essays on the Interpretation of the Hebrew Bible in Honor of David L. Petersen*, edited by Joel M. LeMon and Kent Harold Richards, 333–48. RBS 56. Atlanta: Society of Biblical Literature.

McKay, Heather. 1997. "On the Future of Feminist Biblical Criticism." In *A Feminist Companion to Reading the Bible: Approaches, Methods, and Strategies*, edited by Athalya Brenner and Carole Fontaine, 61–83. Sheffield: Sheffield Academic Press.

Meyers, Carol L. 1988. *Discovering Eve: Ancient Israelite Women in Context*. New York: Oxford University Press.

———. 2013. *Rediscovering Eve: Ancient Israelite Women in Context*. New York: Oxford University Press.

Meyers, Carol L., Toni Craven, and Ross Shepard Kraemer, eds. 2000. *Women in Scripture: A Dictionary of Named and Unnamed Women in the Hebrew Bible, the Apocryphal/Deuterocanonical Books, and the New Testament*. Boston and New York: Houghton Mifflin.

Newsom, Carol A. 1989. "Woman and the Discourse of Patriarchal Wisdom: A Study of Proverbs 1–9." In *Gender and Difference in Ancient Israel*, edited by Peggy L. Day, 142–60. Minneapolis: Augsburg Fortress Press.

———. 2012. "Women as Biblical Interpreters before the Twentieth Century." In Newsom, Ringe, and Lapsley 2012.

Newsom, Carol A., Sharon H. Ringe, and Jacqueline E. Lapsley. 2012. *Women's Bible Commentary*. 3rd ed. Louisville, KY: Westminster John Knox Press.

O'Connor, Kathleen M. 2006. "The Feminist Movement Meets the Old Testament: One Woman's Perspective." In *Engaging the Bible in a Gendered World: An Introduction to Feminist Biblical Interpretation in Honor of Katharine Doob Sakenfeld*, edited by Linda Day and Carolyn Pressler, 3–23. Louisville, KY: Westminster John Knox Press.

Olson, Dennis. 2006. "Untying the Knot? Masculinity, Violence, and the Creation-Fall Story of Genesis 2–4." In *Engaging the Bible in a Gendered World: An Introduction to Feminist Biblical*

Interpretation in Honor of Katharine Doob Sakenfeld, edited by Linda Day and Carolyn Pressler, 73–86. Louisville, KY: Westminster John Knox Press.

Osiek, Carolyn. 1985. "The Feminist and the Bible: Hermeneutical Alternatives." In *Feminist Perspectives on Biblical Scholarship*, edited by Adela Yarbro Collins, 93–105. SBLCP. SBLBSNA 10. Chico, CA: Scholars Press.

Phipps, William E. 1988. "Eve and Pandora Contrasted." *Theology Today* 45:34–48.

Pressler, Carolyn. 1993. *The View of Women Found in the Deuteronomic Family Laws*. BZAW 216. Berlin and New York: Walter de Gruyter.

Sakenfeld, Katharine Doob. 1985. "Feminist Uses of Biblical Materials." In *Feminist Interpretation of the Bible*, edited by Letty Russell, 55–64. Philadelphia: Westminster Press.

Scholz, Susanne. 2010. *Sacred Witness: Rape in the Hebrew Bible*. Minneapolis: Fortress Press.

———, ed. 2013a. *Feminist Interpretation of the Hebrew Bible in Retrospect*. Vol. 1, *Biblical Books*. Recent Research in Biblical Studies 5. Sheffield: Sheffield Phoenix Press.

———, ed. 2013b. *Feminist Interpretation of the Hebrew Bible in Retrospect*. Vol. 2, *Social Locations*. Recent Research in Biblical Studies 8. Sheffield: Sheffield Phoenix Press.

Schüssler Fiorenza, Elisabeth. 2001. *Wisdom's Ways: Introducing Feminist Biblical Interpretation*. Maryknoll, NY: Orbis Books.

Stanton, Elizabeth Cady. 1993. *The Woman's Bible*. Foreword by Maureen Fitzgerald. Boston: Northeastern University Press. Originally published in 1895 and 1898.

Thimmes, Pamela. 1999. "What Makes a Feminist Reading Feminist? Another Perspective." In *Escaping Eden: New Feminist Perspectives on the Bible*, edited by Harold Washington, Susan Graham, and Pamela Thimmes, 132–40. New York: New York University Press.

Trible, Phyllis. 1978. *God and the Rhetoric of Sexuality*. OBT. Philadelphia: Fortress Press.

———. 1984. *Texts of Terror: Literary-Feminist Reading of Biblical Narratives*. OBT 13. Philadelphia: Fortress Press.

———. 2003. "Not a Jot, Not a Tittle: Genesis 2–3 after Twenty Years." In *Biblical Studies Alternatively: An Introductory Reader*, edited by Susanne Scholz, 101–6. Upper Saddle River, NJ: Prentice Hall.

Weems, Renita. 1995. *Battered Love: Marriage, Sex, and Violence in the Hebrew Prophets*. OBT. Minneapolis: Fortress Press.

Yee, Gale A. 2003. *Poor Banished Children of Eve*. Minneapolis: Augsburg Fortress Press.

Yoder, Christine Roy. 2001. *Wisdom as a Woman of Substance: A Socioeconomic Reading of Proverbs 1–9 and 31:10–31*. BZAW 304. Berlin: Walter de Gruyter.

18

Gender II

Womanist, Mujerista, *Asian Feminist, and Genderqueer*

> I am black and beautiful,
> O daughters of Jerusalem.
> *Song of Songs 1:5a*

For many, feminist criticism failed historically to address the undeniable realities of race and class, as well as nonnormative gender identity. Consequently, other interpretive approaches to the biblical text began to emerge, not so much as offshoots but as critical partners with their own histories of origin and development. This chapter highlights certain critical approaches that have drawn from but also critiqued feminist criticism from the contexts of race and transgender perspectives. But like feminist criticism, each one exercises a hermeneutic of suspicion as well as a hermeneutic of hope for a more inclusive and just community.

WOMANIST INTERPRETATION

The theologian and civil rights leader Howard Thurman tells of his illiterate grandmother regularly asking her family to read the Bible to her. Thurman asked why she never asked them to read from Paul's Letters. She explained,

> During the days of slavery . . . the master's minister would occasionally hold services for the slaves. . . . Always the white minister would use as his text something from Paul. At least three or four times a year he used as a text: "Slaves, be obedient to them that are your masters . . . as unto Christ." . . . I promised my Maker that if I ever learned to read and if freedom ever came, I would not read that part of the Bible. (1996, 30–31)

Her telling statement testifies to the challenges of biblical interpretation for African Americans during the time of slavery up to the present: the Bible has been both a source of liberation and a tool of oppression, sustaining white supremacy throughout U.S. history (see chap. 20). For African American women in particular, the reality has been more complicated. Deborah King refers to "multiple jeopardy" experienced by women of color: oppression multiplied by the intersecting lines of racism, classism, and sexism (King 1993). Such manifold realities were not, historically speaking, fully understood and addressed by (white) feminism (hooks 1984, 140). Partly in response, many African American women developed a particular kind of black feminist critique called "womanist."

The term "womanist" was popularized, though not originated,[1] by the author Alice Walker, who developed a four-part definition of the word that spoke to the personal, historical, and religious experience of African American women. Below is her complete definition:

> 1. From *womanish*. (Opp. of "girlish," i.e. frivolous, irresponsible, not serious.) A black feminist or feminist of color. From the black folk expression of mothers to female children, "you acting womanish," i.e., like a woman. Usually referring to outrageous, audacious, courageous or *willful* behavior. Wanting to know more and in greater depth than is considered "good" for one. Interested in grown-up doings. Acting grown up. Being grown up. Interchangeable with another black folk expression: "You trying to be grown." Responsible. In charge. *Serious*.
> 2. *Also*: A woman who loves other women, sexually and/or nonsexually. Appreciates and prefers women's culture, women's emotional flexibility (values tears as natural counterbalance of laughter), and women's strength. Sometimes loves individual men, sexually and/or nonsexually. Committed to survival and wholeness of entire people, male *and* female. Not a separatist, except periodically, for health. Traditionally a universalist, as in: "Mama, why are we brown, pink, and yellow, and our cousins are white, beige and black?" Ans. "Well, you know the colored race is just like a flower garden, with every color flower represented." Traditionally capable, as in: "Mama, I'm walking to Canada and I'm taking you and a bunch of other slaves with me." Reply: "It wouldn't be the first time."
> 3. Loves music. Loves dance. Loves the moon. *Loves* the Spirit. Loves love and food and roundness. Loves struggle. *Loves* the Folk. Loves herself. *Regardless*.
> 4. Womanist is to feminist as purple is to lavender. (Walker 1983, xi–xii)

Walker offers a richly multifaceted "definition" of womanist: mature, outrageous, discerning, willful, courageous, serious, responsible, loving. For Walker, womanism is a certain shade of feminism.

Since Walker's definition, different shades of "purple" have blossomed as African American women have appropriated Walker's definition in religious contexts. Many have built on Walker's emphasis on "survival and wholeness of entire people," claiming womanism's concern for the empowerment of all who suffer marginalization, "male and female." Womanism, in other words, offers an inclusive model for "envisioning human liberation" (Riggs 1994, 2). Others take a more particularistic stance by focusing primarily on the empowerment of African American women. Some have found Walker's reference to women's love of other women "sexually and/or nonsexually" to be problematic (e.g., Sanders 1989). But loosely in common among self-identified womanists is the expressed aim to address the intersecting dimensions of gender, race, and class in the multitudinous

---

1. For the antecedents of Walker's definition, see Junior 2015, xi–xiii.

contexts of oppression (Junior 2006, 39; 2015, 39–75). For many, womanism is also a deeply spiritual matter; it encourages black women to ponder God in affirmation of their whole selves—mind, body, and spirit, personal and collective. Indeed, womanism regards the experiences of black women as a fundamental resource for reflecting on and talking about God (Riggs 2015).

Distinctive of interpretive approaches discussed so far, "womanist" is equally a matter of personal identity as it is an interpretive outlook. That is to say, while all "womanists" are by definition African American women, not all African American women, be they theologians or biblical interpreters, consider themselves "womanists" (Junior 2015, 125–31). In any case, womanists find solid grounding for their work from the early examples and literature of African American women who labored as abolitionists, suffragists, political activists, and ministers throughout the nineteenth century.[2] Together, they objected to African American women being hypersexualized, masculinized, and dehumanized by the slaveholding economy (42–43).

Womanist Interpretations

New Testament scholar Clarice Martin identifies three "assumptions" that shape womanist biblical interpretation: (1) the Bible is a "life-giving" and "empowering resource"; (2) the Bible is a "pervasively androcentric, patriarchal text"; (3) the "reality and effects of multiple, interlocking ideologies and systems of hegemony and domination [are] inscribed within the biblical traditions . . . and within traditional . . . Eurocentric critical exegetical theories and practices" (1999, 656–57). In working with these assumptions, womanist interpreters typically engage in four tasks: (1) recovering texts and their ancient contexts, (2) reclaiming texts related to Africans and "blackness," (3) challenging feminist scholars "on the subject of race," and (4) addressing the effects of biblical interpretation on African and African diasporic communities (657).

In practice, however, womanist biblical interpretation has not been so systematic. Individual womanist interpreters, whether biblically, theologically, or ethically trained, have emphasized only one or another of these elements. But what they have in common is the aim to interpret texts in the light of African American women's experiences of various interlocking forms of oppression. As Hebrew Bible scholar Renita Weems succinctly states, "Victimized by multiple categories of oppression (e.g., race, gender, class) and having experienced these victimizations oftentimes simultaneously, women of color bring to biblical academic discourse a broader, and more subtle, understanding of systems of oppression" (1993, 220).

In one influential study, for example, womanist theologian Delores Williams rereads Gen. 16 and 21 through the eyes of Hagar, an Egyptian slave woman (and hence of African descent), and draws parallels between Hagar's story and the daily struggles of African American women. Motherhood, poverty, homelessness, and expendability are connecting themes that make Hagar a kindred spirit. Hagar's plight is one of surrogacy that connects well to the life struggles of African American women in American history. Her

2. For a discussion of these important figures, see Junior 2015, 12, 39–53.

story is about the miracle of survival. In her words, "Many black women have testified that 'God helped them make a way out of no way.' . . . The female-centered tradition of African-American biblical appropriation could be named the *survival/quality-of-life tradition*" (1993, 5–6).

In her book *Just a Sister Away*, Renita Weems, who in 1989 was the first African American woman to receive a doctoral degree in Hebrew Bible, explored the lives of various biblical women from Hagar and Sarah to Elizabeth and Mary, creatively reconstructing their conversations, emotions, and actions in ways that align with the commonalities in women's experiences (Weems 1988). Her more academic work, *Battered Love*, explores how the prophets, particularly Hosea and Jeremiah, deploy the metaphor of marriage in sexually violent ways; she expresses grave concern over how such texts can incite domestic abuse today (1995).

One might think that the Bible would be written off as a tool of oppression and violence by womanist interpreters. But Weems articulates well the reasons why African American women continue to regard the Bible as meaningful and even liberative.

> Where the Bible has been able to capture the imagination of African American women, it has been and continues to be able to do so because significant portions speak to the deepest aspirations of oppressed people for freedom, dignity, justice, and vindication. Substantial portions of the Bible describe a world where the oppressed are liberated, the last become first, the humbled are exalted, the despised are preferred, those rejected are welcomed, the long-suffering are rewarded, the dispossessed are repossessed, and the arrogant are prostrated. And these are the passages for oppressed readers that stand at the center of the biblical message and, thereby, serve as a vital norm for biblical faith. Therein is a portrait of a God that oppressed readers can believe in. (Weems 1991, 70–71)

For Weems, biblical interpretation has to do not only with retrieving those voices in the Bible with whom African American women can identify, but also with examining how the text arouses and shapes their yearnings for liberation and wholeness.

For womanists (and many other interpreters), the authority of Scripture is no static quality of the text itself. "People have power, not texts" (Weems 2003, 26). To speak of biblical authority is to speak not of the texts themselves but of particular readings that reorient readers, transforming their way of being and doing in the world (1991, 64). The biblical text can mediate lived reality as much as lived reality mediates the reading of the text. Interpreting the Bible should be a liberating activity that nurtures the reader's capacity to move from complicity to responsibility in the face of oppressive realities and relationships. But this can also involve "resistance against those things within the Bible and in culture that undermine one's innate sense of identity and basic instincts for survival" (Riggs 2015).

This partnership between appropriation and resistance can be seen with Howard Thurmond's grandmother. Because African Americans were forbidden to read during slavery, the study of the Bible was made possible only through listening and memory. The Bible thus became the "talking book" (Callahan 2006, 1–20), a book that could also be "talked back" to, that is, critically engaged (Gafney 2013, 197). The result of such critical engagement was the generative practice of *retelling* the Bible, an interpretive strategy that enabled listeners and storytellers to measure what they had *been told* about God, reality, and themselves through the Bible in light of what they have *experienced* of God, reality, and themselves (Riggs 2015).

Biblical narratives that have been particularly important for womanist interpreters include the stories of Hagar, Hannah, and Ruth. As noted above, the story of Hagar vividly illustrates the plight of a female slave of African descent who struggles to survive in a patriarchal household. The story of Hannah is that of a woman who courageously pleads her case directly to God, bypassing established male authorities, as she prays for a child and ultimately offers him (Samuel) to God's protection. Her prayer is a testimony of God's vindication and liberation, a celebration of Hannah's vindication and God's victory (1 Sam. 2:1–10). Hannah's story bears witness that God alone bestows the fullness of personhood (Riggs 2015). The book of Ruth is another story of a foreign woman (Moabite) struggling to survive, a displaced widow who by her wits and courage becomes the ancestress of King David.

GENESIS 1–3

What, then, about the creation texts? While feminist criticism has laid much of the groundwork, a womanist reading strategy specifically raises the issue of race with respect to how human beings are framed within the text. What color, for example, does one imagine humankind to have as one reads Gen. 1:26–28? For Caucasian readers of Genesis such as myself, the default perception is invariably white. But anthropologically, our human ancestors in sub-Saharan Africa were anything but white. Early *Homo sapiens* had dark skin, produced by an abundance of the pigment eumelanin in skin cells. With the loss of hair, human skin became dark, thereby providing protection from the damaging effects of ultraviolet radiation (UV). The variation in skin color that has evolved can be explained by the tradeoff between protection from UV and the need for some UV absorption for the production of vitamin D.

If we place Eve in the context of human evolution, she is black, united to her male partner by flesh, bone, *and* skin. Equal and beautiful. The beauty of black skin is echoed in an anonymous poem published in the first African American newspaper, *Freedom's Journal* (1827), that alludes to the Song of Solomon (1:5) beginning with these words:

> Black I am, oh! Daughters fair?
> But My beauty is most rare.
> Black, Indeed, appears my skin,
> Beauteous, comely, all within. . . .[3]

Can the image of a black Eve be a source of liberation for readers? Much depends on how one reads her character in the garden story. A womanist reading might stress her courageous and "willful" spirit in challenging God's prohibition. Her engagement with the serpent evinces her own wisdom (Gen. 3:2–3). Her desire for wisdom cannot be thwarted.

---

3. "The Black Beauty," in *Freedom's Journal* 1 (June 8, 1827): 52.

But then comes the crushing pronouncement: "He shall rule over you" (3:16bβ). How might the scene be read from the history of injustice perpetrated against African American women? Perhaps by seeing Adam suddenly turn white at the pronouncement, not out of fear but out of supremacy, thereby making the punishment ever more tragic, horrific, and reprehensible. The horror suffered by countless black women enslaved economically and sexually by their white "masters" was incalculable. Indeed, the divine pronouncement "He shall rule over you" historically served as justification not only for subordinating women, regardless of race, in marriage but also for exploiting women of African descent. Think also of the sexualized objectification of black women through the social myth of "Jezebel," which labeled African American women as sexually promiscuous and immoral. White slave owners used the Jezebel image as legal justification for raping their slaves and forcing procreation on them.

Such a reading of God's punishment of the woman invites resistance. Indeed, there is no other option, particularly in view of the biblically grounded vision of true community, a community in which freedom is realizable for African American women. Such freedom shatters the curse of "multiple jeopardy" with its interlocking "bars" of oppression.

> I am YHWH your God who brought you out of the land of Egypt,
>   to be their slaves no more;
> I have broken the bars of your yoke
>   and made you walk erect. (Lev. 26:13)

With such freedom comes a "wholeness" for an "entire people" indeed.

This somewhat detailed discussion of womanist interpretation lays important groundwork for highlighting comparable reading strategies developed by women of other racial backgrounds, in particular *mujerista* and Asian feminist. As will come clear, many of the challenges addressed in these interpretative strategies intersect with those treated in womanist interpretations.

MUJERISTA INTERPRETATION

As womanist is to African American women, so *mujerista* is to Latinas, women of Latin descent living in the United States. Derived from the Spanish word for "woman" (*mujer*), *mujerista* interpretations draw from the diverse experiences of Latinas who face sexism, prejudice, and economic oppression on a daily basis. Such readings are shaped by *mujerista* theology, which "draws liberally from the Christian faith to sustain the struggle for liberation and fullness of life, not just individually but also communally" (Isasi-Díaz 2006, 27). Like womanist interpretations, *mujerista* readings adopt a cultural-critical perspective, which in this case focuses on the daily struggles of Latinas, specifically on *lo cotidiano*, "the immediate space" of lived experience (Isasi-Díaz 2004, 92–106). Similar to womanist theology, *mujerista* theology aims to strengthen the "moral agency and self-definition" of Latinas in community (Isasi-Díaz 2006, 28). The communal emphasis is critical: Latina "identity," or sense of belongingness, is shaped by multiple intersecting relationships, including those of family, friends, neighbors, and communities of faith (28). *Mujerista* perspectives acknowledge the relational dimensions of life, for they materially constitute the "kin-dom" of God, *la familia de Dios* (33).

As for biblical interpretation, a *mujerista* approach is intensely interested in the "daily reality of biblical characters," not only gained at the literary level (the world of the text) but also "behind the text," specifically the sociocultural context reflected in the text (Isasi-Díaz 2006, 29–30). Another emphasis in *mujerista* interpretation is the power of words, the mystery of communication. A common saying among Latinos and Latinas is "*Tu palabra me basta* (Your word is sufficient for me)" (30). Words reflect the richness and power of relationships. Indeed, for words to be truly efficacious, they need to be embodied, as they are, most powerfully, in the liturgy of the Eucharist.

Genesis 1–3

How would a *mujerista* perspective read the creation accounts of Genesis? Regarding Gen. 1, such a reading might focus on the creative power of God's word in fashioning the universe. God's creative word in Genesis is the word before all other words: "Let there be light," marking the first act of creation. God's word brings forth light and life in abundance. In the Priestly account, the efficacy of God's word is demonstrated throughout Gen. 1, repeated ten times, no less, perhaps to align itself with the Decalogue. *La palabra de Dios basta para el mundo* ("God's word is sufficient for the world").

In addition, a *mujerista* reading would dig more deeply *behind* Gen. 1 to discern what is going on concretely, materially, and daily in the life of the community that produced this text and drew support from it. Perhaps such a reading would point out that Gen. 1 spoke meaningfully to the survivors of exile, who knew fully the pain of displacement. The story of God at work in creation is a testimony of hope for a people engaged in the work of (re)building community, inspired by God's vision of the cosmic "kin-dom." What might have motivated God to create the cosmic "kin-dom"? The text is silent, but a *mujerista* reading might suggest that it was God's desire for relationship, a deep love for others, a love to be modeled by human beings, "made in the image of God." Bearing the image of God in the world involves testifying to the inalienable dignity and moral worth of every individual, females and males.

From the cosmic to the familial, the value of community is also stressed in the garden narrative. The man's very first words in the narrative convey unsurpassed delight in the woman at her creation (Gen. 2:23). The woman's agency in the narrative is demonstrated both with and apart from the man. She is his partner, positioned "in front of" him (*kĕnegdô*), as he is hers (2:18). She thus is a "counterpartner"; she is both independent from and interdependent with the man. Their life is a shared life in the garden, not a life of complete leisure but of work in maintaining the garden and reaping its abundance together.

The tragedy of the story is most acutely felt by the woman. "He shall rule over you" (3:16bβ) constitutes nothing less than an assault on the woman's dignity and agency. A *mujerista* reading of God's punishment laments the pain that has daily afflicted many Latinas by the male embodiment of *machismo*—a position of male superiority and aggression against women, which all too frequently has led to infidelity, sexually transmitted disease, domestic violence, sexual assault, and murder. A *mujerista* reading denounces Gen. 3:16 as counter to God's vision of life, as an impediment to the goal of liberation and wholeness for both men and women. Indeed, "any biblical text that impedes this goal is [to be] denounced" (Isasi-Díaz 2006, 28). Given its sociocultural interests, a *mujerista* reading can point out that Gen. 3:16 in its ancient context is more a justification for the author's own lived experience in antiquity, steeped as it was in patriarchy, than it is meant as a mandate for women and men today.

ASIAN FEMINIST INTERPRETATION

Asian women of various nationalities have also experienced exclusion from circles of power in the church and larger community, and the Bible has often been used to legitimize such marginalization. Yet the Bible is also considered, authoritatively so, to be the "liberating and transforming word" for women, particularly when it is read from the "underside" (Say Pa 2006, 48). For many Asian women, marginalization includes the misery of refugee conditions, migrant labor, sexual harassment, and sex trafficking.

Like Hagar and Hannah for womanist interpreters, the biblical character of Ruth is often lifted up as a model for Asian women (48–49). A foreign refugee (a Moabite) struggling to survive in the land of Israel, Ruth exhibits resourcefulness and courage, as well as family loyalty, a model celebrated and found empowering by many Asian women. There are, however, elements in the story that raise serious concerns, such as Ruth's dependence on marriage for her survival, the dubious means that she and Naomi use to secure a husband, and her unquestioned obedience to her mother-in-law (49). Anna May Say Pa, a Burmese biblical interpreter, asks: Is the character of Ruth a genuine model of liberation for Asian women (2006)?

The verdict is mixed. Although her love for Naomi is estimable, Ruth's total submission to Naomi's will makes her an ambivalent character. Ruth's embodiment of "unreflective self-sacrifice" is particularly problematic (58). Gale Yee sharpens the ambivalence by identifying Ruth as a "model minority" and "perpetual foreigner" (2009, 128–33). As a Moabite, Ruth remains vulnerable to mistreatment by Israelites. That Ruth must toil in Boaz's field "until the end of the barley and wheat harvests" in 2:23 can be taken as exploitative (131). One can read her pledge to Naomi in 1:16–17 as "a verbal contract in which Ruth submits her person to the wishes of her mother-in-law," including accepting Naomi's risky proposal to seduce Boaz on the threshing floor under the cover of darkness, an act of desperation (130, 133).

Ruth is forever a foreigner who models how to behave in Israelite culture by sacrificing herself for her family (Yee 2009, 129–30). But as Katharine Sakenfeld points out, such a model can have damaging consequences.

> Ruth's behavior . . . encourages women to follow cultural expectations by serving others at the expense of their own needs, by sacrificing themselves for the sake of family or friends or workplace colleagues. The danger of such an interpretation may be especially acute in some Asian cultures, where some church leaders are reported to have used the example of Ruth to insist that young Christian women

maintain a traditional cultural practice of serving their mothers-in-law rather than choosing to live as a nuclear family or work outside the home. (1999, 13).

And what about "young Christian women" who also single-mindedly serve their husbands? In either case, the Genesis "curse" in 3:16 could easily be used to impose a posture of "unreflective self-sacrifice" upon women in both the household and larger society. For this reason, too, the punishment should be denounced. But life *in* the garden, the life of mutual flourishing, provides both a precedent and a vision for the people of God across genders.

GENDERQUEER INTERPRETATIONS

Gay and lesbian, as well as transgendered, bisexual, intersex, and other sexual minorities (LGBTI-Q)[4] deeply question the heterosexual bias that pervades Scripture and most interpretations of Scripture. It is easy to see why. "Male and female" created in "the image of God" in Gen. 1 falls into a rigidly binary construction of sexual and gender "identity" that favors procreation and heterosexual intimacy. By most accounts, Gen. 1–3 does not offer good news for sexual minorities because of its bias toward heteronormativity: "the dominant belief system that relies on fixed and binary genders and the certainty that heterosexuality is the norm that occurs naturally, that is, apart from cultural influences" (Hornsby 2016a, 2)

Building on the insights of feminist criticism, "genderqueer"[5] criticism broadens the hermeneutical lens to include all gender identifications within its purview. Informed by queer theory, genderqueer criticism calls into question the essentialized nature of sexual categories or identities, categories that claim to be based on inherent, "natural," or divinely ordained attributes. Such criticism looks at the "spaces in between" the socially constructed categories of "man" and "woman," the different and manifold shades of sexuality and sexual expression (Guest 2012, 12). This is not to deny that there are biological differences between male and female sexes. "The problem is the *significance* that gets attached to various body parts and reproductive capacities" that become "concretized" into a "rigid binary" (81). From an inclusive gender-critical perspective, the traditionally rigid divide between sex as something biologically determined, that is, associated entirely with birth genitalia, and gender as a matter of socialization breaks down.[6] Because sex and gender carry social import, both reflect their own cultural construction. This means that heterosexuality is not a "natural" given but a matter of cultural constraints and compulsion, given the way it has divided the world between male and female as mutually exclusive categories (Butler 1999, 8–18). But biology does not determine destiny, as trans people can testify (Hornsby 2016a, 10). Genderqueer readings question not only the gender

---

4. The acronym refers to lesbian, gay, bisexual, transgendered, intersex, and queer, a loose grouping that is not meant to minimize their distinctions. The hyphenation indicates that "queer" perspectives question and resist all identity labels (Guest 2012, 30n15).

5. I use the term inclusively here, although legitimate objections have been raised regarding its limiting scope with regard to "trans people" (see Hornsby 2016a, 10).

6. Contra Bird's discussion of Gen. 2–3 above.

binary ("man" and "woman") but also the sex binary ("male" and "female"). As feminist criticism begins with a hermeneutic of suspicion, so genderqueer criticism begins with a hermeneutic of "hetero-suspicion" (Guest 2012, 82).

Genderqueer analysis addresses the underlying cultural biases that give birth to normative constructions not only of the feminine but also of the masculine. Masculinity, like femininity, is regarded as a cultural way of being rather than as something biologically or innately wired. A case in point is the Deuteronomistic Historian's account of the love shared between Jonathan and David (1 Sam. 18:1–3; 20:17; 2 Sam. 1:26). Is there a homoerotic aspect to David's love for Jonathan, a love that surpasses "the love of women" (2 Sam. 1:26)? The question remains open, but regardless, the narrative does not condemn the "love" shared by two men but celebrates it, blurring thereby the binary division between "man" and "woman" as they are stereotypically construed. As for God, how does one account for divine masculinity, in some cases even hypermasculinity? Are biblical depictions of YHWH's violent fury and willingness to violate Israel a product of imperial rule? Does such language reflect ancient Israel's political context of ruthless domination by the Assyrian and Babylonian Empires? More specifically, what does it mean for males to worship a deity made in the image of the male? What does it mean when the metaphor of marriage between husband and wife is used to describe the relationship between God and Israel, particularly in prophetic literature, when both partners are deemed male? Are homoerotic anxieties reflected in the account of God's choosing to reveal only "his" backside to Moses (Exod. 33:21–23)? Such questions are powerfully posed by genderqueer analyses, and the answers inevitably turn toward the nature of gender/sex construction.

What light does a genderqueer analysis cast on Gen. 1–3? A most critical light, as one would suspect, but the insights are more than simply deconstructive. Such an analysis would highlight God's creation in Gen. 1 as a rigidly binary world, beginning with night and day and culminating with the "foundational binary pairing of man and woman" (Guest 2016, 21). One could also add the binary between God and creation. Creation, thus, is essentially about boundary making and binary formation. Nevertheless, as Deryn Guest points out, the Priestly account is not so reductive "in the beginning": the pre-creative state that exists prior to God's first act of creation (1:2) is one of "formless fluidity" (23). Is such a state inimical or indifferent, menacing or benign? The text is openly ambiguous and, thus, open to interpretation. In any case, the text forthrightly acknowledges God's presence in the primordial mix, specifically God's spirit/wind/breath (rûaḥ) "hovering." Here God is present, intimately connected to těhôm ("Deep") within this boundary-less, "queer" reality (25, 40). Such an interpretation of Gen. 1 is not necessarily the result of reading *against* the "grain" of the text. It is more the case of reading the text "backwards" (43–44).

Regarding Gen. 3, a highly ambivalent binary is established between the man and the woman: "For your husband shall be your desire, but he shall rule over you" (v. 16b; AT). Whereas the primordial couple was inscribed as physically complementary in 2:24 (both are of "one flesh"), now desire and domination characterize the heterosexual binary. What is the connection between the two: the original and the resultant state of gendered reality? First, both heterosexual desire and dominion are matters of cultural construction.

A genderqueer critic might point out that, before the "fall," nothing is said about the woman's sexual desire for the man, or for that matter the man's sexual desire for the woman (except for the allegedly later etiological addition of Gen. 2:24). Heterosexual desire, it could be argued, is a consequence of the "cursed" world. "Desire for a husband is thus an element within a disordered world out of tune with itself and its creator" (Guest 2005, 149–50). In such a disordered world, heterosexuality itself can be construed as a matter of coercion, comparable to the man "ruling" over the woman. Indeed, the woman's desire for the man reinforces and indeed "guarantees" her submission to him (Stone 2000, 64). By mitigating male oppression within the marital relationship, sexual desire makes it (somehow) acceptable. Female "desire" is "the pill meant to soften the blow" of male domination (Guest 2012, 106).

A genderqueer analysis of Gen. 2–3, steeped as it is in heterocentric language, exposes heterosexual desire as a means to construct and maintain patriarchal control of female sexuality, particularly the female capacity for reproduction. The categorical distinction between male and female is one that, as Gayle Rubin has persuasively argued, is based not on "an expression of natural differences" but rather on the "suppression of natural similarities" (1974, 180). To turn this claim around, is there anything in the garden story that might relieve such "suppression"? Indeed, there is. The man's exultation over the woman after her creation does not dwell on or even mention anything that distinguishes the woman from himself. What he recognizes and celebrates are the "natural similarities" (Gen. 2:23). Common "bone" and "flesh": that is what the man celebrates about the woman. No reference, veiled or otherwise, is devoted to what distinguishes the two sexually or biologically. There is no reference to genitalia. Nothing is said about her reproductive capacities. For the moment, at least, there is no "compulsory heterosexuality" at play (Guest 2012, 110). Instead, it is similarity, and similarity alone, that prompts the man's cry of joy. Here is a case of sexual difference being "suppressed," or better, unrecognized. Perhaps this is to be expected within the logic of the narrative, for the ʾādām had negatively assessed the other animals in his search for a match. But now success: a creature made in *his* image, as it were, a creature fashioned "from" him who can now be "with" him. It is as if the narrative itself admits that gender division comes later. Regardless of what happens later, it is the likeness and not the difference between these two creatures of God that launches the human community. Can that community admit persons of "bone and flesh" whose sexual and gender "identities" do not fit within the heterosexual paradigm? The ʾādām's first words may very well provide an opening.

BIBLIOGRAPHY FOR CHAPTER 18

Womanist Interpretation

Callahan, Allen Dwight. 2006. *The Talking Book: African Americans and the Bible*. New Haven: Yale University Press.

Cannon, Katie Geneva. 1995. *Katie's Canon: Womanism and the Soul of the Black Community*. New York: Continuum.

———. 2001. *The Womanist Theology Primer: Remembering What We Never Knew; The Epistemology of Womanist Theology*. Louisville, KY: Women's Ministries Program Area, Presbyterian Church (U.S.A.).

Cannon, Katie Geneva, Emilie Maureen Townes, and Angela D. Sims, eds. 2011. *Womanist Theological Ethics: A Reader*. Library of Theological Ethics. Louisville, KY: Westminster John Knox Press.

Coleman, Monica A. 2013. *Ain't I a Womanist, Too? Third-Wave Womanist Religious Thought*. Minneapolis: Fortress Press.

Floyd-Thomas, Stacey M. 2006. *Deeper Shades of Purple: Womanism in Religion and Society*. New York: New York University Press.

Gafney, Wilda C. 2013. "A Queer Womanist Midrashic Reading of Numbers 25:1–18." In *Leviticus and Numbers*, edited by Athalya Brenner and Archi Chi Chung Lee, 189–98. Texts @ contexts. Minneapolis: Augsburg Fortress Press.

hooks, bell. 1984. *Feminist Theory from Margin to Center*. Boston: South End.

Junior, Nyasha. 2006. "Womanist Biblical Interpretation." In *Engaging the Bible in a Gendered World: An Introduction to Feminist Biblical Interpretation in Honor of Katharine Doob Sakenfeld*, edited by Linda Day and Carolyn Pressler, 37–46. Louisville, KY: Westminster John Knox Press.

———. 2015. *An Introduction to Womanist Biblical Interpretation*. Louisville, KY: Westminster John Knox Press.

King, Deborah. 1993. "Multiple Jeopardy: The Context of a Black Feminist Ideology." In *Feminist Frameworks: Alternative Theoretical Accounts of the Relations between Women and Men*, edited by Alison M. Jaggar and Paul S. Rothenberg, 220–36. 3rd ed. New York: McGraw-Hill.

Martin, Clarice J. 1999. "Womanist Biblical Interpretation." In *Dictionary of Biblical Interpretation*, edited by John H. Hayes, 2:655–68. Nashville: Abingdon.

Mitchem, Stephanie Y. 2002. *Introducing Womanist Theology*. Maryknoll, NY: Orbis Books.

Riggs, Marcia Y. 1994. *Awake, Arise, and Act: A Womanist Call for Black Liberation*. Cleveland: Pilgrim Press.

———. 2015. "Womanist Hermeneutics and Ethical Reflection." Lecture given at Columbia Theological Seminary on March 12, 2015.

Sanders, Cheryl. 1989. "Roundtable Discussion: Christian Ethics and Theology in Womanist Perspective." *Journal of Feminist Studies in Religion* 5, no. 2 (Fall): 83–91.

Thurman, Howard. 1996. *Jesus and the Disinherited*. Boston: Beacon Press.

Walker, Alice. 1983. *In Search of Our Mothers' Gardens: Womanist Prose*. San Diego: Harcourt Brace Jovanovich.

Weems, Renita J. 1988. *Just a Sister Away: A Womanist Vision of Women's Relationships in the Bible*. San Diego, CA: LuraMedia.

———. 1991. "Reading Her Way through the Struggle: African American Women and the Bible." In *Stony the Road We Trod: African American Biblical Interpretation*, edited by Cain H. Felder, 57–77. Minneapolis: Augsburg Fortress Press.

———. 1993. "Womanist Reflections on Biblical Hermeneutics." In *Black Theology: A Documentary History*, edited by James H. Cone and Gayraud S. Wilmore, 216–24. Maryknoll, NY: Orbis Books.

———. 1995. *Battered Love: Marriage, Sex, and Violence in the Hebrew Prophets*. OBT. Minneapolis: Fortress Press.

———. 2003. "Re-Reading for Liberation: African American Women and the Bible." In *Feminist Interpretation of the Bible and the Hermeneutics of Liberation*, edited by Silvia Schroer and Sophia Bietenhard, 19–32. New York: Sheffield Academic Press.

Williams, Delores. 1993. *Sisters in the Wilderness: The Challenge of Womanist God-Talk*. Maryknoll, NY: Orbis Books.

Mujerista Interpretation

Isasi-Díaz, Ada María. 1993a. *En la Lucha* [*In the Struggle*]: *A Hispanic Women's Liberation Theology*. Minneapolis: Fortress Press.

———. 1993b. "La Palabra de Dios en Nosotras—The Word of God in Us." In *Searching the Scriptures*, vol. 1, *A Feminist Introduction*, edited by Elisabeth Schüssler Fiorenza, 86–97. New York: Crossroad.

———. 2004. *La Lucha* [*The Struggle*] *Continues: Mujerista Theology*. Maryknoll, NY: Orbis Books.

———. 2006. "Communication as Communion: Elements in a Hermeneutic of *Lo Cotidiano*." In *Engaging the Bible in a Gendered World: An Introduction to Feminist Biblical Interpretation in Honor of Katharine Doob Sakenfeld*, edited by Linda Day and Carolyn Pressler, 27–36. Louisville, KY: Westminster John Knox Press.

Asian Feminist Interpretation

Chung, Lee Oo, ed. 1992. *Women of Courage: Asian Women Reading the Bible*. Seoul: Asian Women's Resource Center for Culture and Theology.

Kwok Pui-lan. 2000. *Introducing Asian Feminist Theology*. Cleveland, OH: Pilgrim Press.

Sakenfeld, Katharine Doob. 1999. *Ruth*. Interpretation. Louisville, KY: John Knox Press.

Say Pa, Anna May. 2006. "Reading Ruth 3:1–5 from an Asian Woman's Perspective." In *Engaging the Bible in a Gendered World: An Introduction to Feminist Biblical Interpretation in Honor of Katharine Doob Sakenfeld*, edited by Linda Day and Carolyn Pressler, 47–59. Louisville, KY: Westminster John Knox Press.

Yee, Gale A. 2009. "'She Stood in Tears amid the Alien Corn': Ruth, the Perpetual Foreigner and Model Minority." In *They Were All Together in One Place? Toward Minority Biblical Criticism*, edited by Randall C. Bailey, Tat-siong Benny Liew, and Fernando F. Segovia, 119–40. Semeia Studies 57. Atlanta: Society of Biblical Literature.

Genderqueer and Masculinity Interpretations

Butler, Judith. 1999. *Gender Trouble: Feminism and the Subversion of Identity*. 2nd ed. London: Routledge.

Creangǎ, Ovidiu, ed. 2010. *Men and Masculinity in the Hebrew Bible and Beyond*. The Bible in the Modern World 33. Sheffield: Sheffield Phoenix Press.

Goss, Robert E., and Mona West, eds. 2000. *Take Back the Word: A Queer Reading of the Bible*. Cleveland: Pilgrim Press.

Guest, Deryn. 2005. *When Deborah Met Jael: Lesbian Biblical Hermeneutics*. London: SCM Press.

———. 2012. *Beyond Feminist Biblical Studies*. The Bible in the Modern World 47. Sheffield: Sheffield Phoenix Press.

———. 2016. "Troubling the Waters: *Těhôm*, Transgender, and Reading Genesis Backwards." In Hornsby and Guest 2016, 21–44.

Guest, Deryn, et al., eds. 2006. *The Queer Bible Commentary*. London: SCM Press.

Hornsby, Teresa J. 2016a. "Introduction: The Body as Decoy." In Hornsby and Guest 2016, 1–12.

———. 2016b. "Gender Dualism, or The Big Lie." In Hornsby and Guest 2016, 13–20.

Hornsby, Teresa J., and Deryn Guest, eds. 2016. *Transgender, Intersex, and Biblical Interpretation*. Semeia Studies 83. Atlanta: Society of Biblical Literature.

Hornsby, Teresa J., and Ken Stone, eds. 2011. *Bible Trouble: Queer Readings at the Boundaries of Biblical Scholarship*. Semeia Studies 67. Atlanta: Society of Biblical Literature.

Nestle, Joan, Clare Howell, and Riki Anne Wilchins, eds. 2002. *Genderqueer: Voices from Beyond the Sexual Binary*. Los Angeles: Alyson Books.

Rubin, Gayle. 1974. "The Traffic in Women: Notes on the Political Economy of Sex." In *Toward an Anthropology of Women*, edited by R. Reiter, 157–210. New York: Monthly Review Press.

Stone, Ken. 2000. "The Garden of Eden and the Heterosexual Contract." In *Take Back the Word: A Queer Reading of the Bible*, edited by R. E. Goss and M. West, 57–70. Cleveland: Pilgrim Press.

———, ed. 2001. *Queer Commentary and the Hebrew Bible*. JSOTSup 334. Sheffield: Sheffield Academic Press; Cleveland: Pilgrim Press.

———. 2013. "Queer Criticism." In *New Meanings for Ancient Texts*, edited by Steven L. McKenzie and John Kaltner, 155–76. Louisville, KY: Westminster John Knox Press.

Whitehead, Stephen M. 2002. *Men and Masculinities: Key Themes and New Directions*. Cambridge: Polity Press.

19

Empire

> To be colonized is to become a stranger in your own land.
> *Susanna Barkataki*[1]

Empires, by definition, sustain themselves through subjugation, something that ancient Israel knew all too well. Ruled by a seemingly endless succession of foreign powers throughout its turbulent history, ancient Israel persistently suffered the brunt of imperial domination. The four kingdoms allegorized in the form of a statue in Daniel's dream provide stark testimony to the imperial burdens that ancient Israel experienced century after century (Dan. 2:31–45). When Israel had its own kings, the surrounding empires, including Egypt, were always at its doorstep. No wonder. Geographically, ancient Palestine was part of the land bridge between Egypt and Mesopotamia, or more broadly between Africa and Asia, and hence geopolitically served as a buffer zone for these ancient superpowers. Remarkably, amid the trauma of imperial subjugation, ancient Israel produced an unprecedented corpus of literature, a graphic testimony that the victors do not always write the last word of history.

Politically, however, ancient Israel was not simply a victim of imperial rule. For a brief period of time, Israel existed as a small and often divided kingdom that harbored its own imperial dreams (e.g., Amos 9:11–12; Isa. 2:2–4; Ezek. 37:24–28). When native kings ruled, many Israelites suffered, as when Solomon enslaved his own people to implement his building projects (1 Kgs. 5:13; cf. 9:22) or when peasant farmers were conscripted into military service (e.g., Mic. 2:8; Smith-Christopher 2015, 97–99). And one cannot forget the Canaanites, the indigenous of the land who were forced to coexist (if they survived) with an emerging Israelite population. Ultimately, however, the monarchy proved to be a failed experiment, with the end of national sovereignty of northern Israel in 722 BCE and of Judah in 586 BCE. Each "kingdom" suffered the national trauma of widespread destruction and deportation (Albertz 2003, 45–111).

The governing question of this chapter is, *What do biblical texts "do" when read through the lens of imperial subjugation and its aftermath?* The question, often posed in variant forms

1. http://www.huffingtonpost.com/susanna-barkataki/how-to-decolonize-your-yo_b_6776896.html.

by postcolonial critics, draws from the complexities of history, culture, and political ideology, both ancient and modern. An accompanying question is *whether the text in question (and the Bible as a whole) facilitates, accommodates, or resists imperial oppression and its legacies.* Postcolonial perspectives, like other perspectives, situate the text within the context of political and social power, in this case imperial power and its consequences. Such study includes within its vast coverage the biblical text's historical context vis-à-vis imperial power, as well as what has been done with the text from antiquity to the present to oppress and exclude others. Yes, lamentably the Bible itself has often been, and continues to be, a "colonizing text," repeatedly authorizing "the subjugation of foreign nations and lands" (Dube 2000, 15).

BACKGROUND

Although it began with a specific focus on European colonialism, postcolonial study today is an umbrella that covers a variety of approaches that together share a critical perspective on empire and colonialism, anywhere and everywhere (Auga 2014, 14). Its historical reach is staggering, ranging from Babylonian to British Empires, from ancient Assyria to modern America and the State of Israel (see Raheb 2014),[2] not to mention socio-economic forms of power that extend beyond national boundaries, such as transnational corporations in service of global capitalism. Colonialism thus is not a thing of the past; its consequences or legacies continue to define the contours of cultural life throughout the world, including North America. Racism in the United States, for example, is in part a colonial consequence (see chap. 20).

Regarded as the founder of postcolonial study, the Palestinian-born literary theorist Edward Said scrutinized how the West politically and literarily constructed the "Orient" as a negative inversion or foil of the West. Through "a web of racism, cultural stereotypes, political imperialism, and dehumanizing ideology," the various peoples of the East were cast in one way or another as barbarians (Said 1979, 27). Because "the Orient is . . . the place of Europe's greatest and richest and oldest colonies," it is also "one of its deepest and most recurring images of the Other" (1). As Said and so many others since him have demonstrated, "othering" a people is fundamentally an act of distortion and thus violence: "By othering we mean imagining someone as alien and different to 'us' in such a way that 'they' are excluded from 'our' 'normal,' 'superior' and 'civilized' group. Indeed, it is by imagining a foreign 'other' in this way that 'our' group can become more confident and exclusive" (Holliday et al. 2010, 2). "Othering" is an act of exclusion that reduces a human subject into a group object constructed to possess a universalized identity, all in order to elevate the subject that is doing the "othering" to a level of superiority. The construction of the other plays a zero-sum game of identity construction that establishes and sustains various forms of discrimination, such as racism, sexism, and ableism. Put another way, "othering" is an act of essentializing the subject: it constructs homogenized descriptions

---

2. It is critically important to distinguish between ancient Israel and modern Israel, between "Israelite" and "Israeli." The former refers to the community referenced in the Hebrew Scriptures, whereas the latter refers to the modern State of Israel.

of a particular group such that the group is seen to share an unchanging nature that can be readily categorized, objectified, and in many cases commodified.

According to Gayatri Chakravorti Spivak, "othering" is an act of "epistemic violence": the "remotely orchestrated, far-flung and heterogeneous project to constitute the colonial subject as Other" (Spivak 1988, 281). Such violence is conducted through discourse, or more broadly through the production of knowledge that serves to exclude and effectively silence othered voices within Western dominant cultures. Such silenced voices are those of the "subaltern," populations existing at the margins of established political structures (283–85). Epistemic violence is the consequence of "knowledge" that divides the world into rigid categories and consigns to oblivion those who do not fit. The subaltern are the disenfranchised who never fully consent to the dominant culture but whose voice has been rendered mute. "Can the subaltern speak?" asks Spivak. No, they cannot, for the unmediated voice of the subjugated cannot be heard in the (post)colonial context (308).

Broadly put, postcolonial criticism is focused on how imperialism and subalterity coexist, that is, how the "imperial powers impose their control on foreign lands and how the dominated respond" (Dube 2000, 47). *Postcolonialism* does not mean that colonialism is now over and done with. Quite the contrary. Even as a thing of the past, colonialism "did not simply consist of geographical and political domination but also included cultural and economic structures that persist to this day" (48). The legacies of empire are alive and well today; they continue to shape the current cultural, economic, and political landscape. The United States and China are now considered the two global empires of today. Many lay claim that global capitalism is itself an empire. In any case, one is tempted to claim that "empire" is more a verb (a participle!) than a noun: "empiring" has to do with the continued disempowerment of peoples and persons as manifest, for example, in white supremacy, male sexism, economic oppression, and ecological destruction. "Empiring" and empowering are polar opposites.

But there is more. Between these polar opposites, between the imperial master and the "subaltern," between the center and the margins, lies a creative "hybrid" space. It is here that the discourses of both the dominant culture and the subaltern are worked out in relation to each other as a mode of coexistence. As a central concept in postcolonial criticism, "hybridity" refers to this ambivalent space between accommodation and resistance. The Indian-born Harvard professor Homi K. Bhabha describes hybridity as the "sign" that indicates "the productivity of colonial power, its shifting forces and fixities" and, at the same time, reveals the "strategies of subversion that turn the gaze of the discriminated back upon the eye of power" (1994, 159–60). Hybridity, in other words, testifies to the fact that subjugated peoples are never rendered entirely passive (unless they are exterminated). The marginalized often make use of the intellectual and literary forms developed by the dominant culture, not simply by appropriating them, but also by transforming them in ways that make space for their own agency.

The Hybridity of Royal Propaganda

The same goes for the dominant culture's use of marginalized discourse. Imperial powers often engage subject peoples in ways that draw from the subject people's own symbols and patterns of discourse to (re)authorize their dominance, while also acknowledging the limits of their own political constructions. A spectacular example is the Cyrus Cylinder, an inscription placed in the foundations of the city wall of Babylon shortly after the Persian king's conquest of the city in October of 539 BCE. Below is an excerpt:

> I am Cyrus, king of the world, great king, mighty king, king of Babylon, king of the lands of Sumer and Akkad, king of the four quarters of the universe. . . . After entering Babylon in peace, amidst joy and jubilation I made the royal palace the centre of my rule. The great lord Marduk, who loves Babylon, with great magnanimity, established (it) as (my) destiny, and I sought to worship him each day. My teeming army paraded about Babylon in peace. . . . I took great care to peacefully (protect) the city of Babylon and its cult places. . . . The great lord Marduk rejoiced in my deeds. Kindly he blessed me, Cyrus, the king, his worshipper, Cambyses, the offspring of my loins, and all of my troops, so that we could go about in peace and well-being. . . . I also gathered all their people and returned to them their habitations. And then at the command of Marduk, the great lord, I resettled all the gods of Sumer and Akkad. . . . May all the gods whom I have resettled in their sacred cities ask Marduk and Nabu each day for a long life for me and speak well of me to him; may they say to Marduk, my lord, that Cyrus, the king who worships you, and Cambyses, his son, . . . I settled all the people of Babylon who prayed for my kingship and all their lands in a peaceful place.[3]

The Cyrus Cylinder is royal propaganda through and through (Kuhrt 1983). While asserting himself as king of the "universe," Cyrus portrays himself not as a foreigner (i.e., Persian) but as Babylonian, practically a native and specifically as Babylon's savior. He is called by Marduk, no less. Here the Persian monarch deftly adopts Babylonian religion, specifically Marduk worship, to solidify his claim over Babylon, even though his native god is Ahura Mazda, the god of Zoroastrianism. Nevertheless, Cyrus and his successors claimed their right to rule Babylonia by virtue of Marduk. In the Cylinder, Cyrus recounts how he has restored the land: captive peoples are resettled; all the gods are returned to their sanctuaries; peace is restored. Cyrus has inaugurated a Pax Persica for the good of Babylonians, his subject peoples. But there is a catch hinted at in the Cylinder: Cyrus requests that "all the gods" beseech Marduk for "a long life for" him. A "long life" for Cyrus means a long life for the new empire, whose eventual extent was unprecedented in the world, far exceeding the Neo-Babylonian Empire. Moreover, the final petitions in the Cylinder acknowledge that the new empire depends on the cooperation of its resettled peoples for its existence.

The Cylinder, in short, illustrates well the self-proclaimed "benevolence" of colonial action. Similarly, the edict attributed to Cyrus in 2 Chronicles and Ezra has Cyrus authorizing the rebuilding of the temple by virtue of YHWH's authority.

> [2] Thus says King Cyrus of Persia: "YHWH, the God of heaven, has given me all the kingdoms of the earth and has charged me to build him a house at Jerusalem in Judah. [3] Any of those among you who are of his people—may their God be with them!—are now permitted to go up to Jerusalem in Judah and rebuild the house

---

3. Translation by Piotr Michalowski in Chavalas 2006, 428–29.

of YHWH, the God of Israel—he is the God who is in Jerusalem; [4] and let all survivors, in whatever place they reside, be assisted by the people of their place with silver and gold, with goods and with animals, besides freewill offerings for the house of God in Jerusalem." (Ezra 1:2–4; cf. 2 Chr. 36:22–23; Ezra 6:3–5)

Regardless of its historicity, which is questionable, the edict is crafted in such a way as to validate Cyrus's sovereign rule from the point of view of the exiles: it is YHWH, not Marduk and certainly not Ahura Mazda, who has blessed Cyrus with universal dominion and, in exchange, has commissioned him to release the captives to return home and rebuild the temple.

Such royal pronouncements, whether directed toward Babylonians or Jewish exiles, mark a merging of foreign imperial claims, on the one hand, and indigenous interests, on the other. Cyrus *chose* Marduk (and YHWH?) to *choose* him as king of the world, a hybridizing move that meets his subject peoples halfway. The emperor adopts the religion of his subject peoples for the purpose of advancing imperial interests throughout the land. As for the *other* side of the hybridized discourse, the books of Ezra and Nehemiah recount the slow and painful process of restoring order, from repairing Jerusalem's infrastructure to establishing social and religious stability. The chief protagonists in the accounts who bring about such order (i.e., Zerubbabel, Ezra, Nehemiah), not coincidentally, all come from Persia. From the imperial point of view, the restoration of order in Palestine serves to sustain the order of the regime, whose success lasted over two hundred years.

Civil Disobedience in Exodus

The complex work of negotiation between the aims of imperial power and the strategies of survival on the part of subject peoples can give rise to new forms of cultural discourse and practice, forms that cannot be predicted, let alone dictated, by those who wield imperial control. A certain kind of discourse that flourishes within such creative, hybrid space is that of "mimicry," which "marks those moments of civil disobedience within the discipline of civility; signs of spectacular resistance" (Bhabha 1994, 172). Mimicry both discloses "the ambivalence of colonial discourse" and "disrupts its authority" (126).

Although not a particularly subtle example of mimicry, one thinks of Shiphrah and Puah, the first to commit civil disobedience in the Bible, in Exod. 1:15–21. These two midwives do not protest outright, thereby defying Egyptian hegemony. Rather through duplicity and "sly civility" they perform their own successful "defensive warfare" (see Bhabha 1994, 172). The two women, moreover, not only lie in order to disrupt imperial ambitions to commit genocide; they also demonstrate all too well the fine line between "mimicry and mockery" (123): Egyptian women are just not as "vigorous" as their Hebrew counterparts (wink).

A Subversive Lament

Psalm 137, a communal lament, performs a more subtle act of mimicry against imperial designs.

[1] By the rivers of Babylon, there we sat and also wept,
     as we remembered Zion.
[2] Upon the poplars there we hung our lyres,
       [3] for there our captors asked us for sounds of song, our mockers[4] for mirth:
         "Sing to us one of the songs of Zion!"
[4] How shall we sing YHWH's song in a foreign land?
[5] If I forget you, O Jerusalem, then may my right hand fail;
[6] May my tongue cleave to my palate if I fail to remember you,
     if I do not elevate Jerusalem above my chief joy.
[7] Remember, YHWH, the Edomites on the day of Jerusalem,
     how they cried, "Tear it down, tear it down to its foundations!"
[8] O daughter Babylon, you devastator,[5]
     how fortunate is the one who repays you in kind
       what you have dealt out to us.
[9] How fortunate is the one who seizes
     and shatters your infants against the rock. (AT)

An imprecatory or cursing psalm, Ps. 137 articulates rage against imperial violence in disturbingly graphic terms (vv. 8–9). But there is more to this psalm than simply a fantasy of revenge. There is also subversive mimicry. Rodney Sadler argues that what is going on is akin to the subtle subversion illustrated in the African American slave story of "colored Pompey," composed by Peter Randolph (ca. 1825–97), a former slave.

> I could only think . . . of the man who owned colored Pompey. This slave-holder was a great fighter (as most of them are), and had prepared himself for the contest with great care, and wished to know how he looked; so he said, "Pompey, how do I look?" "Oh, massa, *mighty.*" "What do you mean by 'mighty,' Pompey?" "Why, massa, you look noble." "What do you mean by 'noble'?" "Why, sar, you look just like one *lion.*" "Why, Pompey, where have you ever seen a lion?" "I seen one down in yonder field the other day, massa." "Pompey, you foolish fellow, that was a *jackass.*" "Was it, massa? Well, you look just like him." (Randolph 1999, 65)

The story is a masterpiece of subtle subversion. A "great fighter" inquires of his slave regarding his physique. Pompey showers him with compliments, but his master is not satisfied as he chides Pompey's alleged lack of knowledge. But no. Pompey's presumed ignorance actually "functions as his shield" to effect a "momentary reversal of the power dynamics" (Sadler 2014, 451). "In the end," Sadler concludes, "Pompey's story is a poignant example of how the oppressed 'playfully' resist in situations where they are otherwise completely disempowered" (451). It is, to borrow from postcolonial analysis, mimicry at its subversive best.

Sadler argues that Ps. 137 functions in much the same way. The Babylonian taskmasters taunt a group of exiles, requesting them to sing a song of Zion, a song that celebrates Zion's majesty and inviolability, an exercise in humiliation. But the psalmist does not

---

4. This word is difficult since it is a *hapax legomenon*. One plausible solution is to derive the word (noun?) from *hll III* ("make a mockery"), which fits nicely in context. But this is far from certain. See the discussion in *HALOT* 1700–1701.

5. Read *haššôdĕdâ* for MT *haššĕdûdâ*, "devastated one."

revert to passive weeping or painful silence. Rather, a song is sung, one that calls upon a dramatic reversal of power, whereby the victors become the victims of imperial violence. It is a song whose subversive impact would have been missed by the Babylonian captors who may not have understood Hebrew well enough to see through the song's "aural allusions" that phonetically mimic (!) the language of a Zion song (Sadler 2014, 453–56).

Daniel and Divine Sovereignty

Another example of mimicry is found in the first six chapters of the book of Daniel, which adapt the genre of the court tale, a Neo-Assyrian (i.e., imperial) genre, for the use of subtle subversion. The figure of Daniel is profiled as a model for Jews living in the Diaspora who must find that "sweet spot" between accommodation to and resistance against imperial domination (Newsom 2014, 15–16; Smith-Christopher 1996, 20–21). The rulers as portrayed in Daniel, for example, succumb to fits of rage yet are also repentant and remorseful; they are subject to humiliation yet also appointed by God to rule "over the kingdom of mortals" (4:17 [14 MT]). Moreover, nestled within the court-tale genre is the dream of the four-kingdom statue, which foretells the cataclysmic demise of all earthly empires in one shattering blow by the unhewn "stone" that "became a great mountain and filled the whole earth" (Dan. 2:35). The dream as interpreted by Daniel is vivid testimony to divine sovereignty ultimately trumping all earthly sovereignties, a case of imperial subversion undertaken through divine imperial victory. This can cut both ways. While the allegorical dream depicts the destruction of earthly empires, its context within the court tales of Dan. 1–6 can also serve to ideologically stabilize "the *system* of Gentile imperial rule . . . by showing how it can be consistent with claiming the ultimate sovereignty of the God of the Jews" (Newsom 2014, 16). God's sovereign rule, in other words, is demonstrated not only in the destruction of empires but also in the choice of certain Gentile kings to rule "over the kingdom of mortals" (4:17 [14]). While destabilizing earthly empires, divine sovereignty can also serve to legitimize foreign imperial rule. When it comes to hybridity, there is neither pure accommodation nor pure resistance.

The power of postcolonial analysis lies in its capacity to reframe interpretive considerations within the context of inequity, particularly the kind of inequity generated by "empiring." *What does it mean to read texts as acts of negotiation meant to foster subject formation and agency in the face of oppression? Do such texts favor resistance, accommodation, or more often something in between, something "hybrid"? Can texts, depending on how they are interpreted, cover the spectrum between resistance and accommodation? Can they be hijacked for imperial purposes as much as they can be marshaled to motivate resistance?*

GENESIS TEXTS

Examining the creation texts from a postcolonial perspective calls for acknowledging first and foremost that even these texts were not composed in a vacuum; they too were codified and read in a time of empires, whether they are to be placed in exilic or postexilic historical settings. While precise historical dating of either Gen. 1 or Gen. 2–3 is far from certain, it is safe to say that both existed in their near final form by the time of the Persian period (550–330 BCE), more specifically between the sixth and fifth centuries (see chap. 12 above). As a frame of reference, we will examine these two texts in light of Persia's imperial ambitions.

First, a little bit of history from a colonial perspective. The Neo-Babylonian Empire (626–539 BCE)—responsible for destroying Jerusalem in 586 BCE, including the temple, and for deporting a substantial part of its population—was defeated in 539 BCE by Persian forces at the site of Opis, east of the Tigris. The Persian king Cyrus the Great (Cyrus II) entered Babylon peacefully and presented himself as the true king of Babylon.

What was left of Judah after the Neo-Babylonian period was developed through Persian support and control into a "secondary state," the province of Yehud, whose boundaries were significantly smaller than the former southern kingdom. As part of the Persian satrapy of *Eber-Nari* (Akkadian; Aramaic ʿăbar-năhărâ, "Beyond the River," as in Ezra 4:10), Yehud was allowed to function semiautonomously as long as it provided requisite financial and labor support to the empire. Under Cyrus, emigration from Babylonia to Yehud began slowly and sporadically. Once a critical mass of immigrants from Babylonia settled by the end of the sixth century BCE, tensions flared between the newly arrived and the those who never were exiled, the majority of the population prior to the Neo-Babylonian period. Such conflict thwarted initial plans to rebuild the temple, even though Cyrus had permitted the rebuilding in 538 BCE. It was not until 520 that serious work on the temple began, with the prophetic support of Haggai and Zechariah as well as the imperial support of the new Persian king Darius I (522–486 BCE).

Although there may have been plans to restore the province to some vestige of the Davidic "empire" under the appointed governors of Sheshbazzar and Zerubbabel (Ezra 2:2–5:14; Hag. 2:21–23), such aspirations never panned out. Instead, after a period of several decades of Persian reign, the province of Yehud became locally and primarily led by the high priest, descended from Jeshua/Joshua, with the rebuilt temple (the Second Temple) now fully operational by 515 BCE (Ezra 4–6). The temple not only solidified worship of YHWH in Yehud; it also served as a symbol of Persian domination (Berquist 1995, 235). The new temple served a number of functions in addition to the renewal of worship, including financial administration and imperial governance. The temple "was a work of the people as well as a work of the Persian imperial government" (63), in other words, a centralized hybrid space for religious and social order for the fledgling province.

Genesis 1

In the face of empire, the concern for Sabbath, the culmination of the creation account, is set in stark relief. Sabbath practice served as a marker of communal identity, a practice that likely originated during the time of exile in Babylon, along with circumcision, another identity marker. That such practices took root on foreign soil suggests that they functioned in part as survival strategies, fostering communal cohesion in response to Babylonian pressures to assimilate. The same goes for the Priestly ethos that pervades Gen. 1, which frames creation as a cosmic temple (see chap. 8 above). It is possible that such a priestly picture of creation served to relativize or replace the Babylonian (and/or Persian) cultic system by elevating the Priestly worldview to a cosmic level. Creation is claimed by Israel's God ('ĕlōhîm), not by Marduk or Ahura Mazda.

In the shift from Babylonian to Persian imperial regimes, and with it the change in social status from captivity to release for the Judean exiles, Gen. 1 can be read as an account of transition, specifically a cosmic transition from disorder to order and from emptiness to plenitude, made possible through cosmic collaboration. The waters and the earth are co-opted by God to bring about life in all its multitude and variety. The divine assembly, too, is enlisted to create, specifically to fashion humankind in God's image. Through it all God acts as the cosmic emperor, the King of the universe, issuing edicts of creativity to "his" subjects in order to structure and populate the cosmic domains of life.

From a postcolonial perspective, the goals of creation and the means by which they are reached may well reflect the pressing need among the (former) exiles to restore the land for the sake of their livelihood, to repopulate it as well as to reestablish order, all done through God's imperial decrees. In Gen. 1 the domains of land, sea, and sky are, in effect, *colonized* with life. Analogously, perhaps, Yehud is to be colonized with erstwhile exiles with the Persian Empire's blessing. It is easy to imagine a colonial edge to the imperative blessing "Be fruitful and multiply and fill . . ." (Gen. 1:22, 28). Indeed, Gen. 1:28 is "one of the most significant biblical texts in the development of colonialism" (Brett 2008, 32), construed as a "divine charter for colonization" by the likes of John Locke and David Livingstone (20). Is Gen. 1, then, a form of imperial mimicry writ cosmically? One wonders.

Much has been said about the "democratization" of human dignity through the "image of God" in creation. What was often deployed to designate the king as a divine image is now universalized to designate humanity as a whole. Every individual, male and female, thus stands tall with royal stature, each bearing inalienable worth and identity, each displaying an imperial aura, as it were—clearly a "liberating image" for former exiles (Middleton 2005). Now they are masters of their own domains, called to exercise dominion to reestablish order.

But the postcolonial critic must ask, What about the *others* who were inhabiting the land of Palestine during the Babylonian exile? The land was never empty; it remained populated by people who were never exiled as they continued to eke out their living in the wake of Babylonian and now Persian hegemony. Their voices can be heard in Lamentations and in parts of Third Isaiah. See, for example, the following passage:

> [1] Thus says YHWH:
> "Heaven is my throne and the earth is my footstool;
> what is the house that you would build for me,
>   and what is my resting place?
> [2] All these things my hand has made,
>   and so all these things are mine," says YHWH.
> "But this is the one to whom I will look,
> to the humble and contrite in spirit,
>   [the one] who trembles at my word.
> [3] Whoever slaughters an ox is like one who kills a human being." (Isa. 66:1–3)

One can easily imagine this text being marshaled against any ambitious plan to rebuild the temple in Jerusalem. According to Isa. 66, a temple is not needed; it is rendered obsolete, along with its sacrificial system, by the ultimate temple that is creation itself, both heaven and earth. The message seems compatible with Gen. 1, which also depicts creation as a temple. But the Priestly account does not make any polemical move that could be construed as anti-temple. Far from it: Gen. 1 launches a narrative trajectory that culminates with the completion of the tabernacle in Exod. 40, the forerunner to the temple. In comparison with Isa. 66, then, Gen. 1 proves to be more of an imperial, if not hybrid, text.

Is Gen. 1 good news for the subaltern? Was it good news for the people of Yehud? It is impossible to answer one way or another with certainty, given the social and religious complexities rapidly emerging during this turbulent time of settlement, repopulation, and conflict. Good news for whom? Many of the returning exiles, arriving with imperial blessing, clearly had restoration on their minds, including restoration of the temple and the priestly order. Genesis 1 could have served as a cosmic paradigm for establishing such order, a cosmic *imperial* paradigm of communal order. As for the indigenous folk, those left behind during the exile, such a cosmic paradigm might have been felt as an imperial burden. The "people of the land" got along just fine without the Judean elite wielding their power and without the Jerusalem temple demanding costly forms of religious observance, that is, until the exiles started returning with texts authorizing their ascendancy, including Ezra's Torah, which likely included Gen. 1. One wonders.[6]

Nevertheless, the power of Gen. 1 is by no means limited to its production or use in the imperial context of the Persian period. If it facilitated imperial interests in its early "career," it could have later moved favorably toward the interests of the nonelite. The God of Genesis is no conquering tyrant but a cosmic collaborator. The emphasis on all humanity created in "the image of God" is conveyed without hierarchical distinction and exclusion. But is such language essentialist? Perhaps, but it may be the kind of *strategic* essentializing that (ultimately) is meant to be inclusive and egalitarian, or at least should be. In its own way, the divine edict to be "fruitful and multiply" could be a move toward realizing the flourishing of all life. Yet the postcolonial critic who is ecologically aware could easily ask whether such a mandate has an imperialistic cast from the perspective of creation (see chap. 16 above). Can the (nonhuman) subaltern speak?

Genesis 2–3

The agrarian God of the garden is quite different from the cosmic king in Gen. 1. YHWH Elohim is a hands-on deity, planting a garden and forming the *ʾādām* from the loose soil. In the vast Mesopotamian hierarchy of divine deities, YHWH Elohim might be seen as a candidate for membership among the lesser gods (the Igigi), who in the Mesopotamian

---

6. One wonders whether Isa. 66:1–3 is an attempt to turn the cosmic temple program of Gen. 1 against itself. If Gen. 1 functioned, in part, to give support for rebuilding the temple in the Persian period, Isa. 66:1–3 deployed the notion of God's cosmic temple precisely to muster resistance *against* building a temple. Or the converse might be the case: Gen. 1 adopted the cosmic temple imagery developed in Isaiah in order to promote Priestly order in the land. Either way, cosmic temple imagery became a matter of contestation in the Persian period.

tale of Atrahasis attempt to rebel against their divine overlord, Enlil, because of the hard work of canal construction (see Dalley 1989, 9–13). Not so in Eden. God works unbegrudgingly in the dirt.

This anthropomorphic figuration of the divine in Gen. 2 is distinctly unimperial. God is a farmer who puts the ʾādām in charge of a garden and even provides a partner. For the agrarian listener, this characterization of God establishes a sense of solidarity, even partnership, between God and the human being, who is created to work the soil (2:15b). Moreover, the man and the woman are created as solidary (as opposed to solitary) individuals; they are mutually interconnected biologically and vocationally. They are, put simply, fully "with" each other (3:6, 12). But are they essentialized with respect to their respective geneses? Yes, the man, as the ʾādām, is essentialized at the moment of his creation (2:7). He is inextricably tied to the land. His vocation as a worker of the soil is written into his "genetic" identity, as it were, groundling that he is. The fact that he continues to be referenced as the ʾādām after his genderized transformation is testimony to his essentialized identity. It turns out, after all, to be his proper name (4:25; 5:1–5). But it is not his burden to bear until he is punished for disobedience (3:19). The woman is not named until after the "fall": she is "Eve, because she was the mother of all living" (3:20). She bears the burdens and privileges of maternity.

But in the beginning, both the man and the woman are simply characterized by common "bone" and "flesh," that is, they share common physical characteristics, while nothing is said, upfront at least, about subordination. Could it be that life *in* the garden is untainted by "othering"? Perhaps. In any event, the punishment that follows the couple's act of disobedience changes everything, particularly God's pronouncement against the woman in Gen. 3:16b. Has the woman now become "other" to the man: subordinate, objectified, and essentialized as inferior? At the very least, "Eve" has been frequently construed that way in the course of the text's reception. Through the discourse of punishment, the Yahwist has committed "epistemic violence," thrusting the woman into the patriarchal world of male domination while turning her "desire" against her. In the narrative, the woman is caught in a double bind: her unwelcomed subordination and her desire for the source of her subordination. Resistance seems futile.

The final outcome of the story depicts an exile of forced migration, and it begins with expulsion from the garden into the harsh world of painful subsistence for both the man and the woman. It is a world that proves to be increasingly violent. In the following chapter, Cain kills Abel, whose very name (vapor) suggests subalterity, and violence only escalates thereafter. With fratricide as the first official instance of "sin" (4:7), the narrator claims that violence begins at home before it spreads. The epistemic violence of the curse leads to physical violence among human beings to the point of near annihilation. Along that line, the Tower of Babel story (Gen. 11:1–9) could be construed as an ambitious resistance movement on the part of human beings to breach the boundary of the divine even as it ends in further splintering of the human community.

How does God come out in all of this? God the gardener, who delighted in the intimacy of the garden community, strolling cheerfully during the comfortable part of the day, turns into God the evictor, who thrusts the human tenants out into a world of hardship and conflict, a world where life itself becomes a burden laced, to be sure, with a measure of blessing. Has God become an imperial tyrant? It is a fair question, coming from a postcolonial perspective, and from a theological perspective too. But both perspectives might conclude, if there can be a conclusion, by lifting up the garden and life therein as vision of life together *without* violence, without exclusion, without the curse of "othering." That may be saying more than the Yahwist ever intended or imagined, but that's perfectly fine. Let the garden vision of flourishing life, human and nonhuman, be the vision of justice and reconciliation that motivates and sustains resistance against the "polarities of power and prejudice."

The words of Homi Bhabha are appropriate to conclude our discussion on postcolonial criticism, words that offer a pragmatic rationale for keeping a critical eye on, and a resilient stance against, the consequences of "empiring":

> I do want to make graphic what it means to survive, to produce, to labor and to create, within a world-system whose major economic impulses and cultural investments are pointed in a direction away from you. . . . Such neglect can be a deeply negating experience, oppressive and exclusionary, and it spurs you to resist the polarities of power and prejudice, to reach beyond and behind the invidious narratives of center and periphery. (1994, xi)

Critically asking what is central and what is peripheral in the biblical text may be the beginning of exposing and resisting the invidious narratives of power that beset the world today.

BIBLIOGRAPHY FOR CHAPTER 19

Albertz, Rainer. 2003. *Israel in Exile: The History and Literature of the Sixth Century B.C.E.* Translated by David Green. Studies in Biblical Literature 3. Atlanta: Society of Biblical Literature.

Auga, Ulrike. 2014. "Resistance and the Radical Social Imaginary: A Genealogy from Eastern European Dissidence to New Social Movements; Connecting the Debates between Activism and Postcolonial, Post-secular and Queer Epistemology and Theology." In *Resistance and Visions: Postcolonial, Post-secular and Queer Contributions to Theology and the Study of Religions*, edited by Ulrike Auga et al., 5–30. Journal of the European Society of Women in Theological Research 22. Leuven: Peeters.

Bailey, Randall C., Tat-siong Benny Liew, and Fernando F. Segovia, eds. 2009. *They Were All Together in One Place? Toward Minority Biblical Criticism.* Semeia Studies 57. Atlanta: Society of Biblical Literature.

Berquist, Jon L. 1995. *Judaism in Persia's Shadow: A Social and Historical Approach.* Minneapolis: Fortress Press.

Bhabha, Homi K. 1994. *The Location of Culture.* Abingdon: Routledge.

Boer, Roland, ed. 2013. *Postcolonialism and the Hebrew Bible: The Next Step.* Semeia Studies 70. Atlanta: Society of Biblical Literature.

Brett, Mark G. 2008. *Decolonizing God: The Bible in the Tide of Empire.* The Bible in the Modern World 16. Sheffield: Sheffield Phoenix Press.

Carter, Warren. 2013. "Postcolonial Biblical Criticism." In *New Meanings for Ancient Texts*, edited by Steven L. McKenzie and John Kaltner, 97–116. Louisville, KY: Westminster John Knox Press.

Chavalas, Mark W., ed. 2006. *The Ancient Near East: Historical Sources in Translation.* Malden, MA: Blackwell.

Dalley, Stephanie. 1989. "Atrahasis." In *Myths from Mesopotamia: Creation, the Flood, Gilgamesh and Others*, 9–38. World's Classics. Oxford: Oxford University Press.

Donaldson, Laura, and Kwok Pui-lan, eds. 2002. *Postcolonialism, Feminism and Religious Discourse*. New York and London: Routledge.

Dube, Musa W. 2000. *Postcolonial Feminist Interpretation of the Bible*. St. Louis: Chalice Press.

Holliday, Adrian, John Kullman, and Martin Hyde. 2010. *Intercultural Communication: An Advanced Resource Book*. London: Routledge.

Kuhrt, Amélie. 1983. "The Cyrus Cylinder and Achaemenid Imperial Policy." *JSOT* 25:83–97.

Middleton, J. Richard. 2005. *The Liberating Image: The* imago Dei *in Genesis 1*. Grand Rapids: Brazos Press.

Newsom, Carol A., with Brennan W. Breed. 2014. *Daniel: A Commentary*. OTL. Louisville, KY: Westminster John Knox Press.

Raheb, Mitri. 2014. *Faith in the Face of Empire: The Bible through Palestinian Eyes*. Maryknoll, NY: Orbis Books.

Randolph, Peter. 1999. "Plantation Churches: Visible and Invisible." In *African American Religious History: A Documentary Witness*, edited by Milton C. Sernett, 63–75. 2nd ed. Durham, NC: Duke University Press.

Sadler, Ronald S., Jr. 2014. "Singing a Subversive Song: Psalm 137 and 'Colored Pompey.'" In *The Oxford Handbook of the Psalms*, edited by William P. Brown, 447–58. New York: University of Oxford Press.

Said, Edward W. 1979. *Orientalism*. New York: Vintage.

———. 1993. *Culture and Imperialism*. New York: Vintage.

Smith-Christopher, Daniel L. 1996. "Daniel." In *New Interpreter's Bible*, edited by Leander E. Keck et al., 7:19–152. Nashville: Abingdon.

———. 2015. *Micah*. OTL. Louisville, KY: Westminster John Knox Press.

Spivak, Gayatri Chakravorti. 1988. "Can the Subaltern Speak?" In *Marxism and the Interpretation of Culture*, edited by Cary Nelson and Lawrence Grossberg, 271–313. Urbana and Chicago: University of Illinois Press.

Sugirtharajah, R. S. 2002. *Postcolonialism Criticism and Biblical Interpretation*. Oxford: Oxford University Press.

———, ed. 2006a. *Voices from the Margin: Interpreting the Bible in the Third World*. 3rd ed. Maryknoll, NY: Orbis Books.

———. 2006b. "Postcolonial Biblical Interpretation." In *Voices from the Margin: Interpreting the Bible in the Third World*, edited by R. S. Sugirtharajah, 64–84. 3rd ed. Maryknoll, NY: Orbis Books.

———, ed. 2008. *Still at the Margins: Biblical Scholarship Fifteen Years after the Voices from the Margin*. London: T&T Clark.

20

Minority

> My parents loved the soil, the earth, the outside, and in their garden I saw the freedom they felt with it. The garden announced to them and the world that they were absolutely free to be themselves.
>
> *Willie James Jennings*[1]

This chapter follows naturally from the previous two chapters simply because the reading strategies discussed here also have to do with interpreting the Bible through the lens of inequity and thus power. Minority criticism addresses the multiple locations in which biblical interpretation takes place, particularly in North America and specifically in places not dominated by "majority" interpreters, meaning white and mostly male interpreters. Minority (or "minoritized") voices in biblical studies include, but are by no means limited to, African American, Asian American, Native American, and Latino/a interpreters.

The term "minority" is often associated with race and/or ethnicity. Derived from the 1997 Office of Management and Budget standards, the United States Census Bureau identifies and defines five categories of "racial ethnicity":

White—A person having origins in any of the original peoples of Europe, the Middle East, or North Africa

Black or African American—A person having origins in any of the Black racial groups of Africa

American Indian or Alaska Native—A person having origins in any of the original peoples of North and South America (including Central America) and who maintains tribal affiliation or community attachment

Asian—A person having origins in any of the original peoples of the Far East, Southeast Asia, or the Indian subcontinent including, for example, Cambodia, China, India, Japan, Korea, Malaysia, Pakistan, the Philippine Islands, Thailand, and Vietnam

Native Hawaiian or Other Pacific Islander—A person having origins in any of the original peoples of Hawaii, Guam, Samoa, or other Pacific Islands[2]

---

1. Jennings 2010, 2.
2. See http://www.census.gov/topics/population/race/about.html.

Reading critically, what do you find missing from the list? What do you find lumped together? Are some categories too general? Others too specific? Where do you find yourself on the list? Some have suggested a distinction between non-Hispanic white and Hispanic white.[3] Others might contend that placing persons of Arab descent (Middle East) under a category that also covers those of European ancestry is too broad. In any event, what actually are "racial" categories? The Census Bureau states the following:

> The racial categories included in the census questionnaire generally reflect a social definition of race recognized in this country and not an attempt to define race biologically, anthropologically, or genetically. In addition, it is recognized that the categories of the race item include racial and national origin or sociocultural groups. People may choose to report more than one race to indicate their racial mixture, such as "American Indian" and "White." People who identify their origin as Hispanic, Latino, or Spanish may be of any race.[4]

The Census Bureau recognizes that such "racial categories" are neither exhaustive nor mutually exclusive. According to the Pew Research Center, the Census Bureau for the 2020 Census is considering expanding the categories to include White; Hispanic, Latino, or Spanish Origin; Black or African American; Asian; American Indian or Alaska Native; Middle Eastern or North African; Native Hawaiian or Other Pacific Islander; Other.[5]

The fluidity and diversity of such categories indicate that "race" or "ethnicity" is a socially constructed designation. A lot of interracial or in-between space exists among these categories. Moreover, the ideological deployment of racial categories has led to devastating effects in the lives of people through the institutionalized practices of discrimination. Racism is the result, whereby population groups become racially defined and deemed inferior. Consequently such groups, particularly people of color, are oppressed and excluded.

Because the term "race" is itself ideologically charged, I will use the language of "minority," in line with a recent volume of essays on "minority biblical criticism" (Bailey, Liew, and Segovia 2009a).[6] Being a "minority" is the result of "minoritization," which has not so much to do with numbers as with the unequal distribution of power.[7] "Minoritization" is "the process of unequal valorization of population groups, yielding dominant and minority formations and relations, within the context, and through the apparatus, of a nation or state as the result of migration, whether voluntary or coerced" (Bailey, Liew, and Segovia 2009b, ix). Like the social and economic disparities that exist between the empire and the

---

3. Which itself is too narrow for Hispanics or Latinos/as. According to Barreto, the census assumes that Latinos/as would identify themselves as "Hispanic" ethnically but as "white" or "black" racially, excluding those who would identify themselves as Asians or Native Americans (2014, 76). But see the following description below.

4. See http://www.census.gov/topics/population/race/about.html.

5. See http://www.pewresearch.org/fact-tank/2015/06/18/census-considers-new-approach-to-asking-about -race -by-not-using-the-term-at-all/.

6. This collection has as its aim not only to delineate the broad contours of "minority biblical criticism" but also to forge alliances among a diverse array of minority interpreters, including African American, Asian American, and Latino/a critics. Lamentably, little is said about Native American biblical interpretation (cf. Bailey, Liew, and Segovia 2009b, 24).

7. According to latest projections, by 2044 "non-Hispanic whites" will be in the minority, displaced by those of "Hispanic origin" and African Americans. See http://www.usnews.com/news/articles/2015/07/06/its-official -the-us-is-becoming-a-minority-majority-nation.

subaltern (see chap. 19), the disparities between the majority and the minority have to do with who is dominant over whom. The harsh legacies of slavery, internment, forced migration, and segregation continue to minoritize certain groups of people in America, particularly African Americans, not to mention impoverishment, the prison system, corrupt legal systems, job discrimination, and environmental injustice.

In terms of race and/or ethnic origin, minoritized communities must operate fundamentally with a "double consciousness," a phrase originated in 1903 by the great African American sociologist and historian W. E. B. Du Bois:

> It is a peculiar sensation, this double-consciousness, this sense of always looking at one's self through the eyes of others, of measuring one's soul by the tape of a world that looks on in amused contempt and pity. One ever feels his two-ness,— an American, a Negro; two souls, two thoughts, two unreconciled strivings; two warring ideals in one dark body, whose dogged strength alone keeps it from being torn asunder. (1994, 2)

Being both American and Black, a member of both the dominant and the minority cultures: this burden of double identity, according to Du Bois, can also be a strength, an opportunity for merging the "double self into a better and truer self" (2), or as David Levering Lewis in his biography of Du Bois aptly coins, a "proud, enduring hyphenation" (2009, 281). A "hyphenated" existence is what one could call a form of hybrid existence.

While able to traffic between two (or more) cultures, communities of color in particular continue to be marginalized, pushed to the periphery of the center of economic and social power, all structured to ensure white access and privilege. Nevertheless, it is there in that space of marginality where creativity can flourish, offering "the possibility of radical perspectives from which to see and create, to imagine alternative, new worlds" (hooks 1990, 341). Again, this sense of "marginality" sounds similar to "hybridity" (see chap. 19). Indeed, there is something distinctly "imperial" about the dominant culture in America. It is called "white supremacy," and it remains alive and well. Racial injustice is America's original sin, "still the black man's burden and the white man's shame" (King 1968b, 270).

As North America continues to grow in diversity, so the "double consciousness" of minorities has become more a "multiple" consciousness. To be a minority person, to adapt an observation by cultural analyst Mary Louise Pratt, is "to live in more than one [system]. . . . The image for [minority] is . . . a multiplying of the self" (Bailey, Liew, and Segovia 2009b, 8). Such multiplication constitutes the formation of various centers of perception, self-expression, and creativity within a larger culture structured around a dominant center.

Not all minorities, of course, are the same, and neither are the members within each minority group. The experiences of internment for Japanese Americans and of enslavement and segregation for African Americans are wholly different, but they are not unrelated, given the exercise of white supremacy in bringing about both. Racial stereotyping (or "racialization") is varied across minority groups, although each instance of it has been deployed for the purpose of discrimination and social oppression. The so-called model minority stereotype, in particular, has been used against Asian Americans to exclude them from affirmative action programs, while at the same time "shaming" other minorities

(Bailey, Liew, and Segovia 2009b, 11n5; Yee 2009, 128–30). The cultural formation of well-defined racial-ethnic groups that, in turn, minimizes differences within them is frequently underscored by a divide-and-conquer strategy implemented by the dominant culture. Among Asian Americans, there are Japanese Americans, Filipinos, Southeast Asians, Chinese Americans, and Korean Americans, all in various classes and generations of living in American society. The same goes for Latinos/as in North America: there is a wide division between Mexican Americans and those who have roots in Central America, which comprise different nationalities, cultures, and ethnicities. Among African Americans, there are those of Caribbean descent in addition to those who trace their lineage directly to Africa, itself a continent of diverse cultures.

All three population groups came to the United States in different ways and circumstances: Africans came to America as slaves. Asians came as immigrants, many as indentured servants early on. Latinos/as came initially as conquerors and empire builders and more recently as immigrants, some as migrant workers. And Native Americans or the indigenous peoples of the Americas (i.e., the pre-Columbian inhabitants of North and South America) did not come at all but instead suffered the arrival and domination of others, including their containment on reservations at the hands of the U.S. government. Nevertheless, certain connections exist within the wealth of differences among these groups: "A Vietnamese American worker in the garment industry may have more in common with a Latina household maid or an African American cabdriver than a Japanese American Ivy Leaguer" (Bailey, Liew, and Segovia 2009b, 18). What they all share in common is the experience of suffering the "ravages of white supremacy" (21).

MINORITIES AND THE BIBLE

The various histories of minoritized groups with the Bible are equally complicated and intertwined. Associated with white power, the Bible was used as a tool of oppression and yet remained an object of appeal and attraction for enslaved Africans. Since the text was associated with white supremacy, oppressed groups knew that to gain power "they would have to gain access to this text and give allegiance to it" (Bailey, Liew, and Segovia 2009b, 21). It was the "Good Book," the "Talking Book," and the "Poison Book" all in one (Callahan 2006). No wonder. In the hands of plantation owners and abolitionists, the Bible was used to justify both slavery and emancipation. Biblical interpretation by minoritized groups in America became "both a means of assimilation and a means of resistance to oppression" (Bailey, Liew, and Segovia 2009b, 21). A "canon within the canon" has been and remains unavoidable, as it is for anyone, oppressed and dominant alike. The exodus account, the story of Israel's liberation from Egyptian hegemony, has been a foundational text for many oppressed groups, particularly for African Americans. But that too is not without its challenges from other interpretive vantage points, such as one shared by Native Americans who see the "God of Liberation" inextricably tied to the "God of Dispossession" and genocide (Warrior 1991). All in all, the diverse ways minoritized groups have met the challenges of suffering and surviving in the United States continue to sharpen their hermeneutical lenses for interpreting biblical texts in context.

Key to minority biblical interpretation is the practice of contextualizing the text—of interpreting the biblical text in light of its ancient culture and history as well as in light of one's own culture and history. Composition and interpretation are seamlessly related. This rules out any claim of a universal, objective interpretation of the biblical text, for every interpretation is contextual, even as the biblical text is contextual. How might this work?. Through dialogue, the kind of dialogue that utilizes but also reaches beyond the analytic approaches such that one can evaluate their exegetical implications for minority as well as dominant communities. To reside only in analysis imposes a "screen of silence" for the sake of "objectivity and universality" (Bailey, Liew, and Segovia 2009b, 30). But to move beyond analysis you need to accept the invitation to pause and ponder who you are as a biblical interpreter, where you have come from, what are your places of belonging-ness, why you are engaging the biblical text, and for whom.

Minority biblical criticism demands *transparency* in the hermeneutical enterprise. Transparency cannot be done abstractly but is practiced concretely—personally, locally, culturally, as well as globally. Such transparency can itself be revealing, as much as the biblical text can be revelatory. Transparency shows that biblical criticism is not as straightforward and self-evident as one might think. Engaged biblical criticism can be "highly convoluted," immersed as it is "in differential relations and discursive frameworks of all sorts, yielding tensive and conflicting positions under a sense of critical engagement on and from all sides" (Bailey, Liew, and Segovia 2009b, 31). What stands out in this somewhat convoluted statement is its final phrase: "engagement on and from all sides." That is to say, "what is needed . . . is a diverse variety of readings, each one shaped and nuanced by the social status, the cultural baggage, and the historical experience of each reader" (García-Treto 2009, 71), minority *and* dominant, I might add.

Particular topics that minority critics lift up as experiential contexts for biblical inter-pretation include migration, exile and diaspora, borders and borderlands, minority and dominant groups, "othering" through ethnicization and racialization, and the ravages of global capitalism (Bailey, Liew, and Segovia 2009b, 30). Some of these themes resonate well when we consider, once again, the Genesis creation accounts in the light of various minoritized contexts.

GENESIS 1 IN AN AFRICAN AMERICAN CONTEXT

Creation in Gen. 1:2 begins in "darkness" (ḥōšek), and the first act of creation is "light" (v. 3). What, then, is the relation between "light" and "darkness"? One prevalent ten-dency is to view the "darkness" as something bad, evil even, which is then suppressed, contained, or dispelled (take your pick) by the creation of "light." Such negative connota-tions can easily bear racialized overtones, a racialization of primordial creation in which being Black is associated with darkness and whiteness with light. Such a metaphorical framework, writ globally, lent justification for the colonization of the "dark continent" by Europeans as they brought the "light" of Christianity to Africa. White superiority, moreover, continues to associate Blackness with evil and ignorance. Hence the element of "darkness" in Gen. 1 is often vilified.

The destructive cultural legacy of racial colonialism and discrimination prompts reexamination of such an exegetical assumption. Does "darkness" denote evil in Gen. 1? If it does, then darkness would have no place in God's creation, declared "very good" (1:31). But darkness does have its place. Light is created (or unleashed) and then "separated" from the darkness (1:4). Light does not destroy or dispel the darkness. Instead, light and darkness become integral parts of an alternating rhythm from which "day" and "night" are derived, thereby defining the very rhythm of creation.

The issue of racialization, however, is not that easy to resolve simply with careful exegetical examination. One could say, rightly so, that the elements of light and darkness, and from it "day" and "night," are "separate but equal" in God's creation. But such language derives from the language of racial segregation.[8] The issue challenges majority exegetes to be careful in the way they use language to talk about the biblical images of "light" and "dark." Darkness does not mean Blackness, and conversely light does not mean Whiteness.

One of the most significant passages in Gen. 1 for African Americans is Gen. 1:26–27, the creation of humanity in God's image, "a strong grounding motif for the universal worth of all humanity" (Sadler 2010, 71). A suggestive modern parallel is found in the famous poem by James Weldon Johnson (1871–1938),[9] "The Creation," a retelling of the creation of humanity according to Gen. 1 with imagery drawn from Gen. 2. It begins:

> And God stepped out on space,
> And He looked around and said:
> I'm lonely—
> I'll make me a world.

And so God created the universe in richly poetic fashion, occasionally punctuated by the divine exclamation, "That's good!" After all is created, God declares, "I'm lonely still." And so:

> Up from the bed of the river
> God scooped the clay;
> And by the bank of the river
> He kneeled him down;
> And there the great God Almighty . . .
> Like a mammy bending over her baby,
> Kneeled down in the dust
> Toiling over a lump of clay
> Till He shaped it in His own image;

8. The phrase points to a legal doctrine in U.S. constitutional law that justified segregation derived from an 1890 Louisiana law, which actually used the phrase "equal but separate." See https://en.wikipedia.org/wiki/Separate_but_equal.

9. James Weldon Johnson was an American author, educator, lawyer, diplomat, and civil rights activist. He was appointed by President Theodore Roosevelt as U.S. consul in Venezuela and Nicaragua from 1906 to 1913. In 1934 he became the first African American professor to teach at New York University and later was professor of creative literature and writing at Fisk University.

Then into it He blew the breath of life,
And man became a living soul.
Amen. Amen.[10]

Johnson's retelling of creation, including that of humanity, brings together elements from both Genesis accounts: "image" and "dust/clay." A "man" is created, endowed with God's "breath of life." But Johnson goes further than simply integrating the two stories. God's masculinized profile is mixed with the feminine: God is like "a mammy bending over her baby." In so doing, Johnson "playfully" ascribes "divinity to marginalized African American female flesh" (Sadler 2010, 71). Moreover, the intimate work of creation by God involves "toiling" and kneeling "down in the dust," recalling the hardship of manual labor but done with dignified resolve.

The "image of God" in Gen. 1, moreover, becomes critically important in Martin Luther King's discourse: "Man is a child of God made in His image, and therefore must be respected as such. Until men see this everywhere, until nations see this everywhere, we will be fighting wars" (1986a, 255). Human violence signals a tacit denial of this fundamental assertion about humanity's inviolable relationship to God.

This may sound applicable to each and every person, regardless of minority or majority status, but from an African American perspective it carries a critical significance in view of what has been done with another Genesis text, the "Curse of Ham/Canaan" in Gen. 9:18–27. Noah curses Ham (or Canaan in an earlier version) because he has been sexually violated when he was drunk (v. 22). Once Noah discovers this, he utters a curse against Canaan.

"Cursed be Canaan;
    lowest of slaves shall he be to his brothers."
He also said, "Blessed by YHWH my God be Shem;
    and let Canaan be his slave.
May God make space for Japheth,
    and let him live in the tents of Shem;
    and let Canaan be his slave." (9:25–27)

This curse story is intended as an etiology that justifies the Canaanites' servitude and loss of land to the Israelites ("Shem"). But this passage was interpreted in the seventeenth and eighteenth centuries by Euro-Americans to justify the oppression of African peoples during the slave trade and thereafter. The "sons of Ham" were regarded as African, thereby providing theological rationale for enslaving Africans (Sadler 2010, 73). In conjunction with this text, moreover, the "mark" that God placed upon Cain to protect him from being murdered after committing fratricide (Gen. 4:15) was often interpreted to mean that God turned Cain Black. Here, too, black skin was deemed the result of God's curse, even though the text makes quite clear that the "mark," whatever the author had in mind,[11] was meant to provide protection. But for whites, from slaveholders to segregationists, the

10. Johnson 1927.
11. For the interpretive possibilities, see Mroczek 2015.

"mark" provides justification to dehumanize blacks. In both cases, Gen. 4:15 and 9:25–27, biblical texts were used as proof texts to "otherize" African Americans into a position of inferiority. Such interpretive violation spilled over into Gen. 10, known as the Table of Nations but interpreted as a Table of Races, with the descendants of Ham assumed to be the ancestors of Africans (vv. 6–20). But Ham, as well as Shem and Japheth, are never associated with color in the biblical literature. In the stark background of racist readings of Genesis texts, the *imago Dei* passage stands out in stark contrast.

A Japanese American Reading of Genesis 2–3

On February 19, 1942, in response to the Japanese bombing of Pearl Harbor, President Franklin D. Roosevelt signed Executive Order 9066, which allowed for the imprisonment of over 120,000 people of Japanese ancestry living in the United States. Japanese Americans were placed in isolated camps throughout the western states solely on the basis of race and without due process of law.

Frank Yamada reads the garden story of Gen. 2–3 through the lens of internment, an act of national "security" motivated by prejudice and paranoia (2009). He considers readings that regard human maturation as the point of the narrative to be deficient since they gloss over the dissonant themes of disobedience and judgment that conclude the story. In addition, Yamada finds the character of God to be problematic: God seems to set an arbitrary restriction for the primal couple out of fear that they will become divine themselves. Ruling "by control and arbitrary command," God exhibits a degree of "divine paranoia" (99, 110). But what Yamada finds most curious is that despite the death sentence uttered by God for committing disobedience (Gen. 2:17; 3:3), the couple survives, and that may be the surprising point of the story. The narrative thus is most concerned about "human survival in the midst of adversity and hostile authority" (102). It is a story of expulsion from home and the hardship that follows. Through the eyes of those who suffered internment, who were expelled from their homes for being ethnically associated with Japan as the United States entered another world war, a distinctly human and often overlooked aspect of the garden story comes to light: the tenacious will to survive in the land of displacement and arbitrary judgment.

Regardless of whether one agrees with Yamada's treatment of Gen. 2–3, it illustrates well how the unique experiences of Japanese Americans can shape the reading of the text in new ways. More broadly, the themes of home, migration (or expulsion), and exile figure prominently in the reading of Scripture among many Asian Americans. This includes, for example, the migrations of Koreans to the United States and the challenges of surviving as one generation paves the way for the next, as parents try to ensure their children's future in a land that is foreign in their eyes, yet in their children's eyes is a land that has become not so foreign and more like home.[12]

---

12. For a breakdown of generational differences among Koreans/Korean Americans and how they can influence biblical interpretation, see Ahn 2014.

Latino/a Readings of Genesis 1–3

Similar concerns are evident in Latino/a readings of the Bible, coupled with the vexing question of "identity." An exile, an immigrant, a migrant, an alien, a refugee—in any event, being a stranger in a strange land is emblematic of Latino/a experiences in the United States (González 1996, 91–102). To be sure, a "diaspora hermeneutic" is one that Asian Americans and African Americans also share, but each in their own way. Jean-Pierre Ruiz, of Puerto Rican descent, describes his community as "a people on the move," a diasporic community formed by the massive migrations of Latin Americans to the United States, a "big story" filled with countless "little stories" (Ruiz 2011). Such stories begin with various places of origin: Cuba, Mexico, Guatemala, Puerto Rico, Venezuela, to name only a few. For many, the United States is a "borderland" place where life is marked by vulnerability and dependence, a landless existence, such as that faced by Abram and Sarai in a "tale of a desperate family at a border crossing," in Gen. 12:10–20 (Carroll R. 2013, 19).

The categories of race and ethnicity have always been ambiguous and pliable for Latinos/as (Barreto 2014, 78). The Latino/a existence in the United States is bilingual and bicultural. For many, the social process of *blanqueamiento*, or "whitening," an ideological change in self-perception, has functioned as "social pressure-relief valves allowing for social ascendancy" in North America (78).

Such ethnic hybridity is commonly called *mestizaje*, a term derived from *mestizo*, which originally referred to those of mixed Spanish and indigenous heritage.[13] For Latinos/as, the term embraces the complex interface between cultures, the breaking down of social boundaries and territorial borders, not to mention racial/ethnic categories. *Mestizaje* refers to living on a daily basis "in between" cultures, such as in between traditional Mexican culture and the dominant Anglo culture in the United States. The cultural trade-off, however, is that in such a *mestizaje* reality one is not fully identified with either culture; on the one hand it is a life of felt alienation, and on the other it is energizing creativity, by which new forms of culture can emerge and indeed have emerged (see Anzaldúa 2007). In either case, the notion of "home" becomes ambiguous amid the harsh reality of homelessness (Hidalgo 2014, 180–81). At the same time, the familial ties that bind, the strengths of the extended family, help define what "home" is amid homelessness for many Latinos/as (see González 1996, 103–14).

In addition to the complex social reality of Latino/a life, there is also the theological reality of liberation, specifically God's preferential option for the poor, which figures strongly in Latin American theology. As with African American appropriation of the exodus account, stories of God's concern for the disenfranchised in the Bible come into contact with the ravaging effects of economic globalization in the South today, causing many to be "on the move," seeking gainful and meaningful work, or simply surviving. Call it "making do" amid situations of duress (Hidalgo 2014, 181), or simply *resolviendo* (García-Alfonso 2014, 155). For many Latinos/as, work is a vexing issue: Is work itself a form of

---

13. *Mestizaje* is frequently paired with *mulatez*, which refers to the cultural mixing of Spanish and African heritage. See González 1996, 77–90.

punishment, a curse handed down by God because of Adam's sin? No. Was there work in the garden before the act of disobedience? Indeed, yes. So what does the gift of Sabbath mean in an economy where jobs are scarce or are predominantly menial? The Sabbath command to rest presupposes a six-day command to work (Exod 20:9), a command that remains unfulfilled for many because of the lack of meaningful job opportunities.

In tandem with Yamada's emphasis on the primal couple's will for survival in and outside the garden, even under the threat of death, a Latino/a treatment of Gen. 3 might (slightly) recast the narrative as a story of tenacious *resolver*: "a way of facing life, of understanding life, its value and its requirements for survival," as one is thrust into a new reality, a reality that requires change in "the patterns in one's life" (García-Alfonso 2014, 155). The expulsion from the garden amounts to a forced emigration from one's home of origin into a strange land, with its own challenges and hardships. If Eden was the couple's home, now they are homeless as they strive to subsist beyond Eden, while sustained by God. The pattern of movement continues with Abraham and Sarah, Israel's ancestors, sojourning hither and yon, emigrating and immigrating as they cross borders between Egypt, Philistia, and Canaan with only a promise of blessing to sustain them along with their wits and their resolve.

GENESIS 1 REVISITED

The questioning of essentialized identities in minority biblical criticism leads me, a white male exegete, to view the *imago Dei* anew. Much traditional exegetical reflection has tried to identify what is it about humanity that uniquely "reflects" God. Is it rationality, intelligence, language capability, or social/cultural power? Such suggestions are typically cast in terms of innate human capacities that correlate with, or "reflect," mirrorlike, some quality of God. But the hermeneutical move to de-essentialize and diversify human "identity" or sense of belonging leads me to rethink the issue entirely. The mirror metaphor, I now find, is too limiting. More suggestive and generative is the image of prism. Perhaps the "image" language is not a matter of reflection of a singular aspect of the divine in a singular aspect of the human but a prism refracting the various ways human beings, beginning with their gendered diversity ("male and female"), are capable of conveying the manifold character of God in relation to the world. When sunlight, for example, is refracted, it is bent, but since all the colors of light do not bend at the same angle, a visible spectrum is formed by a rich variety of colors.

The move from mirror to prism in imaging the "image of God," is, for me, a move toward a radically inclusive anthropology in which all communities are represented, equally so, each made "in God's image." Since the text makes explicit that the image of God is related to gendered diversity ("male and female"), then it is not a major leap to extend such diversity to other forms, encompassing the vast spectrum of humanity. The other thing about a spectrum is that each color is not rigidly distinct. Rather, one emerges from the other with areas of blending at the boundaries. The colors, in other words, are "fuzzy" at their respective boundaries. People, too, are as fuzzy as they are diverse.

In the image of God he created them,
   male and female he created them
Cuban and Caribbean, African and Anglo,
   Latino and Indian, Asian and Indigenous,
      mestizo and *mulatto*.

The list goes on.

BIBLIOGRAPHY FOR CHAPTER 20

Ahn, John J. 2014. "Rising from Generation to Generation: Lament, Hope, Consciousness, Home, and Dream." In *The Oxford Handbook of the Psalms*, edited by William P. Brown, 459–74. New York: Oxford University Press.

Andiñach, Pablo R. 2009. "Latin American Approaches: A Liberationist Reading of the 'Day of the Lord' Tradition in Joel." In *Method Matters: Essays on the Interpretation of the Hebrew Bible in Honor of David L. Petersen*, edited by Joel LeMon and Kent Harold Richards, 423–40. RBS 56. Atlanta: Society of Biblical Literature.

Anzaldúa, Gloria. 2007. *Borderlands/La Frontera: The New Mestiza*. San Francisco: Aunt Lute Books.

Bailey, Randall C. 1991. "Beyond Identification: The Use of Africans in Old Testament Poetry and Narratives." In Felder 1991, 165–84.

———. 2003. *Yet with a Steady Beat: Contemporary U.S. Afrocentric Biblical Interpretation*. Semeia Studies 42. Atlanta: Society of Biblical Literature.

Bailey, Randall C., Tat-siong Benny Liew, and Fernando F. Segovia, eds. 2009a. *They Were All Together in One Place? Toward Minority Biblical Criticism*. Semeia Studies 57. Atlanta: Society of Biblical Literature.

———. 2009b. "Preface" and "Introduction." In Bailey, Liew, and Segovia 2009a, ix–x, 3–43.

Barreto, Eric D. 2014. "Reexamining Ethnicity: Latinas/os, Race, and the Bible." In Lozada and Segovia 2014, 73–94.

Callahan, Allen Dwight. 2006. *The Talking Book: African Americans and the Bible*. New Haven: Yale University Press.

Carroll R., M. Daniel. 2013. "Reading the Bible through Other Lenses: New Vistas from Hispanic Diaspora Perspective." In *Global Voices: Reading the Bible in the Majority World*, edited by Craig Keener and M. Daniel Carroll R., 5–26. Peabody, MA: Hendrickson Publishers.

Copher, Charles. 1991. "The Black Presence in the Old Testament." In Felder 1991, 146–64.

Du Bois, W. E. B. 1994 [1903]. *The Souls of Black Folk*. New York and Avenel, NJ: Gramercy Books.

Felder, Cain Hope, ed. 1991. *Stony the Road We Trod: African Americans and the Bible*. Minneapolis: Fortress Press.

García-Alfonso, Cristina. 2014. "Latino/a Biblical Hermeneutics: Problematic, Objectives, Strategies." In Lozada and Segovia 2014, 151–64.

García-Treto, Francisco O. 2009. "Exile in the Hebrew Bible: A Postcolonial Look from the Cuban Diaspora." In Bailey, Liew, and Segovia 2009a, 65–78.

González, Justo L. 1996. *Santa Biblia: The Bible through Hispanic Eyes*. Nashville, TN: Abingdon.

Hidalgo, Jacqueline M. 2014. "Reading from No Place: Toward a Hybrid and Ambivalent Study of Scriptures." In Lozada and Segovia 2014, 165–86.

hooks, bell. 1990. "Marginality as Site of Resistance." In *Out There: Marginalization and Contemporary Cultures*, edited by Russell Ferguson et al., 336–43. New York: New Museum of Contemporary Art.

Jennings, Willie James. 2010. *The Christian Imagination: Theology and the Origins of Race*. New Haven and London: Yale University Press.

Johnson, James Weldon. 1927. "The Creation." In *God's Trombones: Seven Negro Sermons in Verse*, 17–20. New York: Viking Press.

King, Martin Luther, Jr. 1986a. "A Christmas Sermon on Peace." In *A Testament of Hope: The Essential Writings and Speeches of Martin Luther King, Jr.*, edited by James Melvin Washington, 253–58. San Francisco: HarperSanFrancisco.

———. 1986b. "Remaining Awake through a Great Revolution." In *A Testament of Hope: The Essential Writings and Speeches of Martin Luther King, Jr.*, edited by James Melvin Washington, 286–78. San Francisco: HarperSanFrancisco.

Lewis, David Levering. 2009. *W. E. B. Du Bois: A Biography*. [1868–1963.] New York: Henry Holt & Co.

Lozada, Francisco, Jr., and Fernando F. Segovia, eds. 2014. *Latino/a Biblical Hermeneutics: Problematics, Objectives, Strategies*. Semeia Studies 68. Atlanta; SBL Press.

Mroczek, Eva. 2015. "Mark of Cain." http://www.bibleodyssey.org/people/related-articles/mark -of-cain.aspx.

Page, Hugh R., Jr., ed. 2010. *The Africana Bible: Reading Israel's Scriptures from Africa and the African Diaspora*. Minneapolis: Fortress Press.

Ruiz, Jean-Pierre. 2011. *Readings from the Edges: The Bible and People on the Move*. Maryknoll, NY: Orbis Books.

Sadler, Rodney S. 2010. "Genesis." In Page 2010, 70–79.

Warrior, Robert Allan. 1991. "A Native American Perspective: Canaanites, Cowboys, and Indians." In *Voices from the Margin: Interpreting the Bible in the Third World*, edited by R. S. Sugirtharajah, 287–95. 2nd ed. Maryknoll, NY: Orbis Books.

Yamada, Frank M. 2009. "What Does Manzamar Have to Do with Eden? A Japanese American Interpretation of Genesis 2–3." In Bailey, Liew, and Segovia 2009a, 97–118.

Yee, Gale A. 2009. "'She Stood in Tears amid the Alien Corn': Ruth, the Perpetual Foreigner and Model Minority." In Bailey, Liew, and Segovia 2009a, 119–40.

21

Disability

> In truth there is no such thing as a life without disabilities.
> *Jürgen Moltmann*[1]

It is only fitting that a discussion on disability perspectives follows the chapter on minority reading strategies. Like "race," the label "disabled" is fraught with stereotype and prejudice, both personal and institutional. What is the first image that comes to mind when you hear the word "disabled"? Perhaps someone bound to a wheelchair? You might think of the iconic "international symbol of access," which was designed in 1968 and is used widely to designate parking spaces, vehicles, and public restrooms reserved for special access.

Exegete the image. Note the proportion in size between the person and the wheelchair. Does it look realistic? How is the person figured in relation to the wheelchair? What is "he" doing? Is the person active or passive?

1. Moltmann 1998, 110.

Compare now a proposed revision that is currently in use in the state of New York:

Describe what is different about this image. Is the "disabled" person passive or active? What do the "knockouts" in the wheels communicate? Note also that the wheelchair is proportionately smaller than in the original symbol. The human figure in the second image, moreover, is given a more robust shape and energetic posture. The proposed revision clearly shows the disabled person in motion and in control.

Now for the critical reflection. For all that can be said positively about the revision, does the image of what appears to be a wheelchair-bound driver racing toward the finish line—a Paralympics athlete—include persons who depend on a motorized wheelchair? Does it suggest an exclusionary sense of independence for many deemed disabled? Does the older, standard image leave more to the imagination, making it the more inclusive of the two images? Which image yields a greater sense of dignity to the "disabled"? To complexify the issue further, it should be noted that only a small percentage of people considered disabled actually use a wheelchair. For better or worse, the wheelchair has become the most pervasive symbol for disability.

Like race, gender, and sexuality, "disability" is more a social identity marker than a diagnostic category. Like the perspectives discussed in the previous chapters, disability has to do with interpreting and evaluating human differences based on presumed or real physical features (Avalos, Melcher, and Schipper 2007b, 3). The term itself does not refer simply to a set of physical conditions but considers how "social, political, religious, environmental, and other structures contribute to the *experience* of disability" (Moss and Schipper 2011b, 2, emphasis added). On the one hand, persons deemed disabled are frequently "minoritized" by society, as the designation assigns greater value to those persons—bodies—that are more "abled," however that is defined. Like racism and sexism, negative valuation and social marginalization of disabled bodies is rampant; it is called "ableism." On the other hand, unlike being identified Black, Asian, female, gay, or by one's ancestral lineage, being "disabled" connects universally with embodied experience.

All life potentially suffers disability, or more broadly impairment,[2] of some sort at some point in time, at least by old age. As a form of human limitation, "'disability' is actually more normal than any other state of embodiedness" (Creamer 2009, 32). Limitation and loss, physical and cognitive, are inevitable. Disability or impairment is an integral part of living. Bodies are vulnerable and finite, but they are us. My body is not something I simply possess; it is part of who I am.

DEFINITION

The wide coverage indicated by the term "disability" is evident in the definition offered by the World Health Organization:

> Disabilities is an umbrella term, covering impairments, activity limitations, and participation restrictions. An impairment is a problem in body function or structure; an activity limitation is a difficulty encountered by an individual in executing a task or action; while a participation restriction is a problem experienced by an individual in involvement in life situations. Disability is thus not just a health problem. It is a complex phenomenon, reflecting the interaction between features of a person's body and features of the society in which he or she lives. Overcoming the difficulties faced by people with disabilities requires interventions to remove environmental and social barriers.[3]

"Disability" lies at the intersection between body and society, between societal participation and physical capacities. It is often arbitrarily defined. Left-handedness was once considered a disability, and left-handed children were painfully forced to become right-handed in earlier generations. From injury and chronic illness to deformities and undesired body characteristics, "disability" covers a wide range of physical differences and mental conditions deemed limiting by shifting societal norms, as measured against an ideal image of what the body should be able to do and be. Some have argued that in a male-oriented society, being female itself counts as a disability or impairment (Fontaine 2007). In a society that identifies the perfect body as male (including God's "body"), then, yes. And if the ideal body is considered to be "white,"[4] then persons of color would also be deemed "naturally" deficient or disabled, illustrating just how socially arbitrary and contingent, not to mention damaging, the term "disability" can be.

Generally speaking, "disability" readings of the Bible ask *questions about the body* and how it is profiled and valued in the biblical text. More specific issues include *health, wholeness, and social inclusion and exclusion.* What *social criteria determine* who is disabled and who

2. Some disability perspectives make a categorical distinction between "disability" and "impairment," the latter being medically or biologically based and the former oriented toward social experience, including the experience of discrimination (Moss and Schipper 2011b, 3–4; cf. Melcher 2007, 115–16). In this chapter, both terms are used interchangeably with the understanding that disability is, broadly speaking, "a product of the ways that cultures use physical and cognitive differences to narrate, organize, and interpret their world" (Moss and Schipper 2011b, 4).

3. See http://www.who.int/topics/disabilities/en/.

4. See, e.g., Leonardo da Vinci's iconic drawing *Vitruvian Man* (1490), https://en.wikipedia.org/wiki/Vitruvian _Man.

is not? What *attitudes or perspectives does the Bible hold* that persons with disabilities would find problematic?

ANCIENT NEAR EASTERN AND BIBLICAL BACKGROUND

In certain Mesopotamian creation myths, the raison d'être for humanity's creation was to labor on behalf of the gods. Through human toil, the gods find rest from menial work. There is one creation myth, however, a Sumerian account from the third millennium BCE, that tells of the gods creating distinctly disabled human beings, each one of whom is given meaningful, productive work (Walls 2007, 17). In the myth of Enki and Ninmah, a man with defective hands is appointed as "a servant to the king." A blind man is assigned to the "musical arts"; a man with damaged feet becomes a "silversmith"; a "woman who could not give birth" is placed in the service of the queen; and a person created without a penis is assigned the role of standing "before the king." In each case, "a social position and productive active role is provided for Ninmah's purposefully malformed children" (18). These "disabled" creations are not marginalized. Rather, these "non-normative human bodies" retain their dignity. Are they disabled?

Of course, the myth proves to be more the exception than the rule. Many disabilities in the Bible, for example, are deemed impediments to service in the priesthood:

> [17] Speak to Aaron and say: "Anyone of your offspring throughout their generations who has a *defect* [*mûm*] may not approach to offer the food of his God. [18] For no one who has a defect shall draw near, one who is *blind* or *lame*, or one who has a *mutilated face* or *a limb too long*, [19] or one who has a *broken foot* or a *broken hand*, [20] or a *hunchback*, or a *dwarf*, or a man with a . . . [5] *in his eyes* or an *itching disease* or *scabs* or *crushed testicles*. [21] No descendant of Aaron the priest who has a *defect* shall come near to offer the Lord's offerings by fire; since he has a *defect*, he shall not come near to offer the food of his God." (Lev. 21:17–21 AT; cf. vv. 22–23)

From impaired eyesight to damaged testicles, such physical "defects" are automatic disqualifiers, only some of which, however, would actually present challenges to performing priestly duties. Through the lens of gender analysis, such disabilities have much to do with compromised masculinity. The fully "abled" or ideal *masculine* body is a body devoid of such injuries and impairments; it is a bona fide priestly body, according to biblical tradition.

Comparable is the description of Absalom, the son who would be king at the expense of his father. "In all Israel there was no man [ʾîš] to be praised so much for his beauty as Absalom; from the sole of his foot to the crown of his head there was no defect [*mûm*] in him" (2 Sam. 14:25 alt.). Here, masculine "beauty" and lack of "defect" converge (see also Dan. 1:4), the same for feminine "beauty" (Song 4:7). But as "beauty" lies in the eye of

---

5. The questionable term *těballul* is a *hapax legomenon* (it only occurs once in Biblical Hebrew), so an accurate translation is impossible, although it clearly refers to something that impairs eyesight, perhaps something like a cataract or more broadly a "growth."

the beholder, so also the "defect." The term for "defect" (*mûm/mě'ûm*) can also refer to a moral deficiency, as evident in Job's self-oath: "If my step has turned aside from the way, and my heart has followed my eyes, and if any stain [*mě'ûm*] has clung to my hands" (Job 31:7). The "defect" here is a moral stain, a "damn spot," to quote Lady Macbeth (*Macbeth*, act 5, scene 1). What is deemed a "defect" is never purely descriptive.

Infertility

In the biblical world, and more broadly the world of antiquity, what was regarded as a disability can be quite different from what would be considered a disability today. Take infertility, for example. For women in the ancient world, the most common "disability" was barrenness, a condition that could threaten the very livelihood of women, given their primary biological and social role in procreation (Schipper 2007, 104–13; Raphael 2008, 53–54). In the ancient world, infertility was attributed primarily, if not exclusively, to women. For example, the first thing we know about Sarah other than her family lineage is that she was barren (Gen. 11:30). So also Rebekah, Rachel, Hannah, and Samson's mother (Gen. 25:21; 29:31; 1 Sam. 1:2; Judg. 13:2–3). From a narrative standpoint, their common condition serves as a point of tension and suspense, particularly in Genesis, where God's blessing to Israel's ancestors includes progeny (e.g., 12:2; 13:16; 15:5; 26:3–4; 28:14). Yet Sarah remains barren, until Gen. 17:16–17.

Fertility was often considered a sign of God's blessing and help (Gen. 4:1). A large family, the "fruit of the womb," was highly valued, a source of human happiness (Ps. 127:3–5). Not only does Abraham laugh at the prospect of having children, so also Sarah, and she is the one castigated for doing so (Gen. 18:10–12). By depicting infertility as a threat to the ancestral blessing, the Yahwist highlights God's power to overcome all odds (Baden 2011, 21).

Although often assumed to be a manifestation of divine punishment, the "disability" of infertility in the Hebrew Scriptures is by no means treated uniformly. On the one hand, the condition was considered in some sense "normal," a given fact of familial life (Gen. 29:31; Deut. 7:14). Conversely, fertility was considered the result of divine intervention, of God "opening" the womb (Baden 2011, 14–15). As for Sarah, Rebekah, Rachel, Hannah, and Samson's mother, their barren condition is not said to be the result of punishment or curse. They are simply barren, "a fact of their existence" (Baden 2011, 18). On the other hand, infertility was sometimes regarded as a state not unlike an illness, as in a particular blessing in the Book of the Covenant, a blessing made contingent on proper worship. "You shall worship YHWH your God, and I will bless your bread and your water; and I will take away *sickness* [*maḥălâ*] from among you. No one shall miscarry or be barren in your land; I will fulfill the number of your days" (Exod. 23:25–26). Here, barrenness is aligned with "sickness" (Baden 2011, 19). Elsewhere, it is a condition that requires healing, such as when Abraham prays to God for healing Abimelech's household (Gen. 20:17–18). In this case, infertility is regarded as a form of punishment.

Barrenness was often a cause for social denigration. The barren woman could be an object of scorn, as in the case of Peninnah taunting Hannah for being childless (1 Sam. 1:6). Conversely, a woman's social esteem and status was heightened through childbirth, as in the case of Hagar vis-à-vis Sarah: "When she saw that she had conceived, [Hagar] looked with contempt on her mistress" (Gen. 16:4). In Isaiah, barrenness serves as a metaphor for exile; fertility, conversely, signals restoration (Isa. 49:21; 54:1).

In sum, the "disability" of infertility is a complex, nuanced issue in the Hebrew Bible. The Bible is not consistent regarding the origin or cause of fertility and infertility. Literarily, infertility serves various functions, from an impediment to realizing God's blessing. It can serve as a metaphor for communal devastation. Sometimes infertility is simply a given condition of human existence, other times a form of divine punishment. The lesson learned? One simply cannot impose modern categories of disability, or narrow theological conclusions, for that matter, upon these ancient texts. Careful comparison is required.

"Disabled" Figures

Speaking of comparison, there are a few "disabled" characters in the Hebrew Scriptures that do not necessitate rejection or pity. Moses complains of being "slow of tongue" (stuttering?), to which God responds: "Who gives speech to mortals? Who makes them mute or deaf, seeing or blind? Is it not I, YHWH?" (Exod. 4:11). Moses' speech impairment, with help from Aaron, presents no obstacle to fulfilling God's mission in liberating the Hebrews. Indeed, Moses is elsewhere considered the ideally "abled" individual, one who suffers no debilitation: "Moses was one hundred twenty years old when he died; his sight was unimpaired and his vigor unabated" (Deut. 34:7). Apparently Moses suffered none of the disabling effects of old age.

Jacob, after his wrestling match on the banks of the Jabbok, walks with a limp due to having suffered a dislocated hip (Gen. 32:25–32). But this is no "disability" in any debilitative sense: indeed, no mention is made of Jacob's disjointed hip after the incident. Instead, the patriarch's limp is construed as a sign of God's covenantal blessing, memorialized by a particular dietary practice (see Wynn 2007, 96–101).

Perhaps the most well-known "disabled" individual in the Hebrew Bible is Mephibosheth, son of Jonathan, grandson of Saul, who suffered a crippling accident at birth: "Saul's son Jonathan had a son who was **stricken** [*nĕkēh*] in his feet. He was five years old when the news about Saul and Jonathan came from Jezreel. His nurse picked him up and fled; and, in her haste to flee, it happened that he fell and became lame.[6] His name was Mephibosheth" (2 Sam. 4:4 alt.). After the long and torturous extermination of the "house of Saul," David shows kindness to the only surviving member of the Saulide lineage by restoring Saul's property to him and by having him eat at his table (9:1–13). Mephibosheth, "lame in both his feet," the narrator repeatedly states, may be an object of pity, but he is also an object of suspicion from David's perspective. His "disability" in the narrative serves to mask his potential threat to David's kingdom. His presence at the king's table is required, not only as a sign of David's magnanimity but also as a way of keeping him under surveillance (cf. 16:1–4; 19:24–30).[7]

---

6. Literally, became "limped" (root *psḥ* in the Niphal).
7. For a trenchant and detailed discussion of this account, see Schipper 2006.

Spectrum of Disabilities and Social Attitudes

The Bible's frequent reference to the blind, lame, deaf, and mute represents a spectrum of sensory, mobility, and speech impairments. A quick survey reveals a variety of attitudes toward such disabilities. As signs of weakness to be disdained, the "blind" and the "lame" are referenced in a taunt against David and his intention to secure victory over the Jebusites in Jerusalem in 2 Sam. 5:6–8 (see Ackerman 2011). On the other hand, Leviticus prohibits mistreatment of those less "abled." The reason? Because God is to be revered. Respect for the disabled in Leviticus is thus given the highest ethical backing: it is a duty commanded by God, no less. "You shall not revile the deaf or put a stumbling block before the blind; you shall fear your God: I am YHWH" (Lev. 19:14).

Job prides himself in assisting the blind and the lame, who are associated with the needy: "I was eyes to the blind, and feet to the lame. I was a father to the needy, and I championed the cause of the stranger" (Job 29:15). Job makes this declaration to acknowledge the well-deserved esteem and honor he once enjoyed from the community (vv. 11, 20–25). Caring for the disabled, in addition to the needy, the widow, and the orphan, serves as part of Job's list of righteous deeds, all marshaled to demonstrate his past "glory." As objects of his compassion and pity, the disabled are included with all who suffer deprivation of one sort or another, casting them as dependents upon the goodwill of individuals with the means to care for them.

In the exilic literature of Isaiah and Jeremiah, however, there is a heightened sense of solidarity with the "disabled." In the so-called Book of Consolation in Jeremiah, "the blind and the lame," along with mothers in labor, are emblematic of the exiles or the Diaspora community (Jer. 31:8). In Isaiah, God's servant Israel is commissioned to be a "light to the nations," thereby curing the blind and releasing the prisoners, both having suffered from "darkness" (42:6–7). God describes servant Israel as "deaf" and "blind," whom God intends to heal (vv. 18–20). The harsh reality of exile is an experience of deep deprivation, of disablement, so much so that it is likened to being deprived of sight and hearing.

To conclude our overview, brief as it is, Sarah Melcher offers a "disability liberation ethic" drawn from the Hebrew Scriptures, an ethic affirming that God is no less a creator of the "disabled" (Melcher prefers the term "impaired") than God is of the "abled," not unlike the Sumerian myth with which we began our discussion (2007, 127–28). Prophetic texts that stress God's restoration and healing, such as Isa. 29:15–24, command central attention. But the one text that gives fundamental theological justification is found in an exilic text:

> Woe to you who strive with your Maker, earthen vessels with the potter!
>   Does the clay say to the one who fashions it,
>   "What are you making"? or "Your work has no handles"?
> Woe to anyone who says to a father, "What are you begetting?"
>   or to a woman, "With what are you in labor?"
> Thus says YHWH, the Holy One of Israel, and its Maker:
>   Will you question me about my children,
>   or command me concerning the work of my hands?
> I made the earth, and created humankind upon it;
>   it was my hands that stretched out the heavens,
>   and I commanded all their host. (Isa. 45:9–12)

The "abled" and the "disabled" are found equal in God's sight, rooted as they are in God's free handiwork. To drive the wedge of social inequality between the two is, in effect, to question the very integrity of God's creative work. Thus here is an appropriate place to reconsider our two creation accounts in Genesis.

CREATION ACCORDING TO GENESIS

How might one interpret the creation accounts in Genesis from a disability perspective? To be sure, there is no specific language of "defect" or impairment found within these two texts, quite in contrast to the Sumerian creation myth discussed above. Nevertheless, these two biblical accounts prominently feature the creation of humankind and hence highlight significant anthropological implications. Both stories shape the physical and cultural contours of human embodiment in significant ways, with body normativity being of critical importance.

Body Made in God's Image

We begin, once again, with Gen. 1:26–28.

> [26] Then God said, "Let us make humanity in our image, after our likeness, so that they may rule over the fish of the sea, and over the winged creatures in the heavens, over the domestic animals, over all the land, and over everything that crawls on the land."
>
> [27] So God created the human being in his image,
>   in the image of God he created "him,"
>   male and female he created them.
>
> [28] And God blessed them, and God said to them, "Be fruitful and multiply; fill the earth and subdue it and rule over the fish of the sea and over the winged creatures in the heavens and over every creature that crawls on the ground." (AT)

How does the human body reflect God? Does being "made in the image of God" presume an "abled" body? Can a "disabled" or impaired body reflect God's image just as readily? These are questions that normally do not present themselves upon the text, since throughout much of the history of biblical interpretation, the focus has been on the human power of rationality or reason as providing an essentialist link to God. Disability criticism, however, widens the link to include bodily implications, breaking down the Platonic contrast between mind, body, and spirit.

The language of "image" (ṣelem) and "likeness" (děmût) in vv. 26–27 may well have bodily implications, as suggested by the discovery of a life-size statue in northeastern Syria bearing a bilingual inscription from Tell Fakhariyeh (or Fekheriye). The statue represents a certain King Had-yitᶜi of the ninth century BCE, which was fashioned to serve as his stand-in in the temple of Hadad, his patron deity, a storm god. On the king's skirt is engraved an Akkadian text translated into Aramaic. The Aramaic inscription refers to the king's "likeness" (*dmwt*) and "image" (*ṣlm*). Although it remains difficult to distinguish the meanings of these two parallel terms,[8] it is at least clear that that together they suggest some degree of similarity between the king and the statue that represents him. Does the analogy extend to God in Genesis? Does the human body in some sense resemble God? Does God have a body? It appears that the Priestly author, while avoiding the kind of blatant anthropomorphizing one finds in Gen. 2–3 (see below), retains some sense of bodily connection between God and humankind. This does not necessarily mean that the Priestly author envisioned God as a royal male with a flowing white beard. But at the very least, the Genesis text affirms a corporeal association of some sort between God and humanity.

As for a disability reading of this passage, the next question to be posed is whether an ideal body is assumed by the text. More specifically, what human abilities or physical capacities does the *imago Dei* presuppose? At least two things are specified in the text: (1) dominion over creation and (2) procreation to "fill" it. The text implies that God's image is evident in the human fulfillment of such tasks. Conversely, the language of limitation or impairment is utterly absent. The text, by implication, endorses the seemingly limitless power of human expansion and control over creation. From a disability (and ecological) perspective, however, the text is highly problematic in its abject disregard of human limitation. On the one hand, the human body matters in Gen. 1, given the language of "likeness" and "image." On the other hand, human capacity over and against the rest of creation is highly valued. Not so in Gen. 2–3.

Body Made of "Dust"

Human limitation lies at the core of this human origins story, a tale of failure, growth, and messy consequences. Limitless physical power and cognitive prowess are not the hallmarks of life in the garden. Various limitations beset the primal couple. First and foremost, the tree of knowledge is deemed off-limits; divine knowledge is prohibited by God—a prescribed cognitive and moral limitation, one could say. Physical existence is also limited, since humanity is created from the "dust of the ground" (2:7). "You are dust," God reminds the groundling (3:19; cf. Eccl. 3:20). Death is inevitable; it is the ultimate limitation.

The punishments laid out in Gen. 3 illustrate certain "disabling" consequences. It is the snake's "disability" that is the most dramatic: it is destined to crawl on its "belly," eating "dust" (3:14). The woman suffers from the debilitating pain of childbirth, a temporarily disabling condition that can bring the woman to the brink of death (v. 16). The *ʾādām* suffers from exhausting "toil" in his work with the soil, to which he shall ultimately return in death (v. 19). That, too, could be construed as disabling for the man, or more broadly disabling of the once symbiotic relationship between groundling and ground.

Despite or because of the limitations that define the human condition, the Yahwist narrative also celebrates bodies. Body imagery pervades the narrative (Estes 2016, 6). Not only do the two human beings have bodies made of "flesh" and "bone" (2:23), but also

8. See Garr 2000; Millard and Bordreuil 1982.

God has a body. Without apology the story revels in depicting God anthropomorphic-ally. God's actions are key: God plants, shapes, breathes, cuts, builds, and strolls. One can easily imagine God getting dirty, working the soil to cultivate a garden and to fashion a human being, all to show, in part, that God is the ablest body in the narrative.

A certain physical intimacy, moreover, is celebrated in the creation of the groundling, from the hands-on activity of shaping a human body from the soil to the divine kiss that animates the body. If God had worked with Georgia clay—part of my own geo-ecological context—in fashioning humanity, God's lips would be dripping red![9] All in all, an inti-mate, bodily God is portrayed from start to finish in this creation narrative. Bodies matter.

Physical intimacy among humans is also celebrated, founded upon the common sub-stance shared by the woman and man, "flesh" and "bone," and the joining of flesh (2:23–24). Moreover, the common substance shared by the groundling and the ground also marks a bond of intimacy enacted in the work of cultivation. The earth, too, is corporeal; it also has a body. The narrative acknowledges no division between body and spirit. The "living being" (*nepeš*) describes the human creature as a unity (2:7). It is not that we *have* bodies; we *are* bodies (see Creamer 2009, 57). Analogously, it is not that we possess life but that we are alive.

Reading the garden story for its corporeal implications reveals certain nuances that might otherwise be overlooked. The creation of the woman from the man exemplifies the paradox of loss and gain. The man, in order to become a man, must experience physi-cal loss in order to gain a fully physical partner (Estes 2016, 14). What appears to be a *disabling* act on the part of God—surgical removal—turns out to be *enabling* by providing companionship and mutual intimacy, as well as the man's sexual identity.

More surprising, perhaps, is the initial consequence of eating the forbidden fruit of knowledge in Gen. 3:7. The opening of the eyes implies that before eating, the man and the woman were blind in some sense. In a paradoxical twist, the disobedience committed by the primal couple turns out to be a self-enabling act, one that, yes, makes them fully human: eyes opened and self-aware. Is awareness of their own nakedness an enabling or disabling consequence? Perhaps both. While nakedness, or the awareness thereof, is what distinguishes human beings from nonhuman animals, it is also what compels the couple to hide themselves in shame from God. Nevertheless, it is precisely the gain of such knowl-edge that makes them more "divine" (v. 22).

The Yahwist creation narrative details the limitations that beset human existence. Some are evident from the outset, such as death and finitude. Others happen consequen-tially, as found in God's punishments. Questions naturally arise: are disabilities God's curse, the consequence of disobedience? This would be a highly problematic conclusion for people with disabilities, as well as for those who care for them. The Yahwist, how-ever, is highlighting certain *universal* "disabilities," or limitations endemic to embodied existence, whether "abled" or "disabled," impaired or nonimpaired. When it comes to the body, what it can and cannot do, normativity *includes* physical and cognitive limitations. This seemingly simple tale of humanity in the making complicates what is meant as ideal or even "normal" for the human body. By doing so, it breaks down the binary between

9. Thanks to Kate Brearley Buckley for suggesting such a riveting image.

"abled" and "disabled" (Estes 2016, 5). Human existence is marked by limitation and imperfection.

Jean Vanier, founder of L'Arche, an international federation of communities spread over thirty-five countries for people with intellectual disabilities and those who assist them, has this to say about society's valuation of the human body:

> The image of the ideal human as powerful and capable disenfranchises the old, the sick, the less-abled. For me, society must, by definition, be inclusive of the needs and gifts of all its members; how can we lay claim to making an open and friendly society where human rights are respected and fostered when, by the values we teach and foster, we systematically exclude segments of our population? (Vanier 1998, 45)

Vanier goes on to say, "A society that honors only the powerful, the clever, and the winners necessarily belittles the weak. It is as if to say: to be human is to be powerful" (46). Are the groundling of dust, the woman in labor, and the man in toil fully made in God's "image"? Yes, they are, limitations and all. So also those who are less abled. May our critical engagements with Scripture affirm nothing less.

BIBLIOGRAPHY FOR CHAPTER 21

Ackerman, Susan. 2011. "The Blind, the Lame, and the Barren Shall Not Come into the House." In Moss and Schipper 2011a, 29–46.

Avalos, Hector. 1995. *Illness and Health Care in the Ancient Near East: The Role of the Temple in Greece, Mesopotamia, and Israel*. Atlanta: Scholars Press.

Avalos, Hector, Sarah J. Melcher, and Jeremy Schipper, eds. 2007a. *This Abled Body: Rethinking Disabilities in Biblical Studies*. Semeia Studies 55. Atlanta: Society of Biblical Literature.

———. 2007b. "Introduction." In Avalos, Melcher, and Schipper 2007a, 1–9.

Baden, Joel S. 2011. "The Nature of Barrenness in the Hebrew Bible." In Moss and Schipper 2011a, 13–27.

Creamer, Deborah. 2009. *Disability and Christian Theology*. Oxford: Oxford University Press.

Estes, Joel D. 2016. "Imperfection in Paradise: Reading Genesis 2 through the Lens of Disability and a Theology of Limits." *HBT* 38:1–21.

Fontaine, Carol R. 2007. "'Be Men, O Philistines' (1 Samuel 4:9): Iconographic Representations and Reflections on Female Gender as Disability in the Ancient World." In Avalos, Melcher, and Schipper 2007a, 61–72.

Garr, W. Randall. 2000. "'Image' and 'Likeness' in the Inscription from Tell Fakhariyeh." *IEJ* 50:227–34.

Junior, Nyasha, and Jeremy Schipper. 2013. "Disability Studies and the Bible." In *New Meaning for Ancient Texts*, edited by Steven L. McKenzie and John Kaltner, 21–38. Louisville, KY: Westminster John Knox Press.

Melcher, Sarah J. 2007. "With Whom Do the Disabled Associate? Metaphorical Interplay in the Latter Prophets." In Avalos, Melcher, and Schipper 2007a, 115–30.

———. 2011. "A Tale of Two Eunuchs: Isaiah 56:1–8 and Acts 8:26–40." In Moss and Schipper 2011a, 117–28.

Melcher, Sarah J., Mikeal Parsons, and Amos Yong, eds. Forthcoming. *Disability and the Bible: A Commentary*. Waco, TX: Baylor University Press.

Millard, A. R., and P. Bordreuil. 1982. "A Statue from Syria with Assyrian and Aramaic Inscriptions." *BA* 45:135–41.

Moltmann, Jürgen. 1998. "Liberate Yourselves by Accepting One Another." In *Human Disability and the Service of God: Reassessing Religious Practice*, edited by Nancy L. Eiesland and Don E. Saliers, 105–22. Nashville: Abingdon.

Moss, Candida R., and Jeremy Schipper, eds. 2011a. *Disability Studies and Biblical Literature*. New York: Palgrave Macmillan.

———. 2011b. "Introduction." In Moss and Schipper 2011a, 1–12.

Olyan, Saul M. 2008. *Disability in the Hebrew Bible: Interpreting Mental and Physical Differences*. Cambridge: Cambridge University Press.

———. 2011. "The Ascription of Physical Disability as a Stigmatizing Strategy in Biblical Iconic Polemics." In Moss and Schipper 2011a, 89–102.

Raphael, Rebecca. 2008. *Biblical Corpora: Representations of Disability in Hebrew Biblical Literature*. LHBOTS 445. New York: T&T Clark.

Schipper, Jeremy. 2006. *Disability Studies and the Hebrew Bible: Figuring Mephibosheth in the David Story*. LHBOTS 441. New York: T&T Clark.

———. 2007. "Disabling Israelite Leadership: 2 Samuel 6:23 and Other Images of Disability in the Deuteronomistic History." In Avalos, Melcher, and Schipper 2007a, 103–13.

———. 2011. *Disability and Isaiah's Suffering Servant*. New York: Oxford University Press.

Vanier, Jean. 1998. *Becoming Human*. New York: Paulist Press.

Walls, Neal H. 2007. "The Origins of the Disabled Body: Disability in Ancient Mesopotamia." In Avalos, Melcher, and Schipper 2007a, 13–30.

Wynn, Kerry H. 2007. "The Normate Hermeneutic and Interpretations of Disability within the Yahwistic Narratives." In Avalos, Melcher, and Schipper 2007a, 91–101.

Yong, Amos. 2011. *The Bible, Disability, and the Church: A New Vision of the People of God*. Grand Rapids: Eerdmans Publishing.

22

Theology

Language about God is kept honest in the degree to which it . . . surrenders itself to God.

Rowan Williams[1]

Theological interpretation is a crucial, if not culminating, step in the exegetical enterprise, since it builds on everything that we have done so far, from textual analysis to contextual exploration. The operating assumption in this chapter is that theology is both comprehensive in its scope and integrative in its work. To quote Anselm of Canterbury (1033–1109), theology is "faith seeking understanding,"[2] and "seeking understanding" is ever ongoing and all encompassing, whether it is understanding the world, ourselves, others, or the biblical text. Simply put, the task of theology is to relate everything there is, reality as we know it, to God. It asks what the text says about God, the world, and humankind, all bound up together. The question of human identity, for example, is bound up with the question of God. Anthropology, in other words, is theological. Just ask the Yahwist. The "earth . . . and all that is in it" bears a certain relationship to the Creator. Ecology is theological. Just ask the psalmist (Ps. 24:1). Racism, which denigrates the "image of God," is a theological issue as much as it is a matter of social justice. Just ask any minoritized person of faith.

Methodologically, theological interpretation does not follow a step-by-step procedure so much as adopt an orientation that engages the interpreter from the outset. While theological interpretation acknowledges the constructive role of the interpreter, particularly in relation to one's view of God and the world, it begins by attending closely to what the text says about God and the world, about how God and the world are inscribed in the text. In the exegetical venture, the interpreter encounters in the text a "strange new world" whose otherness should never be lost (Barth 1957). In the theological venture, the God encountered in the text points to the God beyond the text, the God who is "wholly other"

---

1. Williams 2000, 8.
2. From *fides quaerens intellectum*, the original title to Anselm's *Proslogion* as referenced in his preface. See Anselm 1998, 83–87.

(Otto 1958). This means that theological interpretation is never satisfied with simply providing a description of what the text says about God. Theology involves the exercise of reason (*logos*), whose fruits can be found in doctrine, creeds, treatises, and confessions. For our purposes, however, the theological task is to begin making sense of God and the world with the biblical text. Our point of departure, thus, is the text's "theo-logic," its own reasoning about God.

For persons of faith, God is the definitive, all-encompassing source of meaning that informs and forms their lives. In God, the past, present, and future are inextricably linked. And because knowledge of God and knowledge of the self are intertwined, a theological interpretation of the biblical text fully acknowledges the context and role of the interpreter while also affirming the text's otherness: its ancient roots, specific ways of communication, and peculiar claims. Theological interpretation is meant to bear relevance and as such can address issues of contemporary urgency. As both descriptive and constructive, theological interpretation works with the text and at the same time reaches beyond the text; it attends to the text's own claims about God and the world in dialogue with the interpreter's own world and experience. Theologically, the text informs, shapes, and challenges the interpreter who seeks theological understanding. The theological interpreter does not stand aloof from the world of the text as a dispassionate observer any more than the interpreter can stand detached from his or her own world. On the contrary, the theological interpreter has a vested interest in the text, for it is out of the impulse of "faith seeking understanding" that one treats the text as a partner in dialogue rather than merely an object of scrutiny.

Theological interpreters are boundary crossers. According to James Mead, biblical theologians walk a "tightrope" between history and theology, between ancient text and contemporary reflection.[3] I would, however, replace "tightrope," which signals only caution and danger, with "interface." Theological interpreters thrive on the interface between biblical scholarship and theological inquiry, between ancient text and contemporary context. As much as they are focused on the biblical text and its ancient context in order to be biblical, they are also engaged with theological discourse to be theological.

Theological interpretation builds on many of the various approaches and contexts discussed in the previous chapters, including even the historical. The biblical text is the product of a diverse community whose own history involved the struggle for theological understanding amid the vicissitudes and challenges of its common life. Theological understanding or discernment is never a static, self-contained given. It is always a process, and as such, it is historical, and historical study uncovers, however partially, some of the dynamics that lie behind the text's theological and literary development.

The integrative and broadening work of theological interpretation, moreover, engages the various theological perspectives that the scriptural texts themselves bear. It acknowledges the irreducible diversity of Scripture in all its dimensions: textual, literary, historical, and theological. Such diversity, however, is not a matter of isolated differences haphazardly put together. The Bible's diversity is ultimately a *canonical* diversity, which means that the text's location in relation to other texts invites deliberate and lively theological

3. Mead 2007, 93.

interaction (see chap. 13). As the interpretive net is cast ever more widely, the literary context becomes the canonical context once the entirety of Scripture is caught up in the hermeneutical dialogue. Theological reflection, however, casts the net even more widely to address matters of faith and practice in light of what the text, in dialogue with other texts, says about God and God's relationship to the world, including ourselves.

ORIENTING QUESTIONS

As the interpreter continues to explore exegetically the contours and contexts of the biblical text, three interrelated questions from the theological perspective offer guidance:

1. What is the text's *"theo-logic,"* that is, how does the text inscribe God's character and relationship to the world?
2. What is the text's *"cosmo-logic,"* that is, how does the text inscribe the world in relationship to God and humanity's place within it?
3. What significance does the text have for the interpreter regarding *faith and practice*?

Exploring the text's "theo-logic" is preferable to simply stating the text's "theology." The latter suggests something monolithic and abstract. The former is an invitation to dig deeply into how the text constructs or "reasons" its theological perspective(s). The same applies to the text's "cosmo-logic." Its scope is broader than a strictly anthropological orientation. The text's "cosmo-logic" constructs a world, no less, and in so doing imparts a particular anthropology embedded within the world that the text inscribes. As God and world are ineluctably related throughout Scripture, so the text's "theo-logic" and "cosmo-logic" are inextricably tied together in the particular discourse of the text.

The third question acknowledges the interpreter's theological context. It invites the interpreter to make sense of the text in ways that bridge the past and the present, to make the text theologically compelling to communities of faith today, beginning with the interpreter's own community. A theological interpretation, in short, highlights how the text makes sense of God and the world while inviting readers to do the same. It is a theological *meditatio* on the text, a reflective inquiry into the text's significance for the life of faith. To press a visual metaphor, theological exegesis is about "putting on" the text as with a pair of glasses (or contact lenses); looking through it to "see" God, the world, and oneself more clearly and to act accordingly.

GENESIS ACCOUNTS OF CREATION

What do we "see," then, through the creation accounts of Genesis? Like looking through two different lenses (bifocals?), how does the interpreter theologically appropriate two very different portrayals of God, creation, and human identity? We have already explored how differently God is profiled in each text. Genesis 1 profiles a royal God who issues commands that bring creation, from the cosmic to the human, into being. Genesis 2–3 portrays an intimate deity who gets dirty, strolls through the garden, and creates companionship. Are such contrasting portrayals contradictory? Does one diminish the import of the other? First, let's look more keenly at their distinctions.

The "Theo-logic" of Genesis 1

In Gen. 1, theology and cosmology are bound together: God is revealed in and through the creation of the cosmos. As the first verse makes abundantly clear, God is the creator of "heaven and earth."[4] God creates a cosmos that makes life possible and sustains it. In so doing God discloses a preferential option for life itself, life manifest in great diversity ("kinds") and plenitude ("be fruitful . . ."). The "very good" that concludes God's creation is an affirmation of creation as a self-sustaining whole (1:31). God's approbation at the end, as well as throughout the process of creation, underlines God's satisfaction, perhaps even joy, in creation.

How God made it so reveals something of God's modus operandi in the world. While creation begins with command, God's word is by no means sufficient, according to Gen. 1. God commands *and* creates—such is the rhythm of creating: word and deed, divine intent and creational result. Such rhythm imbues creation with telos, with purpose or direction, whose fulfillment is found in the plenitude of life. To make life happen, moreover, God works collaboratively *with* the elemental powers of creation, the earth and the waters. God enlists the earth to bring forth vegetation and land animals (1:11, 24). God enlists the waters to bring forth marine life (v. 20). The God of Genesis is no Marduk, the conquering deity who destroys before creating, who conquers before constructing. While God may appear transcendentally aloof in Gen. 1 (cf. Gen. 2–3), God remains positively oriented toward creation.

As for the seventh day, God's "rest" marks the completion and indeed consummation of creation. One might ask, Did God need to rest? The fact that "Sabbath" fundamentally means cessation need not imply that God grew tired by the seventh day and was in need of recovery. Rather, divine "rest" formally marks the completion of creation: structures are established, stability is set, and life is launched. From God's purview, creation now has the sufficient conditions to continue in its life-sustaining goodness. God's "rest" marks the culmination of God's approbation of creation (1:31) and the readiness on God's part to let creation fill itself with life in all forms ("kinds"). The fact that this day is set apart as holy is reflective of God's own holiness vis-à-vis the world. God is set apart, transcendentally so, yet remains in relationship with creation. God is no deist.

As for divine intent or rationale, nowhere do we find a specific reason enumerated in Gen. 1 regarding why God created the universe, why there is something rather than nothing, light rather than darkness, structure rather than *tōhû*, life rather than emptiness. Did God suffer from loneliness? Was God in need of relationship? Does God need a world to be God? The text is tantalizingly silent on such matters. It certainly admits of no compulsion on God's part: God simply created. Period. Such theological reticence suggests at least that God created out of complete freedom. Creation was not a necessary or compulsory venture. Rather, it was (and is) a gracious and free act of God.

---

4. Cf. Gen. 2:4; 14:19, 22; Ps. 134:3.

The "Cosmo-logic" of Genesis 1

If Gen. 1 were put to music, the result would be something like a Bach organ fugue, full of contrapuntal variations filling every nook and cranny of a towering Gothic cathedral. But instead of resounding notes, we hear divinely spoken cadences reverberating throughout an intricately ordered universe.

Creation in Gen. 1 is a differentiated and diverse whole, a well-ordered universe that is both stable and self-sustaining. Its stability is due to its structure as defined according to discrete domains. Creation is self-sustaining due to the blessings of seeds and sex, making possible botanical succession and animal procreation. God has fashioned, in short, a *creating* creation, a cosmos that is both dynamic and interdependent. Such are marks of creation's integrity: structured, stable, dynamic, and creative. Creation is both firmly established and actively ongoing; one could perhaps say "evolving." It is all, according to God's own declaration, "very good," acknowledging creation's intrinsic value. Creation is not, ultimately, an arena of conflict between good and evil. Creation is good from the get-go.

As we saw in chap. 8 (above), the chronological layout of Gen. 1 reflects the spatial framework of the temple/tabernacle. The temple is truly a microcosmos, and the cosmos, in turn, is a macrotemple. Biblically speaking, then, creation is God's first temple. While the inner sanctum was considered the holiest part of the temple/tabernacle, the whole structure was also deemed holy—holy by degree.[5] Similarly, what the seventh day adds to creation's integrity is a measure of holiness to the entire structure. Just as the tabernacle's integrity, indeed its holiness, is dependent on God's holiness, made spatially manifest in the "holy of holies," so creation's integrity (its "goodness") is infused with a level of holiness because of the final, holy day. On the seventh day, God's holiness and creation's wholeness are bound together!

Genesis 1 engenders an awe and respect for creation's sacred integrity, its order and its diversity, its vitality and vastness. This is what Gen. 1 elicits from its readers, at least this reader. A respect for God's creation has no greater biblical warrant than here "in the beginning." Respect for creation is tantamount to reverence of God, the creator of all. Creation is God's holy sanctuary; the "depths of nature" are truly sacred.

Genesis 1 and the Doctrine of *Creatio ex Nihilo*

Creation "out of nothing" (*ex nihilo*) is a fundamental claim of the Christian doctrine of creation. Hence it is fair to ask whether the cosmos according to Gen. 1 is created "out of nothing." Genesis 1 seems to suggest not, since *tōhû wābōhû* and the watery depths (*tēhôm*) designate the primordial conditions in which God begins to create (Gen. 1:1–2). God does not begin with "nothing." Nothing is said of God creating the abyss. But the issue is complicated: it is also clear from Gen. 1 that God does not fashion the world simply out of primordial substance. The creation of light, for example, seems to come out of nowhere (1:3). Creation, moreover, is established by God's word, not by God simply shaping something from cosmic mishmash. Theologically, the doctrine of *creatio ex nihilo*

---

5. See Jenson 1992; and most recently Hundley 2013.

serves to highlight the qualitative difference between creation and creator, the former being entirely and absolutely dependent upon the latter.

Creatio ex nihilo is not just a claim about cosmic origins; it is also an affirmation of God's power to bring forth life out of death, to constitute a people from being no people, to triumph over the grave. In its historical context, Gen. 1 is a bold testimony of hope in God to bring order out of chaos and thus to restore a people from exile. Genesis 1 offers a cosmic vision for a community in hope of rebuilding itself, a hopeful vision for those ready to begin the great collaborative work of restoration. The God of "in the beginning" is also the God of "new beginnings," ever and always. That is the striking theological claim of Gen. 1: regardless of whether God created *ex nihilo*, God can create *ex vetere* (out of the old), from whatever is present, even from chaos, making "all things new" (Rev. 21:5).

Humanity in Genesis 1

On the anthropological level, the "image of God" is a powerful testimony that no person is a second-class citizen. Every individual, regardless of gender, race, ethnicity, and ability, has intrinsic worth, indeed royal worth, given the rhetorical setting of "God's image" in Near Eastern antiquity (see chap. 10). Genesis 1 claims humanity as the closest thing to a theophany on the earth. As much as the God of the heavens in Gen. 1 is de-anthropomorphized (at least relatively so as compared to Gen. 2–3), humanity is "theo-morphized" on the earth. Relatedly, humanity is "blessed" with the divinely ordained responsibility to exercise "dominion" for the purpose of reflecting God's creative and sustaining ways in creation. That crucial responsibility is contextualized in 1:29–30, where both human beings and nonhuman animals alike are given the nutritional bounty of the land to share, not to hoard. As there is no place for a conquering Marduk in Gen. 1, so there is no place for an imperialistic humanity exploiting creation, God's cosmic temple. Humanity is called to be a creative and sustaining presence, as God has been and is from "the beginning."

IN THE GARDEN (GENESIS 2–3)

Genesis 2–3, by way of contrast, has no cosmic orientation and no royal profile either of God or of humanity. Instead, this second creation account unfolds in an agrarian setting, and humanity's origin is distinctly earthbound. The theological, cosmological, and anthropological differences are stark. But before we explore how they might converge, a few further observations of the theological distinctiveness of the garden story are in order.

The "Theo-logic" of Genesis 2–3

The Yahwist account is no baroque fugue; it is more an improvised jazz tune. This deceptively simple tale provides an intimate, earthy portrayal of God. God does the gardening, sculpting, and hands-on vivifying. The God of the garden does not flinch at getting dirty, whether it's planting a grove of trees or shaping a human form. God is both farmer and potter who also performs major surgery when necessary. Most intimately, God performs mouth-to-nose suscitation to bring the groundling to life, a very tactile portrayal of human creation, contrary to Michelangelo's depiction on the ceiling of the Sistine Chapel in Rome. God also asks questions (Gen. 3:9, 11, 13; 4:9–10).

Transcendent, royal majesty is not the hallmark of this depiction of the Deity; instead, God is profiled anthropomorphically in quite vivid ways: God is intimate and tender, vulnerable yet tenacious. The God of the Yahwist wants the best for the garden community and finds creative ways to make it happen. Indeed, God is something of an experimenter, trying out different ways to advance creation. Recognizing that the creational situation is "not good" for the groundling, God creates a community from the ground up in order to assuage Adam's loneliness. The first attempt is unsuccessful. The second, however, is a resounding success. In both attempts, God allows the human being to determine his relational destiny by naming the creatures God has fashioned. And so the saga continues, sometimes unpredictably so.

Perhaps most striking in Gen. 2–3 is that God acts without mediation or reluctance in the narrative. Unlike Enlil in the Mesopotamian tale Atrahasis, YHWH Elohim does not hesitate to do the messy work of creation. The lesser gods of Babylonian mythology, the Igigi, rebel at having to perform the menial labor of canal building (see Dalley 1989, 9–13). Humanity, therefore, is created to do the work and to provide rest for the gods. Not so in Genesis. The God of the garden welcomes the dirty work of creating. God revels in the joy of toil.

The intimate picture of God in community is, however, fractured by the couple's disobedience. Division and alienation erupt between God and human beings. Out of concern (fear?) that the ʾādām will become "like one of us," God expels the couple from the garden, barring them from the tree of life. God turns judge by punishing each guilty party: serpent, woman, and man. Overall, one can speak of the dynamic life of God in Gen. 2–3, as much as one can speak of evolving human life in the garden. Whether inside or outside the garden, God remains ever responsive to the ongoing changing situation at hand, intimately involved in whatever happens. The last thing that God does before the expulsion is clothe the couple, preparing them for the harsher world beyond the garden. Even in judgment, God continues to do the work of providential care. Far from Aristotle's notion of the divine, the God of the Yahwist is the "moved mover."

The "Cosmo-logic" of Genesis 2–3

The creational setting of the Yahwist account is distinctly agrarian: a grove of fruit-bearing trees located at a central water source. This garden, moreover, is populated by various animals, including the man and the woman, all part of a community sharing the common substance of the "ground" (ʾădāmâ), their source of material origin. Children of the earth they all are. As the source and substance of primordial life, the ground is a central character in the plot. The Yahwist's drama is the drama of dirt, the drama of earthly life in development. Genesis 2 has only two classes of being: divine and animal, creator and creature. It is only in Gen. 3 that the humans distinguish themselves as different by partaking from the tree of knowledge and thereby achieving a heightened level of self-awareness. Now there are *three* kinds of life in the garden: divine, animal, and human. Humans are the only animals that require clothing.

Humanity in Genesis 2–3

The plot of human development takes a tragic turn. Alienation is the result of human disobedience, alienation from God and from each other: fear and blame take hold. The garden community becomes fractured, and the eviction of the couple is deemed a necessary act so that the divine realm is not threatened (3:22). Classical theology identifies this with the origin of sin itself—"original sin." Curiously, the word "sin" is not used in the garden narrative; it occurs for the first time in connection with Cain's murder of his brother, the object of his jealous rage (Gen. 4:7). The second reference to "sin" is in connection with Sodom and Gomorrah (13:13; 18:20). Sin in Genesis has its roots in physical violence, which is not the issue in the garden.

Disobedience in the garden is driven by the desire of groundlings to be godlings (3:5; cf. 3:22), the desire to transgress the divide between creator and creature. At that divide, according to the Yahwist, is the attainment of self-consciousness. The narrative depicts consciousness emerging painfully with the self-awareness of nakedness ("eyes opened"), as well as the capacity to remedy the situation (making clothes). Gaining the capacity to discriminate between what is good and what is bad begins with self-knowledge. Consciousness emerges, the Yahwist claims, from a profound sense of self-awareness of one's own vulnerability, an ironic result of wanting to become divine.

The garden story is all about the emergence of the human, God's "anthropos project," whose results so far have been decidedly mixed. The Yahwist account is an etiology of how the human came to be human, a development filled with promises and pitfalls. From the Yahwist's perspective, our scientific label *Homo sapiens* is far too self-congratulatory. Yes, we have become "wise," but our self-classification is only half right at best. The other half is humankind's disobedient side: we are also *Homo inoboediens*. Both, according to the Yahwist, refer to one and the same species.

The Yahwist account of creation offers a poignant and profound understanding of the emerging complexity of becoming human, imbued with more a sense of tragedy than that of triumph. At the same time, the Yahwist elicits a yearning for intimacy and community accompanied by the frustration that such intimacy is all too easily threatened or thwarted. In such yearning there is hope, the hope that community remains possible, for humanity's origin is rooted in the community of all life, groundlings that we are. Indeed, such a story of origin points ultimately to the destiny of consummation, with the merging of the garden and the city and God's dwelling on earth in Rev. 21–22. The painful fracture of community in Gen. 2–3 presses the hope for reconciliation among human beings and with creation itself.

Theological Convergences of Genesis 1 and 2–3

Although the profiles of both God and creation in these two narratives could not be more different, the biblical editors saw fit to juxtapose them, one immediately following the other. They are not meant to be treated "scientifically," as is clear from the outset, since they so blatantly contradict each other, as for example, in the way they present the sequence of creation. The framers of Genesis clearly saw a deeper truth at work by combining these two accounts, one that is deeply theological and anthropological. Together these two stories illustrate the complexity of both divinity and humanity. God is at once magisterially transcendent and scandalously immanent: God wields a royal scepter yet also carries a garden spade. God's commanding presence in Gen. 1 is matched by God's intimate, accommodating presence in Gen. 2. While God's word in Gen. 1 finds its fulfillment in the outcome of creation (cf. Isa. 55:10–11), God allows the ʾādām to determine the direction of life in the garden through naming. God endows creation with freedom and purpose. God is no micromanager.

Creation, too, has its converging elements in these two stories. On the one hand, creation is completed, as marked by the seventh day. On the other hand, creation is ongoing, as evidenced in the improvisational, even experimental, side of God's creativity. Creation is both established and open-ended, dynamic and stable, founded and ongoing, ordered yet improvised. Together these two stories testify to the dynamic complexity of creation.

The same goes for humankind. Humanity is both created in "the image of God" and fashioned from creation's soil. Humankind is elevated to near divinity and yet firmly bound to creation. Humanity is both groundling and divine-like. One way of thinking theologically about how these two stories work together is to reflect on what would be missing if we did not have one or the other account. Without Gen. 2–3, we might be tempted to see ourselves as entirely separate from creation, self-transcendent like God, image bearers that we are. In Gen. 1, humility and vulnerability are not the hallmarks of humanity. On the other hand, without Gen. 1, one might be tempted to see ourselves as not much different from all the other creatures of the earth, except for being the most problematic. Today, it is tempting to view humanity as an invasive species. Genesis 1 affirms that humanity can have a positive and powerful role vis-à-vis creation, and in Gen. 2 that role is best served in preserving creation (2:15). Humanity holds creation's promise yet can so easily be creation's problem. Such is the common wisdom shared by both accounts being set side by side!

BIBLIOGRAPHY FOR CHAPTER 22

Allen, Leslie C. 2014. *A Theological Approach to the Old Testament: Major Themes and New Testament Connections*. Eugene, OR: Cascade Books.

Anselm. 1998. *Anselm of Canterbury: The Major Works*. Edited by Brian Davies and G. R. Evans. Oxford World's Classics. Oxford: Oxford University Press.

Barth, Karl. 1957. "The Strange New World within the Bible." In *The Word of God and the World of Man*, translated by Douglas Horton, 28–50. New York: Harper.

Birch, Bruce C., Walter Brueggemann, Terence E. Fretheim, and David L. Petersen. 2005. *A Theological Introduction to the Old Testament*. Nashville: Abingdon.

Brown, William P. 2009. "Theological Interpretation: A Proposal." In *Method Matters: Essays on the Interpretation of the Hebrew Bible in Honor of David L. Petersen*, edited by Joel M. LeMon and Kent Harold Richards, 387–405. RBS 56. Atlanta: Society of Biblical Literature.

Brueggemann, Walter. 1997. *Theology of the Old Testament: Testimony, Dispute, Advocacy*. Minneapolis: Fortress Press.

Dalley, Stephanie, ed. and trans. 1989. "Atrahasis." In *Myths from Mesopotamia: Creation, the Flood, Gilgamesh and Others*, 9–38. Oxford World's Classics. Oxford: Oxford University Press.

Eichrodt, Walter. 1961–67. *Theology of the Old Testament*. 2 vols. OTL. Philadelphia: Westminster.

Fowl, Stephen E. 1998. *Engaging Scripture: A Model for Theological Interpretation*. Malden, MA: Blackwell.

Goldingay, John. 2003, 2006, 2009. *Old Testament Theology*. Vol. 1, *Israel's Gospel*. Vol. 2, *Israel's Faith*. Vol. 3, *Israel's Life*. Downers Grove, IL: InterVarsity Press.

Hanson, Paul D. 1982. *The Diversity of Scripture: A Theological Interpretation*. Philadelphia: Fortress Press.

Hasel, Gerhard. 1991. *Old Testament Theology*. 4th ed. Grand Rapids: Eerdmans Publishing.

Hundley, Michael B. 2013. "Sacred Spaces, Objects, Offerings, and People in the Priestly Texts: A Reappraisal." *JBL* 132, no. 4:749–67.

Jenson, Phillip P. 1992. *Graded Holiness: A Key to the Priestly Conception of the World*. JSOTSup 106. Sheffield: JSOT Press.

Kaiser, Walter, Jr. 1991. *Toward an Old Testament Theology*. Grand Rapids: Zondervan.

Mead, James K. 2007. *Biblical Theology: Issues, Methods, and Themes*. Louisville, KY: Westminster John Knox Press.

O'Day, Gail R., and David L. Petersen, eds. 2009. *Theological Bible Commentary*. Louisville, KY: Westminster John Knox Press.

Ollenburger, Ben C., ed. 2004. *Old Testament Theology: Flowering and Future*. 2nd ed. Winona Lake, IN: Eisenbrauns.

Otto, Rudolf. 1958. *The Idea of the Holy: An Inquiry into the Non-rational Factor in the Idea of the Divine and Its Relation to the Rational*. New York: Oxford University Press.

Preuss, Horst Dietrich. 1995–96. *Old Testament Theology*. 2 vols. Translated by Leo G. Perdue. OTL. Louisville, KY: Westminster John Knox Press.

Rad, Gerhard von. 2001. *Old Testament Theology*. 2 vols. Translated by D. M. G. Stalker. Introduction by Walter Brueggemann. OTL. Louisville, KY: Westminster John Knox Press. Originally published in English in 1962–65.

Vanhoozer, Kevin J. 2008. *Theological Interpretation of the Old Testament: A Book-by-Book Survey*. Grand Rapids: Baker Academic.

Waltke, Bruce K., with Charles Yu. 2007. *An Old Testament Theology: An Exegetical, Canonical, and Thematic Approach*. Grand Rapids: Zondervan.

Williams, Rowan. 2000. *On Christian Theology*. Challenges in Contemporary Theology. Oxford: Blackwell Publishing.

Zimmerli, Walther. 1978. *Old Testament Theology in Outline*. Atlanta: John Knox Press.

PART IV

Communication

23

Retelling the Text

There are two things on which all interpretation of Scripture depends:
the process of discovering what we need to learn,
and the process of presenting what we have learnt.

Augustine[1]

It has been said that while hermeneutics is all about "getting the point" of the text, the art of communication (or "rhetoric") is all about "getting the point across." This final chapter addresses the latter. Communicating the text involves retelling the text, and retelling the text culminates the process of engaging the text exegetically. Believe it or not, you already began the process of communicating the text when you translated it (see chap. 4). Now, however, the aim is no longer to communicate the Hebrew text by replicating it but to communicate it in a different genre and to a specific audience. Communicating the text is your opportunity to *retell the text in a way that you believe needs to be heard at this time and in your context.* What you find to be central to the text as you retell the text should arise naturally from the text and your work with the text, yet also in response to the needs and concerns of people today. No interpretation is final, to be sure, but for now you have the chance to communicate your understanding of the text with clarity, conviction, and creativity, to retell the text with a message that you want others to hear.

Below are a few questions and issues to consider as you take up the challenge of communicating the text:

1. *Whom are you addressing as you communicate the text?* How would you "exegete" your hearers (e.g., congregation, students, participants)? *What form of communication would be most effective* (e.g., sermon, Bible study, lecture, art)?
2. *How can the text's claims or affirmations inform your Bible study or sermon?* Can your presentation *move your hearers* in a way similar to the way the text encountered and moved its earliest hearers or readers?

---

1. *De doctrina christiana* 1.1.1; trans. R. P. H. Green in *Saint Augustine: On Christian Teaching*, Oxford World's Classics (Oxford: Oxford University Press, 1997), 9.

3. *Are the text's central concerns intelligible or meaningful to the cultural and religious experience of your hearers?* If not, why not? Are there ways to bring the text and your community closer together?

4. All of us read from a particular social location or place. A way to broaden your perspective is to consider *how the text might be heard today by others whose social location differs from your own.* For example, how would this text sound to someone living in poverty, or to a physically challenged person, or to someone of different ancestral background, gender, or sexual orientation?

Prior to your exegetical work on the text, you developed a self-exegesis, a profile of your "hermeneutical" self that provides insight into the influences that have shaped the way you read and interpret the biblical text. Now that you have also done significant exegetical work on the text, you are invited to "exegete" the community you plan to address in your communication of the text. For congregations, I recommend the handbook *Studying Congregations* (Ammerman et al. 1998), which offers ways of studying communities in terms of their culture and the dynamics of congregational life. An effective preacher is one who knows the congregation, not just pastorally on an individual basis but also in terms of how the congregation is organized, how power is exercised and distributed, how decisions are made (i.e., polity), and what challenges the church faces within its larger social context (e.g., demographic location). Whenever I am invited to preach or teach in a congregation that is not my own, the first thing I do is study the congregation's Web site and exegete its mission statement, which will reveal much about the church's priorities. Notice also, for example, the kind of educational programs it offers on a regular basis, committee structure, the kinds of events the church hosts, and so forth. The Web site will tell you a lot about the congregation's public face. From the pictures posted, what is the racial or ethnic makeup of the congregation?

This is all to say, before you decide how you are going to communicate the text, get to know your audience. For communication to be effective, for your word to be on target, you should know something of your target audience. Below are two examples of how I would communicate or retell the texts of Genesis. The first is a sermon, the second a lesson plan.

"GOD THE GARDENER"
A SERMON
Context

I envision this sermon as preached at a rural Presbyterian church on the Sunday before Earth Day (April 22). The congregation is small and racially mixed, located in middle Georgia (south of Atlanta). Many of its members, both black and white, work in the agricultural industry or on family farms, some of which are becoming organic. A newly formed creation care committee or "green team" aims to start a community garden on the church's grounds but is facing some stiff resistance from other members of the church.

Hermeneutically, I draw primarily from an ecological approach to the Genesis text (see chap. 16), combined with literary analysis (see chap. 11) and theological reflection (chap. 22). One section of the sermon also applies a canonical approach (see chap. 13) that brings together a variety of other texts sharing a common metaphor.

Texts

Genesis 2:4b–15
Romans 8:18–23

Sermon

"In the beginning there was a farm." That's the opening description on the Web site of a very unique place tucked away within the city of Atlanta: Oakleaf Mennonite Farm, a church-managed community garden that draws from the garden of Eden story for its inspiration. I took my class there once, and right after we parked, the director strode up to us and asked point-blank, "So what do you think God's original plan was?" We all looked at him and then at each other with bemused looks of confusion, wondering what to say, and before anyone of us made an attempt to respond, he answered his own question: "God's original plan was to hang out in a garden with a couple of naked vegetarians!" And that was our introduction to the farm. (We did keep our clothes on during the tour.)

Our introduction to Oakleaf Farm may be a fitting introduction to the garden of Eden story. It is a tender, intimate portrait of creation, a primordial focus on the family. Yet how to read the narrative continues to be a contentious issue among readers today. Is the story historically true? Was there an actual Adam, along with an Eve and a talking snake? Was there a time in which perfect harmony existed between humans and animals after which everything fell apart as a result of human disobedience? Posed this way, I would have to say No. I do not read the story literally, whether historically or scientifically. Humans were not created first and then the animals. There was never a time on Earth when nature existed in perfect harmony. Suffering and death have always been around since the beginning of life on this planet.

Nevertheless, I would claim that Gen. 2–3 *is* historical in a very fundamental way. It illuminates a dynamic of human history that tends to repeat itself time and again, namely, the temptation to overreach for power and to shirk our God-given responsibilities, invariably with tragic results. This ancient tale yields a truth that has endured throughout history. It provides a profound insight into the aspirations and tragedies that mark our evolving relationship with God and the world around us. For me, that makes the story all the more profound, all the more true.

Let's look at the plot and its characters. If God is King of the cosmos in Gen. 1, commanding creation into being, then God is King of the compost in Gen. 2, working directly with the soil to create life. In Eden, God wields a garden spade instead of a royal scepter. The God from on high becomes the God on the ground, a down-and-dirty Deity. This is clear from the very beginning. The garden story begins with a barren stretch of land, a land of lack: no rain, no plants, no tiller (v. 5), as if to say simply: "In the beginning there was dirt." But as any gardener knows, soil is the source of life. The soil bears the potential for growth, depending on its composition. The soil in Gen. 2 is abundantly fertile; it provides the groundwork of all creation, no less, including human creation.

Adam was fashioned from the soil, out of moist "dust." Mineralogists call it "clay," whose intricate structure may have provided the original scaffolding for microbial life. Genesis calls it "ground" (Hebrew ʾădāmâ), so that makes Adam a groundling. That, in fact, is the meaning of his Hebrew name ʾādām, taken as he was from the ʾădāmâ (ground). A child of "dust" is Adam, the groundling fashioned from the "ground," just as the word "human" comes from the Latin word *humus*, the fertile, organic layer of the soil. Adam, in other words, is composed of compost.

You will not find Adam's genesis faithfully depicted by Michelangelo, where a clean, white Adam and the bearded God are about to touch with outstretched fingers. Instead, we read of God performing something more like mouth-to-mouth resuscitation. We find God's muddy hands at the potter's wheel, working the clay and shaping flesh, and God's mouth infusing breath and animating flesh, creating "a living being." If God were working with soil right here in Georgia, God's mouth would be dripping wet with red clay! Imagine that in the Sistine Chapel.

Adam is given an explicit task. God the gardener not only plants a luxuriant grove but also transplants Adam with the expressed purpose "to serve it and preserve it" (2:15), a translation that is better than "to till it and keep it" (NRSV). This garden requires labor: harvesting the fruit and tending the trees. Not that it was backbreaking work, but it was work nonetheless, and Adam was put there for just such a purpose: to "preserve" or sustain the garden. God the gardener and Adam the gatherer, raker, and pruner. And think about it: by consuming the fruit, Adam spread the seeds throughout the garden.

So God has a green thumb. Did you know that God's agricultural prowess can be found throughout the Bible? God plants more than a pristine garden in Eden. God is also known to "plant" a people. The exodus is, botanically speaking, a transplantation:

> You brought them in and planted them on the mountain of your own possession,
> the place, O Lord, that you made your abode,
> the sanctuary, O Lord, that your hands have established. (Exod. 15:17)

Or as we find in a psalm:

> [8] You brought a vine out of Egypt;
> you drove out the nations and planted it.
> [9] You cleared the ground for it;
> it took deep root and filled the land.
> [10] The mountains were covered with its shade,
> the mighty cedars with its branches.
> [11] It sent out its branches to the sea,
> and its shoots to the River. (Ps. 80:8–11)

Or from Chronicles:

I will appoint a place for my people Israel, and will plant them, so that they may live in their own place, and be disturbed no more. (1 Chr. 17:9)

And even from Paul, who credits God alone with growth:

So neither the one who plants nor the one who waters is anything, but only God who gives the growth. (1 Cor. 3:7)

God the gardener. Gardening is a quintessentially divine activity that no other metaphor or title can fully capture. Yes, God is savior, deliverer, liberator, redeemer: God is all these, but missing from such titles is the sense of organic connection with the earth and with a people that only the title "gardener" can fill. To save is to save *from*, to deliver *from*, to liberate *from*, to redeem *from*. But in order to save, redeem, liberate, and deliver, God also works *with*. God works *with* creation, *with* the soil, *with* the fecundity of the earth, *with* body and flesh, to bring forth new life. God: creator, redeemer, sustainer . . . and gardener!

As people of faith, we affirm that creation is good, indeed "very good," created by the living and loving God. But we are also realizing that creation is subjected to a degradation of our own making. Creation is "groaning," Paul states. In our time and place, creation is groaning under the crushing weight of our collective consumption, groaning at the pollution we've spilled into streams and oceans. We must learn to live more sustainably, or creation will be irreversibly damaged. By poisoning the land, we poison ourselves. God's world was created good, but now God's world is groaning deeply, a creation that waits with eager longing for its full redemption, as do we for ours. The two go hand in hand. It is amid creation's goodness and groaning that we must work to "serve and preserve."

John Calvin, the founder of the Reformed faith, had this to say about our text, specifically the verse that states, "The LORD God took the man and put him in the garden of Eden to serve it and preserve it" (Gen. 2:15 alt.):

The custody of the garden was given in charge to Adam, to show that we possess the things which God has committed to our hands on the condition that being content with a frugal and moderate use of them we should take care of what shall remain. Let him who possesses a field so partake of its yearly fruits that he may not suffer the ground to be injured by his negligence; but let him endeavour to hand it down to posterity as he received it, or even better cultivated. . . . Let every one regard himself as the steward of God in all things which he possesses. Then he will neither conduct himself dissolutely nor corrupt by abuse those things which God requires to be preserved. (Calvin 1965, 125)

If we endeavored to hand our land "down to posterity as [we] received it, or even [in a] better" condition, we would no doubt be in a better place than we are now, and we could rest assured that our children, and our children's children, would be safe and would prosper. But there is no assurance of that anytime soon.

But there is hope. God calls us to be grateful stewards of the land's abundant gifts, guardians of the land's integrity. Yet there's more: as cultivators of the land we are practitioners of new life. We are partners with the land, not just its managers. E. B. White speaks of his wife, Katherine, an avid gardener, who every year without fail in the fall began to plot next year's garden.

I . . . used to marvel at how unhesitatingly she would kneel in the dirt and begin grubbing about, garbed in a spotless cotton dress or a handsome tweed skirt and jacket. She simply refused to dress down to a garden: she moved in elegantly and walked among her flowers as she walked among her friends—nicely dressed, perfectly poised.

The only moment in the year when she actually got herself up for gardening was on the day in fall that she had selected, in advance, for the laying out of the spring bulb garden—a crucial operation, carefully charted and full of witchcraft. . . .

Armed with a diagram and a clipboard, Katharine would get into a shabby old Brooks raincoat much too long for her, put on a little round wool hat, pull on a pair of overshoes, and proceed to the director's chair—a folding canvas thing—that had been placed for her at the edge of the plot. There she would sit, hour after hour, in the wind and the weather, while Henry Allen produced dozens of brown paper packages of new bulbs and a basketful of old ones, ready for the intricate interment. As the years went by and age overtook her, there was something comical yet touching in her bedraggled appearance on this awesome occasion, . . . her studied absorption in the implausible notion that there would be yet another spring, . . . sitting there with her detailed chart under those dark skies in the dying October, calmly plotting the resurrection. (E. B. White 1979, xvii–xix)

So it is with God the gardener, who refuses to dress down in the garden of creation yet grubs about in the soil to bring forth life, who grounds us in hope for the new creation, and cultivates in each of us a love for the land from which we came and to which we shall return. Let us begin "plotting the resurrection."

"IN THE BEGINNING": LIVING IN THE COSMIC TEMPLE
A Lesson Plan for Three Sessions on Genesis 1

Context

Over the years I have found that an effective lesson plan depends on good questions and engaging activities. This lesson plan is annotated with a measure of content, which draws from the preceding chapters of our exegetical work. It is designed to cover three Sunday morning or Wednesday evening sessions for adults (i.e., three weeks total) in a large, well-educated congregation that has resources for strong educational programming.

Hermeneutically, the lesson plan draws from various approaches, beginning with articulating "first impressions" (see chap. 3), and concludes with a structural analysis (see chap. 8). Also included are reflections drawn from historical analysis (see chap. 12), literary analysis (see chap. 11), translation (chap. 4), science (chap. 15), and theology (chap. 22). In practice, of course, these approaches cannot (and should not) be categorically distinguished. The key is integration.

Text

Genesis 1:1–2:3

Objective

To demonstrate that Gen. 1:1–2:3 has more to do with how we live our lives than with explaining the origins of the universe scientifically. Participants will gain a deeper understanding of the text in its historical context and theological significance as well as be able to draw implications for their own life and work in God's creation.

Needed Supplies

1. Newsprint on an easel or a whiteboard with markers
2. At least three different Bible translations (e.g., KJV, NIV, NRSV, NJPS)
3. A scientist or two on hand to explain things in Session 2 (see below)
4. Optional: TV or projector connected to the Internet

Session 1: Introducing Genesis 1:1–2:3

A. First Impressions

Read Gen. 1:1–2:3 from the NRSV as an abbreviated *lectio divina* exercise: after participants are settled into a relaxed position, read the text two times slowly. After the first reading, ask participants to share out loud particular words or phrases that caught their attention. After the second reading, ask for adjectives or phrases that describe the character of creation presented in Gen. 1:1–2:3. You could ask the following questions: *What kind of world has God created in Genesis? What are you thankful for about creation?*

B. Historical Background

Share briefly that Gen. 1 was likely written either near the end of the exile or soon thereafter. After reviewing some history, including life in exile and the end of the Babylonian Empire, invite participants to imagine how Gen. 1 could have been understood in the wake of exile. The exiles experienced the national trauma of Babylonian invasion and deportation as nothing less than a cosmic upheaval that left the land devastated, with the temple lying in ruins, much of the city razed to the ground, and the community stripped of its national and religious identity. *What would it mean to former exiles to see themselves "made in the image of God" (1:26–28)? What would it mean to claim that God transformed "chaos" into life-sustaining order?* Genesis 1 offered a cosmically hopeful vision for those ready to begin the great work of restoring their community, a vision that affirmed both the divinely endowed worth of every individual, made in "the image of God," and the goodness of creation.

C. God's Ways of Creating

Ask participants to describe in their own words how God creates according to Gen. 1. Follow-up questions might include these: *Does God create by word alone?* What does God do to bring forth, for example, plants in vv. 11–12? What role does the earth play in this creation? The waters? Look at vv. 20 and 24. *What about the creation of humanity in v. 26? Does God work alone or collaboratively in the creation of life?*

What image of God comes to mind in Genesis 1 (e.g., king, artist, architect)? Imagine what could be going through God's "mind" when God affirms that something is "good" or "very good." *How is creation "good" in Genesis for God? How is creation "good" for us?*

D. *Translation Issues*

1. With different English translations made available to the group (e.g., KJV, NIV, NRSV, NJPS), have each translation of Gen. 1:1–3 read out loud by a different person. Ask participants to identify the differences among the translations. Explain how the first verse in Hebrew is actually a temporal clause that leads directly into the second verse, which leads to the third.

2. "Formless [and] void" (NRSV). Explain what the Hebrew sounds like: *tōhû wābōhû*— what grammarians refer to as a "farrago": two alliterative words combined to give a meaning other than their constituent parts" (see chap. 4). Have the participants pronounce the Hebrew a few times, and then ask them to think of examples of English farragoes (e.g., topsy-turvy, mishmash, hocus-pocus, vice versa). *So what is the text trying to describe with* tōhû wābōhû? A watery mishmash, primordial soup? Given that v. 2 is a description of a precreative condition, *does Gen. 1 claim that God creates "out of nothing"?* Discuss.

3. The meaning of *rûaḥ* (pronounced *ruakh*) in Gen. 1:2. List translation options, such as "spirit," "wind," "breath." Which meaning fits the context best? You could point out that the following verb has its biblical parallel in Deut. 32:11 with the image of the mother eagle "*hovering* over its young." (I contend that "breath" is the best translation in context because it corresponds to God's *uttered* commands throughout the account.)

For a kinesthetic take on this issue, try this breath exercise. Have participants practice deep breathing several times and then instruct them to hold their breath as you read Gen. 1:1–3. Explain that when you get to the command "Let there be light," they can release their breath. (Don't read too slowly!) Point out that this may be the sense of the text: God's breath is held, suspended over the watery mishmash, until it is released in the form of a command, and repeatedly so thereafter as God "speaks" creation into being.

E. *Conclusion*

1. Ask participants to share what insights they have gained in this preliminary study of Genesis:

> How has the discussion deepened your appreciation of this opening chapter of the Bible?
> What new questions do you have?

2. As a preview to next week, explain that they will explore whether Gen. 1 can be understood scientifically. Ask them, for example, to become familiar with the big bang model of cosmic evolution. You could provide a couple of Internet links to help explain the big bang.

Session 2: Genesis as Science?

A. *Introducing the Discussion*

Read this quote from well-known writer Marilynne Robinson: "If ancient people had consciously set out to articulate a worldview congenial to science, it is hard to imagine how, in terms available to them, they could have done better" (1998, 39). Ask participants to respond. *Is Gen. 1 "congenial to science"? In what ways? How not?*

B. Genesis 1:1–2:3 as an Account of Cosmic Origins

Does Gen. 1 lay claim to scientific truth? If you have any scientists in the group, have one briefly describe the following items. (This you should arrange at least a week in advance through personal invitation.)

1. The big bang
2. Age and evolution of the universe
3. When life began
4. The place of humanity in the evolutionary schema

Or you could find and present Web-based videos or discussions of these matters.

C. Questions of Comparison

1. *What connections or parallels do you see between the Genesis account of creation and the account given by scientists concerning cosmic evolution?* Examples are the big bang and the creation of light (1:3), the origin of life in the sea, developments toward complexity, humanity as an evolutionary latecomer.

2. *What collisions between the biblical and scientific accounts have you noticed?* Examples are in the sequence of creation: plants before marine life, creation of the earth before that of the sun, creation completed in six "days."

3. *Do you read the Genesis text any differently now that you know more about cosmic evolution from a scientific perspective?* Have participants give examples.

D. Return to the Robinson Quotation

1. Ask participants *to reassess their initial response to the quote from Marilynne Robinson.* What are the pitfalls and possibilities of trying to understand Gen. 1 scientifically. *If Gen. 1 isn't modern science, then is it still relevant?*

2. As a preview of next week, share that you will explore the relevance of Gen. 1 for today. Next week's "assignment" is to *think about how Gen. 1 can be relevant today.*

Session 3: The Relevance of Genesis 1

Introduction: Ask participations to share what thoughts they had this week on the possible relevance of Gen. 1 for them. *Is it possible for Gen. 1 to be relevant today if it has little to do with modern science?*

A. Structure as Key to the Meaning of Genesis 1

1. Ask participants if they see evidence of an overall structure in Gen. 1:1–2:3. Are there correspondences between the various days? Write on newsprint the following structure, asking participants as you fill it out to name what was created on each day:

Day 1	Day 4
Light	Lights
Day 2	Day 5
Sky	Aviary life
Seas	Marine life
Day 3	Day 6
Land	Land animals
Vegetation	Human beings

Day 7

Invite participants to notice the correspondences between the domains listed in the left-hand column and the members of those domains in the right-hand column. *Is it a perfect symmetry?*

2. *Why is the seventh day set apart?* Reread Gen. 2:1–3. *What is unique about this day?*

3. There is more to this symmetry than meets the eye. Draw horizontal lines between the days.

Day 1 ——————— Day 4

Day 2 ——————— Day 5

Day 3 ——————— Day 6

Day 7

Again, the seventh day stands alone. Notice that a threefold space is constructed between the lines, with the seventh day "inhabiting" the final, open-ended space. Ancient readers of Genesis would readily recognize this threefold pattern. Here it is:

Day 1 ——————— Day 4
Porch
Day 2 ——————— Day 5
Nave
Day 3 ——————— Day 6
Holy of Holies
Day 7

Point out that the chronological architecture of Gen. 1:1–2:3 reflects the spatial architecture of the temple or tabernacle, a threefold space consisting of the porch, nave, and the holy of holies. Explain the significance of the holy of holies in the temple, the inner sanctum where God is said to reside (see chap. 8). God's residence in the temple corresponds to God's "rest" on the Sabbath. *What is the significance of this overall arrangement for creation according to Genesis?* Creation is God's cosmic temple!

B. Our Place in God's Cosmic Temple

1. Read Gen. 1:26–28. Ask participants how they would describe humanity's relationship to creation. *What does it mean to be made "in the image of God"? What images (!) come to mind?* Are we "mirrors" of God's presence, called to "reflect" God's presence? How so?

2. *What does it mean to exercise "dominion"?* You may want to cite Lynn White's 1967 article, arguing that this passage is the fundamental cause of our ecological crisis, giving license to exploit the earth (see chap. 16 above). Ask participants if they believe this. *What are other ways of interpreting "dominion" in Gen. 1? If we are created to reflect God's ways on earth, what precisely are God's ways in creating? Does God need to conquer in order to create?* (You may want to reference Marduk's role in the *Enuma Elish*; see chap. 10 above).

3. *What does this mean today? If we were to truly regard creation as God's cosmic temple, how would we treat it?* What are the *ecological implications* here? Discuss.

C. Sabbath

1. How does the final day fit with the creation account as a whole? *Is there something climactic about this final day? How so? What is the purpose of this last day?* Does God rest because God is tired? Discuss.

2. Read the Sabbath commandment in Exod. 20:8–11, which is, perhaps not coincidentally, the longest commandment in the Decalogue. In light of this commandment, *why is creation ordered according to seven days? Is it to make a scientific or historical point? Or is meant to be a model for human conduct?* The order of God's creation models the weekly rhythm of work and rest for human beings. *What implications does keeping the Sabbath have for creation? What implications does seeing creation as God's cosmic temple have for you?*

D. In Conclusion

Ask participants what they have found meaningful about Gen. 1:1–2:3. *How do they see the text differently? How do they see their lives differently in light of the Bible's first chapter?*

BIBLIOGRAPHY FOR CHAPTER 23

Calvin, John. 1965. *A Commentary on Genesis*. Translated by John King. London: Banner of Truth Trust.

Robinson, Marilynne. 1998. *The Death of Adam: Essays on Modern Thought*. Boston: Houghton Mifflin.

White, E. B. 1979. "Introduction." In Katharine S. White, *Onward and Upward in the Garden*, edited by E. B. White, vii–xix. New York: Farrar, Straus, Giroux; Toronto: McGraw-Hill Ryerson.

White, Lynn, Jr. 1967. "The Historical Roots of Our Ecological Crisis." *Science* 155:1203–7.

Resources for Communicating the Text

Ammerman, Nancy, et al., eds. 1998. *Studying Congregations: A New Handbook*. Nashville: Abingdon.

Bracke, John M., and Karen B. Tye. 2003. *Teaching the Bible in the Church*. St. Louis: Chalice.

Brown, Sally A., and Luke A. Powery. 2016. *Ways of the Word: Learning to Preach for Your Time and Place*. Minneapolis: Fortress Press.

Griggs, Donald L. 2003. *Teaching Today's Teachers to Teach*. Nashville: Abingdon.
Long, Thomas G. 1989. *Preaching and the Literary Forms of the Bible*. Philadelphia: Fortress Press.
————. 2005. *The Witness of Preaching*. 2nd ed. Louisville, KY: Westminster John Knox Press.
Tisdale, Leonora Tubbs. 1997. *Preaching as Local Theology and Folk Art*. Minneapolis: Fortress Press.

A Glossary of Exegetical Terms

This glossary does not include, e.g., names of textual versions (chap. 5), types of poetic parallelisms (chap. 6), and other matters discussed extensively in the previous chapters. For a more comprehensive list of definitions applying to all aspects of biblical criticism, see Richard N. Soulen and R. Kendall Soulen, *Handbook of Biblical Criticism*, 4th ed. (Louisville, KY: Westminster John Knox, 2011).

acrostic. Composed alphabetically, successive verses of a poetic passage featuring successive Hebrew letters, from *aleph* to *tau*, that begin each line, verse, or section. Examples are Pss. 25, 34, 37, 111, 112, 119, 145; Prov. 31:10–31.

alliteration. The recurrence of an initial consonant sound in two or more words.

allusion. An indirect reference to a text by another text.

anacoluthon. A syntactical inconsistency or incoherence within a sentence, as in a shift within an unfinished sentence from one syntactic construction to another.

anadiplosis. The repetition of the last word or phrase of one line or clause to begin the next line.

anaphora. The repetition of a word or phrase at the beginning of successive clauses or lines, as in Ps. 29:3–5.

Aramaism. A word or idiom used in Biblical Hebrew that is of Aramaic origin.

asyndeton. A feature of Hebrew verse or a line that lacks conjunctions or other linking words (e.g., the *waw* or a subordinate clause marker), as in Ps. 23:1b. The reader must determine how the clauses are meaningfully linked. *See also* parataxis.

chiasm (also **chiasmus**, concentric inverted parallelism). A pattern of words or phrases in which the first and last in a given unit are parallel, the second and the next to the last are parallel, and so forth. The result is a sequence that can be divided into two halves, one in reverse or inverted order of the other. The central element and the opposite ends of the chiasm (*see* inclusio) may be more important than any other part (but not necessarily).

codex. An ancient manuscript in book form with bound pages rather than in scroll form.

collate. To compare manuscripts of a given text in order to reconstruct the original.

colon. A single line or verse unit of poetry.

colophon. Title or other summary at the end or beginning of a unit of text (e.g., Gen. 2:4a; 5:1; 10:1; Lev. 26:46).

conflation. A combining of two textual variants, texts, or traditions, resulting in a new reading.

diachronic analysis. A form of investigation that explores the historical background of the text and its development over time.

dittography. The copying error of repeating a letter or letters during textual transmission. See chap. 5.

doublet. A parallel narrative, perhaps resulting from retelling in oral tradition (e.g., Gen. 12; 20; 26).

ellipsis. The omission of a word or phrase that can be easily supplied by context.

formula. A set of words commonly used in a particular context, such as the "messenger formula" ("Thus says YHWH").

hapax legomenon. A word that occurs only once in the Hebrew Bible.

haplography. The copying error of losing (i.e., skipping over) something during textual transmission (e.g., letters, words, sentences, and even larger units.) See chap. 5.

hendiadys. Two or more words linked conjunctively (by "and" [*waw*]) to express a single concept, which can be translated by subordinating one of the words (e.g., "a city and a tower" = "a towering city").

homoioarchton. Similar beginnings in two words that may lead the scribe accidentally to skip from one to the other, omitting the intervening material.

homoioteleuton. Similar endings in two words that may lead the scribe accidentally to skip from one to the other, omitting the intervening material.

inclusio. A literary device in which the end and the beginning of a passage are similar, if not identical, thus bracketing the intervening material. A chiasm presupposes an inclusio.

interpolation. The insertion of material into a text in the process of editorial growth or textual transmission.

ketiv/qere. Ketiv (what is written) refers to the "inferior" reading that the Masoretes included in the text by featuring only its consonants. *Qere* (what is called/read) refers to the "superior" reading that the Masoretes imposed upon the *ketiv* consonants by adding only its vowel points. Frequently a masoretic notation in the margins indicates the "superior" consonantal spelling, as for example in Ps. 100:3.

lacuna. A physical gap in the text.

merism/merismus. The division of the whole into its parts, frequently cast as two contrasting words signifying a whole or singular concept such as "heaven and earth" = creation.

meter. A consistent pattern of accents in a passage of poetry (e.g., iambic pentameter). See chap. 6.

metaphor. A figure of speech whereby one thing is referenced in terms suggestive of another. See chap. 6.

metonymy. A word that substitutes for another, such as a part for the whole (e.g., "Name" standing for YHWH, as in Lev. 24:11), or the whole for a part, or an attribute for the whole. *See also* synecdoche.

paleography. The study of ancient writing. The style of the letters, for example, can indicate the age of a document.

parataxis. The coordination of clauses without explicit indication of their syntactic relation, particularly characteristic of Hebrew poetry.

paronomasia. A pun or play on words through the use of two similar-sounding words with different meanings, achieving a certain effect, from eliciting humor to imparting profound insight.

prosody. The study of poetic meter, which in Hebrew poetry also includes the study of poetic parallelism.

prostaxis. The tendency to start all the clauses in a passage in the same way. Hebrew frequently uses the prostatic *waw*.

synchronic analysis. A form of investigation that treats the text as having a meaningful integrity apart from the historical and cultural settings that shaped it over time. *See* diachronic analysis.

synecdoche. A part used for the whole, or vice versa.

terminus a quo. The earliest possible date for something.

terminus ad quem. The latest possible date for something.

variant. A different textual reading.

Index of Scripture and Other Ancient Sources

Index of Subjects and Names

CPSIA information can be obtained
at www.ICGtesting.com
Printed in the USA
FSOW03n0311010317
31388FS